FOR
GREAT GETTI[...]
THANKS FOR VISITING US
DOWN HERE IN C.T

LETTERS
TO
KUWAIT

BIG   LOVE

CARLOS

LOOKING FOR BULLETS DOWN THE BARREL OF A GUN
REFLECTIONS OF AN AFRICAN PALEFACE

CARLOS LILTVED

PORCUPINE PRESS

Johannesburg

First published in 2019 by Carlos Liltved
letterstokuwait@gmail.com

Local and Regional retail print distribution by
Porcupine Press
PO Box 2756
Pinegowrie, 2123
South Africa

ISBN 978-0-620-82336-4 (print)
ISBN 978-0-620-82337-1 (ebook)

Design and typesetting by Robin Yule
Cover by Carlos Liltved
Printed and bound by Digital Action SA

In one of his poems //Kabbo* the Bushman remembers the contemplation,
of requesting from his mistress,
a piece of thread,
with which to sew the beautiful buttons she had previously given him,
onto his jacket.
To pluck up the courage

Like //Kabbo, most of us are prisoners to a lesser or greater degree –
enslaved by economics or trapped by circumstance

**This book is dedicated to Gareth Rutherford who spent ten years
in prison in Kuwait.**

May we all have the courage to rise above our circumstances and break free.
Or at least try.

And to the storytellers who keep our memories alive.

* //Kabbo was a Bushman convict released into the service of WH Bleek and Lucy
Lloyd for the purpose of recording the language of Southern Africa's
/Xam people – a race which, by then, had pretty much been wiped out.
The poem is called **//Kabbo's Request for Thread**

Contents

Introduction

The Beginning of a Story

I sent my brother Mick an email the other day reminding him that thirty years ago, he and I did our navy basic training at Saldanha Bay. I had been reminded of this, in turn, by a push of salty air at night. West Coast air. Air that whispered of a change in season.

My brothers and I attended a primary school in Tamboerskloof. During the riots of 1976 teargas wafted up from the city and burned our eyes.

When I started there in 1970, the school bell was still being rung by hand. I remember an orange-haired freckled boy nicknamed "big fatty bell-ringer" grasping the wooden handle firmly with both hands and giving it a good thrashing, first above his head, then between his legs. To me he looked like a grown man, but he could not have been more than twelve or thirteen. I was several months away from turning six.

"Big fatty bell-ringer" later became the postman in Camps Bay. He would deliver our mail on a small motorbike. They said he was a Hell's Angel at weekends. He grew old and thin and then disappeared into the grey mist. Today, not even a freckle remains.

Our old school building still stands on Belle Ombre Road. I drive past it from time to time. Behind it, in the early 1970s, lay a large sloping, weed-infested lot that had been cleared of Victorian houses to make way for a new sports field, netball courts, library and school hall. The boys held gang fights there every break time, returning to class scratching their scalps as grains of sand fell onto their books. Ripped buttons and dirt left by the clumpy roots of grass tussocks – the preferred weapons – all over their light blue summer shirts. I remember the headmaster, his black academic gown billowing behind him, chasing after the fighting boys who scattered like fish.

Just 25 years earlier, WWII still raged in North Africa and Europe. Some of the older dads had been there. In their minds, the bullets had barely cooled. My best mate Robert Kinsky's dad Willi had been on the Eastern Front – a boy soldier, as many of them were. Tall and lean in denim shorts and long desert boots, Willi would grab my belly roll between his thumb and forefinger, give it a good twist and say, "My boy, Adolf Hitler would have known what to do with you." Willi worked us hard, offloading heavy machine components, bulldozer engines and so on. Rites of passage work.

Boysie Gordon's dad had been with the South Africans in the Western Desert. He seemed worn out. We bought Battle Picture Library comic books at the café and played being at war.

Through the 1970s, 1980s and into the '90s, most of our family friends were Germans and Eastern Europeans. They were my parents' colleagues, members of the orchestra and music lovers. Quite a few had served in the *Wehrmacht*. Some were old Jews. Some were East Bloc escapees. I have read Guy Sajer's **Forgotten Soldier**, Hochschild's **Unquiet Ghost** and Svetlana Alexievich. I have a better understanding now, compared to then, of what they went through. Except for Uwe Jaspersen's dad Gunther, I suppose they are all dead and gone. But their memories must have been as fresh then as mine are today. Maybe even fresher.

Cape Town in the 1970s had about 400 000 inhabitants. Today, there are ten times as many people. It was a wonderful place for us to be boys. We arrived there at the end of 1969. Our favourite neighbours were the Fagans who lived in a stately Victorian house across the road, up an alley and over a low whitewashed wall.

When we first met the four Fagan brothers, they had a small, wire-haired dog called Bakkies. He was an old dog and was soon replaced by Spikkels the Dalmatian. For all the studious, disciplined behaviour of the Fagan brothers, their dogs were the opposite. I don't think a single one of their four childhood dogs even learned how to sit. Bakkies, Spikkels, Rocky and the wildest dog of all, Shardik the Bear, were totally out of control.

The Fagans had an old fridge engine that was somehow used to fill gas balloons for birthday parties. Each balloon had a string and they were parked in a herd up against a beautiful pressed steel ceiling in the dining room. Boys – the guests were only ever boys – would grab a string and pull down a balloon. It was splendid.

During the party some balloons popped and some would end up flying over the city, but most were left behind after all the fun and games, softly bobbing against the ceilings throughout the house.

Later, in the still of night, when all but Spikkels were asleep, the balloons lost their gas and slowly descended. Soft pops might then have been heard.

To the delight of the boys in the neighbourhood, Spikkels' poos for the next while contained bits of twisted balloons and string. Nobody picked up poo in those days and for weeks afterwards, once the poo had been rained away or had dried and disintegrated, these twisted pieces of rubber and strings lay around as reminders of the parties. *Koeksisters.*

The Liltved home – that was us – was more bohemian than the Spikkels home. A Liltved boy with his thatched head would, not infrequently, be sent over to borrow an onion, a few eggs or some slices of bread for school sandwiches. The Fagan boys were always neat in their blazers, short hair brushed and damped down, ready for school. Fagan boys were never sent to borrow bread or eggs because Aunty Sheila ran an organised household.

One Easter, however, the single exception occurred. I remember a contingent of worried and rather downcast Fagans arriving at the Liltved home to request a loan of a few Easter eggs. Hannes and Sheila had been up early, hiding about twenty eggs for the boys' Easter egg hunt after breakfast. The hunters had returned empty handed. All the eggs had vanished, presumed stolen.

In those days, in the Republic of South Africa, shops were closed on Sundays and public holidays. The missing eggs could not be immediately replaced and the boys were miserable. We were happy to oblige.

The mystery of the missing eggs lasted until Spikkels began to poo. For weeks afterwards – much like with the balloons – twisted shreds of coloured aluminium foil emerged as reminders. Mostly in the agapanthus. Some had smiling bunny faces printed on them.

Spikkels was poisoned a few years later. Perhaps because he was a bit of a nuisance. The toxin did not kill him but left him with some neural damage. After recovering from the near-death experience, he walked around looking faintly bemused. His forehead would wrinkle up and his jaws would slowly hang open, then snap shut like a sprung trap. By some miracle his tongue always managed to get out of the way. He was like the crocodile in **Peter Pan**.

Mick and I did our national service in 1988 and 1989, the last of the two-year conscripts. In 1990 conscription was reduced to one year and then subsequently abandoned. The prospect of spending two full years in the SADF was a dark storm-cloud that hung over the heads of all so-called "white" boys in South Africa during the 1970s and 1980s. The country's energy was really weird then. A strange zeitgeist. Some headed into exile, some ended up in the townships, some on the border, some in the police, some at Personnel Services in Pretoria and others locked up in the *kas*.

I will tell about Gareth Rutherford and a friend who served with the *Berede*. And Henny Adriaens and perhaps Alan Best. The tales are endless, branching out like a big old tree. Some tragic, some funny, memory morphing them a little, perhaps.

The SADF years certainly had a profound effect on the lives of those who experienced them. Palefaces – "We fought battles *eksê*, and we died *eksê*."

To be completely accurate, the armed forces weren't entirely "white". There were brown people in the navy. I saw dark brown NCOs being trained at Kroonstad while I was there. There were "browns" in 32 Battalion and in the Recces and Koevoet. The SADF took what it needed. It was a beast with mixed moralities and, where necessary, a mixed hide.

One of my Portuguese friends, Miguel, served as an interpreter with 32 Battalion. Others were in the Parabats. Boys with weapons and helicopters killing other human beings in the beautiful African bush. A surfer we knew had both his legs blown off by a bomb from a MiG as he sat on a tank getting a lift during the evacuation from Cuito Cuanavale. Some were navy divers while others did duty in the townships. "Nutria" uniforms and dust. Gross, outrageous injustices.

Mick played sax in the Navy Band and travelled all over the country. It was an adventure.

I did navy basics with Mick and then got sent to the army in Kroonstad. School of Engineers. They wanted me in Angola, but I had other ideas.

Some kids really organised themselves. Three months of basic training in the navy, followed by twenty-one months relaxing at the small craft centre in Simon's Town while "messing about in boats". Lovely.

We organised ourselves. Wouldn't anyone?

We have a friend named Henny, one of those eternally good-natured people, always laughing. He would phone us from an army camp somewhere up north. Using a "gypo-ticky" – a ten cent piece with a piece of thread taped to it – he would make endless free calls with the same coin. We would have just got back from surfing. Henny just laughed, even though it was *kak*. Henny "organised" himself and, instead of going to Angola with the rest of his company, became an HQ driver deployed in Cape Town.

One day Henny was sent with a truckload of hot lunches to the weapons testing range at Swartklip near Somerset West. He parked the vehicle and wandered off behind a nearby tree. A mortar fired into the strong south-easterly wind was blown back overhead and landed right next to his food van. Two men were killed. They had also "organised" themselves. You can try your best, but you cannot organise yourself against sheer bad luck.

My schoolmate Ravenscroft was sent to Panzer School at Tempe where, because of his big *bek*, he was repeatedly beaten up. His only way out was to sign up for four years "Permanent Force" in the navy. In 1983 he was at the Simon's Town dockyard gates when the security police came to raid the offices of the notorious spy, Commodore Dieter Gerhardt. As they did not have the required authorisation, Ravenscroft refused to allow them entry, so they just lifted the boom themselves and went in.

One of the ways of getting out of national service was to feign insanity. However, this could also get you two years in the psycho ward. Gay conscripts ended up there, too. It was all very cruel.

SAS Saldanha is the base where the South African Navy is trained. At that time, back in 1988, the OC (Captain Du Toit) was there because, it was said, he had crashed a vessel, possibly even a submarine, into the quayside at Simon's Town. I met him shortly before I left there. He was a kind man. At that time we knew nothing about the lives of men like him or Admiral Woody Woodburne.

Commander Gus Mostert was moved to Saldanha, apparently for throwing a seaman off the bridge of his minesweeper into False Bay. Gus Mostert was built like Steve Reeves and had sideburns that were like a second set of eyebrows below the eyes. The Saldanha *melktert* ladies went all wobbly at the mention of his name, let alone seeing him in his navy whites.

The GI – Gunnery Instructor van Heerden – was supposed to be in charge of discipline at the base. His eyes welled up when the band played **Cavalry of the Steppes** or **Kinders van Die Wind**. He could not resist a band practice, all the while chain-smoking Gunston cigarettes. A Warrant Officer of death-grey leather. A sort of werewolf-man with a voice to match who, once seen or even heard, could never be forgotten.

A young national serviceman tried to commit suicide by jumping overboard with a twenty-litre plastic jerry can filled with water tied to his leg. He ended up with the jerry can floating next to him. Water does not sink in water. He was fished out of the drink and charged with attempted malicious damage to state property. Not everyone could cope with being conscripted into the SADF.

For us "paleface" conscripts, the options were few: serve, leave the country or become a conscientious objector.

One of the boys I knew at primary school jumped out of the window at SAS Silvermine and died. Another ex-classmate hanged himself on a tennis court fence but was cut down in time by a fellow conscript. In our bungalow, some cried every night and were eventually taken away.

Conscientious objectors and Jehovah's Witnesses were deprived of their liberty for four years. Our childhood Glen Beach pal, Gustav, spent two years in a civilian prison and another two years in military detention (aka the *kas*). During the second two years, dressed in blue overalls and constantly ridiculed, *Blou-Jobs* like Gustav gardened and performed menial work on military bases by day and slept in cells at night.

In general, the English-speaking boys from Cape Town and Durban were anti-SADF, while the Afrikaans-speaking boys from up north weren't. They tended to subscribe to the whole *Volk en Vaderland* apartheid regime propaganda routine. They became *bosbefok* parabats and recces.

As boys we had read our Battle Picture Library comics. **The Call of Courage** and **The Devil's Cauldron** ... "Achtung! Englander! Ack, Ack, Ack!!" ... So, we had an idea of the truth.

Our eldest brother Bill left the country rather than join up.

⌦

Do not love your country more than you love yourself.
Do not love your neighbour more than you do not love yourself.
Do not love your neighbour more than you do not love God.

⌦

Ever since I was a boy I have enjoyed reading people's memoirs. Autobiography is king. David Niven's **The Moon's a Balloon**. Gerald Durrell's fabulous boyhood on Corfu. Bill Bryson's life and travels. Doctor Nansen and Lieutenant Johansen wintering in their hut in Nansen's **Farthest North**, and **Life at the Cape a Hundred Years Ago**, by a Lady.

What is it that is so fascinating about the minutiae of daily life, the pilfering of bits of equipment by arctic foxes, or the eating of walruses? Hemingway in Paris? Or Bill Bryson's teenage outing to a lake near Des Moines? Or a WWII fighter pilot like Pierre Clostermann's own account of how it was? The memories of life, written down, are to me just the best.

My mother's partner Ian's grandfather was a doctor from Scotland who emigrated to Rhodesia. Not much is known about his life other than his name and that he had a tough time in Edinburgh as a student. I have tried to imagine his life, but my imaginings are pure fiction. Ian knows about his own granddad, but his memories will soon be gone. Similarly, in Canada, Tim Rogerson's memories of his dad, the London bomb disposal major. It goes on everywhere. Stories big and small. All eventually fading to nothing.

When I talk to the Fagan boys now, they seem to have limited memories of their own lives, of Easter eggs and party balloons. Anton says he was too busy doing his schoolwork. All he remembers is the endless pages of textbooks. They all worked very hard and got excellent degrees. We did not work so hard at school, but, for now, Bill, Mick and I seem to remember everything.

There are some people who morph memory. One of my dear friends has a memory morphing problem. He says, "Hey Carl, remember when we did such-and-such?" And yet he was never there! He has remembered himself into more than one of my stories. I wonder if I have ever remembered myself into other people's stories. I think adults remember, as real memories, stories they were told about themselves as children. Other stories are "remembered" from photographs.

I was telling Zaan about Spikkels. We were laughing and she said to me, "Carly, you should write your stories down, you know, the ones you tell me."

Why would one, when thinking about a new memory project, gravitate first to those two years in the defence force? Well, why not? Given the random nature of memory, a story could start anywhere.

In 1982 I met a young man named Gareth.
He became my friend.
In 2013 I found him to be missing from my life.
Many friends go missing.
We drift apart.
Marriage, kids, emigration, jobs in other worlds.
Like Peter Gibbons working in the Middle East. Or Hopson in Minneapolis.
Through the network we always know, more or less, where a person is.

Marc Barter came back from Canada. Ingram lives just north of Sydney. Gwain Bayley is in California. Grant Ravenscroft vanished for many worrying years, only to reappear with a wife and grown-up children on a golf estate in England. And so on.

Gareth Rutherford, around whom this web of tales revolves, ended up in prison in Kuwait.
A crime involving a lot of hashish hidden in a spare wheel in the back of his lorry.
After a five-minute trial, Gareth was falsely accused and sentenced to be hanged.
His sentence was commuted to life imprisonment.
He has been in for ten years now.
At time of writing, there is a rumour of release.
But his story is his story, to tell or not to tell.

After making a few enquiries, I found out that Gareth had a hidden device. I began writing to him. I write every month.

And it was through the writing of letters to Gareth that I began to document my own life.

1 March 2013   Letter #1

Zaan made a phone call once, "just rearranging the future," she said innocently
as she put down the phone.
But, of course, she was quite right.
How a phone call can rearrange the future!
As Billy Idol said on his album **Cyberpunk**: **"This is the future."**
We are the future
We are in the future now.

❦

The longing for solitude is a luxury dream
In the most part reserved for those people,
Who live lives which are consistently overcrowded by others.

❦

Martin Abert wrote to me:
Carlos we will go here … it is the yearning.
Changes come at any time … but you must make them.
And we will have this time … together with friends.
Until then, take care … because the time will come.

❦

Why make up a lie when you believe it is true.
I love Autobiography.
But all this time travel back into my past makes me melancholy.

❦

We played a daring game all our lives
Dodging the crossfire
We began to think we were immortal
We never thought it could happen to us

⌘

Dear Gareth

Once upon a time in about 1982, I walked up the grey steps leading into the Longmarket Street Technikon building. You were sitting there a little left of centre. You smiled as I passed by and I thought you looked a bit like Shaun Thompson. I saw you again over the next few days, always in the same place, and I knew that I wanted to be your friend. I liked the look of you.

We became friends. A dear man, gentle and enthusiastic ... a humble, quiet man. One would never have guessed that you had been awarded the Honoris Crux for bravery. An admirable man in every way. A beloved friend.

And over all these years – more than a quarter of a century – I think of you so often. You taught me how to enjoy things. How to make an afternoon Soils Lab Prac seem fun ... and mix the concrete and cast the cubes and do the crush tests rather than dodge just in order to get home. You always had a good attitude. You have been a role model to me and a role model (in absentia) to my daughter Allegra and my partner Zaan's son Nicholas.

"I had a friend at Tech called Gareth Rutherford, a prince amongst men" I tell the kids ...

"I hope that you have a chance to meet him one day."

"I count him on my one hand with the best I have ever known."

"When he was in the army and everyone else was 'ducking and diving' he was the kind of guy who would volunteer for a medics course." I think it's true, but anyway, we all need heroes and you filled that role.

"And when the shit hit the fan in Angola, guess who knew how to do the job? And did it!"

"Fill each unforgiving minute with 60 seconds worth of distance run."

You told me many things that have become melded with the fabric of my life ... who knows how much is accurate and how much gets warped inside the cells of the human brain?

This is how I remember it.

As a boy you did the lighting at SACS. You had an interest in Khalifa, the bloodless sticking of swords and hooks … you helped with lighting for Khalifa shows at the Old Slave Lodge.

I learned about Lance Corporal Rutherford and Ratels and 20mm cannon and the shooting down of running men "like rabbits" … the euphoria of that and then the horror. Anti-aircraft guns limbered down and burning machines and the death of your friends and the sound of the bullets hitting the metal above your head as you helped the dying. I could see it all in my mind's eye. I could smell the cordite and the flesh. And you were sent in your "step out" uniform all over the country to tell moms and dads how their sons had died.

At Tech there was a lecturer called Mr Keyter … you loved to say "Kayterrr" and I would laugh. You did karate and I did karate. You trained at Clovelly and I with Sensei Suleiman Samaai near Bo-Kaap.

Your dad Bonzo made your sandwiches which you shared. He carefully laid cheese and lettuce on the butter to create a waterproof barrier so that the bread would not get soggy from the tomato and mayonnaise. I still make sandwiches in that way. He put in raisins, you called them ticks.

I wondered how it felt receiving the Honoris Crux … a colonel? … a big parade? I saw parades of that sort at School of Engineers in Kroonstad years later. I sneaked around the edge of it all, at the time of the battle of Cuito Cuanavale, doing everything I could to stay out of that place. MiGs and armour and flies in the dry season … no thanks … a friend lost his legs there. I had little faith in Magnus Malan and PW Botha. We fought our war trying to keep their stripes and pips off us, Peter Gibbons and me.

I remember a big car owned by the Carpenter-Frank boys. It was called a Saratoga. It had wings … maybe it was green or greyish silver. I think the front seats rotated to meet you when the door was opened. Maybe that was just a dream.

There were circus elephants and big tents on the Grand Parade … you and I cadged overripe fruit from the fruit sellers to feed them. I remember your hands and your peals of childlike laughter. We pushed bananas into elephant nostrils and they shot the bananas back into their mouths. There were parades on the Grand Parade too. I remember when you got upped to Sergeant Rutherford of the Cape Town Highlanders … I think that Linda with purple hair was there watching. You showed me a photo. I remember when you met Linda.

I dated Pee-Jay Tanfield for a while and for a short time I touched a very different world to the one I knew on the Atlantic Seaboard. I loved the old stone houses. The Tanfields' house. Jacob's ladder. I visited the Tilneys once and I remember that home. Boyes Drive, Quarterdeck Road. The Carpenter-Franks ... Robin and his brother ??? ... Tammy and Peter and Robin Auld. A short time in that place and with all those Anglo-Saxon people living near to Simon's Town ... still glued (albeit with Pritt) to that heritage ... Admiralty House. Dressed stone. The Royal Navy. Obsolete naval gun batteries firing in practice at an imaginary threat. The Brass Bell. There was warmer water there.

I remember your big Chev Kommando that poured out petrol when cornering up Kloof Nek and helping you with some Theory of Structures. I remember your motorbike. I came to visit you once and sailed out into False Bay on your tiny "sinker" ... the wind dropped, and I nursed my way back to Danger Beach from that sharky place. I remember you starting to learn the saxophone.

One of the last times I saw you, you came to visit me in Camps Bay, you told of fixing an old bulldozer in Kommetjie and a fire.

Gareth, I think that you are one of those men who did not mind living in uniform and when the war came again and there was an opportunity for you to make some good money up there in Basra or wherever you went, you went. And you eased your way back into boots and fatigues and surrounded yourself with comrades and big diesel-powered machines.

"Rutherford" ... sounds about right.

But all wars are evil things and one way or another they feast on human souls. Their meat is men and women and families and buildings built in cold or heat and hardship. And the tax contribution of the entire lifetime of a US citizen might be spent on one device that may fly through the air and explode and destroy the home of a family built over hundreds of years in an ancient city and leave nothing but excruciating pain. In a flash, finely carved wood and stone is brutally smashed to splintered wreckage. And humans ... or Ratels and humans as you know from that war in Angola so long ago. That denied war ... "we were never there". And the evil of that bush war didn't seem to hurt you too much, but this one has.

Dear Gareth ... I am so sad that you went there and ended up losing your liberty.

As I have said previously, you are so often in my thoughts. Some years ago I tried to get hold of you, I sent you a few emails but received no reply. I Googled you and read a story about a "50-year-old Briton" who shared your name and got convicted for smuggling hashish. I just put it down to coincidence ... there must be quite a few Gareth Rutherfords in this world.

I thought little more of it and continued with the lightning pace of my work and life and own bitter marital experience and trying to keep my head above water. But mine is a lesser story by comparison.

If you have access to books, then there is one that you should read first ... **Shantaram** by another GR ... Gregory Roberts ... There are others that I would gladly send you if I could. **19 With A Bullet** by Granger Korff ... a Parabat in Angola 1980-1981. **Stirling's Men** by Gavin Mortimer ... and if you ever could find **Stuka Pilot** by Rudel ... well need I say more? These are incredible stories, Gareth. Stories by men who did not give up.

And what I am trying to say is this:

Time passes slowly and very fast. The same time can be measured in milliseconds and millennia. You had a dangerous time in Port Elizabeth's Kwazakhele township where so-called "white" people go to shebeens now. Compared to most people you have had a startling life. No-one can feel it for you, no-one can know what you endure. No-one has your memories or knows what you know. My suggestion is that you make this life of yours into a global bestseller or a book for your boy ... a **Shantaram**. That is a worthwhile thing to make of a bad situation.

Korff wandered the streets of America ... a broken vet of an unlovely African conflict. One day he walked into a centre for Vietnam veterans and they told him to write it all down.

If you can Gareth ... write it all down. Boyhood memories, barefoot in boxer shorts with elastic waist-bands. Yellow grass and dust and flies in Angola. The smell of tea. Loneliness. The small, beautiful things. The scratches and cuts in a thick heavy rubber tyre that crushes the grass and stops in the sand. Even though the vehicle weighs tons, you can easily push your fingers in underneath that tyre. The sand is surprisingly cool. Nothing ahead is touched by that rolling wheel, yet. Remember too, the wheels that follow behind. Remember the hot rim of the exhaust pipe and the seeds in the radiator. The way it felt and the way it feels to be inside your unique you. Write down everything that you can and write it truthfully. Do not sanitise.

Write everything that you can. And that which you cannot write, keep safe inside your head ... bring it out, roll it around and put it away for the day when you can ... and when that day comes ... spend 6 months or a year .... making a book of your life.

Your friend ... Carlos

Chapter 1

The Wind is in from Africa

When I first heard Joni Mitchell singing **Carey** I was left covered in goose-bumps. It was as if someone had stepped on my grave. Even though I lived in Africa, the refrain was just so terribly haunting. It made me yearn for something that I did not even know existed. Even Joni Mitchell who had never, as far as I knew, been to Africa, was affected by its wind.

For now, let me borrow four lines of a verse which are not related to the refrain.

Let's have a round for these freaks and these soldiers
A round for these friends of mine
Let's have another round for the bright red devil, who
Keeps me in this tourist town

What is it that attracts us to people in such a way as to befriend them?

In 1978 I was fourteen and in Standard 7 at Camps Bay High School. The annual school play was the Tim Rice/Andrew Lloyd Webber classic, **Joseph and His Amazing Technicolour Dreamcoat**. It was a sublime production. The entire school got involved. The Munitz family even provided miniature motorcycles for the slave trading Ishmaelites to ride. I was one of the 12 brothers and so was Ravenscroft. Zebulon and Gad, I believe. We became friends. We were never in the same class except during Art and PT. He was a fit cricket and squash playing boy. I was not. We bided our time.

Half way through standard nine Ravenscroft and I began to test the water at night. We would hitchhike into the city or catch a lift with Sakkie Bullard who drove an old *Volksie*. We went to *piepiejol* nightclubs that seemed very grownup at the time. Black walls with UV illuminated, leering cartoon characters painted on them. I saw someone shot once. The music was so loud that I did not even hear the weapon's discharge. The B52s – **Planet Claire**. The music abruptly stopped, and everyone was herded out. It was now 1980. A watershed year, our rites of passage, boys to men.

In the late 1970s and early 80s there were rock festivals at the Rotunda Hotel in Camps Bay. My grandmother had danced at the Rotunda in the 1920s when it sported the largest sprung dancefloor in the Southern Hemisphere. Now, slightly worse for wear, the dancefloor was still there. The Rotunda in the summer holidays at the end of 1980 was a haven of live rock music and Black Label beer and Chesterfield cigarettes. Alan and Stephen and Ravenscroft and I would walk casually into the hotel, dip down a passage which led to the empty, darkened kitchen and bail through the service hatch into a womb of lights and sound and tightly packed jiving young people. John Mair played **96 Degrees in the Shade**. And we naughty boys would flop down into an ancient sofa in a back alcove and drink lager out of "hotel bottles" and descend into heaven.

If I look back now, the problem was that there was simply no parental control. We were free to do as we pleased, and we did. We made our own choices, it was all up to us. I had done quite well at school until then. In retrospect, I did very little schoolwork in my matric year and I am still sad about that. I closed the door in my own face going from a good grade child in the "A Class" to an average grade child in the "A Class" in my final year. I think that Ravenscroft was in the "C Class". He never did much work, so his grades stayed the same. His wonderful charm was matched by a wanton, destructive streak. He would ambush you with a flying shotput ball as you walked out of the showers after a run and then go for your naked body with a "sheep's tail" towel as your brain scrambled attempting to cope with the viciousness of the primary assault. He would take a pair of scissors into the school corridor and cut the straps off random schoolbags. At break time, using a box of chalk and a badminton racket, he would attack his fellow students' paintings as they hung up to dry in the Art Room. Scores of paintings were left with chalk-shaped holes, the result of his rapid-fire volleys. Being innately good, I suppose that I was attracted to this darker "devil-may-care" side of my friend. It was probably a poor decision, but we had a lot of fun. Matric was an absurd year, packed so full of misdemeanours that I still cannot believe we passed.

Much better choices were made by the Fagan boys or my classmate Bayley, the studious, intelligent, guitar playing electronics boffin with whom I shared my walk home.

Friends are normally selected from a group of people with whom a person shares a certain activity or situation. A fellow surfer like Uwe, or a colleague at work, or a neighbour, or a classmate. It was sheer good luck that my parents bought a house near the Fagan home and that made all the difference.

⁕

I think of the boys changeroom at Camps Bay High in 1977, with its tiled floor, as yet unfractured by Ravenscroft's shotput ball attacks. And the small room alongside which housed the office and ablutions of John Donald, the PT teacher. "Chips, here comes Sir!" Berelowitz would call out, and everyone would suddenly be good. JoDo or Sir, as he was known, was a tallish Viking-like man with a bushy blonde moustache. He wore a blue nylon tracksuit with four white stripes and refused to sing hymns at assembly (for which we respected him deeply). He had been a Springbok hockey player in his twenties, and now, at the age of about thirty, he was tasked with teaching us the importance of good physical health.

At this stage of my life, I was still a bit of a "non-co". A "butterfingers" with a belly and a bum. (That was some years before I grew tall and headed off into the night with Ravenscroft.) To avoid playing rugby, I and others of the less physical sort ended up on JoDo's hockey pitch. I was disinterested and hopeless, but not worse than Bernstein. I simply couldn't, and still cannot, understand the point of chasing a ball around a field and trying to get it into a goal or a net or over a post or hit it with a bat or some other variation on that theme.

And so it was that I found myself on the hockey half of the school field running after Gavin Strumpman with a crooked stick in my hand. Gavin was dribbling away from me when something in my wrist caused me to let fly that hockey stick like a boomerang (Crocodile Dundee style) hitting poor Strumpman on the head and causing him to drop like a sack of potatoes. "Litvett!" shouted Donald, "get off my field and never come back!" And I did exactly that, thus ending my sporting career at high school.

In those days, extra-mural sport was compulsory two afternoons a week, so I drifted from table tennis in a back room behind the hall, full of smoking boys, to badminton where Bernstein (who had also left hockey) and I failed repeatedly to hit shuttlecocks with any regularity. Thereafter it was just a small step to drifting off the radar altogether.

But JoDo still had to be faced at double PT once a week!

Double PT was two 45-minute periods, pushed back to back, during which we played touch rugby, baseball, soccer, water polo or "did swimming" in the new school pool.

Mostly, double PT took place on the Camps Bay High School field which remains to this day a most glorious piece of real estate worth many millions. Overlooking Glen Beach and the wide sweep of the bay, it comprises a rugby field beside a hockey pitch encircled by a 400m track. A place of honour and joy for the strong and athletic. A place of misery for people like Strumpman, Bernstein and me.

"Okay, everybody once around," shouted Donald, "Malley and Joubert pick up sides."

Malley and Joubert were athletic lads, usually first in after a quick sprint around the track. They would pick a team each as the boys completed their lap. Lutrin, Liltved, Bernstein and Strumpman would be last in and last picked, spending the rest of the double lesson hopelessly chasing after the ever-moving game, or when called to bat at last, would be instantly out. "Strike One! ... Strike Two! ... Strike Three! ... Ruuuun ... DROP THE BAT!!! ... out."

As double PT finally drew to a close, about ten minutes before the bell, Donald would blow his whistle and say, "Okay boys, to the showers, everybody in the shower, no-one goes back to class stinking. You hear? Not you Litvett, go around again."

And around the field I would go for another 400m as John Donald gathered up the sports equipment, bats, mitts and balls, and then, as I puffed, red-faced, toward the narrow brown brick stairs that led up from the field and towards liberty, Donald would be waiting for me.

"Litvett, when are you going on a diet?" He would grab my belly fat and give it a good squeaky twist. This might seem unduly harsh but in retrospect I realise it was a great kindness, an act of charity and love.

A skinny start: Mick and Carlos 1970

After a skinny start, I put on a bit of puppy fat. The eating regime at our home was conducive to that and the local "corner shops" or "cafes" or "Greek shops" or "Bobby shops" as they were called also did not help. Some of the unkinder boys at primary school would call me "bushman bum". I was plumper at primary school than at high school but never anywhere near the scale of obesity we see today and there was no such thing as OT for poor "motor skills". In general, boys were lean and tough. Plump lads like "big fatty bell ringer" were uncommon.

I remember once reading a Calvin and Hobbes cartoon in which Calvin repeatedly tosses up a baseball and misses it as he swings his bat. "Dad", he says in frustration, "is it true that people get paid for playing silly games?" His dad replies: "Yes, and they become some of the most grossly overpaid humans on the planet."

At Tamboerskloof Primary, boys like me and Bernstein were used as human goalposts during pre-school soccer games. Boys packed their blazers around our feet and there we stood. We were glad to be included.

24 March 2013   Letter #2

Dear Gareth,

If you have access to books, get **East of Eden** by John Steinbeck.

The first page of Chapter 7 has an interesting little essay on the passage of time. I wonder what you would think of it.

At the moment, time is passing at a sickening pace for me … I am never really present in the moment … my mind always occupied with the next set of things to do, or problems needing solution. I wish I could slow it down. I feel like … at this speed I will have nothing to remember of these years … when I am old.

At its own pace, summer draws to a slow close here at the Cape.
A few drops of rain and up pop the first green tips after the hot dry time.
Nasturtiums.
Day after glorious day for a few weeks now it is not too hot anymore …
Light airs, warming sun.

Then on days like today, just when a person is easing into the cooler zone, a great South Easter comes pumping through with all the brutality of high summer. A heavy ground swell smashes into the granite rocks off Bakoven and Clifton and will start to move sand and build us surfing banks for the winter.

In our previous lifetimes, at this time of year, me and the boys would be roving the East Coast surfing and camping.

Mick, Carl and Peter Adriaens

You see, with the change of seasons, at Autumn and Spring, comes a sort of restlessness in the soul. It is an ancient thing. (I wonder if there are seasons in Kuwait or if it is just always hot.)

We would be sleeping on the verandahs of empty holiday homes, camping above the cliffs on the "wild-side" at Mossel Bay (which is now a fully established suburb) and sneaking in and out of the camp site at Cape St Francis without paying. I thought the surf was crowded then, but it was not yet.

Less often we found ourselves up at Elands or Donkin Bay or the Vredenburg Points.

Cold water, lovely, lonely places.

We would surf longboards on the small reef breaks while a little further out we would have an old chlorine jar floating with a gunny sack tied to it. If you followed a rope down to the seabed, there would be a ring-net baited with *viskoppe* or limpets. In between surfing waves, we would take turns and paddle out to the *kreef* trap, to pull up the net and transfer the *kreef* into the sack. At night we slept in Uwe's tent which was actually just the rotted inner lining of a once grander shelter. But it never rained on the West Coast, so we did not care. The rocks got wet with dew at night because they were so salty. We made fires of the old creosote poles we found there. They burned just wonderfully. Black oil would bubble out of those bleached lichen encrusted droppers. We steamed baby crayfish in a paraffin tin and ate them with mayonnaise. The large *kreef* we took back home. We were not kind to them. Alan Best packed the bubbling beasts in wet sacking for the trip back to the city, staring up at us with black beads for eyes and broken feelers. I don't like that sort of thing any more. If you are going to kill it, kill it and eat it, don't mess with lives.

Alan and Mick would catch *galjoen*. They would crush mussels in an orange sack and use that as chum or *lok*. The bag of *lok* was tied to a rope … time and time again they would hurl it out and cast their baited hooks after it. Sometimes we slept in the quarry at Elands and *braaied galjoen*.

Speaking of Elands … There are two rivers on the other side of the Du Toit's Kloof tunnel. One is called the Elandspad and the other is called the Smalblaar. The water in the Cape mountains is the colour of tea. We loved to camp up there. Roll out our sleeping bags onto the white crystal sand and fry trout with flaked almonds over the flames in a little pan with a bit of butter.

My grandmother's tales of camping at Pringle Bay in the 1920s sparked our imaginations. She let us know what was possible … all we had to do was imagine it and grab it. In the 1920s there was no coastal road from Gordon's Bay. The nearest humans were a bunch of Norwegians and other whalers down at the Betty's Bay whaling station. Huge pots of blubber were reduced there. Gentle whales were murdered at sea and cooked down, as they were at Donkergat near Langebaan. Because there was no road my grandmother and her two brothers got a lift by boat on a calm day and camped at the lagoon on the northern end of the beach. They speared sole while wading in the shallow water.

The last evenings have been whale-ish here. As Zaan and I sit on our lofty perch, a bench on the hillside behind her home, and watch the sunset, their puffs are visible far out to sea. Our Southern Right whales swim south for the summer. Why are there whales here now? I guess they are humpbacks or something else. I am so glad that they do not hunt the whales around here any longer.

Some years ago I sailed on a yacht from the Bay of Islands in New Zealand to Noumea, New Caledonia. It is a crossing of about 5 or 6 days' duration. There were 3 of us on board and the watches were long. One evening just before sunset I was alone on deck with gentle trades following from the starboard quarter. As the sea turned to gold there were suddenly a group of sperm whales directly ahead. Seacomber is a heavy 56' steel vessel and I could see them from above as we passed through them. Golden wet and shining whales. Such a sight that has imprinted itself in my memory forever.

One memory leads to the next:

A warm and salty day on Voortrekker II, running before the breeze off Madagascar.

Gareth, what we have experienced in our lives!! We must write it down lest we forget!!

A sailboat running before the wind is quiet in a choppy sea and whales cannot hear it come. On this day our sea was full of hundreds of whales all heading the same way. I was standing on the leeward rail hanging onto the starboard shroud. I saw the whale as we hit it, but the contact was such a glancing blow there was no noticeable impact. We slid past one another. Its black rubber skin almost touched my toes. I saw the open eye followed by bubbles and a big brown cloud of fear as it dived.

On Capri I befriended a man named Nino Febbraio. He had been an Italian submarine commander during the war. As you know, regardless of incoming or outgoing tide, a surface current always runs out of the Mediterranean and a deep-water current always flows in. It is a function of salt.

Nino 1942

In the dangerous days of WWII submarines left the Med shallow and risked being bombed by the Brits operating out of Gibraltar, but they could not do otherwise. The return trip was safe and deep which was much more pleasant for Nino and the crew of Velella. One night after penetrating the waters of the Med, and being a fair distance from Gib, Nino brought the Velella up to the surface for fresh air and to allow the sailors to have a smoke. Only two men at a time were permitted to be in the conning tower. As captain, Nino was one of the first pair. He told me of a silver sea and a moon shining brilliantly. What a relief to be through the Pillars of Hercules and on the homeward run back to loved ones. (Whose loved ones had they left behind in the Atlantic, in life boats or dead? Victorious.) Anyway, all of a sudden, the entire sea before them was full of round disks, glinting dull and menacing, just below the surface. What devilry was this? What new weapon? What web of mines had they just sailed into? "Oh no … the end!" thought Nino.

But it was not the end – the web of mines was just turtles who, knowing nothing of the war, were merely on course for the beaches of Cyprus where for millennia they had laid (and still do lay) their eggs.

Velella was sunk in September 1943 off Salerno. Nino was the only survivor. As he told me, he had been called away to Rome to collect a citation or some honours for his ship and crew. In his absence, Velella was called out to rescue a stricken vessel (another submarine with failed engines) and both vessels were sunk by an allied aircraft, Velella without her captain, towing her sister home. Such are the stories of war.

Nino and I sat in his once splendid, now faded, villa at Punta Tragara on the island of Capri.

We drank iced Tio Pepe and spoke in a language we both understood while his reeking long haired dachshund Vergilio tried to climb up onto my lap. His house was full of swords and pirate treasure and flaking whitewash and mosquitoes.

Writing a letter like this can lead the mind down a labyrinth of memories. One memory leading to the next. It is quite extraordinary what one finds in there and one hopes that the recipient of the letter will find it to be a worthwhile read.

The first time I went to Italy I went there by sail. Uwe, Michel Personnic, Clea and I sailed the brand new 65' sloop Aga Jari from Cape Town to Genova via St Helena and Gran Canaria. I arrived on Capri hallucinating with exhaustion and slept through an entire 24hr period only waking up the following morning.

I have been back to Capri many times. Always with Clea. Clea my girlfriend, Clea my partner in adventure, Clea my bride, Clea the mother of Allegra, Clea my wife.

The last time I was there was in 2003. Allegra, Clea and I stayed in the small guest cottage below Nino's villa. Nino was dead by then. (What the bombs could not do, time did more cruelly.) We spent a few months. At night Clea and I talked and talked and drank gin and smoked Marlboro cigarettes. I was fighting to save our marriage, she was no longer in love with me. My ex-best friend Jacques (Jacq the Knife) had seen to that.

Our daughter, Allegra, tanned nut-brown, hair bleached white, dived for coins in the old submariner's especially deep pool. Her little body was covered in fine golden hair. People could not believe that such a glorious creature could exist. I feel that way today.

A family worth destroying

A decade before that sad period, fresh from our sailing adventure, swimming into the Blue Grotto on New Year's Day, with snow on Vesuvio, we had been the darlings of Capri society ... dining with the brother princes di Grazioli di Sirignano, artists, film producers, advocates and a German princess. Now in 2003, it was the beginning of a slow tortuous process of pain and betrayal. How things have a way of changing.

How we long for things my old friend ... How I long for a day in Naples or the smell of the narrow lanes of Capri. Baking and medieval mustiness. Sun-ripened tomatoes in wooden boxes on cobbles in little *piazzetti* where wild Saracens once raided.

Ciao amico mio ... I will write again.

Carl

p.s. Friends should, of course, be chosen with great care, but often aren't. Never tell today's friend what you do not want tomorrow's enemy to know.

p.p.s. Gordon once said to me: "If you had a dream and it didn't materialise, stop going back there, that dream is in the past."

Chapter 2

Kill the Head and the Body Will Die

I often look at the knuckle of my left forefinger, and the scars there.
There are many scars, all cut by the teeth of men.

When I was in my last year at Camps Bay High School, there was a
menace by the name of Kojak. He had already completed his national service,
an ex-Parabat, perhaps 20 years old. He liked to terrorise school socials and
beat up boys like us.

By 1981 I no longer carried any puppy fat.
I was very tall and slender.
Kojak appeared one evening, a group of us were down at the beach.
He challenged us all and Guy Chicken was the only one brave enough to step
forward.
Together, *en masse*, we could have packed Kojak with ease and taught him a
good lesson.
But we were all too scared.
Guy's blood ended up all over my hands and arms.
Guy is haemophiliac, so it did not clot … wet liquid non-coagulating blood.
It was something I will never forget.

In 1982 I started Karate.
It was the best thing for me.
Suleiman Samaai was my Sensei.
He taught me not to try fancy tricks in a real fight.
He taught me how to strike with the left hand.

I recently tallied them up, the incidents that would readily spring to mind.
I never started a fight, but I defended myself and my friends and strangers

from assailants and would-be rapists and crazed men. And in more recent years with our local neighbourhood watch ... there were many additional physical confrontations: In excess of thirty fights and on top of that, more arrests than I can remember. There is sadly a lot of aggression in South Africa. The bush war and township violence period of the 1970s and 1980s were particularly testy for young men. The crime period of now and recent years requires hyper-vigilance. People sometimes ask me why I carry pepper spray while out running. I reply that it is because of dogs mainly, but you never know. I am not as quick as I once was, and our society is not at all well.

After navy basics and my stint in the army at Kroonstad, I managed to get back to the navy at Simon's Town. This was mid-1988, and for me it was a priority not to be in Angola. I was posted at Works Branch and "pulled duty", one day in four, at BUVLOG with my old friend and AWOL-savant, Peter Gibbons.

Peter had an uncanny eye for seeing holes in the bigger picture. Checks and controls that had been in place and functional for years suddenly had great big open doorways in them. Victuals and petrol were liberated. Duty days became surf days. Work days became surf days. Extra meals were taken at Chefs School. Previously unimagined liberties were taken. Hanging out with Gibbons really gave me the sense that we were undermining the foundations of the apartheid war machine by burrowing from the inside. It was great fun.

During a young man's two-year national service period he was allowed 2 periods of leave: seven days in the first year and 14 days in the second.

One applied to one's Duty Officer. Ours at BUVLOG was a gentle soul named PO Paton. Paton was idling in the navy pending retirement in about thirty years. While requesting dates for our seven days' leave in 1988, Gibbons noticed that Paton wrote in pencil in his leave register. Gibbons noticed things like that.

PO Paton gave us our forms and we went to hand them in, as required, to a very strict SWAN at NoiC. (There were lots of acronyms in the SADF: AWOL, SWAN, NoiC, MUT, BUVLOG and so on, and there probably still are ... SWANS = South African Women's Auxiliary Naval Service.)

For some reason Peter and I had used Tippex on our forms and on seeing this, the very strict SWAN became enraged. "No Tippex on the forms!" Our forms were swiftly torn up into tiny bits which she dropped, unceremoniously, into a little metal waste-paper bin at her feet. I remember to this day, the stiff, cream painted, diamond mesh, behind which she stood, and the narrow wooden counter at which she served. But most importantly, our names had not been entered into the main leave ledger!

We took our "seven days" regardless and went on a delightful week-long surf trip to Seal Point and Cape St Francis in Peter's red VW Combi – a beast of burden and a home away from home. What fun.

I don't know when Gibbons worked it out, but a short while after our return, a few minutes before 10am on one of our duty days, he asked me to come with him to PO Paton's office. He was holding an eraser. At 10am PO Paton left for tea and Gibbons slipped into his office while I kept *sout* (or lookout) at the door. Twenty seconds later we headed off somewhere else. Our leave had been rubbed out and a few weeks later we were back at PO Paton's office, followed by a walk up to NoiC with Tippex all over our forms, which were again ripped to pieces by the angry SWAN and dropped into her bin. Another lovely week-long holiday was had.

The following year, as we were upgraded from lowly seamen to able-seamen and then to leading seamen or "killicks", we, in turn, upgraded Gibbons' eraser trick, allowing ourselves 14-day surf trips to Seal Point and Jeffreys Bay instead. But being stealth flyers, we never sewed the little stars and prestigious anchor badges onto our uniforms. It was a time for low profiles.

LS Gibbons and Lt Mike vd Heever – AWOL (again)

On one of those 14-day AWOLs in 1989 ... Peter, Mike van den Heever, the red Combi and I were buzzing around at Seal Point surfing and camping and generally having fun, when news filtered through to us that there was to be a party at St Francis that evening. We usually drove through to St Francis anyway to drink beer at the big thatched rondavel hotel lounge, so we thought ... *lekker*!

Peter parked the Combi among the other cars on the gravel strip below the house. The three of us eased up the driveway and entered the house unopposed. We had a few beers and laughed and talked with other surfers. It was so nice to have slipped the military and to be away again on the wonderful warm East Coast, but soon enough there were creepy vibes. People were frightened. I left the verandah from where we had been watching the last orange glow turn to inky black and went into the living room. What should have been the hub of a good time was not. Faces looked terrorized as a big Slavic-looking *chokka* fisherman abused his female companion. He lifted her up by the neck and pushed her down over and again. From his crazed mouth, utterances like: "I'm gonna kill you, I'm gonna cut your eyes out" and a whole lot more spewed forth. Everyone was paralyzed. It is so strange how it happens like that. Be it a group of army conscripts unable to fight the draft or a group of onlookers witnessing a mugging or passengers on a hijacked plane, the pussified men are terrified and for some reason cannot act together. After the Guy Chicken incident, I had been trained and had trained myself in these matters and I do not tolerate the rough handling or bullying of women.

Fortunately for me, the crazy fisherman was oblivious to the world around him. I observed him carefully and as his head plunged forward to headbutt his companion, I flicked on the light switch and with a very powerful textbook *maegeri* kick, my heavy upward moving boot connected with his downward moving ribcage. The effect was spectacular as the heavy man flew, hit the glass sliding door with a terrible bang and slid to the floor like a jellyfish. It was one of the few occasions I did not need to use my left hand.

His female companion sprang up instantly and attacked me like a wildcat but was dragged off by our fellow party-goers who had finally snapped out of their trance. The baddy was placed in his car and his girlfriend drove them away. That's how it sometimes was in those days, and the party sprang to life: dancin', smokin' and drinkin' beer.

I was reminded the other day of another episode featuring those same boots by my friend Mike Charles, with whom I shared a house in Vauxhall, London, in 1987. Mike and I and some ex-Rhodesians liked to drink beer at the Prince of Teck in Earl's Court on Friday evenings after work. There were girls there too, mainly expats – Australians, New Zealanders and *Saffers*. The summer evenings were long and warm. Patrons spilled out onto the sidewalk and into Kenway Road. At the time there were three Irish guys, a pair of twins and an almost identical brother, who liked to make trouble there. Those boots were still brand new, recently in from South Africa. Mike and I were standing beside an old-fashioned lamp post sipping beer when I heard running water. Looking down I saw one of the Irish brothers urinating prodigiously onto my feet. Without hesitating, I kicked the pint glass straight up and out of the fellow's hand and then kicked him in the chest sending him flying into the masonry pier between two big glass windows. He went down and stayed down, no more trouble from him. Luckily for all of us that it was not the plate glass he flew into. Meanwhile his pint glass had flown up trailing Guinness, most of which landed on a woman from Johannesburg. Boy, did I get hell in *Joburgese*.

Over the space of a few Friday evenings at the Prince of Teck, I had noticed a very handsome Australian girl, always hugging and kissing a different boy. On the night of the piss and boots, she ended up on the back seat of Mike's Rover and later inside our home. It was well after midnight so, being kind, I made up a bed for her in the attic of our house in Harleyford Road. In a flash her clothes were off, including her leather Aussie bush hat. I was, by then, and since 1986, terrified of AIDS and she was clearly a high-risk area, so I opted out. We gave her breakfast and tube fare in the morning. It was all rather sad because she was a lovely young woman, but I suppose, in the days of our youth, a few of the young women were less restrained. Maybe they had not been properly loved as girls. Some would never believe that they could be loved. Some were just naughty and horny. Some were good and stayed at home. Some changed. The boys were pretty much the same, but more tomcattish.

Many of the stories cannot ever be told, some can ... stories from before the easy times of dating sites and modern arrangements such as "friends with benefits" and "fuck-buddies". They hadn't been invented yet.

21 April 2013   Letter #3

Dear Gareth

A while ago I sent you a letter about submarines and other things. I forwarded it to Suzie and have not heard from her since. I will follow up.

I wonder so often, how you are and what you are doing ... especially on those days when I am not frustrated by my own work and travails.

Today is one of those days ... a shining gem at the tail end of a long summer.

I am down at the little green boatshed at the beach at Bakoven. I have been swimming under the sea, watching the light of the sun playing on the seafloor. It reminds me of a poem by Shelley: **Stanzas Written in Dejection Near Naples**. It is so beautiful.

I have just stood up to get the small espresso pot off the cooker plate and I think ... I love to write ... it is a kind of catharsis ... but writing seems to come of itself ... I do not control the thoughts that write the writing. It comes from a subconscious level within. (My mind has a mind of its own.)

So, my friend, the letters I write to you are what they are. I cannot think to not write things that may make you sad or miss too much. I would rather share these thoughts than not.

Today (Saturday) dawned clear. The hadeda ibis flew over as they do every day at that time, crying their mournful cries and waking all but the heaviest sleepers and the most innocent.

Zaan and I do Table Mountain 2 or 3 times a week in valiant battle against middle age. Today on the way home, I saw that there were dolphins in the bay, so I dropped Zaan at home ... (she had to take her son Nicholas to a guitar lesson) ... and I shot down to Bakoven, jumped on my surf-ski and headed out in pursuit.

There are days my friend, that we must etch into our minds ... and write into our journals for they do not repeat often, and never twice the same way.

I headed out over a flat sea and finally spotted the white splashes and dark bodies of the dolphins on the rising swells a long way off. After some minutes, I was in the herd. Maybe 200 animals, maybe 50 on the surface at any time. The dolphins were whistling like humans and whistling like the highest end of the tiniest dentist drill.

I stayed with them for almost an hour. Big dolphins. Babies glued to their mothers' sides. Dolphins jumping, dolphins smacking their tails together. And as there sometimes are, there were seals amongst them, almost clownish or clowning in their poor-man's imitation of the most elegant afore-mentioned.

I left the herd somewhere off Clifton ... they were headed north, and I peeled off to the south. Being in that crowd was so noisy and splashy and wet. Now suddenly it was silent except for the rhythmic work of my body and the paddle, and the flick of a few drops of water off the tip of the blade at every stroke. And I was thinking of liberty and Gareth as I tapped on home.

Now I sit here in the shed overlooking the shining sea and the eternal rocks that never change. Four small boys have popped into the shed to look at the boats and equipment. Small boys like we were just yesterday. Small boys full of wonderment.

Now this boy sits and tries to write with an old pair of specs that are too weak. Not really able to see the words I write, relying on years of practice in piles of journals. Piles of journals that record many days and nights and maybe when I am an old man and I have some of that so rare and so wasted commodity called "time", I will take them out of their plastic crates and read them all in sequence ... Starting in London in 1987 ... but in none of those diaries is remembered a night in the camp site at Mossel Bay, under a full moon, full of beer, dancing like wild and crazy things to a Juluka cassette playing in a yellow Toyota panel van with the back door open.

The song was called **Africa**, maybe the album was called **Scatterlings**, the words went (to my recollection) something like this:

Son as you grow...
Learn never to trust anyone, learn to trust only stone ...
for this is a hard land ...
and will break anyone who does not learn to live alone.

Carlos

Chapter 3

Mossel Bay

In the 1980s I owned a Mazda 323. On Friday afternoons Mick and I would strap on our boards, collect Mike Mater at his apartment and then Uwe at the boatyard. Traffic out of the city was not a problem then. I would drive the winding 400km distance, through Riviersonderend, Swellendam and Riversdale, as my passengers drank and laughed and finally fell asleep on the long straight past Albertinia.

At about 10.30pm we would pull up outside the Santos Hotel in time for a late Friday beer. We would find our friends Peter or Manuel at the hotel bar and sleep at one of their rented houses, or just roll out our sleeping bags on the stoep of an uninhabited bungalow down at The Point or up on the wild-side. It would be a hard winter at the Cape, but at Mossel Bay, with its glorious weather, the options were plentiful. If we were there for more than just a weekend, tents would be pitched at the campsite overlooking the surf spots of Inner and Outer Pool.

First prize was, of course, to wake up close to the sea engulfed by the sound of the roaring rushing waves as they raced down the rocky point towards the broad sandy beaches at Voorbaai and Hartenbos. We would choose our weekends well … after a cold front … with the wind shifting from north-west to south-westerly and the swell taking 24hrs to get there from the Cape.

How does a person describe the surfing? The crate of damp wetsuits, the wax, picking one's way out over the sharp barnacle rocks. Bracing as a wave swirls and pushes, then selecting the moment to dive into the channel, not losing your fins, and then on your board, paddling like anything to get clear without being nailed by a set. It is the same at Jeffreys and Seal Point and Still Bay … just variations on a theme.

Mick, Carl, Uwe & Peter ... free camping

Carlos, surfing small waves at Mossel Bay

The wonderful feeling of stroking out to sea, into the oncoming swell, towards the break, is one of the finest experiences in life. One or two buddies might already be out, or you might be the first. The pitch and thunder. The boil of the reef below. Lining yourself up and paddling into the peak to find yourself dropping into the take-off and racing down the ever-lifting wall of water ahead. Kicking out and paddling back, the sea fizzing, effervescent all around. And the encouraging hoots of friends as one shared the love of being there, playing between the breaking waves. Playing at the place where the great swells of the southern Indian Ocean finally spend themselves on the hard edge of the African continent.

Sometimes on balmy winter's nights, as we slept, if the swell was a little smaller and less noisy, great whales would creep inshore and we would listen to their hollow tubular blowing.

It isn't like that any longer. There are more whales to be sure, but the surf, like almost everything else these days, is so much more crowded. I wonder often, just before I drift into sleep, whether I will ever again step across those honey brown barnacled rocks at Mossel Bay and launch myself into the channel. I really miss that. And the seals frolicking around, and the dolphins racing through us, and the exhaustion, having surfed away one's last drop of energy. And finally making your way in again to the beach ... through the rock pools, taking the greatest care not to step on the spiny urchins lurking in every crevice.

26 May 2013   Letter #4

Dear Gareth

I hope that you are okay … I think about you such a lot nowadays … every time I run down the road for an early surf … I am stabbed by your loss of liberty … your incarcerated situation stands like a beacon in my everyday … I hate it and I just cannot believe it.

It is quite difficult for me to put these things down on paper without having spoken to you … me who rates liberty as paramount.

I need to go and visit your mom … but my life is running on a treadmill or conveyor belt that is ever speeding up against me … I just never seem to get out to 21 Quarterdeck Road. Dear old Suzie.

It is Sunday evening now … I have been meaning to write to you for some time. I have just finished off some prep work for Monday so that maybe I can sneak in a "dawn patrol" at Glen Beach … tomorrow early bells … I wish we could have a good old chat … I hear the rain in the gutter outside my office … does it ever rain in Kuwait? Let me tell you about the Cape.

It has been a warm May … but the morning air has a chill now and we have had some small swells coming through. The mountains are decked with Proteas.

I walk my daughter Allegra to school at about 07h30 … that is first light now … she in uniform, me in my wetsuit. I have already been down to check the surf. I walk with my long-board under my arm. The grainy wet air is delightful to my Northern European skin. The street lights are golden misty orbs.

Stroking out to sea is one of the most calming things in a land of worry. Living in this country can bear heavily on the human heart. Humanity seems unhappy. Humanity is out of control. Humanity is outrageous. People do many things to stave off reality. For me, peace lies just behind the break line on an early uncrowded weekday morning. Cool, beyond the borders, to be touched by the mercy of the sea.

Early morning at Glen Beach

Glen Beach (we call it our backyard) is nothing like the big peeling hollow wave we used to surf at 365 in the '80s ... now relegated to my dream past. We would put longer boards on the roof and drive out on a cold, still morning, when the booming surf made all else unimportant. Past the pines, scraggy in the gloom, of Ou Kaapse Weg. Out there somewhere Sunset Reef was pluming away. On past Slangkop lighthouse, Outer Kom smoking. Park the *bakkie*, on go the wetsuits, wax up the boards. Scuttle down to the water's edge.

Thick rotten kelp piled high by the sea. Over the rocks and into the water like a group of penguins hurrying to avoid the shore-break. Then 100 metres of slow ploughing through a thick bed of kelp, each rise in swell allowing a few metres of progress. Suddenly we would be clear of the weed and out into the open sea. Cold green water, grey sky and a white dot sun. No orientation other than the sun and the direction of the swell. The huge peak of 365 rising just to the left.

The first man out, the first to take the drop. A twenty-foot face, pitch and toss. A small man down to see the submarines. Number two, placed over the boil drops into the pit. Down, down the long green wall. Endless falling, bottom turn and straighten into a monster cover up. Out into the air, milk the inside section, a long wall building up on the inner reef. Kick out, start to paddle back, adrenalin coursing.

Or surfing at Barley Bay in front of the Camps Bay police station. Paddling back, running the gauntlet, huge walls of white water approaching, duck dives, the waves dragging you back, thick kelp, past the impact zone and then finally the relative calm of the heaving outside sea, sun breaking up the cloud. I still know of no finer thing.

Brother Mick says it is bad to live in the past, surfing at Barley Bay 1992

Glen Beach, I surf the "backyard" now and find the peace of a middle-aged man before the working day and think of my old pal Gareth. Among the close-outs and the peaks and the wedges … a handful of old locals who have known each other for years. I surf there now because I don't have much spare time. No time for long drives. Life has changed.

I was at Home Affairs in Barrack Street last week to pick up Allegra's passport. Poorly behaved snot-nosed small children running around screaming while shell-shocked parents holding new grubby bundles in their arms come to register yet another unneeded baby.

Last week I got stuck in the traffic for an hour and a half trying to get to the airport ... the South Africans were burning plastic portable toilets on the N2 highway by way of protest. Big chunks of concrete had been dropped onto the road as well. Black smoke and melted goo ... it is craziness.

In June I will take Allegra to Arctic Norway for 2 weeks ... I can't wait. I will put on a thick warm padded zip up suit and a pair of Harken gumboots and sleep on the pebble beach in the pale sunshine with my head filled by the wavelets clattering the myriad flat brown stones like little castanets.

When you get back old boy ... we will sit in my garden and talk ... and I look forward to hearing your stories.

I know that this is a bit of a disjointed letter, no polish, but some thoughts nevertheless ... What runs out of my fingertips runs. Next time I will stay off the surf stories. Forgive. Next time I will tell you about Norway.

I hope you have received the previous 3 ... This is Letter 4

Much Love ... your old pal ... C

Brother Mick, a little older, surfing the now

Chapter 4

Into the valley of death rode the four hundred

When I finally arrived in Simon's Town, back in the navy, safe and away from the army's clutches, no one was expecting me. I could have slipped away and no one would have been any the wiser, and my national service would have ended eighteen months early. Similarly, had I never boarded that train to Kroonstad, I would not have been missed. There were no computerised crosschecks in those days. In the days of the Angolan war, with all of its adjuncts, the South African Defence Force was a massive organisation with cracks aplenty to fall through. I did not know this at the time.

Peter Gibbons – AWOL Savant

My old pal Peter Gibbons was posted to the new underground fuel storage depot construction site situated above Seaforth beach. He took me down to the dockyard to meet Mr Price (our boss) at the Navy Works Branch and I was also awarded a sinecure there. Whereas previously Gibbons had loafed alone in his shipping container office, slipping away for surfs and meals every now and then, we now did it together – anything but work. That side of things we left to an extremely conscientious, serious young engineer and responsibility magnet named Johan Redelinghuys.

I took a navy apartment at Waterfall Barracks which I shared with two other national servicemen whom I never saw. The apartment consisted of my bedroom, a small lounge, bathroom and two permanently locked doors leading into the other two bedrooms. After Kroonstad, it was utter heaven. A whole other war! With oak trees and a stream and a huge mess catering and cooking for 400 men of whom more than 100 were seldom present. Some of the chefs ran a food racket and were finally arrested by raiding MPs responding to a tip-off, their car trunks stuffed full of "take-aways". Gibbons sometimes lived with his girlfriend in Rosebank and other times at Waterfall. It was all rather fluid in the navy. There were no passbooks.

I had been back in the navy for about a month when I was sent for by PO Paton at BUVLOG and told that I would, from now, be placed on a "one-in-four" duty watch. A freshly minted NSM lieutenant named West had traded my name for his on the duty roster. I was on duty and he was off for the rest of our time at Simon's Town. West had been part of my intake and I had known him for years, a handsome and charming young man, but sadly he was a member of that unlovely group of people who will *naai* their *maatjies*. "*Naai jou maatjies*" as they say in Afrikaans means literally: "fuck your buddies". Lt West was not the kind of person you'd want in your six. The kind of sneaky individual who becomes increasingly disliked as their lives progress.

Note: in the military there are NCOs and COs.

NCOs are non-commissioned officers: like army corporals and sergeants or navy ABs (able seamen), killicks (leading seamen) and petty officers.

COs are commissioned officers like army captains and majors or navy lieutenants, commanders and captains.

Regardless of how junior, the CO always outranks the NCO. A one-pip army lieutenant outranks the RSM (regimental sergeant major) who is obliged to salute the lieutenant.

And that is why the freshly out of Officers Course national serviceman Lt West could order career NCO PO Paton to use his eraser to his advantage and my chagrin.

By that time, my brother Mick was happy as Larry, playing sax in the Navy Band. Coming and going as he pleased in his red Toyota Corolla.

Over the years people have asked me, "How did you and your brother end up doing National Service both in the navy, both at the same time."

I answer, "The long story or the short one?"

Mick and I had been receiving unwelcome army call-ups every six months for the past few years: School of Engineers Kroonstad, Phalaborwa, Infantry School Grahamstown, Potchefstroom and so on. It was 1987, we had just about completed our tertiary education and were soon obliged to go to the military. I had the idea of writing to our local MP (and head of the anti-apartheid opposition party) Colin Eglin. General elections were to be held in South Africa in a few months and I offered Eglin a deal – I would encourage my friends and buddies to support and vote PFP in exchange for navy call-up papers for my brother and me.

Eglin did not reply so I organised a job in London and, like my brother Bill (who was by then living in California), left the country. And soon, suffering from huge culture-shock and homesickness, found myself working at London Stone not far from the giant Battersea Power Station.

It was a glorious June day in London, when I was summonsed to reception, a trunk call, my mom: Navy call-ups had arrived for both Mick and me. Mine for July 1987 and his for February 1988 the following year. For me they'd come too late!

So I stayed in the Northern hemisphere and Mick came over and joined me towards the end of the year. We went to meet our family in Norway and surfed in France and Portugal before returning to face the SADF in early February.

During those years, a postal slip for a registered letter, home delivered by none other than "big fatty bell-ringer" on his little motorcycle, sent the heart plummeting. There were two national service intakes every year and fresh call-up papers were issued every six months. They had to be collected at the post office and signed for. The envelope had an unmistakable logo on it, in the shape of the Castle of Good Hope. As mentioned before, messing around with military call-ups and conscientious objection got you imprisoned. I didn't fetch mine.

In early February Mick and I were dropped off by our mom at Wingfield military base near Cape Town. Mothers and fathers were saying last goodbyes to their sons. Military men on their best behavior simpered around, barely able to wait for the parents to leave. One or two thousand young men were being sorted. Those with army call-ups (by far the majority) were lined up on the various rail platforms. Navy call-ups were double-checked and those lucky fish who held them were directed to buses parked nearby. I avoided the checks and wandered over to a bus marked Saldanha Bay, climbed aboard and hid at the back until a handful of new conscripts climbed aboard and I blended in.

The 150km bus trip to Saldanha was a pleasure compared to the long, hollow-stomach, troop-train journeys that most conscripts were subjected to. We spilled out onto the parade ground and were seated on the marching gravel, all four hundred of us. A register was called and one by one the four hundred were rearranged in straight line platoons of around thirty men each. In the end there were three left and I was one of them. We were asked to present our call-up papers: "Phalaborwa, get back on the bus!" ... "Upington, back on the bus!" ... and lastly me, with my six-month out-of-date navy call-up.

I explained that I had just returned from Europe and these were all I had received, and I was here to do my national service. What could they say? For now, I was in the navy and I went and plonked myself down with my brother Mick and the men of the (as-yet unformed) 1988 February intake MUT band. In the 1970s and 80s many South African "paleface" schools had "military cadets" (in addition to rugby) as a compulsory extra-mural activity for boys. They were taught how to march and shoot .22 rifles. Some of the cadets played trumpets, drums and cymbals. Some of these ex-cadets were in the band, others were simply young musicians who were already experts on the horn, trombone, tuba and the saxophone

The four hundred were then split into two. Two hundred were brutally herded off, in clouds of dust, insults and abuse, to become marines, while the rest of us, the luckiest conscripts of all – luckier by factors of ten when compared to those who had managed to wangle their way into Personnel Services Pretoria – remained: BLUE NAVY.

A month or so later a van of MPs turned up. They had finally tracked me down. Who'd have thought to look for a missing conscript inside a military training base? Well, they did.

Apparently, I was meant to be in Kroonstad doing my basic training at the Army School of Engineers. I was sent to the armoury to hand in my rifle and ordered to pack my kit. But, the OC, Captain Du Toit was not happy about being bullied by a couple of roughneck MPs and the building plans I was drawing for Commander Mostert's new garage were not yet complete. The MPs were sent away. My rifle was returned to me. I stayed at Saldanha Bay for my three-month period of basic training with the guarantee that I would be railed up to Kroonstad afterwards.

⁕

I arrived at the Kroonstad railway station in the early hours of a Saturday morning. I was the only passenger to disembark. The train pulled away and vanished into the darkness. It was quiet and cold. I stood on the concrete platform in my navy "step-out" uniform beside my big red suitcase. There was no one there to meet me. An aged stationmaster appeared out of the gloom and asked what I was waiting for. He called the army base and about an hour later a duty driver pulled up and took me away.

That was the moment I should have turned around and caught the next train back to Cape Town, but how was I to know?

The driver delivered me to the guardroom where I slept until daylight. It was all shockingly unfamiliar. Men in brown uniforms and brown shiny boots. Foot stamping salutes and harsh voices. I was interviewed by a Commandant named Prins who handed me over to four army rugby stars who had a vacant fifth bed in their bungalow. They laughed as they told me to turn over the filthy foam-rubber mattress that had been allotted to me. The greasy hole on the back of the mattress, once flipped over, was in fact the vagina of a crudely drawn woman. Broom bristles had been inserted into the foam-rubber as mock pubic hair. She was introduced to me as Anna. The rugby stars took turns fucking her.

The rugby stars suddenly vanished and I was left standing around feeling uncomfortably numb when a fresh-faced young fellow named Pepe, taking pity, invited me to rather come and stay with them. "Them" turned out to be four soldiers named Heigers, Sugsy, Gramps and Adriaan De Villiers Pepler a.k.a. Pepe. They also had a spare fifth bed in their bungalow, which I was free to use. Pepe then brought down, from the top of his steel cupboard (or *kas*), a huge box of mother-made chocolate biscuits. Tea was brewed. Lucky I was indeed, my fortunes had changed.

Pepe was a Hekpoort farm boy who drove tractors and lorries on the base. Heigers, a local Kroonstad boy who had "organised" himself, was a cross-country runner who had permission to take runs outside the base. He would run home and spend an hour or so having coffee and *koeksisters* with his mother before running back to camp. Sugsy and Gramps were *sleg-troepe*, which is a bit difficult to define. NAAFI would have summed them up (No Ambition and Fuck-all Interest).

For one or another reason, the men I had just joined were not destined for the "Operational Area" or the war in Angola and were known as "HK" or "HQ Troops". The rugby stars were needed to be rugby stars while Sugsy and Gramps were, as Corporal Mans might have described them: "*Siek, lam en vertraag!*" (and happy to be just that). Nik Rujevic, from the next-door bungalow, had served in the Yugoslavian navy and was therefore suspect, and Paki Bardsley was a Pom.

Another quick note on the military: If a person such as Nik Rujevic had already completed his national service in another country, then he would be credited the months served. Nik was grabbed on a visit to his paternal homeland and forced to spend a year in the post-Tito navy. On returning to South Africa he was collared again and forced to sit and twiddle his thumbs in the SADF for another year. Uwe had served for 18 months in the German navy. He, therefore, on returning to South Africa, was obliged to spend six months at the Navy dockyard at Simon's Town. The period of conscription for paleface males in South Africa was an initial two years followed by an additional 24 months of one to three-month long camps. "*Ou man* campers" were sometimes called up for "Township Duty" or to boost the ranks of large operations.

I spent three months in Kroonstad. Initially it was a very depressing shock to the system. Half-inch-thick discs of ice were lifted off the water in the fire-buckets and rolled away. Corporal Mans would wake us up at around 3am on Sunday mornings, shouting us into lines on the frosty grass. There we would stand, barefoot, in pyjamas or underpants, as he slowly went about taking roll-call. We would wake up on other nights with Commandant Prins in our bungalow shouting *"Wat die fok gaan hier aan?"* at the top of his voice.

After a few interviews with various brasses, and my refusal to go on "Officers Course", I was assigned to the building of a new sports centre on the base. Once the sun came out and the ice had thawed from our hosepipes we would mix cement and lay bricks.

A massive steel barn had been erected alongside a new rugby field. Nominally under the control of a lieutenant named Whitfield and Sergeant Stoop, Paki Bardsley and I supervised a pack of eight to ten criminally insane conscripted *boutroepe* (building troops) from Springs. We were assisted by about five to ten green-clad prisoners from the local prison. These mixers of mortar and carriers of bricks were collected daily from their place of incarceration by Pepe: a crew of tattooed murderers, rapists and villains, some prepared to share their stories, others not. It was a wild place. Homemade bombs would go off with splintered shards of glass spinning through the air. Bricks were hurled at one another. On my first day, for insisting that the prison labour also get their share of the tea urn, a shovel was anonymously thrown at me from a scaffold, gashing the toe of my combat boot.

Surprisingly though, walls went up and toilet cubicles, squash courts and recreation spaces quickly took shape. Door and window frames were set. The *boutroepe* were worried (they were not permitted to bring their rifles to site) as to how they would defend themselves against a "*Khaki*" attack, should the British army suddenly appear over the hill and surprise them while they worked. Kroonstad had been in the bosom of the Anglo-Boer War almost ninety years before and unpleasant memories were apparently still simmering away. Half bricks were dropped down unconnected lavatory pipes and tools were plastic-bagged and hidden in drums of paint for later stealing.

Shortly after my arrival in Kroonstad, one of the first things brought to my attention was that there had been no toilet paper for quite some time.

The idea of asking for some was apparently unthinkable so I did and ended up being marched into the Colonel's office (on orders) by the Adjutant. Being taller than normal I had to duck as I entered his low lintelled office, which I think amused the old warhorse. I was marched out again and taken to a huge storeroom where I was issued with what I had come for. I returned to barracks victorious, carrying a plastic-wrapped cube containing 200 bog rolls on my head.

Thus I realised, that there were, albeit concealed, human sides to this army.

Alice Cooper's song title, **We Got To Get Out Of This Place**, became my mantra.

I was ordered daily to go to the quartermaster and draw a brown uniform.

I never did.

27 June 2013   Letter #5

Dear Gareth

This letter has been written in small bits over the last days.

The first time I came up to Arctic Norway was in 2003 – ten years ago.

The sun shone for a week … 24hrs a day … non-stop … and I was sad to leave my young daughter and my crumbling marriage on the island of Capri. My friend Dag and I walked up far into the high mountains where there are small huts and pools with ice and arctic char and reindeer wandering about.

Ten years later Dag and I are just back from the high mountains … this time near Kvænangen.

We climbed up to play Dotterel songs (from a small MP3 player) to the Dotterels Dag imagined to be there … and they were. Within a few seconds, one of these small speeding plovers whizzed about us and flew off. Their nesting grounds are known, but nobody knows where they migrate to once the male bird has finished raising the chicks. Interestingly the females will lay up to three clutches with 3 separate partners as she follows the summer northwards. Leaving her mate each time as soon as the last egg is laid.

After a few moves we sat still with 4 birds approaching ever nearer … one was ringed and had the black base of the small sunlight detector still attached to its left leg, 2 years had passed since Dag and a colleague put it on … but the tiny BAS Geolog sunlight detector itself was gone. This electronic device (being 0.7g and much lighter than a satellite tracking beacon), if recovered would have told the exact time of sunrise and sunset day after day and thereby the exact global position of the bird could be calculated. But the mystery remains a mystery to those humans who care about where the Dotterels go in the European winter.

Every season in the Arctic has its own flavour. Some years are lemming years as we saw last time I was here. Their tiny carcasses fill the fjords and forest floors. Then birds of prey breed with incredible success. This spring has been a warm spring up here, while Southern Europe has enjoyed almost continuous rain. This year is now a mozzy year. Wrists, necks and ankles are lumpy and itchy. Mozzy repellent is poor armour against the pestilential hordes. Unlike their Southern cousins, the slow arctic mosquitoes are easy to kill but sheer force of numbers means that the war is unwinnable until the calendar moves autumn-wards.

To quote Zaan: "Only time really knows how to fly" and oh-boy that is correct. Up here, with continuous daytime a person can become disorientated. Yesterday we ate dinner at 4pm … *Middagsmat* … as the Norwegians call it. At 18h30 I thought it was about 11pm and I was ready to turn in. I went to bed and slept for what seemed like hours and awoke to find that it was only 8pm. I was convinced that my watch had stopped, but no, just time warp. We then sat and talked until 23h30. I awoke again at 02h30. At that time of day everything goes calm and the light is magical. Like the light of thunderstorms or an eclipse. This morning the fjord at Toppelbukt was the colour of flat shining gold. No ripple, no movement, no sound except for the small birds in the forest behind our hut.

Yesterday I went for a run up in the forest. It was cooler than my previous 2 afternoon runs, when stopping or even slowing down meant mozzy attack. (Me with no shirt on = !!! hundreds of little needles within seconds). For some reason or other there was not a mosquito anywhere and I had the pleasure of being still in the silence, trying to absorb the intense beauty of the russet and dark green arctic pines with their resinous roots and the white barked arctic birch on the downslope with their small heart shaped leaves just twitching in the light breeze. (Why is it that running in other places is such hard work? Lion's Head and Table Mountain seem easy, in Norway, JHB and Beaufort West I struggle so.)

Over the days we have caught and eaten trout, pollock, cod and ocean catfish, and we had some delicious Lofoten Minke whale and seal (*per Norsk* – *Wal* og *Kobbekjott*). The long fillet of the Greenland seal makes an unbelievably delicious, tender and rich stew cooked with mushrooms and onions.

Bubbling away like thick porridge in a big kettle … who would not love a bowl of that with steaming sticky rice to absorb the gravy? So now we are part whale and part seal too.

I am slowly getting used to typing on my laptop PC … now that I have come to terms with laying my palm-heels down and not spider-walking my hands up the keypad … much better.

How does a person relax after such a period of prolonged intensity? Well that is interesting to watch. It comes and goes … a little more each day, with the claws of anxiety loosening their hold, little by little.

I had done a couple of hours of work every morning for the first days up here, then the requirement slacked off. Allegra went off into the mountains to overnight with a group of young friends. I came back from a run in the woods and Dag said: "Now you should rest Kallemann." I put on some warm clothes and went to sit in a chair at the water's edge. A sleepy calm. Chattering gulls and songbirds, soft sunshine on my neck. The Toppelbukt Queen and the older nameless fishing dinghy lying at slack moorings. No sound of lapping water or wavelets on the stones. Within minutes a deep drowsiness overcame me. I flopped down on the upper edge of the pebble beach. It was low tide with the water at least 4m away. When Dag came to wake me, the sea was just a few inches from my knees.

That was the same type of tiredness caused by stored fatigue that came over me when I reached Capri in 1993 (20 years ago) after 7 weeks at sea, when I slept for an afternoon, a night, a complete day, another night and got up only the next morning. This time it was slightly less intense, and I dragged the sum of my body parts up to the log cabin and proceeded to dive headlong into the deepest heaviest sleep of years. Dag woke me to put out a long-line at about 7pm which we did, with me in a somnambulistic trance. After which, I went straight back to sleep. Marie laughed at my clumsy antics as we pulled up the line around midnight, whereafter I went back to the deepest sleep for 8 more hours. Now was that cleansing?? I don't know! Who knows how it works?

While nothing is perfect, it is pleasant to be far from the world of a dying Mandela and the corruption and arrogance and ignorance of our local politicians and their self-serving, gold-grubbing, plundering greed as has destroyed the economies and infrastructure of so many African states.

In 1980 when Dag started in Africa, there were 2 Kenyan Shillings to the Norwegian Kroner. Now there are 14. At the same time, he exchanged 7 Norwegian Kroner for 1 South African Rand ... now it is 0.6 NOK to the ZAR. What a balls-up. If only we could import a professional expat government to put RSA back on the right track: Swiss, New Zealanders, Austrians, Norwegians and Canadians.

Contemplatively hiding up here in the land of the midnight sun ... thinking about the Cape and loved ones ... coffee and cream, soft light, beauty and sadness.

Today Joey and I walked up to the mountain cabin of Tryggve and Lena ... Joey and Lena cleaned ... Tryggve and I fixed the verandah which had failed under an unusually heavy pile of snow this winter past. A no mosquito day again! Why?

Tomorrow if the weather remains good we will go out to Loppa Island on the Queen.

Best regards
C

Chapter 5

The Door to Norway

My father's family is Norwegian. He was born in 1934 and came out to Durban in 1938, just before the war. It was a tough time – his parents needed to make a living, so he was partially raised by a local teenager and learned to speak Zulu before he could speak English.

One afternoon, in about 2001 or 2002, a man rang our Camps Bay doorbell seeking advice on the whereabouts of a good guesthouse in the vicinity. He had a Scandinavian accent, so I asked him if he was Norwegian. Dag, born in Bergen, told me that he lived on a fjord somewhere between Tromsø and Alta, over a thousand kilometres inside the Arctic Circle. He was working on contract as a lecturer in Sea Fisheries Technology at the University of Namibia. He and his wife Marie and their three daughters were renting a house in Windhoek. By way of welcome, Marie had been held up at gunpoint in their own garden, with one of the would-be robbers being shot in the back by a neighbour. Dag and Marie had both lived and worked in Turkana, so they were not much bothered by the incident, but now with Dag's tenure at UNAM drawing to a close, his family had returned to Norway and he was in Cape Town hoping to buy a summer cottage here before heading back to the Arctic and setting up a business building *Hytter* or timber homes.

Dag and I chatted for a few hours. He stayed with us for two weeks, bought a house in Hout Bay and over the next ten years, I designed, and he built, 30 new houses and timber structures in Norway. Twenty-nine of them north of Mo i Rana and one south of the Arctic Circle in Lillehammer. It was a busy time for work and raising children. A door had opened wide for me to properly connect with my Norwegian roots.

⌘

In 1987 I went to Southern Norway to meet my grandfather for the first time. He lived in the picturesque coastal town of Arendal. We met and embraced, "Carl, I knew you would be the first to come," he said, and the tears flowed from us, and for a long time neither of us could speak. Two strangers embracing, one seventy-six, the other twenty-three, in the absolute love and acceptance of who each other are: the father of the father, the son of the son.

In the winter of 1993, with thick snowdrifts in windblown curves, packed against the wooden homes and down the alleyways of Arendal, and great loads of dirty ice bulldozed into the fjord, I wrote down the life of my grandfather, Rolf Liltved.

Rolf's father, Petter Thomas Liltved Rasmussen, came from Liltved near Fausing in Denmark. He married Kitty Ørum and they had nine children: Sofie, Eilif, Karl, Rolf, Petter, Rut, Anna Marie, Kitty and Tor.

Rolf was born at Sandefjord, a coastal town known for its whaling companies in the old days. They moved to Kitty Ørum's home town Arendal, bought a central building where they lived and worked and changed the family name to Liltved.

Rolf's *morfar* (maternal grandfather) was a captain on his own sailing vessel, which he sailed world-wide with a crew of ten to twenty men. In 1925, at fourteen, Rolf left home. "I was too young to go to sea … but I did so anyway".

He joined "the rotten wooden ship Anfin". The Anfin could not get decent crew and took men from the local jailhouse because "the boat was so ill". The Anfin was full of "bedbugs, cockroaches and rats". They set sail with a cargo of "timber for the mines".

In 1926, at 15 years of age, Rolf sailed to Northern Siberia and returned with a ship carrying a cargo of timber to London. He "got sick on a night watch" and "lay down on the ice-cold deck". When he woke up, he "could no longer stand up". He was taken to see a doctor in a hospital in Rotterdam where he collapsed. The captain arrived to take him back to the boat, but he could not move. Later he was carried by two crew members to a taxi and taken to the Norwegian Consulate. Nobody knew what was wrong with

- 57 -

him. The consul dismissed him saying: "Cripples like you, we will never send home!"

Rolf was placed in an upper bunk on a ship named Balzac. A kind old man gave Rolf the bottom bunk. He was offloaded in Kristiansand in October 1926 and, still unable to walk, was carried home on a stretcher.

Rolf told me that in the 1920s in the Russian port of Murmansk, the offloading of the ship was done by a continuous line of Russian women. Up one *landgang* (gangplank) empty handed, down another. Each with a heavy sack on the shoulders. He gave one of the women a pair of silk stockings. Contact with foreign seamen was forbidden. She was removed from the group and he never saw her again.

Rolf told me that one day in a Russian port, he traded a shirt and a bottle of vodka for a recipe for yellow margarine.

In 1927 Rolf left home again, with a walking stick, and went to the West Coast of Norway to Kopervik. He sailed to Russia and Siberia in the summer of 1927. Then in winter he sailed with the "Monkey Nut Line" from Senegal. "A lot of coal bricks from England to the Canary Islands. Fruit and wine from the coast of Spain went to North Africa and Palestine. I signed off in England leaving the ship Steinsaas at this point."

Rolf told me that on the trip from Senegal, water was so scarce on-board ship that crew members were only allowed to drink water from a tank high up above the deck. They had to climb up onto the tank and dip for water using a long ladle. There was no fresh water for washing.

In 1928 he sailed on a ship named Ulstaed, one of a group of 3 ships carrying coal to Australia where there was a coal strike in progress. The other 2 ships fell foul to spontaneous combustion. The Ulstaed was the only one to reach Australia. "I was 18 years old – 61 days at sea".

On the way to Australia, the Ulstaed stopped at Durban to re-victual and take on bunker coal. Here he said to his crewmates: "I will settle down in Durban".

In 1930 Rolf attended "cook and steward school" in Oslo before joining a tanker as Chief Steward.

In 1933 he married my grandmother Birgit (Bibi) Solberg and my dad Øystein arrived in January 1934.

Rolf then made some money whaling one season off Madagascar and 2 seasons in the Antarctic on board the Sydney Smith before re-joining his wife in Norway. In the spring of 1937, nine years after his first visit to Durban aboard Ulstaed, Rolf got "the papers in order" and went over to the South African Embassy in London to apply for immigration to the Union of South Africa.

On 30 April 1938, their passports were stamped "Cape Town" and on 18 October 1938, at Durban: "The Point – Port Natal".

01 August 2013   Letter #6

Dear Gareth,

31 July 2013

I spoke to my brother Mick just now. One of our pals, an excellent surfer, fit, handsome, charming and seemingly relaxed individual, just ended up on the table with his heart in the hands of the "heart-tiffies" as they "emergencied" to repair the stress damage. With an ideally situated home (a stone's throw from the beach), a great job, a couple of small kids and a beautiful wife … The "Living the Dream" man.

I was reminded of an email I received once from my dear friend Priceless, who was worried that people might get the impression that all I do is hang around with "Captain Holiday and Co."

He wanted me to tell about the real stress in my life, in other words (and in his words): "The number of Texan plains I smoke in my windowless office each day, the loads of coffee with that muddy layer of sugar sloshing in the bottom, the disposable cups littering my desk. You know, that 'Welcome to the real world' kind of stuff. Late nights up before the computer to make up for the surf time, work hard, eventually make money and then hand it over to the heart mechanics at the age of 45."

Today I got up early, finished and emailed some urgent drawings. I then freewheeled my bike down to the lookout above the Glen Beach. It is so warm with the NE Berg winds blowing for 2 days. There is plenty of swell about but the waves were lousy. No matter how I turned my head, I could not make them better. I rode home, collected Allegra, drove her the 1.5 minutes to school and went back to the beach lookout, the waves were definitely no good … (but such is the longing for surfing that it must be considered a very real addiction). As a second choice, Zaan and I went for a run, at 08h30 … late.

⚜

Our society has changed so much. The so-called "white" people of the Atlantic Seaboard do not, as a rule, walk their own dogs any more. They hire so-called "aliens" to do it for them while they whiz off out of their palaces, in their capitalistic frenzies, to do the necessary in order to make the money to feed the beast. I wonder if they wonder why their dogs and their hired "aliens" are getting flabby. I could tell them because I have found out. When you run late … i.e. out of the starting blocks at about 08h30 … you come across the so-called "aliens" not walking the dogs as arranged, but rather sitting on the benches and in the pretty places along the mountain track, above upper Fresnaye, playing with their mobile phones. Huge smiles and polite hellos as they message back and forth to Burundi and the Burundians and to the Congo and the Congolese … ha ha ha … you gotta love it.

⚜

When one lies awake at 3am in the old Masonic Hotel in Kamieskroon it is very quiet except for, from time to time, the ripping, tearing sound of huge rubber tyres on the tarmac. The night-shredding trucks heading north for Namibia or back.

Up in the hills, on the red granite koppies, out in the cold night midwinter air, *kokerbome* stand unmoving.

Up in the hills on the gravel pass leading to Leliesfontein it is hard to camp because darkness comes early in the winter and the owls screech so terrifyingly that you end up in the old Masonic Hotel, because you did not know that the screeching belonged to the owls until some time after.

When I lie awake at 3am in my bedroom because I had too much coffee too late, trying to work too long, and the stress is too horrible to live with, and the inside of my head is operating like some type of crazed insect hopping from one thing to the next, what I hear is the sea. It is quiet but ever present. "*Thalassa*" (the Sea) cried Xenophon's men, but my beloved sea does not help me then.

When you lie awake at 3am in a prison in Kuwait, is it hot? … is there air-con? What is it like out in the desert beyond those walls? What is it like

- 61 -

beyond the beyond? Are there barking geckos like you find in every wild place in Namibia? Are there the burned-out corpses of tanks which had their turrets blown off their shoulders in 1991 by Yankee depleted uranium shells in Operation Desert Storm? Where did all that depleted uranium go? Does it still kill?

Half life … … where does the other half life go?

The winter is quite summery this year … South easterly winds have been blowing at times. On Sunday 14th (a day after Granny Dinny's 110th birthday), Zaan and I watched a pair of giant humpback whales launching themselves up into the air. Over and over and over … tens and tens of times. Huge white flukes, huge bodies, crashing back into the sea about a kilometre off Bakoven. Massive white explosions in the white capped Atlantic.

We never got to Loppa Island on the Toppelbukt Queen because one does not trifle with the white capped Atlantic at home or in the Arctic.

At sunset this evening … as the sun went down behind the horizon, a southern right breached over and over and over in the sea below, far off.

22 July 2013

When I got up on Monday morning at 06h30, the full moon hung over the sea …

Because I have not been paid for 2 months and I am very stressed.
In an act of rebellion, I start the week by going surfing down at Glen.
This should not be an act of rebellion … this should just be the way.
Today, a thick iron cloud holds the Twelve Apostles in an icy grip.
An opal moon makes an opal mark on the grey above,
But down near the horizon the sky is clear,
There are one or two stars and a big planet glittering,
And a sea of mashed white moonlight,
They say more aeroplanes end up in the sea than submarines in the sky …
and they are quite correct.

"Living the Dream", surfed at Glen Fri, Sat, Sun and Monday morning. Up Lion's head on Friday evening … shirtless in the light rain … I love that cool … Sunday after surfing Zaan and I parked the *bakkie* near the lower cable station and caught a cab to Constantia Nek. We walked along to Kirstenbosch and then up Nursery Ravine. We breakfasted on coffee and Norwegian

Chocolate on Smuts' Track before walking to Maclear's Beacon and then down in the cable car.

Sunday 27 July 2013

Zaan has a friend named Redwan, he was born in France … His father was a Moroccan diplomat's son and his mother a German au pair. Redwan's father went back to Marrakesh. Redwan grew up and became successful at banking. Along the way Redwan began to collect red wine. (I also like to collect red wine but never more than half a dozen bottles.) Redwan collected wine and as his collection grew, he could bring himself to drink his wine less and less because once it was drunk it was gone. Soon enough Redwan owned 10 000 bottles and a carefully climate-controlled cellar. He could go in to his cool dark cellar and look at his wine and breathe in the cool musty air.

One day Redwan got promoted and had to move from his home in Switzerland over the Alps to Munich. His 10 000 bottles of red wine were carefully packed at great cost by a specialist company and slowly trucked up the Mont Blanc pass (or similar) where an un-seasonal blizzard brought traffic to a halt. All of Redwan's carefully packed red wine froze and was destroyed. 10 000 bottles of expensive wine, carefully selected and purchased, never to be enjoyed, *puza* down the drain. There's got to be a lesson in that somewhere I think, but I haven't got a handle on it yet.

Into August we must fly – we submarines

Adios Amigo
C

Chapter 6

Lost Dreams of Yellow Margarine

In July 2013 as I left Oslo for South Africa, my uncle (also Rolf Liltved) gave me my grandfather's old passport and a large envelope of old documents. Rubber stamps and dates and signatures were the order of the day back then, so, sitting in our green boatshed at Bakoven, I collated my grandfather's life before and during the War, and after.

Arendals Politikammer – "good for voyage to all foreign countries" – Expiry date 1 March 1940. South African Police, Durban – Registration applied for, Reg. Certificate 29026 to be issued. A Marseh of the Union Whaling Company confirms that Rolf Liltved "has been in our employ for 2 and a half years … a man of sober habits, of good character and has during the time he has been with us given full satisfaction".

And that was before the war. During the Second World War, things got far more serious for a man with a heavy foreign accent in a British colony with German submarines sinking ships all along the coast. Rolf Liltved's every move had to be reported and recorded. A portion of 1942 looked like this, all stamped and dated:

1 January 1942 – Rolf Liltved reports: "Leaving for Cape Town".

12 January 1942 – Arrives at Good Hope Hotel, Loop Street, Cape Town.

21 January 1942 – Employed at Imperial Cold Storage. Resident at 4 Duke Street, Observatory, Cape Town.

28 February 1942 – Rolf Liltved reports, "Left employment at Imperial Cold Storage and is leaving for Johannesburg".

4 March 1942 – Resident at Fattis Mansions, Loveday St, Johannesburg.

9 March 1942 – Business Address: Southern Eng. Supply, Denver, JHB.

1 April 1942 – Resident at East London Hotel, Loveday St, Johannesburg.

25 April 1942 – Resident at Room 33, East London Hotel, Loveday St, Johannesburg.

25 April 1942 – Miners Phthisis Certificate issued.

23 June 1942 – Rolf Liltved reports, "Leaving for Durban for indefinite period".

25 June 1942 – Resident at Astoria Hotel, Durban.

29 June 1942 – Change of address – Windsor Court, Toledo Ave, Durban.

11 July 1942 – Rolf Liltved reports, "Leaving for Johannesburg".

12 July 1942 – Resident at East London Hotel, Loveday St, Johannesburg.

21 July 1942 – Business Address: Dorman Long, Germiston.

1 September 1942 – Resident at Minerva Mansions, Kerk Straat, JHB.

It was a time of huge upheaval and no doubt, a period of great stress, the likes of which we cannot imagine

⁙

Rewinding a little, we turn on some light music and the misty framed background of hope.

In 1938 my grandparents, Rolf and Bibi, settled in Durban with their four-year-old son Øystein. They were so busy that my father was pretty much left in the care of a sixteen-year-old Zulu boy (his lifelong friend Shikonia Ngema) who lived on top of their block of flats. My father spoke only Norwegian and Zulu when he arrived on his first day at school, where the other little boys called him Oyster and instantly assumed him to be a German spy. And so began yet another Anglo-school career of many cruel canings. Just like Wilfred Thesiger, Roald Dahl and all the rest.

Rolf and Bibi set up South Africa's first yellow margarine factory using the Russian's recipe, but yellow margarine was deemed a threat by the South African Dairy Board and their enterprise was quickly shut down in defence of butter production (yellow margarine only appeared back on the shelves in the 1970s when I was a boy).

With their dream destroyed, Rolf and Bibi became the proprietors of the Killarney Restaurant, but it was not the same, the magic was gone. There was tension within their marriage and without: there were rumblings and then war.

By 1943 the family was no longer in Durban. Misadventures had been numerous. Rolf was by now working at a Transvaal munitions factory and engineering works called Dorman Long Vanderbijl or Dorbyl as it is still known today. Here he stumbled across a pro-German Ossewa Brandwag plot to "blow up" the plant. He reported the conspiracy to his superiors and soon found his own life to be in danger. He was sent, for his own safety, to the copper mines in Northern Rhodesia.

6 March 1943 – "leaving for Roan Antelope Copper Mines Hotel, Luanshya, Northern Rhodesia".
12 March 1943 – Transit Visa (in passport) Southern Rhodesia.
12 March 1943 –Visa (in passport) for Northern Rhodesia.
10 April 1943 – Certificate of Registration No. 475 issued – Luanshya, Northern Rhodesia.

On one of his return trips from Luanshya to see his wife and son – Rolf told me and my brother Mikael – he arrived home unexpectedly and found Bibi in bed with his best friend. "In those days," said Rolf, "I had arms like you, Mikael, and I weighed almost 200 pounds. I knocked him down with one punch. I turned around and never went back."

Rolf told me that one day down in a copper mine, there was a rock fall.

Some steel bars gave way and he was trapped beneath fallen rocks. He lay pinned down and delirious in a pool of water while "rats danced Wiener Waltzes to beautiful music". He walked with a limp ever after.

Towards the end of the war and back in Durban, Rolf worked at the docks as a welder on the "great hospital ship Gerusalemme". He worked alternating 24-hour shifts for a prolonged period and became dependent on what he described as "narcotica".

The life of a man. A trail of breadcrumbs in the form of rubber stamps in travel documents.

WWII is over ... Rolf reports: "Leaving the Union from Durban on board the SS Inge Maersk."

28 February 1946 – Rigspolitet, København – (passport stamp)
5 April 1946 – Halsingsberg – (passport stamp) – Sweden
9 April 1946 – Utrest over Mon – (passport stamp)
9 April 1946 – Østfoldbanen – (passport stamp)
30 April 1946 – Ration Card Issued – København – (passport stamp)

And on and on it went, a life of unsettled wandering. In 1947 Rolf left for Canada where he "worked for 3 years on and off". He was involved with "fishing for scallops". In British Columbia he was asked to work on the construction of a channel for a fishing port. There were periods in Canada and Alaska, and periods at sea on various ships.

In 1949 he married his second wife Bitte who gave birth to Rolf jnr. Bitte had her own daughter, Thorhild, and their marriage was not atypically Norwegian.

In 1960 he took over the family restaurant, which he and Bitte ran until a heart attack finally slowed his pace in 1970. Rolf died in 1995. A man of courage and resilience not often found anymore. Anti-fragile. A wonderful man to have had as a grandfather, but too far away.

Listen to the old man speak of all he has been through.

And I did, and I loved every word.

❦

Footnote 1: The Timavo and Gerusalemme Incident (source unknown)

On 10 June 1940 Italy was about to declare war on the Allies but nobody in Durban knew that except the crews of the Italian ships Timavo and

Gerusalemme who had received a coded radio signal to that effect.

The two ships put hurriedly to sea at noon with papers faked to make it seem as if they were bound for Cape Town but, as soon as they were over the horizon, they altered course for Lourenco Marques which was a neutral port and offered sanctuary from the allied forces.

Later that night the news of Italy's declaration of war reached Durban and South African airforce planes began to search for the two ships. The Timavo was found 150 miles north-east of Durban during the night and headed at full speed towards the Zululand coast after a bomb was dropped and warning shots were fired.

The Timavo later grounded herself about 5 miles north of St. Lucia Bay and her crew was captured and brought back to Durban. The ship herself could not be salvaged but some of the cargo was saved. The Gerusalemme, in the meantime, managed to reach Lourenco Marques where she was interned until the Italian surrender, after which she returned to Durban to be converted into an allied hospital ship.

<hr/>

Footnote 2: The Timavo and Gerusalemme Incident (source unknown)

The Gerusalemme had quite a chequered life. She was one of two Italian ships in Durban when Mussolini declared war. The other was the Lloyd Triestino ship Timavo. Both vessels received notification the day before and left port hurriedly. Timavo had indicated that she was bound for Cape Town and indeed did head south but as soon as she was below the horizon she turned and headed north for Mozambique. She was intercepted and her skipper beached her just north of Leven Point on the Zululand coast. Today she is nothing more than a lump of growth covered junk just off the beach.

Gerusalemme was intercepted by the armed merchant cruiser Ranchi and also "beached" near Kosi Bay also on the Zululand coast. I say "beached" because she was close inshore and Ranchi could not get closer to her being a much larger vessel. As soon as the Ranchi moved off the Gerusalemme "unbeached" herself and made it into neutral Portuguese waters off Mozambique. When Italy surrendered she was sent to Durban and converted into a hospital ship. I have often wondered whether the Gerusalemme really did beach herself or simply played a glorious trick on the Ranchi by pretending to be aground!

24 August 2013   Letter #7

Hi Gareth

18 August 2013

On Saturday morning I drove to Gardens Centre, bought a pack of German rolls at Raith, thick with butter and salami and cold meats and tomato and such. I bought an XXXL sweater at Cape Union Mart for your son and headed out to meet Linda and Michael. Linda had told me that Mikey is a big chap.

When I arrived at their home, I was met by Linda and Michael at the gate … Linda is very negative about virtually everything, but your boy seems to be almost magically unaffected. Michael was present for the entire visit. He did not try to escape to his room and computer as boys do these days.

I observed him closely and talked very carefully to him for two hours. There are so many Gareth mannerisms in his way. He must be 6'3" or 6'4" with big hands and slender fingers. Not hands given to hard work like his diesel engine dad, but hands that can gently convert a complex piece of gypsy music from a lined and dotted sheet of paper into a beautiful sound.

I watched him play the first piece and closed my eyes for the second … some old-style Euro type jazz … the kind one might hear blown out by a lonesome bridge busker in Paris … music drifting across the Seine on the mist.

His feet are size 14 like mine.

He is humble and not pushy in any way, no bragging, no show-off bravado. No flippant teenage style answers. Just calm and polite and correct.

He has 2 smelly Labradors that Linda calls his "stink bombs" … she is right. He sits on the couch with one draped over his lap … absently, but lovingly caressing the animal continuously. The other lies on the floor. A big long-haired tabby cat is positioned nicely in the sofa-sunray and floating dust.

As you know, Michael is at Reddam School Tokai. He swims for a swimming club in Wynberg. He does not play rugby (or like rugby) which is a blessing because rugby is undoubtedly a stupid sport ... especially for a man of his size. They would make him a lock or prop and then destroy the cartilage in his knees and ears and spit him out branded: Injured For Life.

Michael is in what we called Standard 7. He looks like a Std 9 or 10 boy because of his size. I was told that he is on a 50% academic scholarship at Reddam.

I gave him my best lecture on the importance of diligent work and the absolute importance of not "closing in advance" any doors, in his own face, as I did when I was a boy.

I gave him my best lecture on the importance of a good education and the importance of remaining globally competitive ... explaining that South Africa hopefully will, but may well not, hold the future that he might ultimately wish for. I gave him my best lecture on becoming energised.

I told him about his father ... I told him about my wonderful friend ... I told him that you loved him and missed him terribly. I told him about my mother's dad who went off to WW2 and did not return to the house ... and how my grandmother always spoke ill of him ... and how my mother had no option but to believe ... and only later in life (as an adult) did she hear from so many strangers about what a wonderful man her father was ... but by then the time was lost. Linda did not want to hear much of what was said but did not try to stop me. I told Michael that he was a big man-sized man now and could hear about these things. I told him that Linda and he and I and you had all had our share of pain. All in our own ways ... some more ... some less.

He did not seem to mind my tears and, like my brother's strong 18-year-old son Keanu, did not shy away from a couple of hugs.

I think that as far as Michael is concerned ... he is well and healthy and well adjusted. His mother complains a lot but will protect him with her life. She is single and he is her life project.

Gareth, creeping into Linda's life is a tough one ... One wrong move and the door will slam shut.

After I left Linda, I drove 12 short minutes to your mom's house. I stopped on Boyes Drive at the top, overlooking Muizenberg, then again at the top of Jacob's Ladder, and again above Kalk Bay. What a glorious and civilised place. Pine trees and buildings and walls built by people cultured in those crafts. It was a lot like an imagined Italy of the old movies. I then dropped down into Kalk Bay's Anglo-Saxon world … That was a fine place to raise 3 boys in the late 1960s and 1970s, a paradise!

I met your mom again for the first time in 30 years … The house is as it was.

The same 3 pictures of you and your two brothers on the dining room wall. Suzie with her leg in a cast.

We had a good chat.

You are in contact with your mom, so you know all the ins and outs.

She is a dear kind soul … and of course, loves you the most of all people.

19 August 2013

I called Linda today to thank her for letting me visit.

She was kind to me but has asked that I respect her privacy. Not to say where she lives and not to give her number away to anyone. It is obvious that she has suffered a lot through all this. I have told her that I will contact her from time to time but will not make a pest of myself.

I do not have her email address … anything can be found out, of course, but Gareth, I am not one given to deceitful and "creepish" behaviour. I will respect Linda's wishes.

In the long run it will be much better if I can look Michael's mother straight in the eye.

I have told her and Michael that I am in regular contact with you and about the occasional visits you receive from Kim and my old Camps Bay High School woodwork pal Yianni. I have told Michael that lines of communication are open.

In my life of observation, as relationships break up, I have seen partners actively try to punish partners. Sometimes it is by making unkind or belittling comments at a dinner party, when the other person cannot retaliate … or by channelling love elsewhere … or by withholding access to the kids … and so on. There are many variations on that theme.

I asked on Saturday and again today for a recent photo of Michael.

Not this time around I am afraid, Gareth … sadly … Linda still needs to punish you, my friend.

Much love

Your old pal, C

Chapter 7

Moving On

Gareth Rutherford, Anglo-Saxon? Anglo-South African more like.

His mum Suzie and dad Bonzo spoke in rather rounded, cultivated British accents and did not allow the weeds of colloquial tongue any foothold. They raised their boys in Kalk Bay near the Anglican Church, and near the former Royal Navy base of Simon's Town. Their children played with the Tilney children and the Tanfields and the Carpenter-Franks. But that is about all I know. Gareth and I became friends after that.

I took a map once and placed a compass point in the English Channel. I then described a circle from inside which all my recent ancestors originate. On my mother's side, my great-grandfather WC Winshaw had a German mother and Irish dad. My great grandmother Ada Charlotte Day was from Hampshire. The Oosthuizen family came from Holland and the Malherbes from France.

Okkie's Medals

My maternal grandfather Okkie Oosthuizen, went to war in 1939 on the side of the British and returned in 1945 to a locked door with six medals to his name. Many Afrikaners were sympathetic to Nazi Germany because of the assistance given to the Boers by Germany during the Anglo-Boer War. But my grandmother had shut Okkie out for other reasons.

⁕⁕⁕

South Africa has played host to many seaborne immigrants from distant continents: British, Dutch, Lithuanian Jews, Italians, Indians, Balinese, Javanese, Chinese, Portuguese, Stinky Cheese. (An incomplete list and in no particular order.) The clicking Khoi and San people were the First Nation indigenes in the southern and central interior, while the darker Bantu tribes moved down, on foot, from Central Africa to the South. These tribal people were disseminated through the southern sub-continent by wars fought by the Zulu king Shaka.

Camps Bay High in 1980 was 45% Jewish, although it seemed like a lot more. Lutrin, Richman, Weintraub, Saacks, Kahn, Kurgan, Marin, Feinstone, Joffe, Rheingold, Hoffman, Bruck, Bloch, Strumpman and Bernstein are some of the names that spring to mind. They were mostly hardworking children. Their community was tight. They all knew each other and shared secret Hebrew names like Gayil and Shmuel. They went to each other's bat mitzvahs and bar mitzvahs and tended to leave the country after graduating from university. They could see the Zuma era coming, years in advance. Cape Town's Jewish population has declined dramatically since those times. Once thriving, some of the largest shuls are now closed. The remaining Jewish kids mostly attend private Jewish schools with fairly tight security.

Our Jew-people, who are so good at business and law and the professions, also added weight to the magnet in the moral compass in South Africa. Five of the fifteen accused who appeared alongside Mandela at the Rivonia Trial were Jewish – Goldberg, Bernstein, Wolpe, Kantor and Goldreich. Jews were significantly over-represented among so called "whites" in the anti-apartheid struggle. They tried their best and have moved on. A diaspora of human stepping stones.

⁕⁕⁕

Thinking back to the Jewish kids in Camps Bay, I just had a laugh. There were some Joffes amongst them. I do not know if they were all related, those

Joffe boys and girls. "Little Joffe's" real name was Seymour and I forget what "Big Joffe's" name was, but he was very clever. There was a small hockey-playing boy (who stood with feet at a quarter to three) named Asher Joffe, but the Joffe that stands out in my memory was the enigmatic and almost invisible "Mad Joffe". "Mad Joffe" was never seen at school, only at the beach. "Mad Joffe" pretended to be a surfer but I don't think he ever paddled out.

One day a photo appeared on the front page of The Argus. It was "Mad Joffe" in a wetsuit with his surfboard under one arm. He was surrounded by mist. A lovely picture, monochrome, evocative. We all laughed and loved it and "Mad Joffe" got his 15 minutes of fame. I sometimes wonder what became of him. He probably moved to California.

23 Sept 2013   Letter #8

Dear Gareth

Sometimes one is forced to stand and fight ... when one has no option.
But if you do have an option, sometimes it is better just to bend with the wind.
Even the most resolute and sturdy of trees may be snapped in a storm.
A storm that has force and direction and subtlety, exactly correct, to be that tree's nemesis.
Other lesser trees will remain standing.

And if you choose to fight, choose your fights carefully.
And be prepared to fight the good fight.
Do not enter into a fight that you do not believe is just.
Do not enter into a fight that you do not believe you can win.
Fight dirty if you need to.
Do not fall into despair.
As Rudel said, "You are not lost until you have given yourself up as lost."

22 September 2013

On Friday afternoon at around 5pm, Zaan and I were in a city apartment, 5 storeys up, overlooking Loop Street. As I peered out of the window into that dappled urban afternoon, I saw snowflakes falling and rising and floating about, like tiny specks of cotton-wool. More and more, filling the air with myriad soft flights until suddenly the greatest hailstorm imaginable tore through that gentle snowy moment with a violence seldom seen in this place.

Soon the streets were white with ice.

The previous days had all been cold and hot, sunny and rainy. Flu weather. Hail in the night like machine-gun fire on our tin roof. During the weeks past, springtime came and we ran up Table Mountain a few times. Proteas thick on the slopes, flowers to soon be blasted by the final sting of winter.

Today is spring again ... I ran on Signal Hill.
There were hundreds of people out and about, joyful in the warm air.
Snow lies thick on the distant mountains.
From Stellenbosch all the way to the Cedarberg far to the north.
What a sight.

"Gareth, learn your Arabic well," I said as I ran,
"that is a superb skill for a Western man."
While musmilmen kill civilians and take hostages
in a Nairobi building this weekend.

Do you get the news?
And the poison gas attacks in Damascus?
What a crazy world.
What jobs you will have translating the news when you get out!

Across the road from Zaan's Camps Bay home is a building development that was completed at the end of 2012. A pair of luxury houses built on a single erf. A few doors up (on the other side) the same person is building another massive house. Security guards were appointed for each project. The first project is complete and residents have moved in, but a pair of guards remain permanently on "our" sidewalk, day in, day out, for months and months, two on, two off. They work in shifts.

The pair I have befriended are both from the Congo. One is from Congo Brazzaville, the other from Congo DRC. They both miss their homes. They both have scant respect for Congo leadership. They are articulate, strong, good-looking men who fiddle with their mobile phones and vie for possession of a single plastic garden chair. In summer they constantly move the chair to the shadiest spot available. In winter they try to stay snug and dry. They have left their loved ones in the Congos in order to earn money to send home. Apparently there are "no jobs" there so they earn a living in South Africa by doing nothing, all day, all night. The X-men (Xhosas) and the Ovambo labour and all the others on the project have worked and drilled and pushed wheelbarrows and passed bricks in a human conveyor belt and cast concrete like crazy for a year while these two men, in their navy-blue fatigues, have done nothing. Over the December break, the others went away, back home, and the building sites were quiet, but the Congolese men stayed behind to continue with their tedium.

All over our country people work as security guards. How awful it is that people must live and earn a living, contributing nothing material to the economy. Making nothing, growing nothing, teaching nothing, fixing nothing, adding no value. It is a negation of an existence.

When we were boys there were no fences to speak of or domestic burglar alarms. Steel spikes and electric wire now surround most of the properties in our suburb. Sophisticated electronic equipment is developed and installed. Like the two Congolese men, all in the hope of keeping thieves and robbers out. Steel wrested from the earth which could be used to build bridges. Electronic engineering that could be otherwise used in the making of wonderful gadgets, instead wasted on keeping unwelcome visitors out. And still they are not altogether deterred, and they try, and are sometimes successful and sometimes not. And we chase them around at night and sometimes we catch them and sometimes we don't. And after those long nights of chasing we wake up feeling scratchy and sullied.

It is amazing how people stole so much less, per capita, when we were boys. And even less when our dads were young. So much has changed in our lifetimes.

Then one might start to think about it and one might find it interesting to note how crime or the perceived threat of crime stimulates the economy. Extra men are needed and employed to do nothing. Extra iron is mined and steel is milled that does no real beneficial work. The thieves steal and the robbers rob and the stolen goods are sold cheaply to people who would not ordinarily be in the market for expensive items such as laptop computers and big flat-screen TVs, and the stolen items are immediately replaced by those who had them stolen ... so more are constantly needed. And the insurance companies become bigger and employ more people who do not really contribute materially to society, but the jobs are created nevertheless. And the premiums go up. And more guards are hired, and policemen and magistrates and prosecutors have jobs but also do not really contribute materially to society. And so, without a doubt, crime creates jobs and stimulates the economy. But what is the ultimate cost?

Then one might start to think a little deeper and ask: "Is this why there is so little real political will to do anything about it?" But more than likely, it is just that those who are in the top anti-crime posts are just not sufficiently competent or energized to do their jobs and the economy is stimulated as a by-product of their poor performance.

I hear on the radio and read in the papers that there are insufficient hospital beds. That there are too few classrooms and not enough good teachers. That there are too few houses and too few jobs. Like the song, it is always "only bad news on Radio Africa".

But actually, if you think about it, there are enough classrooms and jobs and hospital beds and prisons but there are just too many people. Don't dare say it! Shhh!! The elephant in the room.

Seemingly very few people have the courage or capacity to deal with the simple fact that we humans (the best of whom do amazing things) have, like an infestation of rats, become the plague species of our planet. We have bred and continue to breed too much. Sadly, bringing this fact (so essential to the long-term survival of our species) to public attention is somehow taboo. Politicians won't touch it, nor will talk show hosts. Dawkins will. "One child per adult" I say, until we get back down to sustainable numbers.

Some weeks ago I read in the Mail and Guardian about two guys who had, for some reason, made T-shirts bearing the slogan, "I benefited from Apartheid". I did, too, while hating and disrespecting PW Botha and Magnus Malan just as much as I do our current load of corrupt criminal South African politicians. During the apartheid era, however, economies, systems and infrastructure were conceived and set up by we all know who – the bad men. But for all the evils of the apartheid masters, these systems have not yet been totally undermined and destroyed by this current generation of looters. But they are working at it.

What has happened in Burundi and Nigeria and Zimbabwe and Cameroon and Somalia and the Congos over the past decades? Why do so many of their citizens pour into "The Republic"? It is not for the love of xenophobia, Zuma and Z-men that they come. It is because, to a large degree, the apartheid era infrastructure and systems have not yet failed. And so a pair of strong and eloquent Congolese men can still earn a living far from their loved ones while idling their days away on the pavement so they can send a little money home.

Thinking of you, my friend.

A smart *bokkop* photo of you is framed in my living room ... we look into each other's eyes daily.

Carl

Chapter 8

Not Architecture

After we finished school, some of the boys went straight to the army. Some enrolled at universities like UCT and others, like me, studied at a Technikon. I ended up with a National Higher Diploma in Civil Engineering, which sounds impressive but I still ranked significantly below a university graduate.

I loved woodwork and technical drawing at school. I had wanted to study architecture at university. My dad had a semi-pissed and mostly-out-of-work useless architect friend. "Look at so-and-so," said my dad, "he is always out of work … not architecture." And so I was easily steered away. Ravenscroft and I were not on the list of academic achievers. We had wasted our last year at school having fun like the jackass boys in Walt Disney's **Pinocchio**. Ravenscroft went straight to the army. Bayley, Berg and Brand were all off to UCT to study for undergraduate engineering degrees. I lacked the marks to get into university and, sticking with the subject of engineering, enrolled at the Technikon instead. And so began my long career of job-hopping.

When I was a boy, we read Richard Scarry. Through Richard Scarry I understood work to be building roads and dams and ploughing fields and harvesting crops. Scarry's workers clearly added value to the world of man. I now look at work differently. Labour is ploughing fields and harvesting and digging ditches. My advocate friend works hard, studying cases and writing opinions. My parents worked hard learning operas off by heart and performing before audiences. Work is not digging, digging is labour. Above work there is investing and trading. A man I know became very wealthy dealing in stocks and shares. As far as I could tell, he never actually created or added value to anything – he simply shifted numbers and paper about. Financial traders earn huge amounts of money without breaking a sweat. The business world is for the apex capitalists – people who would rather be seen in a three-piece suit than a wetsuit.

When I was a boy I confused sport with games. To this day I remain baffled as to how people can get paid such immense sums of money for playing games like tennis, soccer and golf. I simply cannot see how they add value to humanity. In fact, they do little more than fan the flames of nationalism by way of ritualised aggression. I still do not like games.

I have spent thirty years earning my living in a space between labour and work, designing and building. I have flown by the seat of my pants too much and have been stressed too much of the time. My creative spirit in stocks. If I hadn't wasted that final year at school, who knows, maybe I would have ended up a clever wealthy architect director businessman, but would I have been happier?

Many of my classmates emigrated to Canada, Australia, New Zealand and the USA soon after graduating. Afro-pessimism. To make better lives for themselves. To breed and raise families in countries free from the fear of revolution, the fear of crime and HIV. Looking at Africa's lack of post-colonial advancements, tin-pot dictatorships and civil wars, they were not wrong.

I went to London in 1987 with a similar view but my love for the Cape was too strong. I have had a wonderful and exciting life, but often tense.

There is so much to lose. I write now in Canada. It is so un-stressful here that it is almost dull. I think that one becomes slightly addicted to the vibrant multi-cultural, noisy, undisciplined, dangerous, untidy life in South Africa. It has, however, been extremely depressing to watch the corrupt and useless ANC kleptocrat cadre-regime all but destroy the country.

Now for the flipside, the view from up North, from countries like Angola, Zimbabwe, Somalia and Nigeria from where the almost stagnant economy of South Africa with its massive unemployment, shimmers seductively all gold and pearl. From countries so broken, like moths to a flame they come, men and women, speaking so many languages, to labour, from where my classmates ran: South Africa where the last of Africa's colonial infrastructure still struggles along.

28 October 2013   Letter #9

Dear Gareth

Monday. Awake with the heavy black hyena on my chest.
04h15 ... late for a Monday.
Job list screaming through my mind's mind,
And the two mesh as sleep hastens off into the distance.
I try awhile but it cannot be recaptured.
Oh boyo, another day of chronic caffeine stimulation.
Ah, but no, there is a proven cure.
Quick ... running shoes on and up the Lion's Head.
Through the maritime fog, into the clear sky with swallows and purple daisies.
Maybe it's not so bad.
When I return home, my house smells like Rome.
Some tiny molecule triggers the sense.
It gently pulls and then lets go again.
Away I am ... a hot shower ... and into the work-seat, strap on that desk.
Jot down these words before I start.
It's a lot worse in a Congolese gold mine ...
"Stop complaining you spoilt boy" ... "Okay dad!"
Is it? ... isn't it? ... yes ... it is!

And as the day spins by, and is intelligently handled, the puzzle pieces sort themselves out.

And so Monday flies into Tuesday and whips into Wednesday ... a week flies like only time can.

That's how it has been for me for quarter of a century, give or take some small gaps.

They are mining alluvial gold in Zimbabwe now. A sort of mini gold rush.

The Chinese want ivory – plenty of cyanide available from the gold mining operations.

Over 300 elephants die from deliberately poisoned water holes and hundreds of other animals are "by-catch". The young perpetrators are caught. They were being paid $50 a tusk.

On the 22nd Kim sent your envelope via registered mail from Fish Hoek.

I found a registered mail slip in my letter-box yesterday, along with another one of those Africa-only slips.

SEEKING FOR EMPLOYMENT	
NAME	Robert
GENDER	Male
NATIONALITY	Malawian
AGE	25
JOB	Garden Boy, House Keeper, Painter
NATURE	Punctual, Honest, Reliable and Hard Working
CONTACT NO	084 237 6307

What a story such a little scrap of paper tells. What a tale of sadness and hope, of longing and desperation. A family wrenched apart, the missing of children, a tale of wandering to the end of a continent, so very far from home. A tale of yet another African country with too many men, too few jobs and more humans just breeding out.

Two rhinos a day … every day … so far this year … butchered for their horns.

A little later I will take my bicycle and roll down to the post office to fetch your letter. I look forward to that. Eventually I go in the *bakkie*.

Flashback to … **12 October 2013**

Days of intense hecticness … meaningless work … what has meaning?
Maybe the children of the sun, in the springtime, stretching up and unfolding … every year.

Showing their coloured faces to the bees.
I long for slowing down.

Your mother, Yianni and Kim and I were due to have lunch yesterday. Your mom rain-checked because of her broken leg. Getting old is *kak* from every angle as far as I can see.

Every week I run a few times up in the mountain. If I were 20 or 30, I would get fitter and fitter. But now, a few months shy of 50, the same run does not get easier every time. The process of getting fitter seems to be in direct conflict with the process of getting older.

I was involved in the arrest of a man on Sunday. He was stealing cell-phones on Clifton beach. I have made so many arrests in my life that I cannot remember them all. I handcuffed him to a pole and radioed the police to come and fetch him. To deny a man his liberty ... that has taken on a whole new meaning for me since I have reconnected with you, my friend. It truly terrifies me now.

Thank you for your letter ... there is a lot to learn in there ... a lot of juice to squeeze out.

Last Thursday I was on a pre-dawn flight to Joburg for a day of work. I saw the sun rise over an orange and purple barrage of cloud. Down below, Worcester, Matroosberg, Klein Karoo and away ... into my book. I am reading a most unbelievable travelogue. A young man (Patrick Leigh Fermor) leaves school in 1933 and walks from the Hoek of Holland through proto-Nazi Germany, Austria, the Balkans and to Istanbul over a period of a few years. To quote the famous Led Zeppelin song, "My spirit is crying for leaving." And I am sure that yours cries too, only exponentially more so.

These old Genesis lyrics so often float into my mind.

No cloud, a sleepy calm, sun-baked earth that's cooled by gentle breeze,
And trees with rustling leaves,
Only endless days without a care,
Nothing must be done.

I long for a trip to southern Italy ... an act of pure escapism.
Istanbul-Prague-Vienna.
I land at Lanseria. Normally I go to the city centre, Sandton etc. The

people are so friendly in RSA. It is such a pity that a few bad apples spoil this place with their savage actions.

This Tuesday I was on a pre-dawn flight to Durban for a day of work. I saw the sun rise over an orange and purple entanglement of cloud. Below, the Indian Ocean … Mossel Bay … and again away into my book. I am now reading a most unbelievable autobiography. A young man named Sam Pivnic, growing up in pre-war Poland, is grabbed by Nazis and flung into a ghetto. Then to Auschwitz. He survives and goes on to live and fight in Palestine, eventually reaching a ripe old age in London. Wow, what a tale! Why do I love to burden myself with history?

I go on to Durban to measure up yet another restaurant. Phew! "Be glad for the work," they all say. I understand why people have mid-life crises.

Across the road from Zaan's house, the two Congolese men in blue fatigues wave as I pass. The single white plastic chair is present, on the sidewalk, as always with its one bent leg. It is a lot worse in the copperbelt mines where my grandpa toiled.

A few days ago. The wind blows in from the WSW. Seven kite boarders play in an environment that could kill almost anyone but members of that clan. Big waves, white spray, rough and extremely cold water. My brother Mick is one of the seven. I would love to be number eight … maybe this summer I'll do it. Afterwards he phoned me full of the joy that only exercise in salt water can spark. As you well know, it is a unique and sublime joy. I think that the salt water ionises and realigns all the bad static electricity in the nervous system. I know that my frequent plunge into the Atlantic always makes me feel a lot better.

⌘

When my brother Mick and I were younger we used to joke about the *Wheel of Kharma* and how a human body, a galaxy, a bad deed and a mosquito are inexorably linked due to the dynamic interplay of give and take and the fundamental interconnectedness of all things.

"Instant Kharma!" we would laugh as the firecracker intended for some unsuspecting victim blew up in the fingers of a stealthy assailant.

"Medium Term Kharma" dealt with the "swings and roundabouts" and usually involved girls and activities that were not enlightened or kind.

"Long Term Kharma" encompassed the old proverb, "What goes around, comes around" and might work in cycles of 30 to 60 years or more.

The system of the "Wheels of Kharma" I have in my mind is not unlike one of those renaissance planetary models, but more intricate and less rigid. Millions of interlocking circles and ellipses all set about with arcane symbols … all turning.

Small wheels spinning furiously, big wheels very slowly. And all related by some fantastic governing equation to one another, and ultimately to the largest wheel, the FLYWHEEL.

The A to Ω wheel, (The Wheel of the Start to End of Time).

Wheels which appear small and speedy in the human scale of reference, or "Human Instant Kharma Wheels", might see the smashing of a mosquito being punished by a stubborn bloodstain on a newly painted wall. But one must remember that there are worlds within worlds and that splat represents the largest wheel in the life of the mosquito, as did the last suck of the mosquito represent a quantity of big wheels in the lives of many red and white blood cells and so on *ad infinitum* in a ripple effect which might be extrapolated right through the greater time/space continuum. And thus the Kharmic Wheels of all systems are interlinked like a suit of multidimensional chain-mail to form one giant machine some might call god.

There we are … now it is even later … but I am not tired any more.

Thank you for appreciating the furniture I make. Most people don't even notice, but you did from way over there. Allegra and I had steak and mushrooms for supper. When you are free, you will come for a lekker *braai*. Don't worry, I think your journals are safe.

It is now a week and a day since I awoke with the Black Hyena on my chest … where lurks he now?

Your pal
Oscar L

Chapter 9

Ageing and Death

Dinny divorced Okkie after the war. They were my mother's parents. One day she encountered the local priest up in the village. "You are not welcome in my church anymore," he told her.

Like I do, Dinny kept the coal hot. And a year or two later, when the same priest knocked on her door to cadge donations for a new wing on the church, she asked him to wait. She returned with her revolver in hand. She would weep with laughter as she told us how he "girded his loins by lifting the hem of his cassock and turned and fled in giant leaping bounds" across the lawn and out of the gate.

"Never come back, you bloody-fucking-bastard!" she called out after him as he ran. We loved that story and the dirty little rhymes she taught us boys. "Here's to the memory of Dead-Eye-Dick ..." and so on. She was just the best kind of woman – tough and fun, intelligent and proper. Educated in the university of life and in the reading of countless books. She did not accept anything as given. From first principles, by way of applied logic, she worked things out. I have taught my daughter to do the same.

As boys, Mick and I would arrive at her home in Stellenbosch for a week or so of our school holidays. The weather was always great there – blue skies, warm air and little puffy sheep-like clouds drifting above. Her thick-walled Cape Dutch house was cool inside and the kitchen smelled of shortbread biscuits and lamb and rosemary. As soon as our mom had left, Mick would ask if we could clean her guns. "Can we have some bullets too?" he would ask. "Please?" ... "Please?"

Dinny's revolver

Dinny owned two small Walther pistols and a seven-shot Arminius revolver. We would take the weapons out into the rose garden where her well-tended rosebushes stood in circular dams of mud. Dinny's two youngest grandsons would shoot the mud. I clearly remember the steaming holes, like smoking craters on some cartoon planet, right at our feet.

We then stripped, cleaned and reassembled the weapons. Mick would return them proudly and be thanked. We grew up with guns and so had she, but that all belongs to another story.

Our beloved Dinny grew old, grandmother and mentor, setter of the bar. The matriarch of our family. The yardstick against which one could calibrate one's own yardstick. The moral compass against which one could swing one's own.

Every generation, on average, lives a little longer and fewer die along the way and now there are too many people. At eighty, Dinny began to age. Things that had been easy to do became challenging and then difficult and then frightening. Like driving to Cape Town to visit us, or the long passage to the lavatory at night, or getting in and out of her bathtub. One eye went and then an ear.

Dinny made her doctor promise that if she should become incapacitated, he would finish her off. At some point she suffered a hemiplegia followed by a severe bronchial spasm. The doctor let her down. I challenged him and he pleaded "Christian" – a man of straw. He hospitalized her and using all the magic of modern medicine, they cheated her of death. We fired the doctor, but it was too late. She lay in bed, mostly paralysed and in a semi-conscious twilight, until she was ninety-six.

They did the same to her sister Natty. And my dad. If anything in this world is a sin, it is the keeping alive of those who would be better off dead.

In America in 1999, Dr Jack Kevorkian was arrested and tried. He served eight years of a 10-to-25-year prison sentence for helping to end the lives of terminally ill patients. At their request. This angel of mercy was released on parole in 2007.

Earlier this year, a 104-year-old Australian scientist named David Goodall made the news after travelling to Switzerland for a legal assisted death.

Slowly we are coming around.

It took a long time, too, for people to accept that the Earth is, in fact, not flat.

30 Nov 2013   Letter #10

Dear Gareth

It is 14h30, Saturday afternoon. I have just finished doing my time sheets and month-end invoicing. I am listening to some old anglo-reggae-ska … **I Just Can't Stop It** by The Beat. I don't care for invoicing but now it's done. Ha!

Zaan's friend Redwan is out visiting from München. Yesterday we headed up Table Mountain for a quick calorie burn. Man, was it hot! 07h30 is way too late for a start at this time of year. I think I got some kind of heat stroke because I am still feeling headachey.

Redwan laughed when I reminded him of his frozen wine, destroyed on the snowy Mont Blanc pass. Being a banker, he needed to correct my numbers as misrepresented in a story previously sent to you. Apparently it was only 2000 bottles and the incident happened on some lesser snowy pass between France and Luxembourg. Sorry.

Last weekend was interesting. I was invited as *braaimeester* (barbecue chief) to my first 100th Birthday party. Zaan's grandfather, Eben Stander, had clocked a century and we took my Weber out in the *bakkie*.

Off to Serenitas old age home in Somerset West we went, Zaan and I and her son Nicholas in my van with the *braai* strapped onto the back. Nicholas has just finished his matric exams. We took spans of top grade *winkelwors* (commercially manufactured sausage) and charcoal briquettes and Blitz. The soft white rolls and salads and so on were provided by Zaan's mom. Man, me and Zaan's *boet* AJ grazed so *dik* on *boerie* rolls it was epiiic. The sun baked down and the southeaster blew as we took shelter under a small tree outside Eben's room while the others did the appropriate things inside. AJ ate an entire coil of *boeries* before we even started. He is a gentle ruffian who builds custom Harleys in RSA and Canada. He came out from Hermanus for the day with his Canadian *cherrie* on a gleaming V-Rod. Not one of those horrible big fat Harleys that sound like an endless wet fart. No, this one is *uitsonderlik mooi* (good looking). I am no bike guy, but you are, so let me elaborate because you would like this thing.

Imagine a gleaming "hydroformed" metallic blue frame with the famous 60-degree V Twin Revolution Engine (developed jointly by Harley and Porsche) and overhead cams and a radiator and plenty of chrome. Quite a vehicle to see there at Serenitas among the small white hatchbacks and wheeled walkers.

When I was spending time in Maltahöhe in Namibia, we would make real *plaaswors* (farm sausage) and turn it out through a special nozzle fitted to the old cast iron, crank handle meat mincer. That was delicious. Venison only and coriander and other magical things. Out on the land we would clean and stuff the *dikderm* (large intestine) with fried onions and finely chopped liver and heart and small bits of meat and braai that alongside fresh springbok liver over *kameeldoring* (camel thorn) coals and sleep in the open veld, under the stars, next to the coals. A vast white Milky Way above. *Koringkrieks* six-wheel-driving all over the place.

I remember one evening listening to the sound of jackals as a *gompou* (kori bustard) settled down for the night. Boom, boom, boom. Barking geckoes getting ready to feast on moths and other night crawlers, and a group of *draaijakkals* (Cape fox) almost invisible, shadow-like, creeping, inching in closer for the possibility of a nub of sausage or an overlooked scrap or a spotted genet in a tamarisk tree at 3am.

Wat om my vrinde –
Wat nooit nie verstaan –
As die sterre my toeknik,
En die maan?

Op my ou ramkietjie
Met nog net een snaar
Speel ek in die maanskyn,
Deurmekaar.

My Zaan comes in to work on her laptop. She doesn't really *smaak* the music so I turn it off.

Now I must go in a new direction.

A few years ago I was part of a small group who travelled to Gabon to do some scouting work for an international luxury hotel group who had received the green light from the president, Ali Bongo Ondimba, to set up a number of very exclusive, very eco-friendly, very expensive resorts or camps inside certain Gabonese national parks so that very wealthy people would be able to sit and sip ice-cold champagne in air-conditioned elegance in very remote settings while being served by colonially-neat and disciplined local servants. I am personally pleased that the whole thing fizzled out because the thought of loud Americans and other spoilt, out of touch people walking roughshod in those gorgeous places is anathema to me. Sadly though, ultimately it will come, one way or another.

What I did find interesting at the time was that the people of Gabon had seemingly, as though in some kind of trance, psychologically handed over unquestioned ownership of all state assets to their president. We flew far and wide across vast jungles in one of the president's helicopters, piloted by the president's three French pilots. We landed in the president's national parks where only the president could decide to allow the building of resorts or not.

The late and former president Omar Bongo Ondimba came into office in 1967 and died in 2009 as one of the world's wealthiest heads of state. Ali Bongo, his son, took up the reins after his father's death. Like South Africa's ANC it is a deeply entrenched regime. Ali Bongo by all accounts seems to be a personable fellow, as does our Jacob Zuma, but when a regime is able to retain power for too long the rot often sets in.

In South Africa our president's name has been tarnished by scandal after scandal. An alleged corrupt relationship with Shabir Shaik, an alleged rape of a friend's daughter, alleged corrupt involvement in the arms deal and now a spend of over R200-million of tax payers' money on upgrading his private home. Our media howls. But why our people are so blindly accepting, I do not know.

This week's Mail and Guardian newspaper is so damning that you would think Zuma is sunk … but his back is like that of a duck.

Up, up and away out of sprawling Libreville we flew … the tarmac ending with the manioc a kilometre out of town. Thin jungle becomes thick jungle. We flew over jungle for hours and hours. More trees seen in one day than can be imagined in a lifetime. Three nerdish ex-French military pilots in orange jump suits with black lace-up school shoes on their feet. A big Puma chopper. A landing at Chutes Kongou – a system of seldom visited waterfalls and cataracts. Crossing the river in a tin canoe. A rare blue flower in a heady hot place. The endless tumbling of water. Camouflaged rangers whispering out of the trees. Refuelling at an abandoned airport – Franceville. A dusty clearing near the Congo Border – Plateaux Batéké. The sweating 1890 cast-iron light-house at Ngombe. Elephants knee-deep in massive coastal lagoons – Missala. Thousands of logs washed up on white beaches. Elephants running for cover. Sunset at 6pm sharp. An orange dot plunges into the sea. Night.

Adios for now my pal.
Carly

Chapter 10
Black and White

A while ago, while driving somewhere, I listened to Cape Talk radio's Eusebius McKaiser interviewing a former employee of Grant Thornton who had been "sexually harassed in the workplace".

During the interview, McKaiser repeatedly asserted that the woman – Nerisha Singh – is black, but I did not hear him once state that the alleged perpetrator – Vernon Naidoo – was anything other than male. Eusebius McKaiser, despite his Greco-Scotto-Germano name and pale brown complexion, refers to himself also as a "black" person and really loves to ride the subject. It wouldn't occur to him to discuss the situation in the following way for instance: "Grant Thornton employee/director harassed and frightened by senior colleague". No, the "BLACK/WHITE" issue is McKaiser's hobby horse. It is his gimmick, a gimmick without which, he would be just another articulate, but also-ran, radio personality.

I try my old failsafe and put my black leather wallet down on a white piece of paper. I place my wrist alongside my wallet. Try it for yourself. I am not "white" just as Eusebius McKaiser, Nerisha and Vernon are not "black".

For various reasons, I consider myself most days as being closer to misanthropic than racist. A racist being a hater of a percentage of humanity based on skin colour. A misanthrope, on the other hand, being a person who finds him or herself at odds with the entire human species. But last evening, as I began reading Yuval Harari's **Sapiens** for the second time, I thought, "By Jupiter, I've got it. I am not even a misanthrope. I am just a normal sapient ape living in modern times!"

In the opening paragraphs of **Sapiens**, Harari discusses the socialisation of apes (chimpanzees and humans in particular). Harari discusses clan allegiance and tribal allegiance in our species and how we (Homo sapiens), over millennia, have evolved to kill or enslave any other human, if even slightly different in skin colour, religion, philosophy and so on. In short, and rather sadly, Homo sapiens evolved out of the stone age as an intolerant, merciless and brutal species.

In recent centuries, some humans have tried to disconnect themselves from their brutish stone age "hardwiring". Cultured groups and civilisations rise, but soon enough fall, more often than not to the accompaniment of barbarism and base behaviour: raid, pillage, subjugate, kill, rape, loot and burn. What sorry testimonials we would write for Hitler, Stalin, Genghis Khan, Attila the Hun, Verwoerd or Zuma!

Fortunately, however, there are some who do hold (or have held) the torch of civilisation high: Mandela, Gandhi, Nansen, Schindler, Biko, Nobel, King – and the many of us lesser mortals who would rather follow the path of good than that taken by the likes of Liberia's Charles Taylor.

In earlier times, human allegiances were confined to the members of the cave-clan or to a certain social group within the village, but later, as communication techniques improved, whole populations could (and still can) be swept up by nationalist fervour. Hopefully with the internet and social media, the power of nationalism will grow weaker and the wonders of science will be shared while the evils of ignorance and intolerance fade away.

I have loathed Jacob Zuma and the Guptas, not because their skin colours are a little darker than mine, but because of their purported deeds against our society. I loathed Magnus Malan and PW Botha equally in their day, for the same reasons, even though their skin pigmentation was similar to mine.

ON THE RACK: The former Minister of Defence, General Magnus Malan, and other luminaries of P W Botha's Defence Force have been charged with murder. With the announcements of their arrests the Government's position appears to have shifted somewhat.

Magnus "Ampie Aap" Malan

I find myself today not a racist, and happily not a misanthrope either, but rather a person with a strong sense of territorial aggression and a primal allegiance to those of my own clan, and I am proud of it.

Fortunately (unlike in ancient times) my clan is no longer by necessity a localised group. Some of them I know, many I do not. Some live in my suburb, most do not. Their skin colour, gender or nationalities are irrelevant, but they are all socially responsible people. People who care about others. People who put in more than they take out. They are courteous people. They are conservationists and conservators. They are people who are aware of overpopulation and do not overbreed. People who do not leave their dogs outside to bark when they go out. They are people unencumbered by religious dogma. People who lead organised rather than chaotic lives. They are people who do not race around quiet neighbourhoods late at night on Harley Davidsons or in two-seater V8 Cobras. And they certainly do not divide humanity by grouping humans into "black" and "white".

Constantly focusing on and referring to people by their skin colour (as is epidemic in South Africa) is to me, by definition, racist.

McKaiser sounds a lot like a racist to me.

Defining people by focusing on skin colour, gender, religion, history, physical characteristics etc does not serve society well. Fatty, shorty, white racist, black, woman driver, Chinky, Jew. "Izan your grandpa was a Nazi! Ha, ha, ha." It is time to see a bigger picture and open up the way forward for others to follow.

I have a photograph of John Maasch and myself with three Gabonese rangers in the steamy bush not far from the Congo border. Three quite dark brown (not black), with two reddish-pink (not white) men wearing the broad smiles of camaraderie. The Homo sapiens rangers combat poaching and are involved in building up and socialising new Pan troglodyte (chimpanzee) families from orphaned juvenile chimps (orphaned by bushmeat poachers). The two paleface visitors are also Homo sapiens but carry 2.5 to 3.5% "First Nation European" or Neanderthal genes! All five people are, however, of 100% African genetic origin.

When in Gabon, Zimbabwe, Namibia and Botswana, I never come across any of this Black/White stuff. I never get any of it from Malawians, Congolese, Angolans and other continental Africans I talk to. South Africans like McKaiser are obsessed by it.

In Gabon, the pink, French, 2.5 to 3.5% Neanderthal, male helicopter pilots in orange jumpsuits with shiny black polished shoes are only referred to as *pilotes d'hélicoptère*. Colour is never brought into it. The chopper itself, however, is referred to as *l'hélicoptère blanc* as opposed to the alternative *hélicoptère camouflé*.

25 Dec 2013   Letter #11

Hi GR

14 Dec 2013

The *annus horribilis* of 2013 is drawing to a close. Let us hope that 2014 is our *annus mirabilis*.

There is fighting to be done, no doubt, but may the outcomes be victorious for us, dear friend.

Work pressure has lightened and the past days have been very pleasant.

Every morning for the past five days has been calm.

Each day at dawn I have paddled before the earth has been heated by the sun, causing warm air to rise, causing a local low pressure, causing a maritime fog to ridge in. A refreshing grey fog that has lasted until about 10 or 11am and then mercurially vanished into thin air leaving a gloriously cooled morning. At about 4pm the predicted SE has started to blow south toward Bakoven. Some small white horses dancing in the haze. Nice.

Mornings with Cape dusky and shy west coast Heaviside's dolphins at the extreme southern limit of their range. Yesterday I paddled over a giant Mola mola bigger than a dinner table. A pair of Brydes whales eased past. Seals are everywhere and *sterretjies* rise up from Whale Rock screeching in a massive flight. The sea is full of small fish. It is glorious even at 17 ZAR to the GBP. The rand is now worth "sixpence".

Last evening was what I might call a *rara avis* or a rare bird. I was alone. I sat and played guitar and sang in my stairwell. The acoustics are magnificent and make up for my lack of practice and rusty strings. I played my old songs and then started to Google everything that I could think of. I listened to music and watched music videos. History, facts, castles in Transylvania, Kaiser Wilhelm II, on and on. I had always been intrigued by the haunting images presented by Peter Gabriel in his song **Mercy Street** dedicated to Anne Sexton, so I Googled Anne Sexton and found her poem **45 Mercy Street** below:

In my dream,
drilling into the marrow
of my entire bone,
my real dream,
I'm walking up and down Beacon Hill
searching for a street sign –
namely MERCY STREET.
Not there.

I try the Back Bay.
Not there.
Not there.
And yet I know the number.
45 Mercy Street.
I know the stained-glass window
of the foyer,
the three flights of the house
with its parquet floors.
I know the furniture and
mother, grandmother, great-grandmother,
the servants.
I know the cupboard of Spode
the boat of ice, solid silver,
where the butter sits in neat squares
like strange giant's teeth
on the big mahogany table.
I know it well.
Not there.

Where did you go?
45 Mercy Street,

with great-grandmother
kneeling in her whale-bone corset
and praying gently but fiercely
to the wash basin,
at five A.M.
at noon
dozing in her wiggy rocker,
grandfather taking a nap in the pantry,
grandmother pushing the bell for the downstairs maid,
and Nana rocking Mother with an oversized flower
on her forehead to cover the curl
of when she was good and when she was …
And where she was begat
and in a generation
the third she will beget,
me,
with the stranger's seed blooming
into the flower called Horrid.

I walk in a yellow dress
and a white pocketbook stuffed with cigarettes,
enough pills, my wallet, my keys,
and being twenty-eight, or is it forty-five?
I walk. I walk.
I hold matches at street signs
for it is dark,
as dark as the leathery dead
and I have lost my green Ford,
my house in the suburbs,
two little kids
sucked up like pollen by the bee in me
and a husband
who has wiped off his eyes
in order not to see my inside out
and I am walking and looking
and this is no dream

just my oily life
where the people are alibis
and the street is unfindable for an
entire lifetime.

Pull the shades down –
I don't care!
Bolt the door, mercy,
erase the number,
rip down the street sign,
what can it matter,
what can it matter to this cheapskate
who wants to own the past
that went out on a dead ship
and left me only with paper?

Not there …

Lean enigmatic imagery, none too clear, leaving plenty of meat for the imagination to feed on. Since my earliest days I have always been hung up on the lyrics. Boy, do I love those that hook me: "Welcome my son, welcome to the machine … where have you been, it's alright, we know where you've been." Brother Bill brought it home. Pink Floyd 1975. I was touched at the core and never fully recovered.

16 Dec 2013

My brother Mick's twins, Keanu and Mikaela, turn 19 today. I wrote them this:
    In the 1980s Mick and I started going on surf trips. We went on many. Mick was very clever with his hands. He could make or fix anything. He always had equipment with him. He loved kits. He had a medicine kit containing remedies for various types of pain, Imodium to stop the pooing, Valoid to stop the nausea. He had a surfboard repair kit in a cardboard box containing resin and tape and catalyst and sandpaper and blades. He fixed our boards. He always had leather and needles and scissors and a sharp knife. When the wind blew onshore and the surf got junky, Mick made paper patterns and sewed moccasins or, as if by magic, he would produce small blocks of soapstone for us all to carve. One day while we sat carving soapstone effigies overlooking

the lagoon at Plettenberg Bay, Mick surprised us by producing a three-legged cast-iron pot and cooking us a wonderful hot meal over a tiny fire of twigs. Mick made ponchos and a fine coat out of a blanket. Later he sewed splendid zippered navy-blue suit bags for the Navy Band – I still have one. After the first few camping trips we equipped ourselves with plastic milk crates to store our tin plates, cutlery, mugs, kettle and condiments. Our tent and sleeping bags were always packed. Whenever a cold front and a weekend collided we would mobilise at a moment's notice and head off to Mossel Bay. We roamed the coastline and also camped in the Cape mountains with Uwe and Mike Mater and Alan Best, Henny, Jarome, Pieter Adriaens and so on. We had great fun.

When I left for London in 1987, I needed a travel kit. It started with a small plastic box containing Pritt glue, pencils and a sharpener, pens, a knife, needles and thread, Imodium, painkillers and a long piece of string to use as a washline for socks and *onnies* while on the road. In those days I also carried a small calculator for currency conversions, but now a calculator is standard on every cellphone.

Over the years, items were discarded or replaced. The more interesting things the traveller sticks into his or her journal, the quicker the Pritt runs out. Once, after stitching up my left elbow with a needle and thread, I added proper sutures. All my med stuff is still contained in a 1988 SADF plastic bindle.

In 1993 a Swiss army knife replaced my old pocket knife. I found the new one in the side pocket of a bag I bought at Cape Union Mart. I regret to say that I was not honest enough to return it. I always feared that that knife would have a bad *jundi* but it has served me well, always ready in my pocket on sailing trips around the world.

In Gabon, sachets of Smecta replaced the Imodium. This *muti* is a vital addition to any traveller's kit box. When a dodgy salad leaf makes your gut go liquid, you need to fix it quick-quick.

Now you twins are turning 19 today. Matric is finished and you will fly out into the world. Doors that you cannot even imagine will open. You may well end up working in careers that do not yet exist. My school friend Gwain Bayley studied electrical engineering at UCT. He is now one of the world's top cellphone electronic integrated circuitry inventors with scores of patents to his name. When we left school at the end of 1981, the cellphone had not even been invented. Nor the laptop. And nobody had a PC.

On Saturday I had to think of an appropriate birthday present × 2. Hmmm. Then … aha!

What about a starter pack "kit box" for your lives beyond the nest?

So I went out and bought three boxes – one for each of us. For the past 26 years mine has always been a bit small. The new ones are bigger. I have put into yours some essential items. You can customise the contents as you go along. A nail clipper is a must. A headlamp is vital for finding your stuff in dark youth hostel dorms or sailboat cabins or bilges or when working on diesel fuel pumps in the dark. When Mick and I were young headlamps had not been invented, so we wore our teeth down and gagged as we gripped our Mini-Maglites in our mouths. Isn't it amazing that such a simple thing as a strap-on head-torch had not yet arrived in the shops? You will need a stolen teaspoon for eating yoghurt and honey in Greece. A lighter for burning the ends of frayed nylon cord. A lucky button … already included. A few small padlocks for your luggage. Maybe a pocket compass and so on.

And you will need open, questioning minds as you enter adulthood. You will need to be alert to what is happening around you and to all the wonderful possibilities that exist.

Chapter 11

Daddy Shaw

My mother's mother's mother, Ada Charlotte Day, arrived from England on board the Tantallon Castle. She was a collared and aproned Victorian nursing sister, escaping London for better pay in the colonies. In a thick fog, a few miles short of her destination, the Tantallon struck a submerged reef off Robben Island and foundered. There was no loss of life and the cargo was salvaged before the steamer sank. At the Cape, Ada Day met an American doctor named William Charles Winshaw who was in the service of the British. He had delivered a shipload of mules from South America to Kitchener's army and decided to stay on. It was 1901. The Anglo-Boer War was in full swing and there was nursing and doctoring to be done.

After the war was over, William and Ada met again in the Karoo town of Graaff-Reinet. They had both been sent there to do battle with an outbreak of bubonic plague. They were soon married, and in 1903 my grandmother Virginia – aka Dinny – was born there, followed over the years by her siblings Nancy, Natalie, Bill and Jack.

When I was a youth, the firstborn four were still living on a large Stellenbosch property bought by my great-grandfather in the 1920s. Jack, the youngest son, lived on his protea farm at Kleinmond. Dinny and Natty lived alongside one another, each in their own half of the 18th Century Cape-Dutch home La Gratitude. Nancy and Bill lived in spacious homes between La Gratitude and the Eerste River. It was a heaven for kids on holiday. A long, agapanthus-lined gravel driveway named Virginia Way, with a canopy of jacaranda trees full of cooing doves – linked the three houses. Nancy had a swimming pool and fig trees. There were wide lawns and stately trees, rose gardens and vegetable gardens and bamboo thickets. There were piles of National Geographic magazines, some dating back to before "The War" (there were so many wars). There were bicycles, air rifles, model aircraft and a trout stream at the end of the garden. And if that wasn't enough, the whole package was wrapped in a cocoon of unconditional grandmotherly love, with lots more of the same coming from grand-aunts, a grand-uncle and his wife Dot.

Uncle Bill would tell us fantastic stories about sending his "Dotty off in a gas balloon" and dig through his pockets, saying, "Let me find a couple of bob for you boys." And off we would go, happy on our bikes, with gravel crunching under our tyres. Dinny would give us each a brand-new bank note (always with sequential serial numbers) and we were off to De Wets to buy trout flies or Airfix models or packets of small green soldiers and air rifle pellets. We would spend hours building elaborate split-bamboo forts with watchtowers and moats and plastic soldiers – then shoot them to smithereens, one pellet at a time. Model bathyspheres were lowered into Nancy's pool and trout, illegally caught on grasshoppers, were brought home for the pan.

But those were the halcyon days down at Virginia Way. The tail-end of a golden period before The Twilight of the Gods and after the great flu epidemic of 1918, followed by successes, failures and bankruptcies in the building of a family business.

Son to a German mother and an Irish doctor, my great-grandfather, William Charles Winshaw, ran away from home in Pulaski County, Kentucky, fearing the consequences of purloining a pie. After adventures on rivers and rafts, with hillbillies and horses, he stopped long enough to complete a medical degree in tropical medicine in New Orleans. Next, he made his way to Heidelberg in Germany where he studied the art of making wine. After more adventuring still, he found himself leaving South America with that ship of mules and entering service with the military in South Africa. After the Anglo-Boer War he fought a new battle – a medical one – against an outbreak of bubonic plague at the Cape.

It was wonderful to have a character like WC Winshaw right there, so vividly alive in the memories of his children. The stories of his exploits and adventures never failed to please and never seemed to run out.

Ada Charlotte and Daddy Shaw
My grandmother Dinny is the standing child

During the prohibition years he distilled brandy in Chicago from rehydrated South African raisins. In 1933 he lost his fortune with a shipload of raisins on the Chicago quayside – the prohibition over. During WW2, he and his son Bill distilled brandy in Stellenbosch and shipped it to North Africa in army-sized fruit cans. The brandy was distributed on the Egyptian black market by his youngest son Jack. He had worked as a roadie with Buffalo Bill's Wild West Show, been at the Klondyke and met Teddy Roosevelt while riding with the Texas Rangers. He had punctured an eye on a hook in his attic and had it cut out by his friend as he lay on his back on the kitchen table (I have his glass eyes still). And he shot an eagle that snatched his little red hen – right out of the sky! Our hero, Daddy Shaw.

During the 1918 outbreak of Spanish flu, a quarter of Stellenbosch's population perished. Unwell herself, my then 15-year-old grandmother nursed the entire family back to health.

At times the family were very poor and the children were sent out to fish for trout, shoot Guineafowl and gather mushrooms. It was during those times that Winshaw would board a ship and head for Europe or China.

He would return with loads of cash, ready to start again, and bearing jade bracelets for his daughters, carpets from the east and magnificent Hungarian vases. Perhaps he robbed banks.

In the mid-1930s WC Winshaw began producing wine and went on to found Stellenbosch Farmers Winery (now Distell). He persevered, with all five children employed in the family business, until they finally made it a success. And so it was that through the efforts of these wonderful people, we, as boys, saw the inside of Anne Sexton's house and could lie under the giant spreading yellowwood tree blowing bamboo forts to smithereens.

26 January 2014   Letter #12

Dear Gareth

I hope this first letter of 2014 finds you well. I am two weeks back in the rat-wheel zone fighting my old enemies, anxiety and stress. I dreamed of a land where we could turn back time.

A Happy Holiday

In hopeful preparation for quieter years ahead, Zaan and I opted out of everything normally associated with the festive season. No presents, no Christmas, no New Year, no commitments, no commitment anxiety and so on.

We woke up early and took long runs from Constantia Nek to the top of Table Mountain via Nursery Ravine and Maclear's Beacon and down home via Kasteelspoort.

We paddled our surf skis and we swam in the sea.

We went down to the little green boatshed at Bakoven with baskets full of books and our PCs and my guitar and coffee and bacon and eggs.

We rested and we played.

Zaan is renting out her two houses (as well as a few properties belonging to others) to holidaymakers. This is seasonal work. Lots of enquiries are answered in the same way one has to bait a hook many times before the fish is finally caught. There have been plenty of house cleaning days. It is time-consuming work but not unpleasant. Excited guests check in and happy guests check out and money is made. This year I had a break from my architectural work, which was wonderful. Gordon Verhoef did not arrive mid-December and spring a whole lot of projects on me. This year, aged 75, he just arrived mid-December without the projects.

When I was a teenager I spent a lot of time climbing on and snorkelling off the rocks at Bakoven. This year over the holiday period we had some very warm seas so Zaan and I started free diving (masks and snorkels but no fins). Rough surging water, poor visibility, kelp forests and allowing oneself to be washed around in that salty primal element is such a wonderful flashback to a youthful time of great fun. We climbed through a secret cleft between the massive granite boulders – a passageway more than likely unused since my band of pals last crept through it in 1981, cormorants vibrating in their seaweed and guano nests and crayfish holes (now empty) below. Sadly, the once abundant crayfish have all but gone. The *perlemoen* are poached to hell, their shucked shells litter the clearings. The striped pajama sharks are gone, the *vaalhaai* are gone, the once plentiful ink squirting octopi have gone. Apparently the *kreef* (crayfish or rock lobster) are now up at Hermanus and along the east coast. I don't know about the rest ... scattered like my old school friends.

As the Atlantic water cooled we continued our free diving, but with our surfing wetsuits on and a couple of lead weights – not enough lead to make one under-buoyant and so a game can be played, with the help of the surge, like an inverted Johnny Weismuller swinging from kelp stalk to kelp stalk through the algal forest until finally one's breath is up and you let go and slowly rise up, with all the tiny bubbles, to the surface of the sea.

19 January 2014

Today I drove out to see my old dad. Old, legless and dazed he lies in his hospital bed.

Western medicine tries its best to make it hard for people to die a dignified death.

Propped up with all available remedies at every turn.

What a horror.

Tomorrow he turns 80.

He definitely does not want the party that his wife Gisela will force on him. That was the one firm verbal response I did get out of him.

A long, low, melancholy "Noooo."

Despite his weakened condition, the once grand man of the stage still eats well. He gobbled up his favourite steak and kidney pie and an ice-cold Coke, followed by some kudu biltong and a huge double-sided chocolate biscuit. Like me, appetite is not one of his weak points.

I remember 30 years ago, January 1984, when the old man turned 50. I was 19½ years old then and fifty seemed pretty old. Now 50 is just around the corner. I think my brother Bill was already living in California by then. Mick and I grudgingly went to my dad's birthday party hosted by family friends who lived on an estate in upper Bishop's Court. Mick and I were probably not feeling very well-disposed towards our dad at that time as we had not even bought presents. My mom gave us a beautifully iced birthday cake to take along. "Happy Birthday Øystein," it said. Why she had it made I do not know, but we took it to him.

A few years later at fifty-three, our dad collapsed with a venal thrombosis in his brain. He has effectively been out of action for more than half of my life.

Today is the 26th of January. Bill went to see the old man yesterday. He has become like the Dormouse in **Alice in Wonderland** and keeps falling asleep. Tired and old, he has been in the departure lounge for years. It is now time for him to move on.

Where is the mercy?

Certainly not with the medicine men who are in the business of administering antibiotics and anticoagulants and making their money selling hospital bed space.

May there be mercy soon.

26 January 2014

Early this morning Zaan and I went for one of our regular speeds up Table Mountain. We were back in time to check out guests at 08h30, clean an apartment and check in new guests by mid-morning.

Now, as I write to you, Zaan sleeps on a mattress on the floor under a soft cloth between me and the wide-open window. Thrushes and boubous feed on scraps of yellowtail. Doves tired of feasting lie on their bellies on the sunny, green lawn. I need more tea.

When we do Platteklip we run/walk/scramble as fast as we can from the lower cable station to the upper one. Last week I got in in under 60 minutes again. Zaan was an unbelievable 10 minutes ahead. Who knows what set of circumstances promoted such pace? This morning we did the run/walk/scramble in just over an hour with Zaan about 300m ahead at the end. But that is not the point of the story.

Platteklip Gorge is the most used route up Table Mountain. Some people take black marker pens, Tippex and even spray cans with them to add their names and their moronic messages on the rocks.

This morning, on a rock somewhere near the start of the trail, a person had recently written, "Down with White Supremacy."

"Africa for Africans" was written over and over all the way to the top.

Somewhere halfway up the mountain, a quote attributed to Robert Mugabe boldly stated that "whites" should be driven into the sea.

Living in an ever "globalising" world, being analytically minded and having never seen either a black or a white person, the concept of "whites" and "blacks" and Africans is quite confusing to me. I assume, however, that by "Africans" the Platteklip vandal must mean modern brown-skinned Homo sapiens born on African soil with forebears who were not part of any pre-historic migration out of Africa and into Asia, Europe, the Americas, the Pacific Islands or Australia etc.

Working on that assumption, I would suggest to the writer that, for a month or two, she or he should put aside all their accoutrements of non-African origin, starting with the black marker pen, the hiking shoes and socks and the plastic energy drink bottle. After that, lose all modes of transport powered by electric or internal combustion engines. No more cars, minibuses, trains and so on until we get to the telephone. Bye-bye all phones … No more mobile phone! No more text messages! No more internet and no more PC. "Oh, but I didn't realise!"

I would then invite her or him to ask a friend with a PC or other device with internet capabilities to Google images of the CAR, Somalia, Kinshasa, Congo and so on … corruption, mismanagement, famine, war, economic disaster.

Wherever I am in the world, whether in Norway, Italy or South Africa, I find Africans trying their best to get the hell away from "Africa for Africans".

The sad non-PC reality is: "Africa for Africans" is akin to scuttling one's own ship mid-crossing.

There will always be a few pirates among the crew.

Cheers G ... Kallemann

Chapter 12

Øystein

My dad was a big man with a neatly trimmed beard and a karakul astrakhan hat. He sang and produced operas for a living and was away from home for long periods of time. He looked the part.

In the '70s he performed in Seattle at the Wagner Festival every year. He staged annual operas for the Shah and toured the Benelux countries with travelling productions in buses and pantechnicons filled with sets and costumes. I am not sure how he juggled it all. Sometimes he would be producing one opera while singing in another simultaneously. No wonder he got stressed.

In the late '70s he escaped Tehran, snapping pictures of burning buildings and plumes of smoke with his Kodak Instamatic as he fled. They paid him in cash that time. Notes scraped out of some already looted safe. We boys couldn't believe our eyes when he returned to our home at 45 Burnside Road and popped open his small brown suitcase packed full of banknotes. He handed us piles of money to sort and count. There were a few US dollars and pounds and Deutschmarks, but mostly Italian lira. Strange currency with unheard of denominations – 10 000, 50 000, 100 000. We were in heaven. Believing that we were now multimillionaires, we thought our cares were over. What did we know about the lira and hyperinflation back then?

After his father left, my dad lived with Bibi in a series of flats in Johannesburg. Bibi sewed evening dresses and ran a small haute couture business in Joburg. It could not have been easy being a single mum in a post-war society. After finishing high school, Øystein tried his hand at this and that before landing up in Kenya as an apprentice coffee taster. He must have been 19 in 1953 when he found himself in uniform driving an armoured car. It was the time of the Mau Mau uprising. However, he only told his boys the fun stories. Stories about driving out to Mount Kenya with the ordnance removed from the turret and replaced by a Bren. About surrounding a village with the men and him falling headlong into a pit latrine. And the gift goat and the heat and the joy of driving down to the coast to Mombasa or Malindi and swimming in the sea. We loved his stories and he told them well. In the early 1970s, before TV, his sons and a few sleep-over buddies would listen to his tales, the scenes playing out in our minds as vividly as on any screen.

Finally, after much globetrotting, he returned to set up base back in Durban. It was there, in 1988, that he was poleaxed by the fates. "The bigger they are, the harder they hit," he used to joke. Sadly, "The bigger they are, the harder they fall." And he fell hard.

I remember that I was still in navy summer whites when I flew up to see him. He lay in St Augustine's hospital with its views of the ocean, harbour and city. His memory was devastated. He could remember the Hulett's sugar silos down at the harbour – they were there in 1938 – but he had no idea what the surrounding modern apartment buildings were. We had to coach him and, bit by bit, his memory returned.

During his time in hospital he would tell me different things, other recollections. He told of one night as a young man, laagered in the Kenyan bush, when he and his carefree pals rolled out their blankets and went to sleep, leaving their askari to sit guard up in the branches of a nearby tree. The next morning, they found a dead man lying next to one of the armoured cars. He had a wound in his back, just below the neck. The askari had watched the man creep into their camp around midnight, speared him from above, climbed down and removed the spear, then returned to his post up the tree.

Such tales were told from the story-box previously not opened to his boys. Narratives and unguarded anecdotes in the clouded present, drawn from the crystal past.

Many years later, by which stage his mind had found ways to access his more recent past, I was visiting my dad at his old age home near Stellenbosch. For want of subject matter, I asked him, "Dad, tell me about your time in Kenya." He looked at me with pain and said, "No, that was a time of too much killing." Apparently, the story-box had not really even been opened at St Augustine's.

In Kenya the big teenage Øystein Liltved took a part in a local Gilbert and Sullivan am-dram production and found out that he was meant for the stage.

In 1955 he met my mom in Vienna where they studied together and were married on the Rock of Gibraltar. My mom gave birth to a son in Switzerland, another in Spain and a third in Germany. By 1966 they had three small boys in Europe. It was winter and their rented accommodation Spartan. They began thinking of a return trip to sunny South Africa.

My brave old dad died in 2015. His falls had led to hip replacements and steel-pinned bones. Both legs were ultimately lost to gangrene. I do not believe I ever heard him complain. Not once.

Towards the end he talked of one day going back to Mombasa, or perhaps visiting the Kenyan coast again. Mick went to Malindi last year on a kite-boarding holiday. He sent us a photo of dad which he had pinned to a palm tree, looking out to sea. A snapshot of a young man with a feather of a moustache, sitting at a desk in his Nairobi office, his shirtsleeves rolled up and a tie around his neck, working at a ledger of some kind. A photo lifted from a dead man's box of memories.

2 March 2014   Letter #13

Dear Gareth

15 February 2014

Another day of textbook perfection – but too hot for me.

Full moon and a big heavy swell running. In other years I would not have missed such a perfect surf day. But the surf is so crowded now. We really do not like the crowds. So Zaan and I walk and run the mountain paths where relatively few people go. And we paddle our surf-skis and swim out into the kelp forests. But none of it is a patch on surfing, so it is sorely missed.

A month of intense work has left me feeling very drawn at times. Not hard work, not unpleasant work, but simply too much. Too much pace. Production at a speed too fast. Since the year began I have been working on new Vida coffee shops. V & A Waterfront, Accra Ghana, La Lucia KZN, Pine Slopes and Cresta in Gauteng, Portside Bree St, Edwards Rd in Durban, Durbanville and so on, as well as concepts and presentations for Naspers and an African initiative setting up in Zimbabwe. It is all a blur. What a meaningless waste of a precious month in this, my one and only given life. It is like stealing a tiger's stripes. You cannot steal them without stealing his skin, and that is all he has.

22 February 2014

Last night Zaan's friend Fabrice invited us for dinner at a Cape Town restaurant called HQ. It was quite remarkable. There is no menu. Everyone is served exactly the same meal. The same food is prepared every night, week in, week out. Always a piece of perfectly grilled steak, a lightly dressed salad with roasted pine nuts, a small pile of the most delicious crisp golden French fries and a small pot of Béarnaise sauce. Nobody could want for more. The restaurant is situated in Heritage Square. The old building is a model of crafted complexity inside. The table cloths are paper, the light bulbs are soft white. The restaurant was full of people. Every table full. All over 40 types, like us. At about 9.30pm music started playing. A kind I do not know, but I believe it to be popular in modern times. Beautiful percussion men, a DJ in an island shirt weaving songs. Drumming and tympani so enchantingly intricate. The smell of what I imagined to be a tropical mango plantation drifted in and filled the room. Everyone was smiling as though spellbound. Everybody danced and was still dancing when we left to go and fetch Allegra just before midnight. I felt like a tooth yanked from its socket. For someone who has not licked that side of the stamp for years, it was quite an experience. This morning I feel done in.

1 March 2014

Up Table Mountain we went … a little too late, a day too late. Saturday morning one hour later than usual and some of the apex members of "the great unexercised" were already on the path. To be rapidly overtaken. Noise and shouting and litter. On top, at a quarter to nine, a couple were being married in some quasi-religious ceremony. What a joke. Releasing heart-shaped balloons for God to scrape off the bottom of the clouds later.

In 1995 and 1996 I worked in Athlone for a company called Southern Wind Shipyard. Two years designing the interiors of big expensive yachts. In the afternoons I drove home usually feeling a bit *gal*. So I started running up Lion's Head for exercise. At first it took me a little over 30 minutes and I pared it down to 20. In those years I was one of maybe three or four regulars, and the only person I knew who ran it often. People were, of course, already running the Three Peaks but I never saw them on my shift. Now trail running is a major sport. They run the Puffer from Cape Point to the city. The Bat is a night race which does all three summits, but not via the city centre each time as is the case with the Three Peaks. But I don't care about all that stuff. Even Lion's Head is too busy these days. Twenty or even ten years ago, I would be the first car at the boom in the early morning. Now forty or fifty cars arrive at first light for the pilgrimage to the top. Zaan and I try other ways.

As I was running this week on the gorgeous sandstone of the Table Mountain group and the crunchy decomposed granite gravel of the loop around Lion's Head, I began thinking about the runs I have done in far-flung places and how one grows to love the earth of home. The unstable ground of north New Zealand feels hollow under the running foot. The rock of Norway is hard. Even a jeep track in the Norwegian forest is hard. The rocks in Norway break into big chunks because they are so hard, and you feel it underfoot. You can of course take soft downhill runs on the rotten snow and thick crisp moss of the high arctic mountains in summertime, but then there is always the bounce of the pack on your back. I once ran on a sweating metalled road in the jungle of New Caledonia. Flights of green parrots and humidity. I looped the painter of my little tender around the stanchion of a small bridge – overjoyed at first to be ashore after some days at sea. How far can you run into an unknown jungle? You can only do it by the watch. Twenty minutes in, 25 out. Then swim in the swirling eddies under the light slab of the culvert and slide up into the little boat. It was a place called Yate. The next morning the breeze was blowing straight up the estuary. The tide was low and we got Seacomber's keel stuck in sticky mud. But that has little to do with running upon the earth, which one has come to love. I cannot imagine how you feel, Gareth my friend. Pacing like a caged beast in your enclosure. But you know as well as I do that pace you must, because we live in hope and one day you will be free to experience the Cape mountains again and you must be ready for that day because the Cape waits for you.

This morning, as the season turned, long fingers of mist crept low and long fingers of high cloud layered themselves in such a photogenic way that all cameras were out on the Western Table. A dozen ships lay waiting to enter the container basin. As we watched, two more steamed in from the horizon. From whence came they? I can imagine the green electric hum of their passageways and the smell of the galley and the huge pistons turning over and over all the way from there to here.

Zaan's son Nicholas is done with res and is now in digs with five other guys.

I remember your digs flat in Alma Road – or was it Bognor?

The shared fridge and the pilfering.

And so this is the end of the weekend. Rain rattles in the gutter outside my office door.

All best my old pal
C

Chapter 13

Seacomber ... Up Early, Leaving Yate

Over a period of years, Gordon would phone me up. "We're sailing to New Caledonia," he would say. "Here are the dates." And I would fly over and meet him in the Bay of Islands or somewhere else. In more recent years Zaan would join us, and even Bill and Tess. We dived with manta rays and saw Komodo dragons stamping up the dust, guarding their eggs while drooling their poisonous drool. Indonesia and the Whitsunday islands, Great Mercury Island, Whangaroa, Flores, the Isle of Pines and kangaroos on the beach at MacKay. Wonderful adventures, impossible to have dreamed up by myself.

When I was a teenager, three sister-hulls were being fitted out on a vacant lot just behind Cape Town's famous Mount Nelson Hotel. Gordon, Brian Bayley and Bruno were each building a yacht. It was not far from our home, so I walked past and popped my nose in a couple of times. Bill was there quite a bit. I remember them as large, hard, unfriendly things. Massive, mill scaled, steel shells. Hot metal supported by heavy timber props. Sharp off-cuts, old tyres, scaffold boards and empty oil drums lying around. It took people with real imagination to think of these objects as future teak-decked, blue-sided, tall-masted, white-sailed visitors to faraway tropical lagoons. Gordon, Brian and Bruno had that imagination.

The three sisters were launched and soon parted ways. Across the globe they sailed. Gordon sailed his Seacomber into the Pacific via the volcano fjords of Tierra del Fuego. Then through the Pacific islands and all the way to Japan. Finally, a storm-whipped Seacomber was blown into the old pirate town of Russell (Bay of Islands, North New Zealand) and took a mooring.

Many years later I measured up Seacomber to prepare drawings of her for an onboard yacht manual. The tip of her mast bobbed 20m above the waterline.

From bow to dive-platform she measured just over 17m and her beam was 5m across. (65½ feet tall, 56½ feet in length and 16½ feet in width.) Wide and sturdy, slow but true. A tender was mounted on davits astern.

In May 2007, Celia, Gordon and I had overnighted in the tidal inlet at Yate. We woke to find that as we slept, the breeze had shifted through 180 degrees and had now become an ever-freshening set of easterly squalls blowing straight up the channel from the ocean. The tide was low, but not yet fully out. Time was tight, so we weighed anchor and made way for the open sea. The muddy estuary with its muddy bottom was churned up as we bumped and slurped our escape, then out between the pincer headlands and into what was, by now, a heavy blow.

Soon enough our sails were set as we beat south-east, making way for Noumea. We breakfasted on boiled eggs and buttered toast and espresso with cream, protected from the salt spray by Seacomber's generous dodger. After about 20km of beating, we prepared ourselves for a turn to the south-west, cracking-off and sailing on an easy reach, headed towards île Ouen.

There is a channel between the land at Bay Goro and some unnamed atoll reefs about 2km offshore. But the current coming towards us was so powerful, and the wind from behind so strong, that the entire sea, for a couple of square miles, was full of awe-inspiring standing waves. Giant traffic cones, ten-foot high, moving slowly along. Unbreaking, foam-topped stacks of water, an obstacle course from a TV game, but in real life and under heavy cloud. We pushed through. Gordon steered us well and we popped out smiling, just in time for lunch.

That's how it is with sailing. Tension followed by relaxation, relaxation by tension, then relaxation again. If it isn't a storm, it's the fridge. If it isn't the fridge, then the bright green diesel you bought in buckets from an army black marketeer turns out to be full of plastic lathe-turnings which clog the diesel filters and the motor stops just when you need it to get out of trouble. Remember that beautiful ballad, **Southern Cross**, by Crosby, Stills and Nash? Well, that's the half of it. (And **Sailing** by Cristopher Cross.)

Let me tell you about that half, the wonderful half. Only three aboard. Two asleep and one on watch. Smooth, scrubbed teak underfoot. Seacomber perfectly trimmed, the auto-pilot rams grunting happily, keeping course true. Moonlight bright on the choppy sea, the trades blowing, shirtless, bare back to the breeze, sometimes a ship in the distance but mostly not. Hours pass by – it is so lovely that you just stay on watch. Lines and sheets and winches. Dark wet wood on the leeward side. Checking course against a constellation rising and falling on the weather shroud. The Pleiades, and, of course, the Southern Cross.

21 March 2014   Letter #14

3 March 2014

I saw my first *dassie* in twenty years at the top of Lion's Head today.
A tiny baby one that seemed to be suffering from myxomatosis.
There were three small humans of the Skræling/Khoi/Javanese hybrid type,
Feeding it bits of pink cake.
One of them asked me if it was a squirrel.

HST – The Edge

"There is no honest way to explain it because the only people who really know where it is are the ones who have gone over."

11 March

Last evening at 9-ish Zaan and I were sitting down at the old green boatshed counting our lucky stars. The moon was about half, the sea as calm as can be. Warm air, shirt off. All of a sudden we became aware of a number of ghostly shapes gliding around beneath the water's surface, almost phosphorescent in the pale moonlight. The shapes formed up in a group at the edge of the slipway and one by one a family of four otters slid silently from the sea. They stood up, showing their white chests and faces. They were too shy to come over and drink at our little stream, but clearly wanted to. We sat as still as we could but our human reputation is obviously not good with otters. They slipped back in. One came out again and then they were gone like ghosts.

12 March

I receive this email from Dag in Arctic Norway who has just returned home after three months at the Cape. While here, he hurt his knee on the Vlakkenberg.

Cellphone calls in my Arctic home: "Where are you?" No presentation, no name, poor line... then reception lost... Hmmm, sounded familiar, like my pal Arne Olsen, local fisherman and shaman.

Later the same day: went to see the official shaman with my Vlakkenberg injured knee for comments. His advice: see the Tromsø hospital, another 700km down the fjords, for a 10 min MRA.

Stopped in at Arne's place, found him covered in a flock of at least 2 000 northern Kelp gulls and colourful arctic ducks. All the "feathers" feasting on liver and guts from 800 gentle codfish sitting on his homemade jetty. "Fish for you," he said, pointing at a heap of 10/15 individuals, age 8/10 yrs, averaging 8kgs.

No questions like: "How are you? Where have you been? How was Africa?" Just turning the back on me, preparing his own heap of fish with his son Karl Arne.

Karl Arne sitting on a homemade hammer-hand drying rack for production of the dried Stockfish, a more than 2000-year-old low-tech way of processing the vast marine resources occurring up here.

No more small-talk, time only for action.

I drove home with my share of fish, happy and saturated with impressions, just like the gulls and ducks were, filling their bodies with high energy liver and half-digested capelin sardines from the numerous cod bellies, donated to them by my pal Arne and his son Karl Arne.

What a world of contrasts!
Dag

What a world of contrasts indeed!

Dear Gareth

In Zaan's garden there is a giant pepper tree. The Cape white-eye feasts on the tiny fruit. Bees swarm to its blossom. Birds of many kinds find sanctuary in its fast-growing, twisted branches. We have small lights up there for summer nights. In the dappled shade below that giant pepper tree is a broad, cool, white cement seat with sea-shells and mermaid money and emerald wave-worn glass pressed into its surface. The cool surface will draw the heat of the day right out of you if you let it.

Today as Zaan watered her roses, I sat on that seat and stretched my feet (we had run up TM shortly before, so my feet needed stretching) and as I sat, I watched the little black ants that run around between the fallen pepper leaves and the sunspots. Among the ants, a remarkable little scene played out. One ant appeared to be dragging a fallen comrade. The ant pulled a bit, then let go and ran around the "dead" ant a few times at high speed (as if in extreme distress) and then returned to pulling. It reminded me of that famous Hector Petersen photograph, or a scene from the streets of a Middle Eastern conflict zone that you would know so well. All the pain and tragedy distilled into miniature. Then, as the "dragging" ant went off on one of its frenzied runs, the "dead" ant flipped onto its feet and took off at high speed.

"Now there's a thing!" I thought.

What an unbelievable month of news this March has been, and I am not even talking about the Oscar Pistorius trial. To my mind it is simply filthy to turn such a hideous event into some sort of social pornography for the general public to bet on and slaver over. Lawyers become gladiators before the emperor-judge. Thumbs up or thumbs down.

About a month ago two 16-year-old township girls were murdered by two boys from the same school. Blades and black candle stumps were found at the scene. Almost no media coverage at all of that evil action.

On the 9th of March 35 000 cyclists entered the howmanyeth Argus Tour. A windy day but flanked by perfect days on either side. The luck of the draw. I think they all loved it.

I am sure that you see all this on CNN *ad nauseam*, but I have been intrigued by the missing jetliner. At first I imagined the giant 777 was hijacked and flown to some secret runway where it was to be converted into a massive dirty bomb full of old uranium scrap and flown by fanatical suicide bomber pilots to a European city, all secretly orchestrated by Dr X who is actually CIA in order to give credibility to the ongoing "War on Terror" and thereby justify the burgeoning international weapons trade. We will never know the full extent of their dark and secret workings.

But then Australia reports a major discovery of what appears to be large pieces of debris spotted by satellite. Immediately several countries scramble to search an area about 1500 miles off the coast of Perth, for what may be the remains of Kuala Lumpur to Beijing flight 370.

One of the objects appears to be at least 78 feet in size. It's being called "the best lead right now".

A Navy P8 Poseidon surveillance aircraft returned to Perth just a few minutes ago with "nothing to report" after flying a ten-hour search mission over the Indian Ocean.

Only 3 things are certain:
(1) The Boeing 777 disappeared on March 8th.
(2) The mystery continues.
(3) I went down a little way south once, by yacht, and if the weather turns foul, nothing will ever be found by ship or by air.

Then how about this one – Russia annexes the Crimea.
Adolf Hitler invades Danzig/Poland.
Putin annexes the Crimea.
Scenes from our next attraction – China invades Taiwan/Formosa.
And maybe 100 000 Africans invade Europe every year on leaky boats and in passenger jets and everything in between. Why? Because the West is weak again.

And maybe 100 000 Africans from Zim, Angola, Burundi, Namibia, Nigeria, Somalia and so on invade "The Republic" every year and Kofi Annan tells us, "Twas ever thus," and he is right. Human migration is an ancient and unstoppable phenomenon. Just like invasion and war. That is what mankind is.

On the local scene, Julius Malema's fledgling party the EFF (Economic Freedom Fighters) managed to scrape together the R600 000 required to register and they will appear on the ballot papers in the May 2014 general election. God help us if we ever get Malema as president. He would be even worse than the corrupt thieving clown we have in command at present.

But the most interesting and frustrating news for me was Wednesday's report by the Public Protector on how R250-million was spent on a so-called "security upgrade" to President Zuma's private home. Public Protector Thuli Madonsela was superb in her three-hour presentation of the report, but that slippery eel Zuma will more than likely wriggle off the hook as usual.

I include an article from The Star.

Senior government ministers defended President Jacob Zuma on Wednesday following the release of the damning Nkandla report.

At a briefing in Pretoria, Minister of Justice Jeff Radebe said that, despite Public Protector Thuli Madonsela's findings that Zuma benefited improperly from the security upgrade project, the government maintained that all renovations at his private home were related to security and no public funds were used.

This took place as the DA moved to impeach Zuma, while other opposition parties called for criminal charges to be laid against government officials implicated in the report.

"The private house of the president was built by the president and his family. The retaining wall, cattle kraal and culvert, fire-pool and water reservoir, accommodation for security personnel and visitors' waiting area are all essential security features which ensure physical security and effective operation of security equipment," Radebe said.

He said Zuma started building the home in 2008 and was paying a bond. Zuma became president in 2009.

Radebe said the government was already taking action to recover money that may have been wasted on the project.

The cost for the renovations have ballooned to R215m from the initial budget of R27m.

"The Department of Public Works has finalised the cost of apportionment of the project for recovery of funds from the SAPS and the Department of Defence."

The Department of Defence had set up a board of inquiry to investigate any irregularities that may have been committed during this project, Radebe said.

He said Public Works Minister Thulas Nxesi, Police Minister Nathi Mthethwa and Defence Minister Nosiviwe Mapisa-Nqakula, who have been implicated in Madonsela's report, would not be fired or resign until Zuma pronounced on the issue.

According to Madonsela's report, Zuma unduly benefited from the Nkandla upgrades.

"President Zuma improperly benefited from the measures implemented in the name of security, which include non-security comforts such as the visitors' centre, the swimming pool, amphitheatre, cattle kraal with culvert and chicken run. The private medical clinic at the family's doorstep will also benefit the family forever.

"The acts and omissions that allowed this to happen constitute unlawful, improper conduct and maladministration."

Rejecting what seems to be Zuma's "I saw nothing or heard nothing" approach to the Nkandla saga, Madonsela said he should have been circumspect. She recommended he repay the costs incurred on the non-security upgrades.

Madonsela also found there was no lease agreement with the Ingonyama Trust over land used to build a helipad, among other things – but Radebe denied this.

Madonsela also complained that her staff were intimidated by ministers' interference during the investigation. But Basic Education Angie Motshekga said Madonsela should develop a thick skin.

"There should be no holy cows. We have always said she is free to conduct her investigation, but people also have the right to defend themselves," Motshekga said.

Radebe said the government would set up a team to read the report and formulate a full response.

Zuma had made a proclamation that the Special Investigating Unit probe the Nkandla upgrades, he said, adding the report was expected soon.

"This report will form a basis for disciplinary action and/or criminal charges against implicated individuals.

"The report will be forwarded to the National Prosecuting Authority for prosecutorial consideration."

Apart from condemning Zuma, opposition parties also tried to take advantage of the Madonsela report ahead of the elections.

DA parliamentary leader Lindiwe Mazibuko said she would ask Parliament Speaker Max Sisulu to recall the National Assembly and initiate the process of impeaching Zuma.

"Today is a historic day in our fight against the corruption, cronyism and nepotism which have run rampant during President Jacob Zuma's term of office," she said.

DA Gauteng premier candidate Mmusi Maimane said he would travel to Nkandla on Thursday to open a case against Zuma.

I know that they say one should not hate, but I truly hate Zuma's corrupt ANC government as much as I ever hated Magnus Malan and his cohorts.

Now, after all that ugliness, I will take you back to a beautiful place courtesy of DH Lawrence, Taormina, 1923.

A snake came to my water-trough
On a hot, hot day, and I in pyjamas for the heat,
To drink there.

In the deep, strange-scented shade of the great dark carob-tree
I came down the steps with my pitcher
And must wait, must stand and wait, for there he was at the trough before
me.

He reached down from a fissure in the earth-wall in the gloom
And trailed his yellow-brown slackness soft-bellied down, over the edge of
the stone trough
And rested his throat upon the stone bottom,
And where the water had dripped from the tap, in a small clearness,
He sipped with his straight mouth,
Softly drank through his straight gums, into his slack long body,
Silently.

Someone was before me at my water-trough,
And I, like a second comer, waiting.

He lifted his head from his drinking, as cattle do,
And looked at me vaguely, as drinking cattle do,
And flickered his two-forked tongue from his lips, and mused a moment,
And stooped and drank a little more,
Being earth-brown, earth-golden from the burning bowels of the earth
On the day of Sicilian July, with Etna smoking.
The voice of my education said to me
He must be killed,
For in Sicily the black, black snakes are innocent, the gold are venomous.

And voices in me said, If you were a man
You would take a stick and break him now, and finish him off.

But must I confess how I liked him,
How glad I was he had come like a guest in quiet, to drink at my water-trough
And depart peaceful, pacified, and thankless,
Into the burning bowels of this earth?

Was it cowardice, that I dared not kill him? Was it perversity, that I longed to
talk to him? Was it humility, to feel so honoured?
I felt so honoured.

And yet those voices:
If you were not afraid, you would kill him!

And truly I was afraid, I was most afraid, But even so, honoured still more
That he should seek my hospitality
From out the dark door of the secret earth.

He drank enough
And lifted his head, dreamily, as one who has drunken,
And flickered his tongue like a forked night on the air, so black,
Seeming to lick his lips,
And looked around like a god, unseeing, into the air,
And slowly turned his head,
And slowly, very slowly, as if thrice adream,
Proceeded to draw his slow length curving round
And climb again the broken bank of my wall-face.

And as he put his head into that dreadful hole,
And as he slowly drew up, snake-easing his shoulders, and entered farther,
A sort of horror, a sort of protest against his withdrawing into that horrid
black hole,
Deliberately going into the blackness, and slowly drawing himself after,
Overcame me now his back was turned.

I looked round, I put down my pitcher,
I picked up a clumsy log
And threw it at the water-trough with a clatter.

I think it did not hit him,
But suddenly that part of him that was left behind convulsed in undignified
haste.
Writhed like lightning, and was gone
Into the black hole, the earth-lipped fissure in the wall-front,
At which, in the intense still noon, I stared with fascination.

And immediately I regretted it.
I thought how paltry, how vulgar, what a mean act!
I despised myself and the voices of my accursed human education.

And I thought of the albatross
And I wished he would come back, my snake.

For he seemed to me again like a king,
Like a king in exile, uncrowned in the underworld,
Now due to be crowned again.

And so, I missed my chance with one of the lords
Of life.
And I have something to expiate:
A pettiness.

Have you heard from your boy?
C

Chapter 14

South

In 1988 Uwe was called up to the Simon's Town navy dockyard. Having already completed his eighteen months in the German Navy, atop the masts of the barque Gorch Fock, the SADF now wanted a six-month national service "top-up" to bring him up to the required 24 months. The 65' navy sloop *Voortrekker II* was in for a refit and Uwe, with his years of yacht building experience, was just the guy for the job.

The navy's famous Commander John Martin had rigged *Trekker*, as she was affectionately known, with internal water ballast tanks for single-handed racing and Uwe was tasked with removing the tanks and making her crew-friendly again.

Soon enough the job was done and *Trekker* was back in the water and recommissioned. A phone call or two from Uwe, pretending to be Cdr Martin's assistant, soon had me aboard as crew. We sailed to Saldanha Bay. I remember being tailed one night off Dassen Island by a gigantic phosphorescent shark. We rounded Cape Agulhas and sailed to Mossel Bay. We took part in races and anchored off Clifton Beach at the weekend. We hung out at the yacht club. This was all just so much better than Angola.

After a while I let the sailing tail off so that Gibbons and I could do some 14-day AWOLs. A routine of late breakfasts and surfing and hours of sleeping in between four starched sheets while on duty at BUVLOG, became the order of the day. At that time we were so trim and fit, so well fed and optimally rested, that we should have been awarded medals.

One day in mid-1989 I received a call from a member of the Voortrekker II crew. They were due to sail for Mauritius and one of the crew members, unpopular on-board, had to be replaced. My old pal Lieutenant West got shoved off and I got on. *Trekker* was victualed, loaded with water in 20l jerrycans, sails were packed forward and off we went.

Facilities were rudimentary. There was no functioning toilet on board, so "jobbies" were done over the side, clipped to the back-stay while chatting to the helmsman. There was no plumbing, so all fresh water was worked from the jerrycans stored aft below the deck. Sea water was collected with a bucket and rope. The entire hull was open from the aft companionway right down to the sail-loft forward. There were no internal bulkheads, only ring-frames. The engine was enclosed by some plywood boards directly below the cockpit. We slept in sleeping bags in pipe-cots fitted with lee-cloths. Suffice to say, no home comforts.

The objective was to sail to Mauritius and then race against a flotilla of other yachts back to the Point Yacht Club in Durban. Our sponsors intended to throw parties on the island so we were obliged to pack the aft compartment with cases and cases of liquor, which we lashed with dayglo sail-ties to any available fixing point. The steering gear and quadrant and rudder stock were all packed round with cardboard boxes full of glass bottles. We had no idea just how wet it would get.

The ship's complement was as follows:
Skipper – South African Navy Submariner: Lt Cdr Hanno Teuteberg.
Crew – SADF national servicemen Rob van Wieringen, Gordon Guthrie, Jakes Manten, Rowan Clarke and me.

Hanno drove a submarine for a living and the others were all champion dinghy and keelboat sailors. I could cook.

We set sail in August and turned east. We had barely found our sea legs when we were hit by a massive double cold front with a record low pressure at its centre. One front followed the other for seven days and seven nights. Huge waves, over sixty feet high, towered above us. We sailed with bare poles or a tiny storm jib shackled to the inner forestay. The speedometer needle banged continually on the little stainless pin at max speed – 24 knots. We were probably doing 28. Cloud cover was total and lashing rain swept in while thunder roared around us. The air exploded with white and blue lightning. It zapped and tracked over the deck. As if on some incredible funfair ride, Gordon, Jakes, Rowan and Robbie surfed *Trekker* from one gigantic wave to the next. Down, down, down we would plunge, the needle banging at 24 knots, then at the last moment, before the nosedive and pitchpole, the helmsman would turn away, out of the run, and the wave would pass. We would rise up to the crest and begin the whole performance again. How many waves we surfed, end on end, day and night, is unimaginable – with not one wipeout. After each spell at the wheel, the exhausted helmsman would flop down and sleep. Nothing could wake him.

At the top of each crest there was a brief moment when one had a chance to look around. Huge irregular, jagged mountains of shifting water far away to the left and right, vanishing into the gloom. And great albatrosses cutting through it all with wings like blades. And pintado petrels just going about their day, business as usual, in the teeth of the storm.

I fed the crew with soup and pizza and hot stews, all prepared on a gimbled gas ring. I sat on the weather quarter watching out for the rogue ten-foot chop that tried to poop us and did from time to time.

Down below everything was awash. The navigation equipment had been swamped so we had no idea where we were. The skipper had a sextant but no almanac or sun. The generator, which should have been serviced by the navy dockyard, hadn't been.

Trekker would fill up with water, it was open bilges, there was no floor. The aft compartment had become a mess of booze bottles and *papier-mâché*. We saved them and repacked them as best we could.

Robbie and I would take the starter motor apart twice a day and wind new stainless-steel springs for the brushes (on a pencil). They could only be used for one start. There would be sparks and shocks and cursing and the engine would burst into life and we would pump the *Trekker* dry. Had we dropped a part, the yacht would have filled up with water and sunk. It was right on the edge. Robbie (who now works in guess what? – yacht service and refit on Mallorca) was a magic man.

On we went until, on the morning of the eighth day, the darkness lifted and we saw the sun. The swell dropped and the wind eased. It was a Noah moment, biblical in its magnificence.

Robbie went below and took the SATNAV apart (this was before the invention of GPS). He washed each delicate component in fresh water and dried it carefully. The SATNAV was reassembled and soon after we knew where we were – a pencil cross on a battered chart. All we had to do now was take a deep breath, raise some canvas, point north and a little bit backwards, and head for the Island of the Dodo. Which is exactly what we did.

No sooner had we raised the mainsail than our boom folded in two. We splinted it like a broken bone, using the spinnaker jockey-pole, a bucket and some rope, and under a glorious pink sunset began the journey upwards.

On the thirteenth day out from Cape Town we sighted our green and lofty target, washed our stinking selves with sea water and Badedas and sailed into the busy harbour of Port Louis.

Newspaper articles from September 1989 say that we had made the fastest recorded sail crossing from Cape Town to Mauritius – 22½ hrs quicker than ever before.

Rowan Clarke at the wheel

On arriving at Port Louis, customs officials wanted to confiscate our cargo of wine and spirits. We used some of the liquor as a bribe and smuggled the rest ashore in Grande Baie. Bottles of Bacardi and KWV brandy with damaged labels paid for most of our expenses on the island. A bottle or two of red wine paid for the taxi.

28 April 2014   Letter #15

Dear Gareth

In 1982 I worked in the drawing office at Ninham Shand Civil Engineers in Cape Town. We used snap-off bladed NT Cutters to scrape our errors off the drawing film. A rumour went around the office that NT Cutter blades would soon no longer be available. We all panicked and went out and bought a stack each.

In 1994 I did my last drawings on film – yacht layouts at Southern Wind Shipyard. And then it was over to AutoCAD and the PC.

Today, 32 years later, I still have a few packs of those snap-off NT Cutter blades. I have been using one to try and cut out a deeply imbedded splinter in my right index finger. Still as sharp and shiny as the day they were packaged in Osaka, two years before Alphaville was **Big in Japan**.

April is a funny month in RSA … lots of short weeks and public holidays. Seemingly endless strings of *trekduikers* fly low over the sea. At sunset Zaan and I stop at the top of my mom's road to sit on the warm rocks. Long lines of birds flying low on the water all the way from Llandudno to Clifton.

The weather has been so calm and balmy and the sea as warm as can be. A big great white shark has been seen over the past days swimming around Clifton, Glen Beach and so on. In the last week of 1999, I remember seeing a big shark on three separate occasions. Once off La Med twice on the same paddle, a few days later off Whale Rock and then Bill and I saw it off Glen Beach on 31 December.

13 April 2014

Was it Vincent van Gogh who said, "My love and life are one"? Maybe it was someone else. My love and life are not one. Not enough of the time, anyway. I think something went wrong somewhere. Enough complaining. But how is it that the single activity I love the most is that which I seem to do the least? Surfing!

Surfing takes time and time is what I do not have to spare. If there are no decent banks at Glen, I simply cannot afford to go looking for waves under current work conditions … running on the old hamster wheel so that others may live in style.

Towards the end of last week I finally caught up to a point where Zaan and I could ease off and go surfing in the week. On Thursday and Friday morning we caught low tide at Derdesteen.

Friday's swell was a bit small but Thursday was lovely for longboarding on those cute little left and right mini A-frame wedgy peaks that come sailing in like cue balls (not Q-balls) after having broken around Robben Island 8km out to sea.

An old green Huey chopper with ARMY painted on the side flies low past us, with tourists hanging out of the open doors. Very noisy, freaking out the kelp gulls, but I do find that choppers never fail to be a wonder.

Yesterday we paddled on a flat sea, no waves, but today we had quite an experience on our surf-skis. I had a similar one once, but this was more extreme.

Around 8am we spotted a school of dolphins cruising past Bakoven. They have been around for the past few days. Maybe 70 adults and young ones … not too small but still doing awkward flops and tail flaps. We whizzed down to the shed, grabbed our skis and paddled out at top speed. We were accompanied by a local resident named Robbie Brink. We reached the dolphins off La Med and they turned to join us. For about 20 minutes we all went around and around, back and forth. The sea was a churn of fins and tails and striped sides and slaps and puffing and dolphin faces. So noisy and splashy, with clownish seals jumping out and barking in surprise at the sight of the surf-skis. After a while I noticed a group of 10 or more seals come swimming in from the north. The dolphin school suddenly panicked and turned, and at full tilt they shot off south towards Llandudno. It was a blind racing panic and in the chaos the bow of my surf-ski got hit hard. I was immediately reminded of a previous experience off the 12 Apostles Hotel* and I told Zaan that the only thing that could have spooked those dolphins was a big shark either following the seals or simply coming to investigate.

We headed for the rocks and paddled back just off the beach, through the gap at Whale Rock and along the edge back to Bakoven. The dolphins were far away by then. I did see a big fin pop up three times off Barley Bay but assumed it was a sunfish. As we neared the boatshed I was finding it difficult to keep pace with Zaan. Then I noticed my boat was up to the gunwales in water. When we reached the beach, I found a 5cm x 8cm chunk had been removed from the front of my hull 30cm from the nose of the boat. That's how fast one dolphin was going in its crazy rush to get away.

*Some years ago I was paddling slowly in clear water off the 12 Apostles Hotel. Maybe 8 to 12 dolphins were playing with my ski and in an instant they panicked and shot off at great speed toward Llandudno. I looked down and underneath me was the huge grey head and shoulders of the *tanneman*. It had come to see what the fun and games were all about. I turned for the rocks and crept back along the edge.

21 April 2014

It is Easter weekend. Always up early, us. Up Table Mountain before the other humans. Paddling on the still darkish sea. Yesterday in the early morning we surfed Derdesteen before the southeaster came up. The waves were breaking hard and lovely. Not unlike Sandy Bay. On the drive home we noticed how many flamingos and Egyptian geese there are about in the wetlands. Many pelicans on the *vlei* and quite a number resting on a small muddy island just upstream of the old wooden bridge at Milnerton.

23 April 2014

When I was a boy, and even into my 20s and 30s, Easter weekend meant the beginning of winter. Each year exactly on time, a great cold front would hit the Cape. How many Easter weekend surf trips were spent in soggy tents or trying to stay warm at midnight in the endless stream of hot water provided by the gas geysers of the Mossel Bay Caravan Park showers. Until the camp superintendent Barnie would wake up and chase us out. We would then sit out the night huddled in our damp cars and wait for the dawn. But not anymore. The southeast has been blowing for three days now. No cold front.

On Monday evening the first of the whales came back. Ten or 15 putting on a lovely show in the silver-grey wind-tousled sea.

Towards the end of 2013 I was introduced to the writings of Patrick Leigh Fermor by my friend, the advocate.

Autobiography, travel … a young man sets out in the 1930s to walk from the Hoek van Holland to Constantinople (and then on to Mount Athos). An epic of finely drawn detail set between two World Wars in a Europe that would soon no longer exist.

Never have I enjoyed reading the written word so much. I am reading the third in the series now, **The Broken Road**, which surpasses the other two in the series – **A Time of Gifts** and **Between the Woods and the Water**.

A biography was also written – **An Adventure** by Artemis Cooper – which covers among other things his wartime exploits on Crete and in North Africa.

I will get you a set if you would like and send them via Yianni.

C

Chapter 15

How is it then with Sharks?

Brother Bill, having done so much diving, has undoubtedly had the most close encounters with the "men in grey". If you asked him, he could tell you many a sharky tale. He might tell of a dive somewhere off the coast of Port Elizabeth on a murky reef covered in gorgonian sea fans. He was pottering around looking for the small molluscs he was studying at the time when one of the larger sea fans began to move. It slowly transmogrified into the tail of a massive Great White. He would tell of being pushed firmly down, flat onto his back, by the huge creature. Large gleaming teeth passing over first, then the pectoral fins like the wings of a jet, then the white belly followed by two massive claspers and finally the caudal and then gone. Bill says it vanished like magic into the gloom and he was all alone on the sea bed again.

A large shark in shallow water at Noordhoek

But, if you think about it, living at the seaside, at the tip of a continent, and being in the water so often, our paths must surely cross from time to time. Once in Barley Bay, Alan, Uwe, Mick and I enjoyed the company of a gentle, open-mouthed basking shark. Another time in Mossel Bay, Uwe and I were surfing at Outer Pool. As I came skimming along a large clear face, I passed a great big shark headed the other way. I surfed right onto the rocks and clambered ashore, jumping up and down and waving my board and shouting for Uwe to get out of the water. He did and his life was spared.

A few days later Uwe and I left the water at Gerickes Point because of a big sand-coloured fin and a smaller one behind it.

A sizeable dorsal fin popped up right next to my hand once while surfing on my own one onshore day at Plett. The Keurbooms River was flowing strongly and the waves were lousy and brown with mud, but when you gotta go, you gotta go.

Alan Best was tossed clean out of the water by a huge Zambezi shark as he swam alongside my brother Mick who was sitting in a canoe. They were seven or eight kilometres from the mouth of the Breede River. Upstream! The sharks are there, but seldom seen. It is their place.

One perfect morning Zaan and I drove out to the Turkish wreck at Table View. For a few short years, the final resting place of the *Seli 1* was a great spot for surfing. In 2013 a crew was put on board and they cut her down for scrap before blowing up the last bit of wreckage.

There were probably ten of us out at the *Seli* that morning, laughing and riding longboards on the easy waves. Suddenly it was just Zaan and me. "Wow," I thought, "everyone has gone in – more waves for us!" There were people on the beach watching us and a chopper full of tourists appeared and hovered overhead. They waved at us. We waved back and kept surfing.

About half an hour later the waves petered out with the incoming tide, so we paddled back to shore. As we were stripping off our wetsuits, one of the other surfers came up and asked us if we were mad. He told us that a giant shark had circled us for ten to fifteen minutes as the helicopter flew above. I guess we just didn't see it and we certainly didn't feel it.

Sometimes when you are surfing, everyone in the water can be simultaneously spooked by an ominous sensing. Especially if the waves are largish and there are big sets from time to time.

One such evening, with the Mossel Bay point out of control, Theo

Kotze, Manuel and I sat in the soupy green ocean at Ding Dang, not far from the sharks' favourite take-away at Seal Island. The sun was hanging low as large but infrequent sets moved through. Suddenly we all got "the fear". We felt who was down below. Theo smiled and sang a bit of nonsense to lighten up the moment, *"Hoe ry die boere, drie op 'n drol."* We paddled in, over the rocks and out.

If you want to hear about sharks, ask brother Bill.
He saw one too many and took up botany instead.
Here he is high up in the mountains of the Cape.

31 May 2014   Letter #16

25 05 2014 (The Darling Buds of May)

Dear Gareth

Yesterday I looked up at the big frangipani at my gate. It is full of small, hopeful, newly opened blooms. What warm spell tricked this tree into thinking it was that time, when it should be shedding leaves and rugging up for the winter?

Today Zaan and I ran the loop around Lion's Head. Cold wet air straight off the Atlantic whipped through the grove of pines above the high school. "Rough winds do shake the darling buds of May," I thought and began to hum the 18th Sonnet.

I arrived at 21 Quarterdeck Rd at 12h40, ten minutes late, after trying to track down a third book for you. Your brother Tammy was there with his wife Sally and their two boys, your mom Suzie, your brother Peter and the mother of the Carpenter-Frank boys, Dorchy. Yianni and Kim arrived a little later with so much hot battered fish and *slap* chips from the harbour.

We had a lovely afternoon. Sadly, your son Michael did not join us even though he had been invited. Linda would not let him.

I am sure that Yianni will tell you about the lunch, so let me tell you about the three books I have sent you. They are among the best ever.

(1) **The Forgotten Soldier** by Guy Sajer is a must-read account of the horror of World War II on the Eastern front, as seen through the eyes of a teenaged German soldier. At first an exciting adventure, young Guy Sajer's war becomes (as the German invasion falters in the icy vastness of the Ukraine) a desperate struggle for survival against cold and hunger, and the

terrifying unstoppable Soviet army. One can almost touch the heavy steel materiel "stained by the acid sweat of desperate palms".

(2) and (3) Paddy Fermor's **Time of Gifts** and **Between the Woods and the Water**. Let these books entrance you with their beautiful prose and if you love them as I do, I will send you the third and best of them all ... **The Broken Road**.

Voting day in RSA was Wed 7 May.
Only a very stupid person would vote for Zuma's ANC.
The ANC are in office again ... The great thief Zuma in the No. 1 seat.
The majority of South African voters are therefore stupid people.
Of that there can be no doubt.

I recently picked up a Zimbabwean hitchhiker. He told me that the reason Mugabe gets voted back in, over and over again, is because the Zimbabwean voter realises that Mugabe has ruined the country, so he must therefore be put back into office in order to fix it up. Perhaps, in the historical "group subconscious" of the African mind, a big chief who successfully becomes the big chief by pulling off many cattle raids, is a good big chief. Zuma's corruption and stealing of today is equivalent to the cattle raiding of the African past.

7 May

Zaan's car was packed with kit and four boards on the roof.

Our votes were cast and with little brown marks on our left thumbnails we headed for Mossel Bay. We were among the first in the queue and while the rest of the country stood in long dusty lines reminiscing about how it was last time they voted and the time before, we motored up the Garden Route. Chicken pies from Houwhoek for breakfast.

I had had a few surfs in the past weeks, so I knew that I still could, but the joy of picking my way across the rocks at Inner Pool and then launching into the sea is indescribable. Then turn left and out to Outer Pool. This action is so a part of me, forged into my soul. Like Kalk Bay reef to brother Tammy, I suppose. Big days, small days, winter, summer, autumn, spring, friends ... Uwe, Mick, Mike Mater, Manuel, Peter Gibbons, Colin, Speedy, Bacon, Katzy, Jerram and even Jonathan Paarman once or twice.

Lonely evenings – sunsets over the bungalows – last man out, seals, solitude, joy, exercise, exertion, adrenaline, relaxation and so one could go on for quite a while. In short, happy times.

And so, on that day of voting, two or three of us surfed lovely waves at Outers. Inner Pool was a bit crowded. Inner Pool is always a bit crowded these days while Outer Pool is not.

Zaan and Carly rented a bungalow called *Hemel op Aarde* (Heaven on Earth). It is very comfortable with rolled up towels and crisp sheets. A great view of the surf breaks and a brand-new Weber gas *braai*. Hey, my china. A far cry from those Easter weekend surf trips spent in soggy tents. Or trying to stay warm in the endless stream of hot water provided by the gas geysers of the Mossel Bay Point Caravan Park or sitting huddled in damp cars waiting for the dawn.

8 May

Zaan had a few waves at Inners but some jackasses felt the need to hustle like they were in a surf comp. Why? What's the point? Let a girl have a few waves.

I spend the rest of the day at Outer Pool having a blast. Surfing in a dream. "Skipping over the ocean like a stone." No thinking, no falling off, it's second nature by now I suppose. My knees have been painful of late. By the end of the day my back knee is painful and my riblets are sore from lying on the board. This will pass in a day or so. Surfing with a baker named Bob ... Bob the Baker.

9 May

I paddle out and return within a few minutes as a strong NW spoils the surf. Zaan and I pack up slowly and head for Cape St Francis at noon. We rent a little cottage on the point.

10 May

The offshore is strong. Zaan and I pick our way out via the channel at the back of Seals and surf all morning. I go in again in the afternoon. Waves so easy to surf.

11 May

Small waves at Jeffreys Bay, high tide at lunch time. Sunday, no one in the water at Supers except me. Not the best Jeffreys, but better than Glen Beach ever gets, by a very long call. And warm water too. Lovely surf in the afternoon at Seal Point with Zaan. Zaan disappearing in the silver spray .... Only to reappear like a tiny stick figure way down the line, paddling back grinning with all the boys going, "woo woo!"

12 May

Windy, small swell ... too small at J-Bay ... head back down to Mossel Bay through light rain. Intense driving for Zaan.

We are back at Mossels. I look at this idyllic scene. The rain has headed up toward the Transkei. The sun is shining, perfect waves at Outer Pool. Two guys out ... quite a few seals. After I wax my board, there's no one out.

I couldn't believe that one could still paddle out into perfect waves like this with no one else in the water. I was soon joined by two chaps, but they were of like mind and we surfed more waves than we could imagine in that dream state, with a pack of seals swimming around us and surfing the waves and bumping our feet and fins. One large male kept swimming under my board and blowing up big blasts of bubbles that looked like exploding mercury as the air raced upwards. The swell dropped off a bit as evening approached and I surfed my last wave right up the little rocky inlet that leads out and up onto the beach. Zaan ran down to meet me with a camera full of pics.

25 May 2014

Last night I went to make sure the little green boatshed was locked up tight. A 6m pure west swell was predicted for Sunday morning. I put on my cozzy and stood on my usual rock, knee-deep in the cool clear water. Not a soul around. Fairy lights behind me, waves coming in from the ocean.

News in that an American yacht sailing from the US to the UK has just lost its keel. Four fine yachtsmen gobbled up by the sea. That was always my fear at sea – losing the keel or the rig at night.

I dive and swim in the darkened saltiness and then run up the beach … Ha Ha Ha

31 May 2014

Yesterday we bunked out early and drove through to Muizies for a longboard. The swell had dropped too much so it was not great for surfing. As we walked down to the water's edge I said to Zaan, "You know, I don't really do this for the money, the surfing I mean. I do it for the love." She smiled and replied, "Sometimes it's cold and sometimes it's scary, but I do it to impress my boyfriend." We laughed and waded in.

Adios Amigo
Carl

A Thought on Religion

So quick they are, the men … to take up arms and fight for religion!
Such an easy cause.
AK47s and RPGs

So slow they are, the men … to follow the teachings of the holy ones.
Too much effort, the cause.
Love, Caring and Thoughtfulness.

Chapter 16

Berede

During my time in London, there were parades featuring red-jacketed Chelsea Pensioners who were survivors of World War One. Some were so damaged by what they had gone through that they had been institutionalised back then (1914-1918) and remained in that situation through the Blitz of WWII and right into the late 1980s. They are all dead now.

In WWI, WWII, the Crimean War and many other historical conflicts, soldiers endured long and repeated battle stress. The Somme, Stalingrad, Sebastapol, over and over. For conscripts[1] in the SADF, unlucky enough to end up "going operational", they would have been involved in maybe one or two contacts with the enemy. Some would have been part of a major mechanised push such as Gareth's Operation Sceptic. Others would have seen no action at all.

During the bush war in Angola, the SADF Equestrian Unit, or *Berede* as they were known, were highly active. Armed men on horseback in bush-hats. And dusty men, usually smiling, wearing browns, photographed with dusty motorcycles. And thick thorn bush, maybe a riverbed with a little water in it. Lots of sand. *Berede* could operate where it was difficult to move fast on foot.

We surfed at Mossel Bay with a friend who was part of Gibbons' group. He was one of the *Berede* on motorcycles. Just a normal guy, one of us.

---

1   For volunteers to specialist units such as the Parabats this would not apply and for professional units like the Recces, 32 Battalion and Koevoet this would not apply at all.

One of Us

One day while inside Angola his patrol came across a pair of pastoral Ovambo men. The platoon leader, a two-liner corporal nicknamed *Duiwel-oë* (Devil Eyes) decided to interrogate the men. He did this by pulling sacks over their heads and bayonetting them, little by little, to death. Later in the afternoon, many kilometres away, as the group made ready to bivouac for the night, our friend realised that his rifle was missing. He remembered he had left it leaning against a tree at the scene of the interrogation.

He went to *Duiwel-oë* to fess up. Needless to say: *Duiwel-oë* was unimpressed. He picked up and cocked his own rifle, muttered something about *"fokken Engelsman"* (Englishman), put the muzzle against our friend's temple and pulled the trigger. I remember our friend telling of the darkness of the platoon leader's eyes and the moment of shocked silence, followed by the explosion of laughter at his stupidity in believing that his own platoon leader would actually shoot him.

Our friend was sent back to fetch his rifle. He rode alone through the seething late afternoon bush, following their tracks until at last he found his rifle where he had left it. Nearby lay two bloodstained sacks with protruding legs and feet and buzzing flies. Somebody's fathers, somebody's sons. Our friend made it back to the bivouac at last light. How would his post-traumatic stress compare to that of a Somme survivor or Guy Sajer's "forgotten soldier"?

I have three Ovambo friends in Cape Town. Lukas, Moses and Eric. They were boys living near Oshakati at that time. They herded cattle and sometimes played with weapons that had been left behind by careless or fleeing men.

29 June 2014   Letter #17

My friend … some disjointed thoughts for June.

Yesterday evening as the sun was easing down, a group of whales moved south across our field of vision. Their actions made me think that they were humpbacks, but my eyes are not as keen now as they were a quarter of a century ago. Maybe they were just ordinary old southern rights, but that's still pretty cool. And then as the sun dipped, a brilliant green flash.

Some people say there is no such thing as the green flash, but there is. Zaan and I see it a few times a year sitting on our secret bench tucked away on the hillside above her house. There has to be some light, wispy cloud near the horizon and the moment after the sun disappears, just for an instant, there is a luminous acid flash of green.

We have seen a handful of them this winter, but on 21 June, the evening of the solstice, (the day in Norway they call *Sankt Hans*), a thin layer of cloud lay fractionally above an inky gentian sea. The sun was briefly split in two as it hung there, preparing to dive below the waters. And so we saw, for our first time, a double green flash.

When I first went to Paris in 1987 it was 10 francs to the pound and R3.33 to the pound. When George Orwell was cleaned out by an "unscrupulous and ambiguous Italian with side whiskers", he was left with 47 francs in his pocket which at that time was equal to 7 shillings and 10 pence. And so he went from being a poor student teaching English to outright destitution.

In 1933 he published **Down and Out in Paris and London**, which is where my literary wanderings have led me for this month of June. I am so happy that I have no need for television and that none of my time is wasted on it.

Poverty – now that is an interesting subject.

14 June 2014

Today is my 50th birthday. I don't like my birthday. Last night as the clock struck 12 and I teetered over into my second half century, I was out with SAPS and SANParks and other law enforcement agencies on an operation. There were plenty of personnel and *bakkies,* but to me there seemed to be a lack of cohesive planning. The op was due to end at 02h00 and I felt that for most of those present it was more about overtime pay than anything else. Since I was there on a voluntary basis, I excused myself and went home. It was after 1am and I could not sleep.

Every thought I had, produced another ghastly adrenalin explosion, causing me to be more and more awake with each consecutive blast. In the end I scratched around and found a sleeping pill and within minutes my stress and anxiety disintegrated into a heavenly deep sleep.

Q: What was all the late-night angst about?

A: Homeless people. Their absolute penury. Cold, wet humans on a winter's night, the global hopelessness of it all, and being a parent, and how will I ever escape the boa constrictor's constriction – the stranglehold held over me by my ex-wife. The unfairness of it all. And my birthday ... the annual facing of the fact that a human such as I who has really had an abundance of good fortune and "blessings" in this life would quite possibly have preferred to remain unborn in the nihil.

I have had a few weeks of less work than usual as Vida prepares itself for what it claims will be a massive surge in growth. I await this explosion with 50% trepidation and 50% disbelief. But in the meantime, I catch up on much admin and so on.

Since my twenties I have been running up Lion's Head as exercise. It became my sword and shield in a fight against ageing. Pushing the body hard and fast. There is no hard and fast rule except hard and fast.

Over the years Lion's Head has become more and more crowded with people, so on my 38th birthday I went for a run from the lower cable station to the upper cable station. I did it in 59 min 50 sec – just inside an hour –

and was exhausted. I have done it inside an hour many times since then, and more slowly too. It has become an easy thing to do.

The 13th of June 2014 was a warm day with light berg wind conditions. The mountain is covered in proteas and many beautiful birds. I left a bit late and did the push in 63 minutes. That was okay … room for improvement … but no exhaustion … quite easy at 50.

On the way down in the cable car I was questioned by some middle-aged tourists. They were maybe a bit younger than me, but in poor condition, working for Ritz Hotels. International penguin types living in New York and London. *Homo penguinus.* When I told them about my lifestyle – no commute, a daily run, paddle or surf, living in Camps Bay etc, they said I must be the luckiest man alive. Perhaps I am, but then why so much pain and stress? Why still the longing for the nihil?

Today I became down-in-the-dumps as I often do on my birthday. The "black hyena" comes out for a chew. I exercised at the shed and went swimming in the rough sea. Although everyone else thinks it is cold, it is not. So I swam in the warm Atlantic in the big surging winter swells between the huge granite rocks and the cormorants with no other humans about. I left that place feeling so much better.

Do you remember a cricketer from SACS named Jeremy Tyfield? He is maybe a year or two older than you. A good friend, a tough fighter, gravely ill … soon to be no longer of this world.

On Tuesday I must meet with my ex-wife … that is a dread. Our daughter Allegra came top of the grade again this term. She is a marvel and a delight. I hate my role as "provider", ensnared, chained to the rat wheel … yet the luckiest man alive.

Life is all contradiction and paradox.

Adios Amigo … C

Chapter 17

Maltahöhe

By 1993 I had been out of the SADF for almost two and a half years. I had a team of four men working for me – Motsamai, Chilliboy, Upington and Tony. We fixed up houses. Mick and I bought and sold a few and made a few rand, but it wasn't much. We undertook small contracts for clients, adding bathrooms and decks and altering spaces. Much of what I knew, I'd learned on the army building site at Kroonstad. The rest I made up as I went along. It became a very stressful time and thoughts of suicide were never far off.

One of our closest childhood friends hanged himself without leaving a note. An excellent boy with every prospect in the world, but too sad. The can of worms he had opened would not be re-canned. He had not found a passion or a sense of purpose in his life. He had seen the enemy and he knew it was us.

His death dragged me towards it, but seeing the hurt he had caused to his family also repelled me. In the moment before tipping into sleep I would ask the night that I should not wake up again. It never listened.

It was Uwe who told me it was time for me to get away. To pack my *bakkie* and drive up to his sister's farm near Maltahöhe in southern Namibia.

Farm Daweb, 18 000 hectares of sunny grassland and rocky ridges and drought and cattle and wild animals and birdlife and wind was just the place I needed. Rolf Kirsten and Uwe's sister Rosemarie stood at the kitchen door, waiting with open arms. For over 100 years, the Kirsten family had husbanded their little patch of our planet's skin. They had erected fences and drilled for water, installed pipelines and reservoirs and basins for animals to drink from. A cool shadowy home banished the searing sunlight. Giant pepper trees made shade. There were some permanent pools down in the riverbed where catfish swam and four-leafed clovers grew on the banks. Lucky I was.

Daweb

I was given a room in a shed once used for skinning karakul. At night I drew cartoons. I would wake early and walk across to join Rosemarie and Rolf for a farmers' breakfast beneath a blueing sky still speckled with stars. The orange dawn was barely visible on the eastern horizon. Coffee and smoked gemsbok fillet and butter and jam and cheese and Rosa's homemade bread.

I spent the first weeks walking through the bush removing the snares of poachers. I would pile them up to be fetched later with the Landcruiser. In the end, when I had cleared them all, we had a garage full of useless twisted bits of wire that had been cut from Rolf's fences.

Rolf and I would drive out to the cattle stations and inject vaccine or dehorn as was needed. We would shoot springbok for the pot and collect drinking water in aluminium milk cans at Hochfeld.

Out there in the clean air, red sand, tall grass and nights of stars, I became strong again in spirit.

One day, while out hunting for snares, I came across three poachers and their dogs. Lying low, I watched them for a while through my binoculars. Standing up, I called out and they ran. I gave chase: over the fence, off the farm, down the hillside and towards the nearby shanty town, a muddle of corrugated iron structures that shimmered in its own mirage behind the brick and mortar buildings of Maltahöhe.

I broke off my chase and loped back to the farm where I found Rolf working on his solar panels. We hopped into a Landcruiser and drove to the police station. The policemen were all large Ovambo men from up north, all keen to make an arrest. We followed the police van into an unimaginably dry, dusty and bleak collection of shacks. Poverty on a level even Orwell had never imagined. The three poachers were soon found and identified by the colour of their shirts, each hiding in a chicken *hok*.

Tiny Nama men they were, the clicking progeny of the people who were the first to live here. People for whom only the wild animals had had to give way. Men half my size, almond-eyed and scared. This was not my finest hour. Six months each in prison – a time of being unable to feed their families while I walked free to remove their snares. Snares that tortured and indiscriminately killed beautiful slender-necked creatures, their carcasses often not even collected.

31 July 2014   Letter #18

What a blaze of speed the last while has been. A blurred headlong rush ... like looking up and spinning in an autumn forest.

I just returned from Zimbabwe ... went to measure up two stores in two Spars in the Harare suburbs of Borrowdale and Groombridge. Didn't even get to see the city.

Fly in from CT on Monday 28th ... get there at lunchtime ... fly out at lunchtime on the 29th.

In Harare, omelette is best for breakfast.
It is cold and smells like Norway,
or maybe Norway smells like Zimbabwe in the winter.
It is sadly rundown.
It is sad for all the people because they are so nice and kind.

For what were the African wars of liberation fought?
For bad leaders and worse economies?
For bigger parasites?
For tougher ticks stuck fast in the folds of the hide?
Ticks like Mugabe and next, the Chinese.

5 July 2014

We had quite a bit of rain yesterday. Today is what they call a cold day in Cape Town ... a southerly wind straight off the sea. Grey squalls racing in every so often, interspersed with sunshine. Everyone is led to believe it is freezing so they squeeze their fat and pasty bodies into sweaty black polyester polo-neck jerseys and drive around in steamy cars or sit in their homes and turn on heaters and watch world cup soccer on TV or work in disgusting stuffy offices. Of course, it is very cold for those who are exposed and homeless or living in shacks amid the sub-economic hell on the Cape Flats or up in Ceres, with not nearly enough quality food in their stomachs, but for us it is not cold. This is weather that our northern European bodies adapted to and evolved into millennia ago. One only has to try it out to know. Today Zaan and I went out to run on the mountain. It is always too hot for me to wear a shirt when exerting myself (and I avoid the sun's rays by exercising early in summer) but when those raindrops turn to hard white hail and bounce off my back and cap and arms and bounce onto the path to melt away, then, my friend, that is when one knows that one is alive.

Last night we saw a movie about three teenage boys living by their wits (or lack of them) during a summer in Belgium. We hire wonderful, gentle foreign films from DVD Nouveau. No Yankee-doodle bang-bang stuff for Zaany and Carly.

One cannot imagine how it must have struck our forebears as they turned the corner into Europe and left the future "holy land" behind them, leaving the Levant, onward, westward and upward. What a gorgeous, wooded, verdant place it must have been.

Did you ever notice how different the north and south coasts of the Mediterranean Sea are from one another? The African coast is almost feature-less while the European coast is fretted with peninsulas and promontories and islands too. Apparently before the humans started building warships, Europe was almost entirely forested in oak. Spain, Italy, Greece, France, Germany and all the way up to Scotland.

My name is Carlos Liltved. I am 50 years old. I was born in Spain and was given a Spanish "Christian" name. I have not really enjoyed having a Spanish name. Carl would have suited me better. My brothers and friends call me Carl or Carly. My friend Dag in Arctic Norway calls me Kallemann with great enthusiasm and that is heartening.

I have been a lucky person in many ways and consider myself to be fortunate not to have any jealousy or envy. The only time I feel anything that might fit into that category of emotion is when I hear other people sharing tales of their exciting travels. But then I only wish that I too could have been there.

First day at school – aged 5½

Ever since I was a boy, the thing that has upset me the most has been when people have made me do things against my will – starting with school, sports days, SADF etc. And in more recent years, the distress caused by other people preventing me from doing what I want to do. Or living the way I choose. My ex-wife has caused me much pain, but now that our daughter is sufficiently grown, I must start to try and extricate myself from this short-leashed, rat-wheel alimony-trap of my own making.

I am a man who has only recently stopped feeling like a boy inside. It is a difficult adjustment to make, and I still often feel like a boy. I am a man of strong broad convictions and a boy in self-doubt. I get anxious and stressed if I have to endure inaction, but I am very strong in times of action and might even be what some consider brave. People say that Geminis have dual personalities.

At noon on Thursday I switched on my car radio to listen to the news. Instead of the news, the station had crossed live to the Oscar Pistorius courtroom. Pistorius' psychologist was going on about the three possible reactions humans and animals have when they are startled. "Flight, fight or freeze are the three possibilities," he said, "and the startled organism will react in one of these three ways only."

I have decades of experience in this field and I wonder if Pistorius' medical expert has any of his own experience other than that which was vicariously gained. You, my friend, were awarded the Honoris Crux for your gallant action under extreme stress and enemy fire. You did not Fly, Fight or Freeze. Instead, you Helped – and that's what makes you a special man. A few years later you ran from flying bricks in Port Elizabeth's Kwazakhele township. You took "flight" and hid in a manhole. I would love to hear your thoughts on this matter.

In my life I have had more similar encounters than I could even begin to count, and one almost always reacts in the same way in which two dogs often do before a fight. First, they size each other up. One has to critically appraise one's opponent/s, the situation, the environment and the realistic possibility of "backup". If, for instance, your neighbourhood has been marauded, over and over, by the vicious Momadi Gang, or the Crowbar Gang, and you are chasing a suspect through the dark suburb at 2am, and you chase that suspect into a building site and are finally "startled" by the fact that you have him cornered in a dark room in a half-built house. What then? F, F or F? Well, you can't freeze and you can't flee and you can't fight because the law no longer permits it. And you do not know if you have chased and finally cornered a scared homeless person or a petty criminal or John Mthambo (the chisel man) or a tik addict or a copper thief who is creeping around the neighbourhood while others sleep and you are out on a neighbourhood watch patrol. Now that moment is almost always a nuanced and exquisitely disciplined experience. It is here that you must rely on psychology or induce fear to dominate while overriding the effects of your own adrenalin.

Police officers in first world countries are trained for this. I have learned it somehow. And as much as the cumulative anger against home invasions and criminality will make your inner "caveman" surge forward in attack, the time of Genghis Khan is long gone. The fear of the "Pollsmoor lifestyle" is always present, so one needs other methods. I have mine, like cards in a hand, acquired from a lifetime of observing and testing the waters.

I do not like but do understand the police brutality we have in this country. I work with the police often and I must say our Camps Bay SAPS members have always exercised restraint and courtesy while assisting us with arrests, but their frustration at the failing criminal justice system is big. In today, released tomorrow.

Back to the radio. The other day, while driving, I picked up a bit of a chat show on global food surplus and hungry people. Jay Naidoo was the guest. I did not hear as much as I would have liked as I was doing errands, stopping and dropping etc, but I would like to share my thoughts with you.

I am most compassionate w.r.t. the hunger and suffering of people, but I bet that most of those who go hungry come from families that, for whatever reasons, have unsustainable numbers of children. In other words, more than two. There seems to be some massive global taboo on discussing population control/reduction strategies. Why? I do not know.

If I had the time and resources, I would drive a campaign promoting a "one child per adult" philosophy. I cannot understand why the Bob Geldofs and Bonos of this world choose to spend so much effort and resources on saving babies rather than on education and preventing babies in the first place.

Sadly, like rats, we humans are now the plague species. If we do not reduce the speed of our population growth, we will all perish. Humans are apparently reluctant to look this fundamental issue straight in the eye. They would rather scratch around for every other possible excuse or solution.

Off to Canada in a couple of days.

Adios.
Kallemann.

Chapter 18

Making War on the Fish

Often as I cycle up the Ontario riverside pathways I come across men with long slender rods. I ask them if they ever catch anything and they tell me that they do. I ask them, "What kind of fish?" and they answer, "Many kinds." I ask them if they take the fish home for supper and they usually tell me they don't. I stop for a while to watch as they cast, hoping for a strike, imagining life below the water where the fishes lie. Over and over they cast, waiting for that thrill of a take, for that little squirt of adrenaline they require to lift them for a brief moment out of their human malaise and feel a little excitement as the fishy fish fights for its life at the end of the line.

I passed a paddler off Clifton the other day. He had two lines out. "They're holding a big fishing competition," he told me.

Did anyone ask the fish what they thought about it?

Did anyone ask the fish?

So much of what once was strictly illegal is now just the norm. Homosexuals were flung into prison not so long ago. Young people were jailed for owning a couple of joints. Non-Catholic Christians were tortured by Catholic ones. Muslims were killed for being Muslim. Christians were enslaved by Muslims. Why do they waste so much time on an imaginary god?

In the bloodiest battle of medieval Italy, the men of Florence and Siena slaughtered each other. Now they are friendly neighbours in a pair of Tuscan towns just 80km apart.

And the women who fought for suffrage and children sent down the mines and greenhouse gas and missionaries on Tahiti and medicine to prevent Third World infant mortality without contraception to balance the scales.

Why do we need to go through so much pain to get to what is so blatantly obvious?

City-states unified into nation-states and nationalism was born. At the height of it, Germany brutally invaded Belgium and France and Poland and Russia. Now they are all (sort of) friends. I watch in hope as nationalism dies, as the globalisation of economies and cultures slowly breaks down the borders in people's minds. Nationalism is certainly ignited by US invasions and ISIS and events like the World Cup soccer tournament, but it is less intense than before.

Wouldn't it be wonderful if we could simply drop all the borders so that people could be free to go wherever they please and work wherever they wish? Weren't we all born equal in the eyes of the imaginary one? Isn't this our birth-right?

In the SADF they used to shout at us "*Dis nie 'n reg nie, dis 'n voorreg!*" … "It's not a right, it's a privilege!" … That is, of course, the truth. There are no rights, only privileges, all of which are a function of the civilisation.

And if the borders were to evaporate one day and the world lived under one global government and a Zuma or a Saddam or Hitler came to power, and Big Brother lurked behind a telescreen in every room, then, except for the ruling elite, our asses would be doomed.

Maybe we need nation-states to provide the checks and balances.

No system is perfect.

Afterthought

Politically, I call myself a Liberal Conservative.

I believe in a liberal constitution with conservative penalties for those who elect to transgress.

I believe in capital punishment because it permanently removes the rotten eggs from society – rapists, paedophiles, sociopaths, psychopaths, rhino murderers.

Not nice but necessary ... no repeat offenders.

Outside, the seas are wide and deep.

A piece of scrap iron and a chain are all that is required.

On land, disused mine shafts are plentiful.

The problem, once again, is man.

No system is perfect, least of all the legal one.

Gareth knows.

27 August 2014   Letter #19

Hey Mr Tambourine Man, play a song for me
In the jingle jangle morning I'll come followin' you

Take me on a trip upon your magic swirlin' ship
My senses have been stripped, my hands can't feel to grip
My toes too numb to step, wait only for my boot heels to be wanderin' …

15 August – *Ferragosto*

At the edge of Lake Huron near the small beach resort of Grand Bend in a sun dappled wood called the Pinery on a path near a gentle stream, we met a 96-year-old woman pushing a wheeler. Her 65-year-old daughter had brought her "to do her walk". A walk she has done regularly for 50 years. I detected a slight British accent. The old lady explained that she had been born in Dover and lived thereabouts until after the Second World War. She remembers warplanes going back and forth and seeing an allied fighter chasing and tipping a V1 "doodlebug" flying bomb. She told us that she had been lucky to survive.

Yesterday (14 August) we were in a dragster club warehouse full of souped-up cars and old photos and things. Our neighbour Tim's brother was showing us around. Their dad, after losing two brothers in the war – one in the Navy, another in the RAF in North Africa – emigrated from a ruined Britain to Canada. His choice had been Canada or Rhodesia.

At the age of 23, Tim's dad had been a major in the bomb disposal unit. Have you read **The English Patient**? Tim brought me a German bomb fuse with a date stamp from 1938. His father had defused it in Coventry. A piece of finely crafted technology that had been loaded, flown, dropped and dismantled without exploding. Can you imagine? History in my hands! One of thousands of pre-war Nazi Germany's nasty little ordnance surprises, secretly stashed, along with fighter planes, bombers, tanks and other super modern materiel, awaiting the glorious day when Hitler would unleash his dogs of war on an unsuspecting Europe. An action that affected every one of our families profoundly, changing all our histories. Tim's dad had been lucky too.

"I have returned from Germany with peace for our time," said Neville Chamberlain, also in 1938. How wrong he was.

21 August

"Canada is a place for people who like orderly living," I said.

Zaan replied, "You don't drive around feeling assailed by things that need attention, crying out for maintenance, falling into disrepair, water gushing from the roads, feeling like you are the only one who notices."

We drove down to Port Stanley on the Lake Erie shoreline after a day of intense work. Almost nine hours of non-stop designing and detailing on my part and a day of equally intense house painting, scrubbing and scraping on Zaan's.

Although we were dog-tired, Zaan steered our rented Dodge along the busy highway with consummate skill. The saturated evening light put a golden glow on our world. She was right. No water bubbled from the fire hydrants and water-main stopcocks as it does these days in Camps Bay. A combination of ageing infrastructure plus poor maintenance.

Port Stanley is not wholly unlike the Grand Bend, and it is almost as bland. For me, anyway. Giant lakes that have no visible other side, no surf-skis, no kite-boarders (although conditions are perfect) and no smell of the sea. Few people, too. And no aboriginal people in their tee-pees camped on the beach with curling woodsmoke and salmon drying on racks. Strange.

27 August

Zaan's house is on Anderson Street, Wortley Village, Old South, London, Ontario.
Her house borders a small park.

It is like baby bear's bed – not too hard, not too soft, just right.

There is no fence.

The garden and the park and the sidewalks are full of huge trees.

We are surrounded by them and my office on the first storey is like being in a tree house.

At night a skunk comes to eat our *braai* bones.

Each house is a work of art. Delicate, European, conservative, ideal.

It is very peaceful here for a person accustomed to the diversity of South Africa.

Dogs don't fly at cyclists. Aggression is not noticeable. People don't hoot. Long cycle-walking-jogging paths follow the river's edge through miles and miles of parkland. A linear oasis, a green artery, kicking off only 100m from home. What a joy the cycling has been, whizzing along like a giant school boy on my new red Fuji roadster bike. Ducks and geese abound. Sea gulls, turkey buzzards and osprey wheel overhead. It is summer and the weather is warm. My design work has not abated. Zaan has worked like a Trojan. We have painted and fixed and made nice. We are having a great time.

All best C

Chapter 19

On Luck

Lawrence Green wrote a book named **Karoo** – an unmatchable set of stories about that wide dry place on the other side of the mountain ranges that separate the ocean cooled coastal belt from the interior. The Karoo, a place of outlaws and mad men, of remnant San hunted down by Dutch settlers, of springbok migrations with herds spanning days and the farming of sheep for their wool and meat. Great fortunes were made with ostrich feathers and great fortunes lost.

The unlucky ones and a total loser

I worked there for some time, in the Nuweveld, on the Loxton road, developing a game farm. Here is a story I heard:

A quiet man moved off his farm where the work was too hard. He rented it out to more likely men and moved into a house in the suburb not far from the shops and a video rental outlet. He bought a truck and started a business driving the more desired parts of animals over the mountains and down to the seaside towns.

In one of the seaside towns he would regularly stay at an inn, or a "guest-house" as they have come to be known in modern day South Africa. He and the lady innkeeper soon became friends. One day the lady innkeeper asked him to bring with him, on his next visit, a little jackal poison, as is commonly found on Karoo farms, so that she could kill the neighbour's constantly barking dog. And this he did.

One Saturday morning, months later, while mowing his lawn with his truck parked on a patch of gravel beside the house, he was crept up upon by two groups of men – men from the South African Security Branch and men from the murder and robbery unit based at the seaside town. Both groups of men rushed across the lawn as the quiet man fumbled with the lawnmower's on/off switch.

The people he had rented his farm to were members of the *Boeremag*, a right-wing group who, among other things, were wanted for blowing up a supermarket in Worcester. Unbeknown to him, his farm was their hideout and he was therefore a suspect. Also, the lady innkeeper had used the poison to kill her husband and not the neighbour's dog, and the quiet man had been set-up to take the rap. Neither of the arresting parties was willing to give up their bounty, so he was arrested twice. And there began the living nightmare that became the life of the quiet man. Presumed guilty until proven innocent.

It was the same with my friend, Gareth. The bad luck of being in the wrong place at the wrong time. Even worse if being used as a mule by bad men. Imagine sipping *gluhwein* at a Berlin Christmas market on a Monday evening when Mr Crazy decides to mow it down with his massive Scania lorry. Imagine the excitement while unpacking one's trunks in a stateroom aboard the Titanic.

My brother Bill is now involved with the history of wrecked ships on the South African coast. Along with ingots and coins, the personal effects of unlucky people are sometimes found. A signet ring in perfect condition bearing someone's initials. An ivory-handled hairbrush. Perhaps she drowned. Or made it ashore. Perhaps she walked all the way to Algoa Bay and was rescued. Unlucky one day, lucky the next.

I sometimes wonder how many potential Kelly Slaters are born in countries with no surf. Or Mozarts into homes where there is no music. Or Steve Jobses in rural Burundi. Luck counts for so much. Good luck is the ideal launching pad for sustained, consistent effort.

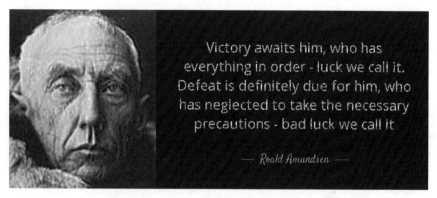

Victory awaits him, who has everything in order - luck we call it. Defeat is definitely due for him, who has neglected to take the necessary precautions - bad luck we call it

— *Roald Amundsen* —

Scott of the Antarctic attributed failure to "sheer bad luck".
Amundsen, on the other hand, planned well and did not trust unto luck.
These days, in the West, I think we see fewer cases of bad luck as a result of science, technology and better forward planning.
But we shall see.
I think that the Canadians have a right to feel lucky.
Planning mitigates against, but cannot defeat, bad luck.

28 September 2014   Letter #20

Dear Gareth

5 September

Today I leave Canada for London.

Zaan and I went for a bike ride up to Gibbons Park and a little further. We had worked like hell all morning getting the last jobs done. Lights and skirtings and measurements for future work. Almost time now to leave.

While out riding, an osprey flew overhead. A month ago, on the day I arrived, an osprey had frightened the ducks and they stayed concealed, packed tight on the opposite bank. Only one duck came to greet us in the hope of a snack. Zaan told me that duck's name is "Little Leader" (Little Leda?).

Today all the ducks were crowding round being fed "hush puppies" by an old woman and her mom. "Little Leader" must have been among them, but they all look similar you know … did I say all? All except one! Today there was one white duck among the brown ones. It had escaped from the duck farm and joined the wild ducks, thus avoiding being made into soup.

Back in Blighty.

Queues at Heathrow airport, a crowded tube to Victoria, then up into Gordon and Celia's lovely flat near Victoria Station. A hot shower, a fresh shirt, socks and *onnies*. A lovely terrace lunch at Santini. Crab pasta – *Gronchio*. Smart uptown city types.

Gordon drives me through Chelsea and out to Petworth. Getting better all the time. He says, "Living in England is wonderful." Maybe that's why there are so many refugees at Calais.

6 September 2014

I went for a long walk in the deer park and took a scenic drive this morning. It was lovely.

I can't connect to the WiFi so I take my laptop down to The Angel, drinking a few pints of bitter as I work. "This is a lovely drop," the publican says as he passes me a glass of hand-drawn ale. And indeed it is. I sit at a big oak table in a big old room watching, with half an eye, the comings and the goings of the village.

I wander around this place absorbing and imagining its history. Henry VIII hunting deer in the Deer Park. Nelson's shipwrights sizing up the oak trees. German bombs falling. Canadians preparing for the D-day crossing to France. I am fascinated by history.

When driving out through London, it's clear that some of the suburbs are economically challenged or depressed. The residents are people who live in the present. When you have five days of money left and ten days until payday or dole day, then you live in the ten-day present tense.

But what about the future?

Ekhard Tolle explains:

This instant is all we have.
The past is no longer in existence, nor is the future.
Only this split second called "the now".

When Allegra and Ella were little girls, I tried to explain to them what time was.
That is not an easy thing to do.
I wrote it down somewhere.
I will try to find my thoughts sometime.

Tolle says that we should "drop the pain and anger of the past like a hot stone and live only in the moment" with "as little regard for the past and future as is absolutely necessary". You may or may not agree.

9 September 2014

The sunset was pretty.
Pure Turner actually, and I should know,
I saw 30 of them in Petworth House on Sunday.

18 September 2014

It is two weeks ago since I left Canada. The days have passed like lightning. Yet it seems like an age ago.

A month in Canada seems like a lifetime in itself.

A lighthouse standing tall in a sea of repetition.

Such is the capriciousness of time.

The two weeks that have flashed by and yet seem like an age have been hard work. Not one night has gone by without working until at earliest 10pm … sometimes 12.

Mostly up at 5 and at the desk by 05h30.

Last night I flopped down at 11 to the sound of rain on the roof.

This morning I slept until 7 … It seemed like 11 when I opened my eyes in a light-filled room.

It was still raining as I ate three boiled eggs and butter and coffee for breakfast. It is really cold and the Atlantic is wild.

It is surely one of the last winter fronts before summer sets in.

20 September 2014

This morning Allegra and I walked up Lion's Head. Afterwards I drove the *bakkie* out to Stellenbosch to see my old legless dad. Amazingly he was in excellent spirits with more clarity than I can remember in a long time. He asked all about Zaan and why she had lived in Northern Canada and for how long, and about Saipan and about who found the house on Anderson Street and when she bought it. He commented on what a good man the Ukrainian president was and also what a "*lekker ou*" our old family friend Hannes Fagan was. CNN was droning on in my dad's room. I left it on and I got updated on many world issues like Scotland, Ukraine and ISIS.

Arriving in Stellenbosch, the oaks are trooping their spring green and the white snow-capped mountains north towards Ceres are truly beautiful. Meerlust, with its oak and palm tree drive and full dam and windmill, was a magnificent sight.

When I left my dad, I drove via the R300 and N1 as I needed to go to Paarden Eiland to run an errand or two. I stopped and bought some lilies and went to see Hannes, that wonderful man. The example to and mentor of so many young people (my brothers and me included) lying there unable to move, staring upward, warmly and lovingly wrapped in puffed glazed-cotton duvets. Listening and speaking softly, just above a whisper, with clarity, memory, humility and, as usual, great kindness. He spoke well of my father, just as my father had spoken of him a little earlier.

Two old men in late autumn, remembering one another.

Too soon my friend, we will be there.

Since I have been back in Cape Town, I have had the pleasure of going up Lion's Head with Allegra 2 or 3 times a week. We leave home at 6 and are back at 7.

She goes off to school and I kick off my day.

During the walks I seem to need to cram her brain with all manner of subjects – geology, history, social anthropology and so on.

I think it is because I feel I had so little time with her during her formative years that I have so much educating that I should have done and could still do.

On Friday morning we were trotting down the jeep track and I was singing (and in so doing, trying to teach her) a more recent addition to our compendium of South African folk songs.

We're Recces we're Recces a long way from home,
We're highly *bedonnered* so leave us alone,
We drink when we're thirsty, we drink when we're dry,
And if you don't like it then fuck off and die!

I noticed by her expression that she would have preferred quiet so, to try a new inroad, I asked her, "Do you know what a Recce is, my love?"

She replied, "Yes, a kind of soldier, dad."

I felt ashamed. I told her to put my morning prattle into a sieve and shake out the rough and the gravel. Perhaps one or two pearls might remain. Perhaps not. I then gave her silence and listened to the robins and thought the following:

For almost every generation they provide a war or a conquest
for the boys and the men,
So that the men might have a place in history.
And so the women and the girls may suffer.
I love history, but I like it vicariously.
I would rather not have a place in it.

All best my friend
Carlos

Chapter 20

Uncle Hannes and Aunty Sheila

In those days, South African paleface children from non-bohemian homes called grownups Aunty and Uncle.

Uncle Hannes and Aunty Sheila Fagan lived with their four sons and a dog in a stately Victorian home overlooking Cape Town's city bowl. The roof was still the original Welsh slate and the walls were softly whitewashed. Teak shutters flanked the windows and the open right-hand leaf of a pair of tall sash doors would welcome you in. It was a home of high ceilings and fireplaces and understated elegance. There was a grandfather clock in the hall. A thousand books lined one wall of the dining room, with its long yellow-wood table and chairs for six (plus extra for visitors). There was a piano in the dining room and a rocking chair and a fireplace with brass suns. Below the house, a dark, cool cellar lived, filled with tools and saws and wood.

Uncle Hannes had been an advocate and then a judge. Aunty Sheila kept the whole kit and caboodle together and did it superbly. To my brother Mick, and many other boys, she was like a second mother. The Fagan home was an open house to the numerous sons of the neighbourhood. Heini, Wynand, Marky, Leon, Sven, Dawie and Ed Stassen, Christo, Lance and the Liltved boys. Girl visitors were very rarely seen.

There was a swimming pool and a TV, a table tennis table and chess and Monopoly, *carrom* and Scrabble. Cricket was played on the upper lawn. "Teatime," Aunty Sheila would call out, and boys came running. Everyone was included. There was never a thought of sending anyone home.

I sometimes think of all the shopping Aunty Sheila must have done in the time before point-of-sale scanners. All the teatimes and packets of biscuits. All the meals and the laundry. And when the Liltved parents went away, one of the Liltved boys might be left there for six weeks. Uncle Hannes and Aunty Sheila never said no.

Who knows what went on inside Uncle Hannes' head. Cases and arguments and sentences to hang. He was vehemently opposed to the government but was trapped in the system with four sons and a wife and so much to lose.

Uncle Hannes was our mentor, always positive, always smiling and active. The human opposite of sloth.

"*Lekker, lekker, lekker,*" was his catchphrase. (Nice, nice, nice.)

He taught us how to sail at the Breede river-mouth and how to hike and camp. He taught us how to capsize and right ourselves and never to walk past a piece of litter. He loaded up bikes and dropped us far away, so we could ride home all by ourselves. He took us up Devil's Peak a few times to spend the night. Later we did it alone. Anton made lists and packed like Shackleton, and off we went, time and again, rucksacks, sleeping bags and tents. The doors had been opened. This was not the stuff of "boys to men" but more "little boys to big boys". I guess we were aged between eight and twelve and that was fine.

But putting all the other good things aside, for me and my brother Mick, the Fagans' cellar was possibly one of the most important single components of our boyhood. A place to learn how to make things. Our foundation in materials and tools.

The Fagan home was a candle to the boy moths of Tamboerskloof.
Uncle Hannes and Aunty Sheila filled the gaps and showed us what was possible.
A place of selfless generosity.
The other end of the spectrum.
A home without conflict.

One day, and I was quite a big boy already, Aunty Sheila said to me, "Carlos, you don't have to call me Aunty anymore." And I never did.

25 October 2017   Letter #21

Dear Gareth

I hope that you are okay. I have not heard from your mom for a long time. I will give her a ring.

I have collected some thoughts over this past month and so will share my life.

18 October 2014
Early this morning I paddled through to Clifton.
The tide was low, so I had to go the long way around, no short cuts.
As I rounded the corner I spotted four Egyptian geese and a seal on the same rock.
The seal heard me and raised itself up, glittering like Lot's wife in the early morning sun.
The Clifton bungalows were still in deep shadow,
And from that shadow came the loud staccato calls of a fifth goose.

We have big birds in the neighbourhood and I love that.
I love the noise they make, it is so primordial.
Guineafowl, hadeda ibis and Egyptian geese,
As well as Steppe buzzards and other raptors at times.
It means that we don't have shotguns like they have in Italy, and that is good.

I remember when reading Steinbeck's **East of Eden**:
Someone arrived at the farm and a chicken was put to death for dinner,
And Steinbeck commented that every time a baby is born,

Or people get together for a celebration or a meal,
A chicken has its head chopped off.

As you know, in terms of numbers, the humble chicken is by far the most successful species of bird on earth. For millions of years chickens evolved without having their eggs boiled or their flesh roasted, but only since humans began cooking chicken meat and eating chicken eggs did chickens achieve this top-dog avian status. As a species they make the ultimate sacrifice to achieve this, but for what? Just to sit in a tiny coop?

It's a fuck-up … but that's a living metaphor for the society in which I live. People work so long and hard – no fun, just stress – so that they may present as being the most successful. The largest house, smartest car – but they are not successful. They die young of heart attacks and cancer. The ultimate sacrifice.

I am having a hell with my ex-wife. Have you had any news from Linda?
The neighbourhood was thick with Jehovah's Witnesses today. Shame.
The Lord is my shepherd, I shall not think.

This morning I paddled out into a stiff steel grey sou'wester with light rain.
A giant half-wheel of refracted light formed a massive and intensely coloured rainbow over Bakoven Rock.
Dolphins shot up to join me as I ran before the chop.
The sea was like paint, one could not see into it.
On the homeward run,
The bow of my new surf-ski reminded me of being on the foredeck of Voortrekker II.
The action was similar, in miniature.
How I remember those nights!
The sea was the same colour too.
There is something wonderful about a South Westerly blow.
I love It.

Gareth. An old spare wheel packed full of hashish. Every time you drove a truck across the border or anywhere else for that matter, there had probably been an old spare wheel or a jerrycan or a bag of tools or a first aid kit lying around. Who knows when they might be the mule. What a terrible story! Like a river to the sea, and the endless ebb and flow of ocean tides, and change of seasons, we all endure the exact same time in minutes, but what different realities those minutes may contain.

This was a thought I had today:
I feed a pair of robins in front of my office … they are quite tame.
One eats a few bits of cheese and then flies off toward the mulberry tree carrying more cheese.
Somewhere sits a big hungry speckled chick.
Sam the cat was hanging around yesterday watching the birds.
A cat to a young bird is like war to a boy.
It does not care a damn about how much hard work and love a mother put in.

I am terribly much looking forward to Zaan's return from Canada. She returns on Wed 29th. It has been quite long, I have missed her a lot. I cannot imagine how you feel. But I am very happy that she has had a fantastic break. Away from the day-to-day chores and routines that prevent one from thinking and reflecting.

A time away like she has had is so important. Perspective can only be achieved from a distance.

For me here in Cape Town, it has been a time of the most intense workload ever.

Tension and stress.

I had a neighbour across the way. He dropped down dead last week. He was only about 57. He commuted weekly, back and forth to Johannesburg, as so many businessmen do. I believe it was supposed to be his last trip before retiring. He never made it back.

My neighbours enjoyed sociable evenings drinking wine on their terrace, talking, laughing. No more wine for Mr Neighbour. He has returned to the place he was during the time of the dinosaurs. I spoke to his widow a few days ago, out walking the dogs. Naturally she is devastated. She told me what I had already guessed. Mr Neighbour died of prolonged exposure to stress.

I have worked on 43 commissioned projects (this includes renovations to existing stores) this year. There were probably about 10 or 15 more preliminary design exercises that never came off.

I do take my short early morning gaps – for me exercise is a non-negotiable. But that time has not been relaxed as the computer in my head uses what should be down-time to work things out. As I have said before, my mind has a mind of its own – a subconscious that goes 13 to the dozen. Since

I have been back from Canada I have scarcely had a night off. Starting at 5-ish in the morning and working until 10 or 11pm.

In addition, I have had to fix up the pigsty at my rental home, 2 Berkley Rd, left behind by our tenant and his trashy entourage, as well as organise the painting of all three properties. It is still not all done. And to add insult to injury, my employers, the people I make rich, simply choose not to pay me for prolonged periods. For some projects they simply don't pay at all. Which drives me nuts. Beg, beg, beg.

The death of Mr Neighbour is the latest in a series of deaths, cancer, heart attacks and strokes in my near circle in this age group. My dad, fucked at 56, Buster Siegelberg, heart attack – dead. Dave Talbot survived his heart attack. Jeremy Tyfield – let's not talk about that. Graeme Clarke, cancer – dead. Chris Gurney, cancer – dead. Solly the painter – dead. Dicky Brink, heart attack – dead. And so on goes the roll. I observe with interest that they are all male.

I spoke to LS of Vida the other day. They are planning a massive expansion trail over the next two years. They want to do 150 projects in 2015. A large design company will be needed. A company called TDC Design is already being negotiated with. My one-man band cannot cope with the sheer load any more. I am like an overloaded little Nissan 1400 *bakkie*. They need a truck. It is time for me to get off before I am added to the roll.

I really feel burned out and need a break.

Some time to recuperate.

The intention is therefore to sell one of the houses (reluctantly, as they have been my life project) and use the money to buy myself some time. It is time for "me time". I have been in flat-out service for too long.

My ex-wife remains unrelenting in her demands. The proceeds of the proposed sale of a house will also kick that can a bit further into the future. The mortgage will also be paid off. That costs me over R13 000 a month, which my ex-wife does not contribute to. I have also been using the bond to pay for all the repairs and maintenance. My mom must also be repaid her loan as she needs to plan for her future years. She came in with that, so I didn't have to sell property at the time of our divorce, but now the time has come. And there are so many other costs. Rates, insurance and massive wads of income tax. The albatrosses we create for ourselves.

In times of stress it is obvious that one should ponder stress and why all of these men become ill or succumb to heart attacks as a result of it.

The authors Neitzel and Welzer are very intelligent people.
They have put together a compelling work called **Soldaten**.
Pages 50 and 51 deal with an interesting subject.
That being: basic human urges, and in this case particularly "autotelic violence".

It is a bit hard to take this out of context, but I quote: "Do we feel the need, for instance, to account for the human sex drive? Do we try to explain why human beings eat, drink and breathe? In all of these core areas of human existence questions may arise as to how people try to satisfy their needs, but we never question the fact that human beings want to eat, drink, breathe and have sex."

We do however question violence. Something that is so core to our maleness. Our governments legitimise it and invade other countries, but it remains strictly forbidden on a man-to-man level in our passive Western society. We can't shake our need of it, so we opt for hidden domestic violence and proxy violence in our movies, TV shows and modern video games. When I listen to men talk about what they would do to an intruder in their home or what should have happened to Oscar Pistorius. It is so close to the surface.

Personally, I am with Darwin, Dawkins and Joe Quirk in sharing a belief that we are all hardwired to the Stone Age. Hundreds of thousands of years of slow evolutionary programming are not simply overwritten in a few centuries of "civilising". Women might not agree but they are hardwired for different things. Things upon which the success of the species equally depends.

To me anger and aggression are two basic human urges. These urges are strong evolutionary success strategies. In simple terms, the more passive would have been wiped out by the more aggressive and the aggressive would have lived to breed out more genes and thus aggression becomes the dominant feature of the species. Whether we like it or not, we are sadly a species of aggression and war.

Modern society – i.e. the corporate world, business, city living, social structures – does not allow, for obvious reasons, men in positions of power to behave as evolutionary human chiefs. They have to go through all the courtesies of disciplinary hearings. The relatively new weight of the female voice in society adds a frustration factor. Tensions and jealousies in the workplace must be contained, and many other restrictive protocols simply tighten and tighten the old pressure cooker lid until finally – bang!

Ordinary men cannot act the way they instinctively should when their wives are caught in bed with their best friends, or when intruders invade.

And so, the stress builds up.

Now I will go and make myself a piece of toast. Hungry now.

All best – your friend – Kallemann

Chapter 21

Adderley's Comeuppance

Today was Canada Day. It is now almost 10pm. I am sitting on the back porch drinking beer and staring up. The sky is royal blue. Between me and heaven is a giant hackberry tree. Its leaves and branches, silhouetted black, move to the breeze. It is very hot.

Fireflies, like little torches, flicker on and off. Four thousand people have gathered down at The Forks to watch a fireworks display. We hear it banging away in the distance. As the darkness slowly thickens, I am thinking about a difficult subject. I cannot remember ever applying my mind to it before. My thinking was triggered by Neitzel's and Welzer's dissection of "autotelic violence" – violence for its own sake. Violence as a primal urge of man. My subject is not this. My subject is, the deep satisfaction of successful violence on a personal level. Not bullying, not sadism, but the pleasure of beating the bully or the "bad guy". The base and carnal gratification in denying a would-be assailant his victory. The feel-good stuff of vigilante movies: Clint Eastwood, "Make my day!"

I have known bullies. In the army we had a guy called Adderley who, as his trademark, wore one black leather glove. Adderley would only stage his appearance once the breakfast queue was already long. He would swagger up to a small soldier near the front, slap him hard on the head, and bounce him out of the line. Adderley would then take his place. The little guy would slink to the back of the queue with his tail between his legs. Nobody did or said anything. They were all too scared. Adderley was a dominator, a bully for power, alpha male, primitive. I witnessed his act on the first couple of mornings after my arrival at Kroonstad. I hadn't quite found my feet there yet, so I watched, indignantly contemplating. But I did not have to contemplate long. That Friday, Adderley and two pals got a weekend pass. As evening fell, they stood, hitchhiking, near Welkom. For amusement they decided to bully a man, a passer-by, at the side of the road. Adderley and his pals were rough guys, but luckily for their victim, a Toyota HiAce full of Friday afternoon beer-sozzled miners pulled over to assist one of their own.

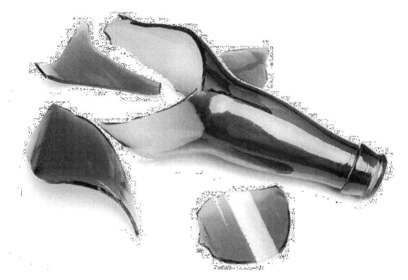

Adderley returned to camp, from hospital, a few weeks later. He must have received over two hundred stab wounds from broken bottles. Each jab by now a raised purple welt, reminders to carry for the rest of his life. A broken bottle had also sugar-scooped the muscle off his right forearm, which had been sown back on. Adderley came back shamed and tamed and queued for breakfast with everyone else.

Adderley was a bully, but the men who attacked him were not. They were men carrying years of pain. Apartheid pain. Bullying, unfair pain. The pain of being separated from their families and working down the mines. The pain of hard living in compounds. Historical poll tax pain. Pain caused by stupid, brutal masters. For them it was just solidarity and revenge, the pleasure of spilling the blood of the oppressor.

In my life I have so often been at that place – not the door-to-door brawling of soldiers liberating a city, but the standing and holding one's own. The bully or bullies before me. The calmness and the summing up. The elegant strike of a cleverly concealed weapon. The spray of blood from a throat. Perfect slow motion as you watch your own foot wrapping around the head of the bad guy. The sheer, unadulterated pleasure of it. No bullying here.

In order to make civilised society work, people are, for obvious reasons, denied the pleasure of taking care of their own dirty work, the taking of the law into their own hands. We all know why this is necessary, but it is certainly the cause of much frustration. The emasculation of the man, the lawyer's letter, frustration, litigation, a complaint to the authorities that is never responded to. The need for violent video games.

I walk around here in Canada and look at all the passive men.

14 November 2014   Letter #22

17 November 2014

Dear Gareth

Allegra turns 17 and writes her maths exam. Suzie Rutherford, 75, passes away. Gareth in a prison far away plays saxophone in memory of his beloved mother and the sound clip is emailed to his friends. The sound clip will be played in a little church in a few days.

Zaany and Carly went for an early run on the mountain and then down to the sea for a swim at Bakoven. The inlet was full of anchovies. Terns were diving at the back. Big kelp gulls going in and under, time and again, learning the diving trick somewhat clumsily. Then coming up again, sometimes three fish in a beak, mostly just one. Glittering anchovies beach themselves like warships at Narvik, only to be nabbed by the small gulls as they bounce all over the sand. We do not swim, only sit and watch, fascinated. Carly thinks about death but only gets the Suzie news today. Coincidence. Carly often thinks about death, perhaps too much. There has been a lot of it around lately. Today the thoughts are sparked by the activity in the water. Small fish, beautiful birds.

18 November 2014

It is full-blown summer now. Very hot.
The only possibility for exercise is early.
"Up before the sun, Recces on the run," sings Zaan.
She should know, she was married to one.
Today the surface of the sea in the dawn light is like this:

Imagine a zebra skin
Imagine the stripes are a bit more like circles
Imagine the black a little bit more blue
Imagine the white a little bit more blue

Camps Bay is full of seals. Maybe 100 small seals float in rafts with morning bellies already stuffed to capacity. It is the time of the anchovy fest. A few dolphins loll about. We paddle our new white surf-skis. As the sun rises up, the sea becomes turquoise. That is how it is now, and Suzie is gone from us forever.

In the still of the arctic summer at 02h30 one can paddle out in a boat to where the mosquitoes aren't. Let us imagine that we are out in a boat beyond the mosquitoes. The midnight sun is obscured by a veil of cloud. It is warm enough and utterly quiet. The surface of the water is like gossamer. The human eye cannot focus on it. Small lures are being cast and trolled and chased by speeding ice blue bolts called herring. The humans murder the herring by throwing them roughly into a plastic bucket. Tiny translucent jewels that are herring scales flake off.

The herrings are fried for breakfast and are delicious. Their spines with head, tail and bristle bones are pulled off the meat. Complete skeletons discarded along with squeezed out lemon wedges.

On the 15th of November we had our first mosquito in our bedroom in Camps Bay. I hunted it in the small hours but could not get it. The next day it came to suck blood from my left foot as I worked in my office. I found its still twitching airframe (so delicate and amazing) on the floor not far from where I had struck at it with one of my new Canada caps.

While writing to you now, I remembered and looked up a piece I sent to you in my 9th letter, all about mosquitoes and life. I risk it for a second time, because of Suzie.

When my brother Mick and I were younger we used to joke about the Wheel of Kharma and how a human body, a galaxy, a bad deed and a mosquito are inexorably linked due to the dynamic interplay of give and take and the fundamental interconnectedness of all things.

The system of the Wheels of Kharma I have in my mind is not unlike one of those old mechanical planetary models, but much more intricate, more involved, less rigid.

Millions of interlocking circles and ellipses all set about with arcane symbols … all turning.

Small cogs and wheels spinning furiously, big wheels rotating very slowly. And all related by some fantastic governing equation to one another – and ultimately to the largest wheel, the FLYWHEEL.

The A to Ω wheel, (The Wheel of the Start to End of Time)

Wheels which appear small and speedy in the human scale of reference are called "Human Instant Kharma Wheels". They might see the smashing of a mosquito being punished by a stubborn bloodstain on a newly painted wall. But one must remember that there are worlds within worlds and that splat represents a huge wheel in the life of the mosquito, as did the last suck of the mosquito represent a quantity of huge wheels in the lives of many red and white blood cells, and so on *ad infinitum,* in a ripple effect which might be extrapolated right through the greater time/space continuum. And thus the Kharmic Wheels of all systems are interlinked like a suit of multidimensional chainmail to form one giant machine some might call god.

Gareth, your Suzie is in our human world no more. It must be the greatest sadness to you. She was a splendid, spirited, intelligent, joyful human being. Much loved by all who knew her well enough.

Her sphere of influence was a happy sphere. She put in more than she took out. She added value. She made the world a better place.

I am sorry my friend.

Carl

Chapter 22

Escaping Kroonies

Hitchhiking back from a visit to my dad in Durban, I was picked up one Sunday evening by the young camp chaplain. He had studied theology at Stellenbosch University and was utterly insane. As we turned off Marais Street, we passed the old WWII Churchill bridge-laying tank and the white-washed guard hut and boom – the border between the world of civilians and madness. Rifle-toting guards appeared – stamp, stamp, salute, salute – the boom was raised and up the driveway we went towards the parade ground.

When I left a few days earlier, the parade ground was lined on three sides by big, leafy trees. On my return, I could not believe my eyes. A yellow wheel-dozer was parked at one gravelly corner and every tree in this once verdant frame had been pushed out of the ground and smashed to bits. "What on earth is going on?" I asked myself.

It turned out that some of the senior NCOs had become worried that the trees would provide perfect cover for an enemy force, should we ever come under attack while on morning parade. One of them had therefore spent the weekend uprooting the trees. I knew that I had to redouble my efforts to get far away from this place.

Every army camp has an officer in charge of the health and psychological welfare of its men. The School of Engineers in Kroonstad had *Welsyn Offisier, Kaptein* Visagie.

"Nobody gets out of here," she told me firmly on my first visit to her office, "but you can try."

"Here are the *verklaring* forms. State your reasons clearly, all forms to be filled out in triplicate, no carbon paper may be used. Name, date and *magsnommer asseblief.*" Followed by a quick forced smile.

The next day I returned my completed *verklarings* to *Kaptein* Visagie. She snapped open a drawer in steel Pendaflex filing cabinet, dropped them in and told me to come back in a week.

The following week she reported that she had received no response to my request that I be posted back to the navy. She ordered me to go to the quartermaster and draw a brown uniform. Holding out three fresh pieces of paper, she said dismissively, "And while you're about it, you'd better fill out another set of forms."

The following week was a repeat of the previous. Every time I went to see her, *Kaptein* Visagie opened the filing cabinet and dropped in the latest set. I could see the old sets stacking up in triplicate.

As the weeks went by I made a few friends around the camp. A kind HQ *troepie* named Rhyno operated the only Xerox machine on the base and he would always make a few copies of my cartoons if I asked. Rhyno's boss was a staff sergeant with a Burt Reynolds moustache and big flappy ears like Dumbo. Dumbo, as it turned out, was a really kind and helpful man too.

It was perhaps my fifth or sixth try and I had very little hope as I knocked on *Kaptein* Visagie's door. Knock, knock, no answer, knock, knock, try the handle. Nobody inside! Grabbing the opportunity, I went over to the filing cabinet and pulled open the drawer labelled I–Q and there they were, all of my *verklarings*, swinging in their little cardboard hammock stapled together in threes. My desperate cries for help had never even been sent.

Utterly indignant, I grabbed them all, walked briskly to Rhyno's office and asked him for a copy of each. I then took the forms back to Visagie's still vacant office and returned them to the filing cabinet.

I was not sure yet why I wanted copies of my forms, sequentially dated, week after week, or how I would use them, but I was due for a four-day pass to Cape Town in a week's time and I thought an opportunity might arise.

Two days after the photo-copying episode, Rhyno told me that his "staff" wanted to see me. Rhyno had told Dumbo my story and Dumbo was appalled. He offered to fax my *verklarings* to *D-Genie* (The Directorate South African Army Engineer Formation), but not from the base as this could be tracked. He would do it from a public fax machine at the Kroonstad post office on Saturday morning. I thanked him for his kindness and as I was headed for Cape Town that weekend, Rhyno copied another set for me to take along.

That Friday I was permitted to leave camp at about 11am. I hitchhiked the 200km to the Bloemfontein airport in a couple of hours and flew home from there.

Twice a week in the early hours of the morning, a long train passed by the Kroonstad army camp. I would be instantly awake, thinking that I was hearing waves washing onto the shore. But now I was back, back in the Cape in winter, and this was the real sea!

Every lucky son has a wonderful kind mom.
A person who can be relied on.
A person who will help her little boy.
A mother could be asked to write a note saying something like, "Dear Mr Donald, please excuse my son from swimming at PT as he has a post-nasal drip. Yours sincerely …"

Donald would sneer and scoff and say, "Get out of my sight!" but he was powerless against a mother's note. There would be no swimming for mother's little Carly that day.

Then, as we get older, a time comes when a mother can no longer protect her son from the harsh realities of life. She still provides good advice and succour, yes, but eventually the pendulum swings and it is then the son who does good things for his dear old mom in return.

At the time of that 1988 four-day pass from Kroonstad, my mother was still very much a force behind the boy. One of her singing students was the secretary to a brigadier in Personnel Services based at the Castle of

Good Hope. She had arranged for me to see him on the Saturday morning. I explained everything and gave the brigadier a set of my *verklarings* (requesting my return to the navy) and told him about my faxing the same to D-Genie in Pretoria. He was furious that a national serviceman should have been yanked from the navy and sent all the way to the army in the Orange Free State. He was furious with *Kaptein* Visagie and told me to go back to "Kroonies" at the end of my period of leave and not to worry.

A couple of days later I flew to Johannesburg and hitched back to camp. I was immediately summonsed before Commandant Prins. He was puce and spluttering. Between the spittle and fury, he informed me that *he* had decided to send me back to the navy with immediate effect. I could "pack up and *klaar out!*"

The Adjutant told me there had been "*BIG KAK!!!*" … and I was gonzo.

27 December 2014   Letter #23

Dear Gareth

Early December 2014

I woke up this morning and went for a paddle. On the way home from Clifton, about a kilometre out to sea, not far from Bakoven Rock, I met up with a white butterfly flying happily along, headed south towards Llandudno. The butterfly would dip down and touch the sea from time to time. This was in exactly the same place I saw an identical butterfly doing the same thing a few days earlier. I don't know why, but I was immediately prompted, internally, to write down the Afrikaans haiku poem as follows:

Onkruid
Vasbyt
Naai-meid
Pielhanguit
Lekker-tyd

Isn't life strange? Steven Pinker discusses this subject in his book titled **The Stuff of Thought**. I am so often amazed at how thoughts are triggered by other thoughts or odd stimuli and how abstruse the knock-on can be from one to the next ... on and on.

Mid December 2014

At present in the RSA we are experiencing what some call "rolling blackouts".
The latest government euphemism is "load shedding".

I work on a laptop PC now. It has a big screen and keypad plugged in. When the power cuts out, I yank out the monitor and continue using battery power. If this country was occupied by Swiss people, I ask myself, would there still be these problems? I mean, is this a function of climate and geographical situation or simply a function of human ineptitude? A French guy I know worked for many years in Congo on oil drilling infrastructure. When I was in Gabon I noticed that all of the oil companies are run by Italians and French etc. It is the same the world over. Expats provide the service of making things work when the local people cannot do it themselves. It is like filling your own tooth. You simply admit that you cannot do it and you go to the dentist. I messed up by trying to be a "home lawyer" before my divorce. Boy, do I pay for that stupidity now. If only our leadership would simply admit their uselessness, put up their collective hand and ask for help. Expat governance! That could save South Africa.

Maybe I could invent a small in-line turbine that would be placed in the irrigation water supply. Turn on the sprinkler, water the garden and an LED bulb would burst into glowing luminescence.

26 December 2014

Today is called Boxing Day. There is a massive sea running and a strong SE wind. It is not a very nice day for those who traditionally visit the beach on Boxing Day.

Well, Christmas came and went. What a big calendar event it was when we were boys. Peeping into wrapped presents that lay tauntingly beneath a decorated but sacrificed baby pine tree (Pinus pinaster – alien – enemy of the fynbos – kill, kill, kill). The tree stood in water in a plastic bucket supported by bricks and rocks. The bucket was wrapped in green crinkle paper to hide its unæsthetic plasticness. The water was a small kindness. Like INRI the tree died anyway (but very slowly because the Pinus pinaster is a tough tree) and was discarded maybe two weeks later, brown branches among the trash with all the chocolates eaten off but some silver *eis-lametta* trimmings still dangling among the needles.

24 December 2014

A supper with Zaan and Bill and Tess and my mom Virginia and Ian and Zaan's son Nicholas – two Hungarian-style ducks and a glazed ham, Brussels sprouts and crisp potatoes and so on. Good company. Glorious victuals.

My pal, if I had the power or a genie in a bottle, you would have been there to share in it.

There are no small kids anymore, so we have a "no presents" rule these days, which takes a lot of the pain out of it. I spent the 24th gardening and working. On Xmas day Zaan and I went for a quiet lunch with her mom and aunt and Nicholas. Allegra was with her mom and the other side of the family. It rained gloriously all day, culminating in a torrential downpour. I gardened until noon and was back in the garden from 14h30 in and through that rainstorm while Zaan drove Nicholas back to his apartment in Stellenbosch. Working and planting and digging and pruning and composting in mud. Wearing only my shorts, a cap and a pair of old trainers. A glorious time of rivulets and earthworms and solitude.

Bephi Govuza aka Rocky our trusted gardener is, like me, also 50 years old and should not be trusted any more (to do work, that is). What did he do while I was away? In a few days I have fixed the irrigation system. I have plugged holes and replaced and cleaned many micro-jet spray heads. I have yanked out much crap and pruned the two olive trees that missed their pruning in the winter when I was away. I have trimmed the overgrowth and so on. I fed the hungry soil with litres of Sea-grow and kelp extract pellets and quenching water. Ten normal sized bags of compost went in and today $12 \times 60dm^3$ bags more.

There are three houses, all with gardens linked via gates. It is a heavenly place in the gardens, but one really needs time. There are thrushes and robins and mulberries in high summer. There are trees and swimming pools. It is not a place of many flowers but there are a few. It is a place of greenness in our seaside suburb where the harsh blue light and harsh white light assail my pale eyes more and more. Sadly, my workload these past years has forced me to neglect my focus on the garden.

This year of 2014 has been a year of many deaths in the immediate spiral around me. Your Suzie went with them. I often wonder about how my death will be. I fear not death and I fear not going back to the peace I had for all those millions of years before I was born, but I do not relish the possibility of a painful, lingering or brutal death. *Thanataphobia* I think the humans call it? A week or so ago, our friend Richard Pooler was taken by Azrael. He was only 66, but as you well know, "There is no man who lives and, seeing the angel of death, can deliver his soul from the palm of his hand." Psalm 89:48.

That is just the way it is.

A week or so ago … maybe three … I was speaking to my friend Craig Matthew about time. He lent me a thick book on the Third Reich and a magazine called the **Scientific American**. The magazine is a Special Collector's Edition (Autumn 2014) dedicated to "time" and is incredibly interesting, if a little complex in places. The book on the Third Reich I have dipped well into – what a time that was, too much horror for now. For the time being I am reading in other areas – Time being one of them. **Moby Dick** being the other.

1

Well, apparently things have been moving forward over the past while. Einstein's Special Theory of Relativity kicked things off nicely with the Twin Paradox, but now there is so much more. The possibility of travelling through time, not into the future or past, but through it! What a tantalising possibility. "Wormholes" have crawled over the event horizons of our imaginations into science.

My crude, pulsing "Big Bang" theory in which all matter and everything collapses along with time into a fraction of a unit of nothingness and then explodes again to form a new cosmos with new galaxies and stars and planets which expand outward (while careening ever onward through the continuum of space-time) until everything once again reaches a point of total gravitational stasis before slowly beginning the massive retracing of steps back, is now the old easy one. There are new hard ones too! That which I can grasp is fascinating stuff.

2

I cannot believe that in 50 years a copy of **Moby Dick** has never crossed my path. Allegra wrapped a paperback copy for me for Christmas. What a delightful and amazing book! I believe it will end up on my bookshelf with the Fermors and the Steinbecks. It was ahead of its time. By the way GR, did you read the Paddy Fermor and **The Forgotten Soldier** I sent?

<hr/>

Mothers and Sons:
Your mother raised 3 and so did mine.
Our homes were filled with other boys and girls as well.
Where did all the food come from?
Can you imagine all the grocery shopping that our mothers did?
Can you imagine the Checkers or PnP checkouts –
one item at a time, no scanners?
Can you imagine the Checkers or PnP carrier bags being lugged into the kitchen?
And the plates and dishes and thousands of meals.
Gareth, the mothers of our childhoods were saints.
And they had a capacity for devotion and love we do not comprehend.

My mother drove down to bring me some cake today.
She pruned a lavender bush while I dug holes and planted things.
She is wonderful, as was your Suzie.
The husbanding of plants is the pastime of hope.

Love Carl

Chapter 23

Virginia's House

My dad was very much part of the building of our Camps Bay home. But then, shortly after we moved in, he jetted off on one of his trips abroad. A few days later a letter arrived, sent from the airport. He wasn't coming back.

It didn't seem to bother me much at the time, but perhaps it did. Perhaps if my dad had been around there would have been less latitude for delinquent behaviour in my last year of high school.

My mom's house was a place of great generosity. Mick built surfboards in my dad's ex-garage and the likes of Alan, Henny, Peter, Mark, Uwe and Michael Mater were always in and out.

Mick making boards in 1988 and still at it in 2018

My mom had a huge casserole which would be filled with *sauerkraut* and German sausages and *kässler* chops. There would be *leberknödel* and potatoes. She called it a *bauernschmaus*. There were oxtail stews and roast chickens and pastry covered steak pies and much more.

I don't know how she did it. Boys and girls sat at the table and laughed and told stories. Girlfriends came and went. I think people felt really welcome there.

When brother Bill refused to serve in the military, he was ordered to leave the country or face arrest. He ended up in San Francisco, sleeping in a basement on a slowly deflating air mattress. It must have been a horrible shock after the vibe at home. But he says he has no regrets about leaving. Eight years he spent working at the California Academy of Sciences – an education.

With Bill gone and his room vacant, many a wandering surfer we met up the coast was invited to come and stay.

Those were the days of high apartheid. South Africa was heavily sanctioned and we were substantially isolated from the world at large. Sometimes, while on our surf trips up the coast, we would come across a backpacking surfer far from home. We would surf with them and if they were nice guys, we would invite them to pop in when they finally got to Cape Town.

Gil Riviere from Yankeeland stayed for a month or two. As did a moustachioed Aussie named Chris. They told us tales of the world. Gil of being locked up in a Nigerian cell with twenty cellmates and pebbles for toilet paper. Chris told us about working as a property assessor in the Australian outback and Ronnie about surfing Malibu boards at Newquay. We learned a lot about the world from those travelling boys and our imaginations expanded.

They slept in Bill's room and ate *bauernschmaus*.

My mother remembers those times with great fondness.

31 January 2015   Letter #24

Can he warm his blue hands by holding them up to the grand northern lights?
Would he not far rather lay himself down lengthwise
along the line of the equator?

———⟨⟩———

Hello Friend

It is 2015 … 1/12th has already gone.
Where to, I do not know.
Even this morning gone.
Zaany / Carly Up at 05h30.
Down to Glen – in the surf at 6 – crowded by 7 – out we get.
Riding bikes on Table Mountain at 07h30 – skidding to a halt at 08h30.
Then a few eggs for breakfast.

I wrote this in my journal a few weeks ago (I stole from Melville at the top).

In mid-December 2014 I met again with LS of Vida. Their proposed expansion drive is going ahead. They want to do 150 projects in 2015. A nationwide design/shopfitting company FVE has been appointed to do all the new Vida stores. I have some projects still carrying over from last year and have been promised the new stores (other than the Vida) such as Strela and Cold Press but this, I assume, will only be one or two. Unfortunately it is nothing I can bank on. I started with Vida in 2006 and it looks like that 8+ year (just over 180 projects) run of work will now draw to a close.

New work, new projects, new possibilities.

How can one be as jaded as I?

Feeling lazy – feel like a surf trip.

Jaded eyes, tired eyes.

Dark rings – I can't do those 05h00 to 23h00 shifts any more.

A New Year letter from the Cape – January 2015

It is the first day of 2015. I woke up early this morning, made coffee, went for a 6km run around Lion's Head, came home, collected Zaan and went for a paddle. In Camps Bay we found a school of the shy Heaviside's dolphin. The sea is cold and a light front has killed the hot air of yesterday. It is a gorgeous day.

Yesterday was the last day of last year. I dropped Allegra and her friend Kelly in Milnerton. They are off to Clanwilliam for New Year. It seems that 90% of the cars on the peninsula are concentrated around Kloof Nek, Signal Hill and Tafelberg Road. The city and surrounds are like a ghost town. The streets of Milnerton are empty, not a soul to be seen in any garden. On the way home, I buy two long Roman Candles from a poor man on Strand Street. While making the purchase two others rushed up to beg, bleary eyed with faces like toffee apples.

They say that no-one promised life would be fair, and it isn't. It is very unfair. For sperms, spores, dandelion seeds and humans. Opportunities vary so hugely. All these guys from some or other African country, far from their homes, shiny and sick and hungry (see Matthew 26:11).

To avoid the traffic jam on Kloof Nek I went up High Level Road. I had my crystal-clear new specs on, so I could see every detail of everything. I stopped at a traffic light and observed a young woman waiting to cross the road. Her eyes the colour of bush honey, her hair dark blonde. Slender arms and a slender, taut body in a loose blue sundress. Flat sandals. A strong face, dusky Slavic, like a Russian, strong, but oh so terribly sad. Sienna lips of pursed sadness. But why and what? Who knows what lies behind any closed door?

The streets of Fresnaye and The Avenues were empty and silent and hot. Silent and hot like the summers of our boyhoods when bitumen melted out of the streets at the edge where the asphalt meets the kerb.

On the way home I looked in wonder at the yachts moored in Clifton bay and the huge grey and black painted houses between Kloof and Nettleton Road. It was like a scene from a James Bond movie. The forever happy champagne and caviar set.

A man fell and died on Lion's Head in the morning. A rock that had not given way for millions of years suddenly did. The Sky-Med chopper flew off with his mortal remains. 2015 was not to be his.

As the day of the 31st progresses the city prepares for a party, but at 6pm the power goes off. PING! Cape Town is dark. It is called a rolling blackout. The ANC's version of African style electricity.

The lights start to come on again at 22h30 in fits and starts.

Zaan and I sat on my upper deck to watch the day make way for the evening. African swallows whizzing and screeching above our heads. A Steppe buzzard salutes us with an unusual turn. Crying hadeda ibis head for home. A moment of crepuscular radiance before the darkening. Was there a flash of green? I forget. Hesperus appears and soon it is night. The suburb stays unlit. We watch a movie on Zaan's laptop before lighting the Roman Candles, which are the kind you can hold in your hand and shoot off maybe 50 or 100 little coloured balls, each with a different sized bang, pop or fizzle. They are a cheap Chinese version of what we once knew (Ronson). These have a massive carbon footprint, and for that matter a massive sulphur and saltpetre footprint as well.

We are asleep long before midnight and wake a little to the sound of explosions. It is now 2015.

At 04h10 my drunken neighbour Kenny returns from some hideous night out and stands on his driveway alternately shouting obscenities at the world and wishing everyone a happy New Year. The 10 or 15 Angolan children renting the villa next door to Kenny's house are doing an all-nighter and are happy for the amusement he provides and wish him happy New Year over and over in return until their parents come out and tell them to calm down.

The other day I was thinking why some people, in their final years at school, seem as though they will undoubtedly succeed in life, and yet don't.

On reflection a school like Camps Bay High (or Reddam or SACS for that matter) is not dissimilar to a small-craft harbour. Some of the boats being prepared for a voyage may look shiny and splendid, but the real test is what happens once they put out to sea. The test for vessel and crew is the open ocean with all its rigours and unpredictability. Only then can one tell whether the boat has been well prepared or not.

Let us hope as our children make their last preparations, that it is a job well done.

Let us hope that they are never over-tested such as you have been, Mr R.

The other day I was also thinking that a large part of me is unhappy because of my enslavement to other people. I believe that I have the right to be happy and live a life in which I define the terms myself. It is my right to be free of my ex-wife and I must be. I cannot take it any longer.

Gareth – 2015 is the year for trying our best to get out and be free.

Carly

Chapter 24

Life at Kroonstad

At Kroonstad HQ there were two NSM chefs – boyfriends named Anthony and Kevin. They shared a room with three other guys, one of them known as *Van Wyk die Priester* who was very religious. They were never allowed to be on duty together and their shifts were long, so their lives were a little strained. They had to be careful in that place.

I would wake up at about 4am and walk across the crisp frosted grass to the showers. I would use up all the hot water in the tiny 50 litre geyser and then go back to bed. I would lie in my bed and listen to the others getting up around 05h30 to do the best they could with 50 litres of, by now, newly heated hot water shared between 30 men. Once everyone had gone off to shower, I would hop out of bed, pull on my clothes, head down to the mess and help the chef on duty get the breakfast ready by putting plates in racks and butter, bread and jam on the table, and milk and cereals out for the men etc. I would, of course, stuff my mouth with grated cheese as I worked, that was the *quid pro quo*. The duty chef always appreciated the help.

One Monday morning I arrived – crunch crunch crunch down the path – only to find Anthony sitting on the doorstep weeping. The door to the kitchen was open behind him, and he pointed inside. "Look, look, in the fridge," he sniffed. I pushed past and went inside.

The fridge was not a fridge in the ordinary sense. It was a sizeable room with white tiled walls and a white tiled floor. The windowless chamber had a heavy insulated wooden door with an old-fashioned chrome lever handle. There were timber shelves against the walls, all neatly packed with eggs and cheese and crates of milk and carrots and other perishables.

I peeped inside and saw perhaps twenty dead springbok stacked in a heap of stiff-legged rigor mortis. The floor was a jelly of dark, congealed blood, perhaps a centimetre thick. Truly the stuff of nightmares for our poor chef.

At their "summary trial", it transpired that a bunch of NCOs had been out hunting and drinking on a nearby farm. Having overshot their quota, and being too drunk and lazy to gut and field-dress their mass kill, they brought the carcasses back to base and dumped them in our cool-room.

The NCOs were let off. "Boys will be boys, hahaha!"

I don't think Anthony ever got over it.

A John Cleese moment outside our bungalow
With Adderley's ex-glove

One day there was great excitement.

A story was being passed around between the men.

Du Pisani and Crowley brought it to Pepler and Gramps and me as we sat outside our bungalow in the wintery Sunday afternoon sun talking *kak* and buggering around with Adderley's ex-glove.

Cpl Mans had been killed earlier that morning in a car crash near Ficksburg.
Everyone was overjoyed.
No more 3am barefoot inspections on the frosty spiky lawn … hahaha!

The senior NCOs had morning tea in their *boma*.
All the *gharrys* were left idling, parked in the road.
Old Landrovers … huge clouds of smoky steam condensing in the cold air.
Why not turn them off?
Because no-one gives a fuck … hahaha!

On Sunday and Wednesday evenings it was Church parade.
Church parade was compulsory.
I had the boys lock me in our room.
Padlocked from the outside.
MPs would come and bang on any locked doors.
"*Ons weet julle naaiers is daar binne,*" bang, bang, bang!
And they would try to peep through the windows but the curtains were drawn.
Hahaha!

We stood guard at night in corrugated steel huts 5' × 5' square. The huts were called *hokkies* and stood on wooden poles raised about twenty feet in the air. There were no windows or door. It was freezing and everything was iced over. A vertical steel-runged ladder was the only way up. We had to stand with our rifles and watch for terrorists. There were acid-yellow lights.

Sometimes a duty sergeant would creep around in the hope of catching a sleeping *troepie*. It was a game of sorts. One night a stealthy sergeant wearing gloves almost caught one of us, but the sleeping man, curled up on the floor of his *hokkie*, woke at the last moment and kicked out in fright. The sergeant flew earthwards. His neck snapped on the cold ground below. A classic knee-jerk reaction.

At the inquest the *troepie* said he thought it was a terrorist creeping up on him.
He said the sergeant should have called up to him, and not crept like that.
The men at HQ laughed.
Hahaha!

Shortly before I left Kroonstad, Lt Whitfield asked me to please stop forging his signature in everybody's passbooks.
Hahaha!

"We fought battles *eksê*, and we died *eksê*."

28 February 2015   Letter #25

Hello old pal

16.6667% of 2015 is already in the past … to me like the crack of a whip.

There was a female Diedericks Cuckoo in the garden today. We have never had one here before.

Yesterday the ocean was full of whales, from Mouille Point to Llandudno we could see them. Off Clifton they looked like new rocks. In the evening, off Bakoven, their spouts and breaching punctuated the white-capped choppy water until the sun had gone to bed and the planets came out.

All night I dreamed of the sea and I played with the reflection of the sunrise in a web of fractured mountains called the Twelve Apostles.

This morning early, the wind was gone and so were the whales. Mitch Brown says they are humpbacks. The news says southern right. If they are southern right whales, then they are early because they should still be down south in February. Maybe they are southern wright wales witch is rong.

This morning Zaan and I stood on a submerged rock and watched a small cormorant hunting, lightning flashes in the shallow water over white sand and little coloured shell fragments. The bird was busy with its breakfast as it darted around our feet. Quick with a fast neck. Ice cold little fishes gulped into the warm stomach of such a clever hunter.

Once while travelling in Umbria with little Allegra in a backpack, we strolled across a piazza. I think the town was called Gubbio, but perhaps it was Perugia or Assisi, or another of those magical places. Allegra was at the age of dummy sucking and had a small twist of soft blanket that was vital to her psychological wellbeing. We stood before a building with ancient weathered stone lions flanking a flight of steps. Allegra's little arm shot out and pointed at the lion on the right. "*Ashgethgoth*," she proclaimed. Then she pointed to the lion on the left and said, "*Ashkêmal*". It was as if she knew them by name from some previous incarnation. My hackles hackled … it was such a creepy moment.

When I was a teenager we moved to Camps Bay. Giant rain-spiders would often come into the house. My mom called them Goofy spiders. You could hear them galloping along on the wall-to-wall carpet. It was my job to trap them with an upturned container, then slide a piece of cardboard under and release them outside. That was creepy, too. We don't seem to get rain-spiders any more.

During those same years huge basking sharks would come close inshore. Every year the boys who lived down at Bakoven would report their return. I remember the time Alan Best, Uwe, Mick and I were out on surf-skis when we saw what might have been the last one to visit. It was swimming slowly just off the Barley Bay take-off spot, its mouth wide open. We sat there with it for maybe 20 minutes, looking into that massive gaping maw. Finally, Uwe decided to jump in and swim with it. In a flash, it was gone. I think they might have all been killed by humans, to make soup.

15 Feb 2015

Today is Sunday the Ides of FEB … one month before the Ides of March. Work has now come in like a freight train. I use the weekends to play catch-up, not too many disturbances. Not enough rest.

Early Feb 2015

Islamic State militants announced that they had beheaded a second Japanese hostage, journalist Kenji Goto, prompting Prime Minister Shinzo Abe to vow to step up humanitarian aid to the group's opponents in the Middle East and help bring his killers to justice. "I feel intense indignation at this utterly cruel and despicable act …" a grim-faced Abe told an emergency cabinet meeting early on Sunday. It is interesting to note that only 70 years ago the Japanese more or less stopped the centuries-old practice of wholesale beheading of prisoners and POWs.

In 2008 three members of a bomb disposal team were killed in the central German city of Göttingen while they were preparing to defuse a World War

II bomb found on a construction site. This was quite an event in modern times as barely a week goes by in Germany without unexploded bombs from World War II being discovered on building sites. Bomb disposal operations are so routine in Germany that no one expected any problems with this one. But hey, one must expect the unexpected and this one made international news. I even heard about it in Cape Town and remember it today.

It is again interesting to note that just 70 years ago the Americans and the RAF stopped routinely bombing German cities. During that war hundreds of thousands of people died as a result of similar bombs dropped from aircraft. It was so common it was almost *de rigueur*.

As Malaysia ends its search for the missing flight MH370 and officially declares the disappearance an accident, many of the families of the missing passengers will not accept this verdict.

Until fairly recently it was not abnormal for commercial ships to go missing and never be heard of again. In WWII it was common. Crew and cargo lost without a trace. It was an accepted fact of life.

In late 2014, 276 female students were abducted by the Islamic militant group Boko Haram in Nigeria. More have been taken since then. I recently read two books about Stanley and Livingstone and their African experiences in the second half of the 1800s. The slavers conducted similar raiding operations and worse. Is Boko Haram or ISIS any more rude than the Catholic Inquisition? I think not.

Where am I going with this? Nowhere, I suppose. Just noting how the human mindset changes.

The human "mindset" ... now that is an interesting thing:

I look at this crazy species of ours. I think that I am one of very few who likes peace and solitude and un-complication. I like to paddle on the sea and run in secluded wilderness places. I like surfing only when very few of my species are in the water. I notice that other people seem to like crowds and stadiums full of their fellow man and vuvuzelas and traffic jams. Most seem to like spawning more than one child per adult (like insects) and keeping smelly dogs. To me it is truly horrible. I guess I am kind of misanthropic.

In Melville's magnificent novel **Moby Dick**, I read at the beginning of Chapter 107: "Seat thyself sultanically among the moons of Saturn, and take high abstracted man alone; and he seems a wonder, a grandeur, and a woe. But from the same point, take mankind in mass, and for the most part, they seem a mob of unnecessary duplicates, both contemporary and hereditary."

I have been wondering why the Arab world is so inflamed with fighting and has been for my entire life and for centuries before. The Balkans too. And I can only conclude that that is what they enjoy. Similar to those who like to go to crowded soccer games, these people have in their "collective subconscious" a love of running around like crazy fools waving AKs and RPGs with LMG ammo belts around their necks. Bombs and rubble. Dust and bullet pock-mocked walls of dusty clay brick. Disorder and chaos. That is what they love.

Meet me at the opposite end of the pavilion, far from the crazy hubbub.

I love autobiographically written historical books and gentle European movies without plots and dolphins. And groups of 2 and 4. Hey man … no wonder I don't fit in!

Now back to the future:

Once when we were boys on holiday at my grandmother's house in Stellenbosch she promised us a Saturday treat – a trip in her Austin Princess to Tygerberg Zoo to see the Chimpanzees' Tea Party.

It proved to be a great disappointment. The ordered, civilised, tea-sipping, wonderlandish party of my imagination turned out to be a muddy slurping-out-of-plastic-tea-pot-spouts and chopped fruit being tipped out of bowls the moment they were served by gum-booted "waiters".

The ANC government has disappointed me in exactly the same way. Only this time it is for real.

Adios Amigo … Carlos

PS. In South Africa the K-word is not acceptable, but there is a new K-word now. Kleptocracy.

Chapter 25

On Rage

I was filled with rage every day for about ten years. There was nothing I could do about it. While anger was the default setting of my psyche, rage often swept in. It took immense self-discipline and a supreme dread of going to prison to keep my behaviour in check. But even so, the rage seeped out and others were affected.

Towards the end of 2007, I was a broken person. For various reasons my wife had taken to the husbands of her close friends in preference over me. I lost almost all my friends in a destructive inquisition to find out who was involved. Eventually I exposed two of them. The affairs had been going on right under my nose. Marriages crashed and burned.

It was difficult to focus on work. Sometimes I would drive out to Dag and Marie's empty holiday home. On one of the beds lay a pile of three or four foam mattresses and I'd creep in-between them, like a sandwich, and cry for hours. Much later I would return home and start with simple tasks, hauling myself back up to the coalface.

I was angry at myself for allowing such a situation to develop and I was angry at my ex-wife and my two former close friends. It is a long and painful tale that spans the great divide between love and hate, and even further still.

I had met my ex-wife in the mid 1980s. It was one of those off-on youth relationships that spanned years. She spent 1988 in Italy and we got together again on her return. I gave her all the trust I had and the love as best I knew how. Trust was no problem for me, but I think that my love toolbox was poorly equipped. There is perhaps nothing more precious in life than the feeling that you are loved. I would say that my trust was raped.

Happy holidays – the lover and my (then) wife … photo credit: the blind cuckold

For years I had planned an early semi-retirement, or rather a life on my own terms.

I had three houses in Camps Bay (all next door to one another) and only a small loan to work off.

If things had gone according to plan, all would have been settled fairly quickly. We would have lived in one house and rented out the other two and lived comfortably off that.

By 2008 I was so hurt and broken that I drafted and signed the most stupid divorce possible. It was all about trying to please people and do everything for our daughter, Allegra.

For ten years thereafter, I worked three weeks out of every month just to cover my ex-wife's housing, alimony and child support. In two of those years I never took a full day off.

People used to say, "forgive her" or "just let it go". But you can't let a thing go while you are being bled through the neck.

In 2015 I sold the first property to get rid of all debt and give myself some breathing space. We then allowed the lawyers to fight it out. The hired guns.

In 2017 I sold the second property and finally paid my ex-wife a 10-million settlement. This year I am finally free. After the paying of the settlement, the rage died.

One year I became so toxic that my dear friend Dag refused to see me. When I asked him why, he came around to my home, read me the charge sheet and left. Not long after, I went to see a psychologist named Stein.

During our first session, Dr Stein's neighbour's dog began to bark. He jumped up and ran to the window of his apartment, pretended to be holding a rifle and fired off two imaginary rounds. "Bang, bang," he said, "how I would love to shoot that dog, but I am afraid of the Pollsmoor lifestyle! Just look at the mess in that yard – the guy lives like a hillbilly."

Our therapy sessions were doomed from the outset. "Pollsmoor lifestyle" indeed, I thought to myself. Those are my lines, lines of the unwell, not lines of the healer. Let me rather self-medicate.

The "Pollsmoor lifestyle"

I am grateful that during those dark years I did not physically harm anyone, or harm myself. I restrained the Norseman in me and swallowed as much of the rage as I could. There were some who presented shoulders to lean on and for that I thank them. I hope that I have finally cleansed my system of the toxic residues left by years of adrenalin-fuelled fury. But one never can tell, the extent of the damage done.

After all those merciless years, I do not feel resentful or angry any more and at times there is even a little remorse, but I do know exactly where that hot coal of hatred lurks, better to be left alone.

Notes in a Diary – 2 May 2004

I am sitting in the shed,
Looking out at the "Rock"
The sea is blue jade and silver white.
I know that salt spray so well.
I know and love its taste and cold touch.
I just sit and watch,
And am filled with an emotion
That I cannot name.
My wife is unhappy with our marriage and the way I am.
And would like to leave me,
But what about Allegra?
This is the situation I have dreaded all my life.
No escape door.
I would like to give her the freedom she desires.
For her own sake.
But what about my best beloved child?

22 March 2015   Letter #26

Hello old pal.

Am I too afraid to ask? ... No good news from Kim ... How are you?

7 March 2015

Today I ran out of my front door, up the Glen to Kloof Nek, around Lion's Head and home again. There is a big sea running. The season is changing. The run is like a meditation. As I ran I remembered the following interlude:

For a time in 1993 I was on a farm in Namibia, near the small town of Maltahöhe. A stress too great for me put me in my *bakkie* and sent me there for solitude. To draw and walk and detoxify, for humanity was taking its toll and I was not ready then (as I am not now) for this life among people.

The local pastor was a German from Bremen, one of those missionary types. Not my kind of guy. His tenure was about to end and before he returned to his home, it was his wish to kill a springbok. Now as we all know, springboks breed fast, and on farms they need to be culled on an annual basis or they would all ultimately starve due to overgrazing. But such culling is farm work and not work for pastors. The farmer, my host, Rolf Kirsten, could not refuse the pastor because of his position in the community even though he wanted to, and so the appointed day came and we went out in a Land Cruiser with a .243 rifle.

After a bumpy drive out to one of the game camps, we stopped and the pastor was helped up into the back with me. Sometimes springbok run and sometimes they simply stand. That day they just stood and stared. The pastor shot poorly and instead of putting his round through the heart just behind the foreleg, he shot the poor creature through the lungs.

Now that is why I remembered the story. Today while out running, it was hot and maybe my breathing was not at its easiest, and I arched my body as I ran just like the pastor's springbok and the two images overlapped – my view of myself at that instant and my memory of that stricken beast.

We helped the pastor down onto the hard, stony ground and made him follow the dark foaming blood-spoor he had caused. Lung blood, getting less and less as we went until it was no more. The pastor was horrified at what he had done. "*O Gott, O Gott, O Gott,*" he moaned over and over.

The Schwartzrand is an unyielding place and there were no tracks.

We never found the place where that springbok finally fell.

What triggers memory? It is such an interesting thing. An amazing thing.

My friend Dag treated me in a strange way this last visit. It was subtle, but I could sense it. We have been friends for many years. At last, on the eve of his departure for Norway, he came to see me. It was laid before my feet that I have become "toxic" to myself and others, and that he felt that a good psychologist was what I needed. Well, that may be very true, but not necessarily for the reasons put to me.

The whole carton of rotten eggs, as presented to me by Dag, was absurd and shan't be mentioned here. Absurd views from a man whose assessments are usually deadly accurate. There were many charges laid before me. I rejected them all, except that of becoming "toxic". Dag's complaint of my "toxicity" was completely fair … the dark and toxic seepage of suppressed anger at my ex-wife and my open-ended alimony trap.

I called my GP Dr Hans and he referred me to a Jungian-type psychologist called Dr Stein who turned out to be an interesting case himself. A guy who makes me look like a buttoned-up suit by comparison. I sense him to be much like me in many ways, just less collared.

So now I have got to go and throw R580 an hour at "the wind" once a week. Have I unwittingly become the "fool" in Proverbs 11:29? What the heck, let's see what comes out of it.

Gareth, don't get me wrong, I do not object to paying for the hour (people pay for mine), but there must be a sense of value found, and Dr Stein must be exchanged for someone different. Something more structured and forthright would be better for me.

What am I? Why a life of angst? Why so much nagging, nauseating anxiety throughout my waking years? First days of term, school sports days, work Mondays, the days prior to a wedding or Christmas, the days leading up to a holiday or just waiting for something to go wrong on a sail crossing. All of that and more. Why so much fighting against the system? What's the point? Is it possible for a chameleon like me – a man of so many shirts – a sensitive human being with it all packed in so tight – to start turning it all over? So much unpacking and repacking of baggage that can never be discarded at any station. Baggage that must be carried, but in the best way possible. What is that optimus?

I have been to see Dr Stein three times so far. Because I am paying, it is my hour. The conversation is therefore naturally skewed or unbalanced. He is the kind of man that one would rather have a balanced conversation with, on equal terms, so to speak, or perhaps not at all. If I met him on equal terms, yes undoubtedly, the ensuing chat would be an interesting one, but a friendship would not be pursued.

How does one step off the rails of their expectation and become toxic to one's friends? How long do we tolerate toxicity before we cut that person off? I bumped into my old friend Uwe the other day. I told him my story and he said he couldn't have put it better himself. Toxic. "Withdrawing and folding in on yourself," he said. What does that mean? I shall have to go back and ask him. I remember how Uwe, my best pal and surfing buddy, eased himself out of our social group. For him it had become too toxic. I think he knew what was going on.

I think back on my own experience and reflect on people who became toxic to me in my life. When we sailed to Italy, the skipper became so toxic that I would have happily shot him by the time we got to the Canary Islands. But after we tied up in port, we talked it out and hugged and it all just vanished in a puff.

I think that we all have, at some time or another, been toxic to others. Like Lady Justice with a pair of scales in the left hand and a sword raised high in the right – when the scales finally tip, the sword then makes the necessary chop. It was like that with an old school friend. I remember it so well. A straw to break the camel's back, then … chop! chop! … he had to go. And my ex-wife's ex-lovers, my ex-wife, my ex-parents-in-law … chop! chop! … and I am very sure that they were overjoyed to chop! chop! me too.

I must say, it was quite an insight that day, having Dag's charge put before me! And on reflection, it is amazing how different one's own view of oneself is when compared to the way one may be seen by others. And on further reflection, it is amazing that we humans, and me as a 1/7billionth part of an incredible but vermin species on a wondrous planet at this instant in this vast expanse of time and space should be so self-involved as to spend hours contemplating these little things.

In life we try things and do things, and usually we try to do things that have meritorious potential. But sometimes, like the pastor and his springbok, we cannot foresee the results of our actions. And like the Schwartzrand, life too, is an unyielding place. Memories warp and disappear with each passing year (paper may keep them for a while) but as a rule, history is rearranged and rewritten or simply lost. And like the dead springbok, we can never tell where the results of our actions might actually have their effect, and whether or not the effect of our actions will bear good or toxic fruit.

Love C

Chapter 26

Lost and Found

Gareth was arrested in 2008 and I have asked myself, from time to time, why it took so long for me to notice that he was gone. Before I started making calls and finding out.

Well, he had removed himself from Cape Town society by working long shifts over in the Middle East. On returning for short periods of leave (a month at a time) he focussed on his immediate family and friends, his mom and son and wife.

I was freshly divorced and, after years of wandering around in an emotional desert, was trying to start a loving relationship with Zaan. It was not an easy time for me at all. Not easy for any of us. My biggest stress, by far, was being separated from my daughter. Being involved with the Neighbourhood Watch and SAPS, I knew what was going down in our suburb at night. It was almost unbearable for me to go to bed at night knowing that I couldn't be right there if she needed me. The choices of my ex-wife had ultimately denied a committed father the right to protect his vulnerable child. We are not talking Canada or Norway here. This was the real deal. Camps Bay homes were being invaded. Luis Momadi – screwdriver in eyeball stuff.

At night, when sleep finally overcame me, I would have nightmares and soak the bed with feverish sweating while holding my breath for long periods then gasping loudly for air. Zaan would shake me awake and say, "Are you okay?" And I would mumble and shift around, trying to find a dry patch to curl up on.

After being in a partnership for 20 years, my emotional-skills toolbox was sorely lacking in what was required for the job. A left-handed screwdriver, some scraps of old sandpaper, a blunt dasco chisel and a ring punch.

In the summer of 2008, Allegra and I went to Norway – father and daughter – to visit Dag and Marie and the family in the Arctic.

5 July 2008

Allegra and I are in Norway
Cape Town → Amsterdam → Oslo → Tromsø → Toppelbukt
1200km by road inside the Arctic circle.
Outside, the fjord is flat and steely,
Gulls and oyster catchers,
Fine rain and rainbows,
Bright green and golden leaves,
Birch and Arctic pine,
Smells of Europe that stop me in my tracks,
Hauntingly reminiscent of something close but intangible
to the human puzzle piece that I am.

Here the sun shines at midnight.
And gently melts the mountain ice.

Time and time I tell myself, I'll stay clean tonight,
But the little green wheels are following me, Oh no, not again,
I'm stuck with a valuable friend, I'm happy, hope you're happy too,
One flash of light but no smoking pistol.

I've never done bad things, I've never done good things,
I've never done anything out of the blue.
I want an axe to break the ice, I want to come down right now,
Ashes to Ashes … etc…

"I want an axe to break the ice." Indeed.

The seventies were done and the eighties opening up.
The enigmatic lyrics of Bowie and Pink Floyd and Genesis
Were cast into the crucible of my teenage mind …
(For better or for worse).

A strange and complex youth was laying down
strange and complex foundations in a strange and complex world.
A human puzzle piece in the wrong puzzle box.

And so into adult life I made my way instead of opting out.
And have done so for another 28 years …
Many opportunities have been thrown away, many not.
Few gambles and much hedging of those few bets taken.
A young man worm-bored by anxiety and fear,
With no faith in the world.

And now, finding it somehow difficult to accept that he is no longer a boy,
The man finds himself taking his first tentative steps into middle age.

Now at Toppelbukt,
I have been given the opportunity
to watch my ten-year-old Allegra, and Dag and Marie's 3 daughters
Aged 18, 20 and 22 …
Four beautiful young women in various stages of taking those
first major steps that set the course of human lives.

And when I say beautiful, there is no Lolita-ish voyeurism here.

Allegra with two of the three Gjerstad daughters

On the one hand I am talking about physical youthful beauty,
Appreciated in the way that one would appreciate

The muscles under the foreleg-skin of a young ridgeback dog.
On the other, and more specifically, the beauty of joyful, smiling,
Ebullient positive energy that would thaw the soul of even the most cynical man.

I notice how confident and unspoilt they all are
And it fills me with joy and hope.
I think my ex-wife was like that,
But sadly, I don't think I could see it then.
No frame of reference.

And that was it:
Now I was focussing on my own life and immediate circumstances.
In survival mode.

Trying to unsink my own ship.
More aeroplanes end up under the sea, than submarines in the sky.

2 May 2015   Letter #27

The Dreamzone

Hello Gareth

Who knows what a person dreams at night, for only a fraction is remembered the following morning.

Last night I had some of the "entertainment style" surrealism that I am used to – "*la fantasia*".

A nun holding a bible high in her left hand. The bible conceals a camera and she is filming a group of young film stars like Brad Pitt and the (old) A Team as teenagers, laughing and joking around a restaurant table. Two CIA agents (one of them a young version of my friend Sedick Hartley with exaggerated cheekbones) watch their antics intently on a PC monitor via a feed from the nun's camera. I know where it all comes from. Zaan and I dropped Allegra and some young friends at a restaurant in Hout Bay. We joked about sitting at a back table and spying on them.

But what about this unusual snippet? Not so light-hearted in the waking moment.

My mother and I are seated at a dark wooden table on a Karoo guest-farm type verandah. I do not look at or see my mother, but I know it is her with me. It is either dawn or dusk. A large, peeled, hardboiled ostrich egg is placed before us. It is translucent, shimmering opal. A black and white male ostrich makes an appearance for a moment in the garden. It looks at us. There is a low rough stone wall between the verandah and the garden.

The egg is suddenly cut in two, in the same way one cuts an avocado in two. The two halves are almost but not quite equal in size. The two yolks look like illustrations of the sun. There is an almost swirling granularity in their orange faces. An arm with a hand holding a large spoon appears over my right shoulder. The yolks are swiftly scooped out and flicked away, into the garden. That is the moment of waking with this most vivid image intact.

Zaan says that dreams are like conversations – some are serious, and some are just "chitty-chat".

25 March 2015

We have an Irish neighbour who likes to drink too much. His name is Kenny. Kenny has just sold his house and will move out at the end of the month.

My old friend Braam Malherbe phoned me a while back as he was taking stock of his friends. We met at the boatshed and had a really good chat. We talked of many things. In 2017 he intends to circumnavigate the globe on the tropic of Capricorn with another old friend of ours Peter van Kets. It will be a fossil fuel-free trip. A row across the Atlantic, walk across South America, sail across the Pacific, walk Madagascar, sail to Africa, walk across the sub-conti-nent and end at Sandwich harbour.

My dad is 81. He lies in an old age home in Stellenbosch, both his legs cut off above the knee. In June 2011, a few days after he had had his second leg amputated due to gangrene, he told me that his wife Gisela had made him change his will. He told me that he was unhappy about this and wanted his old will back. I reprinted his old will and he signed it.

Jonathan and Linda Paarman's son Dane committed suicide a month or so ago. He was about 35 years old. He hanged himself in the garage. I knew him from the age of 3 or 4. Jonathan and Linda live in St Francis. The funeral service was held in Camps Bay.

On Monday I flew to Johannesburg to measure up some restaurants for Simply Asia. The shop at Clearwater was really grubby and oily and sticky. There was a crude steel cage fixed to the wall in the back room. It was full of vegetables and onion skins and crappy stuff.

A few nights ago, I dreamed that "drinky" Kenny (who lives across the road opposite) suddenly popped up at my back wall in Sonia Rees' garden, head and shoulders and a ladder. He hopped over the wall, shouting in his usual sozzled style, waded through my pool and came up to the back terrace. I gave him two glasses of drink. One full of red wine and one full of beer.

I chose cheap glasses as I knew that I would never see them again. He left immediately, shinned up my rocky back wall with both glasses in hand, damaging his suit on the way up. He then stood on the wall and took a flying jump into Sonia's pool. There was a loud splash, then silence. That was a "chitty-chat" dream.

Last night I dreamed that my brother Mick and Jonathan Paarman were planning to ride their bicycles around the world. I drove to Cape St Francis to say farewell. No-one was around at the Paarman home so I looked at some old photographs that caught my eye, lying on the coffee table. The floor of the room was beach sand. Linda then came in and told me that Mick and Jonathan were actually leaving from Cape Town so I drove back. Braam Malherbe was in the Volks Hospital so I went to visit him. I was wearing SADF browns and carrying a beer as I entered the lift. The Volks Hospital was as I remember it in the 1970s. When the door of the lift opened Mick was already inside. He was wearing his white Navy step-outs and looked very smart and young. When we got into Braam's room, Braam was lying in a filthy steel cage, the same one I had seen in the restaurant I had just measured up at Clearwater. His mattress was brown and stained, as were his blankets. That was also a "chitty-chat" dream. One just knows it as soon as you wake up.

The ostrich egg dream was a serious dream and so was this next one. Last night I awoke with someone telling me that I must be very careful to keep my father's new will safe. I could not see who the person was, or even whether it was a man or a woman.

On Wednesday morning Zaan and I went for an early paddle at Bakoven. There have been many dolphins around of late. The sea has been very flat. Zaan saw what she thought was a baby seal on one of the rocks. It turned out to be an otter! Now isn't that something special!

One of the JHB absentee-homeowners down at Bakoven, John "Chick" Legh, is currently having a new sliding gate built to enclose his carport. On the 22nd of March it was the birthday of my old school friend Robert Kinsky. On Wednesday I did not shave so I had an uncomfortable scruffy face all day. Last weekend I gave Jan and Haike advice on their trip to Namibia. We talked of all the places I had been to in Namibia over many years. Swakop, Maltahöhe, Sossusvlei, Sesriem, Etosha, Sesfontein, Ruacana, Duwisib, Homeb, Damaraland, Owamboland, Hobatere, Khowarib Schlucht, Warmkwelle, Ngongo Waterfall, the Naukluft, Brandberg, the Skeleton

Coast and so on. I suggested that they spend their last night at the Waterberg. I remembered the lovely swimming pool there. You, my friend, are in prison in Kuwait, and so often on my mind.

On Thursday I awoke from the following dream. Chick Legh had just built a truly huge and magnificent pagoda/castle/house up on the slopes of the Twelve Apostles above Camps Bay. My brother Mick, Robby Kinsky and I stood outside as dirty teenage boys. I did not see Robby but I knew it was he who was present. Chick appeared and greeted us in a somewhat unpleasant way, but then he became friendly and invited us in. It was a truly magnificent and surreal building that kept morphing as I looked at it. An old stone prison (very similar to Schloss Duwisib) had been erected in the courtyard. Chick Legh kept asking Mick if it was architecturally incorrect to have it there and if he should move it. There was a big swimming pool directly in front of the stone prison. The swimming pool had exactly the same edge/surround to the one at the Waterberg. It was the pool from Coetzenburg. We swam and the water was lovely. Chick Legh gave me a new razor and I took a shower and shaved my face in the shower. Large clumps of blond beard clogged the blades and they had to be constantly sucked clean. The window frames of the house were made from ancient Japanese pine with black wrought-iron ironmongery.

Zaan told me about "Googling" things in dreams. I have subsequently "Googled" hard boiled ostrich eggs, a male ostrich, uniforms, swimming pools, a prison, a man in a cage and so forth.

Yesterday I worked for 12 hours straight, 5am to 5pm. I was exhausted by the intensity of my effort. I slept hard and deep. All I can remember from the dreamzone was that I was carrying a very large dead fish. I had both arms around it. I was in a rudimentary, sepia-tone, municipal building. I was searching for scales I knew they had there. The type of scales that you see weighing luggage in old movies. I needed to weigh the fish.

Today Zaan and I went for an early walk up Table Mountain. Exactly 1hr + 30min. brisk walk from Theresa Ave to the upper cable station via Kasteelspoort. As we walked up Kasteelspoort, in the first few hundred metres up from the Pipe Track, we found three massive "new" sandstone boulders. One of them is cleaved in two – therefore there are actually four. The largest is a huge cubic sandstone monolith of about 3x3x3m at least. They are still coated in dust. Dead and broken plants lie in their wake. Smaller rocks stricken, splintered and smashed. What a glorious event it must have been to see their fall. High school geography in action – weathering and erosion. When I look at the big sleeping lichen-clad boulders on the lower slopes of Table Mountain, Lion's Head or at Betty's Bay, I always wonder when they broke loose and fell and bounced and rolled and finally came to a grinding halt. Well, here are brand new ones. Did anyone else notice them?

It was a busy day, cleaning the apartment and so on. I feel a bit flu-ish. We were in bed by 8pm. I got caught in a dream from 8 to 12. Four hours in a racing, noisy, cybernetic machine. Something like a cross between the underground railway tunnels at Victoria Station on a busy day and the workings of a large clock. The moving parts were more biological than mechanical. Every now and then I would wake up to try to kill the mosquito that was biting us. At midnight I got up and took a sleeping tablet and killed the mosquito in the morning. A fat, blood filled grape hanging from the ceiling – swiftly executed. Why feast like that all night only to be murdered at first light?

On Sunday Zaan showed me an article about Putin as a young man in Dresden. Zaan also suggested that she get a "tablet" to make reading internet articles easier than on her iPhone. She told me that Russell had been dating a Lebanese woman with an Indian ex-husband.

I park my *bakkie* outside Julia the Sangoma's house. The green top of a big acacia thorn tree shows over the white wall. It is Woodstock – it is Golders Green. A southeaster is blowing. The air is scented with the smell of a hot fire and wild herbal things burning. Kameeldoring, I know it so well. Julia greets me kindly and shows me three sandstone rocks getting red hot amongst the flaming logs. She shows me into a rectangular room with a blue painted floor. In it there is an orange plastic bath full of steaming water, a round enamel bowl full of herbs, a wooden chair and a coarse blanket. Julia pours water onto the herbs in the bowl. "This is your room," she says. And in that room, I steam.

I leave Julia's house in the dark and for the first time in a long time I take a different route up through Gardens. For a change I go up Camp Street. Lo and behold – on the edge of the sidewalk are three large sandstone rocks – a fourth lies set back to one side.

During the night I dreamed that I had married into a Lebanese/Indian family. I never saw my bride. The home was full of Levantine types and women in saris. The walls were cracked and the paint peeling. Semflex had been incorrectly applied in an attempt to waterproof the shower. I knew that there was a lot of work needed here and it all seemed dreadful. My old school pal Simon

Wood was there, trying to convince me that a Mercedes Benz side mirror was actually a "tablet" device. At some point a person walked in carrying a framed photograph of Putin and announced, "Vladimir Putin is dead!" In the end Zaan appeared and saved me from the compressed insanity of the house and we made a break for it. We ended up in a park in Oranjezicht. We chose to sit down next to a little stream. The water was clear and it babbled. (The stream was the stream we had seen in Helen Zille's garden a few weeks before.) We had a bottle of whisky with us, but we did not drink any. A dog belonging to some picnickers barked. I caught it and held it by one canine tooth and it stopped barking. All was peaceful thereafter.

I have committed to go and visit my dad in the old-age home in Stellenbosch on Saturday. He is now a denizen of my dreamzone.

On Wednesday night I had many tangled dreams … my dad stopped his Mercedes at the bottom of Burnside Road and waited with Mick while I got out. I noticed that I had a bottle of whisky and half a bottle of Moby Dick rum in the righthand side pocket of my fatigue pants. I went to fetch a bottle of Coke owed to me by the proprietor of a bottle store in Brunswick Road. The neck of the bottle was cracked and leaky. I was offered a wooden carved shower rose in the shape of a horse head instead. I was told that it would only be ready in a week or two. I walked back past the park. A large yellow Bedouin style tent had been erected. The tent had been covered in scrawled ANC graffiti, but the scrawlings had all been covered with white stickers. As I turned the corner, Burnside Road had suddenly become a fantastic scene. Wooden bridges were being built over a sizeable irrigation furrow. There were water buffaloes and "coolies". I was in India. It was around 1900.

On Thursday night I dream about hiring a blue jacket for a function. I put it on and show it to my dad. The jacket is a little tight around the shoulders and my dad asked, "Do you think you could salute in that?" I gave a navy salute and then did a Nazi style John Cleese salute. He shook his head and said, "You shouldn't do that." I then saluted an army salute.

On Friday night I dreamt that I went to my father's cremation. I was happy about that. The dream was drawn in pencil. A very simple cross section through a building with an oven at the bottom and an S-shaped chimney to cool the smoke before it was released into the atmosphere. I was happy that the old man had finally been released from the chains of his enfeebled and legless life.

Today is Saturday the 4th of April. I drove out to Stellenbosch in the rain. I took salami and butter and soft white rolls and Easter eggs and wine and a heavy chocolate cake. Connie and Mrs Fritz were there. Those nurses are humanity personified. My dad was glad to see me. He can hardly speak anymore. I try some English, some German and then some Norwegian. His mind hears and turns over clearly but slowly. It must not be crowded with impatient chatter. He takes a long time to respond. Most of his utterances do not make sense. He eats like a horse. He ate 2 packets of sliced Italian Salami and a buttered white roll. Then some beetroot and carrot salad and potatoes. Physically he is strong with a big strong pumping heart. He loves to see his boys.

The evolution of the human soul ... Julia explains briefly that her understanding is that the "soul" is something that is much larger than the physical body. A much larger and surrounding entity. This being unlike the Christian concept of a soul which fits neatly into the body.

My thoughts on the soul, or spirit whatever it is, are as follows. A few centuries ago humans could not see red blood corpuscles or bicuspid valves because they lacked microscopes. They could not understand the explosive mechanism of a nematoblast or the working of a butterfly's tongue. The world was flat. One day we will understand what a soul is, what a personality is and what charisma is. My theory is that the soul or the spirit or the life force is just as much part of our living mechanism as a leg or an arm. Some people have a large and powerful presence, some are timid and meek ... these are things of the soul. Some people have large and powerful forms, others small and weak ... these are things of the physical body. And as our human physicality evolves, the soul evolves just the same. The caveman had a more primitive soul. The dog has a dog soul and so forth. It is not hard to imagine, really. The soul is the spiritual entity – the life force. When we die, the life force is gone, and the body soon rots away.

7 April

Last night I dreamed that I was working at a filling station. It was 1978 and I was helping my mom do the quantities for the new house she was about to build for us in Camps Bay. I then had to go to a meeting and deliver a dictation. I sat down next to Alten Hulme. It was a steeply raked auditorium. I was poorly prepared and my notes made little sense to me. Some girls in pink leotards were performing a dance up on the stage. One little girl executed a spectacular back flip and landed perfectly. The teacher stopped the dance and awarded her the "oak leaves" on the spot. Thereafter the dance continued, but the dream became somewhat vague, more difficult to pen.

On **15 March** I wrote to you:

How I hate the machine.

What am I? Why a life of angst? Why so much nagging, nauseating anxiety throughout my waking years? First days of term, school sports days, work Mondays, the days prior to a wedding or Christmas, the days leading up to a holiday or just waiting for something to go wrong on a sail crossing. All of that and more.

Some of Julia's magic has worked. All anxiety has gone. I have not had any anxiety since the night of the fire and rocks, and my dreams have gone too. There are only small snatches and snippets left, each a few seconds long at most. No anxiety equals no dreams, or so it seems.

We knew a man called Boesman Pinto who died of TB about a year ago. I dreamed that I was standing overlooking the *dassies* at Bakoven teaching Zaan to gob like I can. Pinto arrived and stood beside us. He hawked thoughtfully and prepared spit. I watched him with interest. Then he spat, and out of his mouth issued a fine deadly mist. In horror, I felt the cold wetness of it all over my face and arms. It has been misty these past days. I have enjoyed the cool.

I dream that it is 11h50 and we have to leave Rhodesia by 12h15. I go into the lavatory for one last pee. I wake up and go for a real pee. I dream I am about to assemble a small prefabricated hut for Zaan. It is a hut similar to the trash hut she has in Canada. I am holding two wall parts. The dream only lasts a second.

I dream a fragment here and there, but these fragments are quickly forgotten. Nothing remains.

Oops … not so fast! The night of 12 April produces this: I live in a 2 bedroomed apartment in a little English town similar to Petworth. The apartment is accessed by a flight of outside steps. I am renting the first room to a now-aged Jannie Reuvers. Jannie, that former paragon of golden youth, is now an elderly man going by the name of Johnny something or other. I ask Jacques Theron and he confirms, "Yes that is Jannie Reuvers."

In order to access my room I have to crawl along a ledge overhanging the road. Against the wall are many of my mother's precious possessions and knickknacks. I enter my room by crawling through a miniature doorway.

One of my mom's paintings is hinged to a frame as a door. I head out to visit the Norwegian mint. I am searched by two Filipino women guards. I go to my friend's office. He opens his desk drawer which is packed with neat fat bundles of used Norwegian Kroner notes. He says that I may not steal any. All the other employees also show me their notes. I am interested in a pile of freshly printed, hot off the press, large 1 Million Kroner bills. They are printed in black ink on lovely grey paper with swirling patterns. I am told that they are "Death Bonds" and that each Norwegian family gets one every time a family member dies. I leave the mint and, as I leave, I am searched again by the same two women. They find only cigarettes and tampons in the side pockets of my fatigue pants.

I return to my apartment. What was a busy road is now the swimming pool area of a guesthouse. A UK tourist woman in an oversized white shirt boasts that she has found a place where she was able to sunbathe naked. She was red as a lobster. Her "mini-me" teenage daughter looks on. The UK tourist produces a small carved Mopani wood rhino and it drops into the pool. I immediately (in my swimming costume) jump in "bomb" style and make a huge juvenile splash. I descend to the bottom of the pool and rest there. The rhino has broken through all 3 planes. The horn is off, and the soles of its feet have also broken off. They look like dislodged tooth crowns. I collect them up with the intention to repair.

Zaan keeps talking about cutting her hair short. I just say, "go for it". She shows me a picture of Meg Ryan and says it is Goldie Hawn. She talks about a movie called When Harry meets Sally, I think of Thelma and Louise. I have just read a book called **The Naked and the Dead** by Norman Mailer. There are a few anecdotes about falling asleep on sentry duty. One of them fatal.

On the night of the 13th I dream this: Uwe and I are in the USA, staying in a hotel. We are about to leave our room when suddenly we notice a man seated at a small table next to the door. He is facing the wall and apparently nodding off. A pistol is placed on the desk just above his right hand. Uwe grabs the gun and it discharges. The man springs up and attempts to block our path. I grab the pistol and fire. The bullet hits him in the centre of the forehead killing him instantly, but it also bounces back at me and lands on my forehead slightly flattened and quite cold. I feel the bullet (which has become tangled up with a few of my hairs) and pull it free. I think that it is odd that the bullet is cold. Uwe and I grab our bags and dash into a parking garage. I have seen footage of the parking lot before (in a news clip perhaps) but it was flooded then. The water has now all drained away, but a fine silt remains on the concrete columns and the floor. I throw the pistol into a storm-water catch-pit. I hear it clattering away down the pipe into the bowels of the earth. We jump into Uwe's car and race off. It is Thelma and Louise's convertible, but it is pink.

And so the dreaming returned and now I dream again. Last night Allegra reported to me (in a dream) that Eddy Kohlani had painted the staircase in her house a beautiful shiny smooth white.

The remnants of my anxiety are gone. Zaan has cut her hair. Zaan and I adore each other. She leaves for Canada on Thursday.

Love C

Chapter 27

Sunshine of Your Love

In Canada, I dream a lot. Hours and hours of quality dreams. My forty-year high school reunion is held in my sleeping head, three years ahead of time. My classmates are all there, just as they were back in 1981. Sammy Munitz with his huge smile, Jenny Marin ticking off the register.

Why am I trying to conceal an AK-47 behind my back? I certainly do not intend to harm anyone. Why do I have three full magazines plus a single spare round? Why do I feel the need to stop and place my six-pack of warmish Carling Black Labels on the flat-topped newel post of the front steps, tear it open and glug down a quick, fizzy beer before entering the venue?

How are photographically vivid dreams like this choreographed? And the pulling at the tough plastic shrink-wrap surrounding the beers, the exact size and feel of the spare 7.62mm bullet and the three metal magazines. Who does the casting? Who writes the screenplay? Who directs? I guess it is all inside me – my dreams that is – but where? A wonderful mystery. A part of us we do not yet understand.

Such an amazing capacity we have for remembering detail, people and things one would imagine to be long forgotten, popping up in an imaginary but detailed place. The blending and weaving. And what about songs?

I believe that our capacity for remembering songs is a function of pre-literary survival. Before writing, everything needed to be remembered inside the head. Early poems and chants would have transferred a tribe's knowledge and lore. Constant repetition and amendment would have kept it vibrant and fresh. Epic poems like Homer's Odyssey, remembered and recited: the culmination.

My brothers and I had a pair of opera singers as parents. As soon as both were out of the house, my brother Bill, four years my senior, would take charge of our dad's Philips record player and the aural terrain of our home would change dramatically. As far as I remember, Bill owned over two hundred records (bartered, bought or misappropriated).

Mozart's **Entführung aus dem Serail** would be replaced by: Cream – **Sunshine of Your Love**, Led Zeppelin – **Good Times and Bad Times**, Pink Floyd – **Welcome to the Machine** ... it was a glorious metamorphosis. Mephisto.

My brothers and me, in the heyday of Cream

I was totally hung up on the lyrics. As a young boy I couldn't catch or comprehend them all, but those that sunk their hooks into me are still inside my head, along with, unfortunately, most of the contents of my school hymn books. I think that some of them possibly did some damage in there.

Bill started with Led Zeppelin and David Bowie and continued by pouring Cream, Golden Earring, Pink Floyd, Deep Purple, Supertramp, Rush, Genesis, Blue Öyster Cult, Yes and even ELO into the mix.

I followed with Cat Stevens, the South African group Rabbitt, Rodriguez, Boston, Joe Jackson, The Police, Van Halen, Fleetwood Mac, The Clash, ZZ Top, Talking Heads, Crowded House, Billy Idol, Dire Straits, U2, Def Leppard, Roxy Music and more.

The imagery was so powerful.
Visions captured by the phrase.
Some repeating almost daily, many lying in wait like torpedoes in their tubes. I am sure that it is the same with most people – if I listen to a song from my childhood, it is there, ready and waiting, instantly recognisable in every detail.

You don't have to live like a refugee
Tea in the Sahara with you
A rebel without a clue
I've heard a rumour from ground control, oh no, don't say it's true
I'm happy, hope you're happy too
There's distance between us
96 degrees in the shade
Parched land, no desert sand, the sun is just a dot
Don't look back
She was a fast machine
It's alright we know where you've been
No one ever dies there, no one has a head
When I was a child I had a fever, my hands felt just like two balloons
What does it take to be a man?
You'll never know just how hard I've tried
It's a nice day for a white wedding
Glorious things of thee are spoken, Zion, city of our God
And I can see those fighter planes
Slapping them down, one hundred, two hundred
Some kind of alien, waits for the opening
I see my Mary Anne walking away
News guy wept and told us, earth was really dying
In my thoughts I have seen, rings of smoke through the trees
And the voices of those who stand looking

Alone again, alone again tonight oh I'm
Alone again, it seems to me that every time I try to change
Say that you say that you'll help me reach the other side

No cloud, a sleepy calm, sun-baked earth that's cooled by gentle breeze
And trees with rustling leaves, only endless days without a care
Nothing must be done.

And all the fat-skinny people
And all the tall-short people
And all the nobody people
And all the somebody people

Anne and her father are out in the boat, watching the water, watching the waves on the sea.

Glamorous indie rock and roll is what I want ... and a beer.
And that's no big ask.

24 May 2015   Letter #28

Hi GR

My old surfing buddy Manuel Maragelis turns 50 on Monday.

A get-together was organised by his wife Jacqui at the Bascule under the Cape Grace Hotel. The evening wind was a north-westerly but warm enough. No jersey required. Big yachts at their moorings. The familiar *ting-ting-ting* of halyards against masts. Clouds and stars and foreign accents and people smoking cigars outside. Just like the First World.

So good to see old pals – the trust, acceptance and deep affection for one another. You could call it love.

I was the only driver there, all the rest were using Uber taxis. Pieter and Honey Adriaens and their sons were all using Ubers – the two boys took Ubers home from two different parties!

I stayed off the booze but not the buffet. I was outclassed and outgunned by a pair of super-efficient eaters – Roly Roland and another giant fellow named Craig. For once I was like the little guy. The three of us guzzled vast amounts of crispy potato *rösti* croquettes topped with fillet steak and miniature bowls of lamb, gravy and mash and mini souffles and prawns on skewers and crispy crab delights and chicken filled spring rolls and on and on. I was 1.5kg heavier this morning.

How is it that a person can be full of ebullient positiveness the evening before and then wake up feeling blue? The same set of physical circumstances, only one day older. Just a chemical wash I guess.

It was a misty morning with a good swell. I went to exercise down at the shed. Oystercatchers and cool air. Soon I felt better – you know "onwards and upwards" … "that's the spirit."

But crime is bad and the ANC is depressing and the power blackouts engender little faith.

Sliding.
Cry the Beloved Country.
My mom and Ian were victims of a home invasion. They survived but are severely shaken.

Ian is in a lot of pain with eight stab wounds, an injured knee, painful fingers where his assailants tore at them as he fought them off, refusing to be tied up with his own washing-line (which was cut down and brought in for the purpose). What would have happened to Ian and Virginia had they been tied up? Four savage young men invade a civilised home and brutally attack an elderly couple. They left the scene after knocking Ian senseless. Virginia escaped to her room, locked the security gate and pressed the panic button. The robbers left in Ian's car with their phones, IDs and Virginia's rings.

Neighbourhood Watch and the CBCSI were there almost immediately. There was so much blood. The stab wound behind Ian's ear has damaged his hearing. The one intended for his heart chunked into his sternum.

For 35 years Virginia has enjoyed her peaceful park of a garden, shared with Guineafowl and bunnies and other critters. Now she fears it, from one day to the next. The result of a selfish, brutal action. Finding a smaller and safer house for them is now a priority.

This is a country with a poor economy.
A relatively small percentage of the population (with nothing much to lose) opt for violent crime.
Brazil is a country with a good economy and plenty of violence:
43 000 gun-homicides in 2014.
That is almost 120 a day … mainly young men under 30.
Packed in cardboard trays and boxed, shiny bullets leave the bullet factories.
Those with human names on them randomly clinking in-between the bullets that miss their targets or simply tear into tin cans and old bowling skittles.

Humans on Earth numbered like this over the past 7000 years.

5000 BC – 5 Million
2000 BC – 27 Million
BC/AD – 170 Million
200 AD – 190 Million
1500 AD – 425 Million
2000 AD – 6000 Million
2015 AD – 7000 Million. Seven Thousand Million

They tell me that if you divide the number of violent acts by the number of people, the Earth is presently a far less violent place than it was at any other time in our human past. Pre-historic raiding parties laying waste, Hittites laying waste, Alexander the Great laying waste, Romans laying waste, Ottoman Turkish invaders laying waste, Huns laying waste, the Mongol Ghengis Kahn laying waste, the Vikings laying waste, World War I and II laying waste and so on *ad infinitum*. Believe it or not, we are surviving more successfully now than ever before. And to make matters worse, we breed unchecked and our babies do not die any more. Yup, we are a successful violent species that makes war on our own species and any others that we might benefit from – whales, trees and tuna. I like reading books. I don't watch TV and I have little hope for the species. I hate the species.

But, what about the individual?

Now that is a different thing altogether – the beautiful thing called HUMANITY. The milk.

On Friday I met my Ovambo friends Eric Fanuele and Mr Moses. What lovely warm-hearted men. And the unbelieveable warmth of the Shona people I was with in Zimbabwe the other day. And the Tswana people up in Gaborone. And the big Afrikaner Stephan who runs Simply Asia stores up in Jozi. And the kindness of the Italians I have known. And my beloved Norwegian friends. And my mom and my brothers and my granny Dinny and Zaan and you, *ou* Gareth.

Where does humanity end and the species start? That is the question.

Love C

Chapter 28

Home Invasion and Compassion

So slowly it creeps up and in that you do not even notice the change.

At first, towards the end of every gathering around a table with friends, somebody would tell a horror story. It started off with tales of a victim in Johannesburg, twice removed. Soon it became once removed. Then suddenly it was here, and everyone stopped talking about it at the dinner table.

Our rude awakening started around 2007 or 2008, courtesy of Luis Momadi and his gang.

Google him and see what kind of man skulks and ambushes and robs and rapes.

"To family members, Luis Momadi was a hard-working husband who always made time for his three children, but at night, when they believed he was out socialising with friends, he was breaking into Camps Bay homes, attacking and robbing residents. Momadi, 29, convicted of rape, robbery, housebreaking, racketeering and money laundering, was sentenced to life imprisonment by the Western Cape High Court."

Compassion for such men?
From me?
No.
I would squash them like bugs if I could.
I suppose it would be much like killing cockroaches.
Squash a few tonight and tomorrow fresh ones arrive,
Only to scurry away when the light is switched on.
Until society turns on criminality with a big stick, there will be no cure.

Headfirst into the *vangwa*
All the way from Mozambique

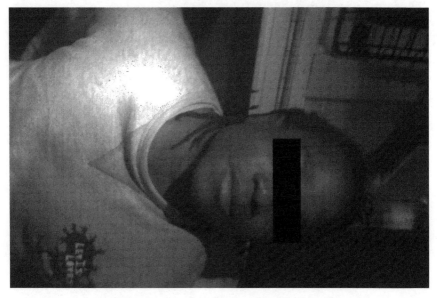

Arrested with his cohorts and a carload of stolen TVs
In today, out again tomorrow – "It's Catch and Release," says Zaan.

Should one have compassion for a man who drives a lorry into a crowd in the name of Allah?
There have been almost 300 school shootings in the USA in the last decade.
Should one have compassion for the poor mixed-up kid who shoots up a school?
If it is your child killed?
Should one have compassion for Anders Breivik?
If it was your child killed?

One evening in 2013, my 80-year-old mom had been out to see a friend. She was dropped at home around 9.30pm and settled down in the upstairs lounge to chat with her partner Ian.

Four men quietly entered the room. My mom's first thought was that someone was playing a practical joke. She quickly realised that this could very easily end in death. One man grabbed my mother around the neck in a stranglehold as he tore the rings from her fingers while repeatedly asking, "Where is the safe?"

The men had brought the washing-line in with them. They held Ian down and tussled with him as they tried to tie him up. Ian, although not a young man, had served in the Rhodesian SAS and managed to fight them off. He was stabbed eight times and badly beaten about the head.

For some reason – perhaps they thought they had killed Ian – the men disappeared as quickly and as quietly as they had arrived, stealing Ian's car as they went. My mom, keeping a very cool head, locked herself behind an internal security gate and pressed the panic button.

The police stopped Ian's car in Hout Bay but the men were not arrrested, possibly in exchange for one of my mother's rings. Next, they drove to the local informal settlement and traded my mother's jewellery for drink. Then off to the harbour where they wrecked the car.

An exercise in absolute futility.

When Zaan and I arrived at my mother's house, Ian was drenched in inky purple blood and wandering around dazed, from room to room, with stab wounds in his chest, arms and behind one ear. Mick arrived next and whisked Ian off to hospital – a brave man who, by refusing to be tied up, probably save my mother's life and his own.

My mom built her home when I was a teenager at Camps Bay High School. There were no fences or gates or burglar alarms back then. One property ran into the next. The homes of Camps Bay are now fortresses of high walls and zap wire and CCTV cameras. Slowly, the evil crept in. And it was allowed in. The good men of the West had become weak and unwilling to assert their right to defend themselves. They never stood together, preferring to watch Tarantino movies on TV instead.

Five years have passed.

Ask my mom or Ian if a day goes by that is not clouded by the memory of that attack.

Ask me about compassion or the lack thereof.

3 July 2015   Letter #29

Hello Mr G

When the (so-called) "white" man arrived in South Africa, at the Cape of Good Hope, the (so-called) "black" man was not here yet. At school they taught us that he was still up around the Kei or the Great Fish River. Pushing downwards and outwards, but momentarily stalled. They taught us that he was unable to cultivate sorghum in the winter rainfall areas, under 200mm per year.

This land down at our tip of Africa was the preserve of the Hottentot and Bushman Khoi. The Khoi died with their language and their lore and their culture and their bushcraft.

Gone.

The (so-called) "white" man killed him.

The (so-called) "black" man and the (so-called) "white" man fought.

The (so-called) "white" man overwhelmed the (so-called) "black" man.

And within a short while, the Great Empires of the Northern Men overran and colonised the brown-skinned countries of the world.

The British, the Dutch, the Germans, the Portuguese, the Belgians.

India, Gabon, the Congo, Mozambique, Batavia, the Spice Islands, China, the Union of South Africa, Rhodesia, Burma ... The list is long, long, long.

But the wheel turns.

Europe cannot seem to stem the tide of the invasion from Africa now.

Calais.

Europe does not seem to like it very much at all ... they rumble and grumble ... and turn to the right.

Down here where we live,
the (so-called) "white" people are fighting a last-ditch battle.
A strangulation of the Afro/European culture.
The (so-called) "black" man is now in command, the land is in his hands.
The continent is largely in the hands of despotic and corrupt men,
Put into power by coups or ignorant, undereducated, populist voters.
There are Pirates in the Wheelhouse.
Electrical "load shedding" is the physical manifestation of the metaphorical "lights going out".
We cling to our civilised handhold.
We love the warm weather and the cheap labour way too much.
We hope against hope.

I work alongside the (so-called) "black" man – we get on very well.

The Species vs. the Individual
The Masses vs. the Man
The Misanthrope vs. the Philanthropist

Early June 2015

The question is: Would I or wouldn't I if I didn't have to?

I believe that the answer is: "No, I would not go."

But waking up in Zimbabwe, in the pre-dawn dark, sitting in a wonky guesthouse room working at a fall-down side table, as the light creeps in, and different robins and other birds herald the morning, and seeing the tired property of the guesthouse in the dawn light, and getting up and taking a walk around, then, then the answer becomes: "Yes I would, even if I wasn't being paid." I guess that I would do it for free.

Yesterday I woke at 04h00. Cape Town was cold and rainy. I delayed getting up and lay in bed for half an hour before kicking into gear. I was in JHB by 09h00 and on site in warm Harare at 2pm.

Charles and Tasi take me to measure up a "going concern". The Doc plans to convert a failing Borrowdale steakhouse into a brand-new Asian delight. It is a difficult "measure up" as there are many columns and curved walls. At 17h15 I am almost done when the restaurant operator arrives. His sleepy staff didn't seem to mind or even notice me as they somnambulated around the place to the soft strains of jazz standards while a few tipsy men claiming to be lawyers chatted at the bar. But the restauranteur wasn't pleased to see me, tape measure in one hand and laser in the other, with a camera and pad on a table nearby. I left him after a bit of slippery obfuscation on my part. I noticed a bubble full of "What the fuck are you doing here?" hanging in the air above his head. The sun set over the parking lot as I stuffed down two slightly stale chicken pies for supper. Lucky picked me up and whisked me away into the night. The traffic was quite heavy and, with no streetlights, an experience with typical African charm.

In due course I was delivered to a guesthouse somewhere outside town. What must have been a gorgeous home is now sadly falling into a Third World condition. No maintenance and few available skills in that department (or available cash). Both bath taps fall off onto the worn enamel tub at first touch. The toilet cistern is empty. I open the stopcock. I take a hot bath and wash my body and hair with a cake of Lifebuoy Soap. The toilet flushes and I head out, wonderfully degreased after a greasy afternoon in the restaurant. I head out towards the main house. I am the only guest. My hosts' names are George and Locadia. They are lovely and warm. I spend some hours at their reception desk converting my measurements into an "as-built" drawing. At 10pm the generator sputters and stops. No lights. No power. I return to my room, led by George with a tiny torch. A stream of water is running out from under the door. The room is flooded. I change to another room and, using my cellphone as a torch, I go to bed. At 22h30 the Harare grid comes back to life and my bedside lamp flickers on next to my head. I switch on my PC and work until midnight. It is a difficult drawing and I need to crack it before I can sleep.

I am up at 04h30 and back at work before 05h00 after an extremely odd night, wondering if someone had placed a *jundi* on me. My head itched the entire night and it felt as though an army of biting bugs was crawling through my hair. I swatted and scratched and feared that I would be covered in blood and crushed insects in the morning, but I found neither. As soon as I stood up all traces of the symptom vanished instantly. I cannot explain it other than that my using Lifebouy soap instead of shampoo caused this extreme itching.

The guesthouse calls for description:

Once upon a time in colonial Rhodesia, a family of European extraction carefully built a fabulous home on a large property in a gorgeous location just outside Salisbury. The roof was shingled with tiny flat tiles. The eaves were trimmed upwards with a slight pagoda-style tilt. The garden was set out with rose beds, hydrangeas, agapanthus, oak trees, lilies and a clay topped tennis court with a practice wall to one side. A swimming pool lay above the court and half a dozen thatched guest *rondavels* were built around the pool. Below, stables housed the horses and (so-called) "white" people had Anglo-Afropean fun. Pimm's No.1 Cup and bubbles etc. A large staff of grooms, gardeners and house servants probably also had a great time. They were probably well treated and had not yet cottoned on to the notion that they might also have desires above and beyond their collective lot. That was Rhodesia. Then there was the war after which Zanu-PF took up office and ultimately were (to quote Lucky) "IN POWER". The economy crashed to a point where a loaf of bread cost a trillion Zim dollars. The Zim dollar has now been replaced by the US dollar and the economy is slightly better. But as long as The Great Dictator and Zanu-PF remain in corrupt command, the ship remains doomed (much like Zuma's RSA).

The Tennis Court

The towels are very white and the sheets are ironed perfectly. The large verandah surrounding two-thirds of the house is polished a bright black. These three features stand in stark contrast to the general tone. It seems that for these, and other things like the mowing of lawns, the required skills have been retained. However, the poles of the tennis court fence stand rusted and bent. The gate lies where it fell twenty years ago. The net and clay surface are long gone. The pool is a greenish soup. The snapped off cast-concrete head of a Botticelli Venus stands on a broken steel drinks table observing the slow decay. The hydrangeas look as only untended hydrangeas can. The last roses display themselves among speckled orange hips. The African trees and bamboos are grand and wonderful. It is all wonderful, actually.

As Dag says, "Spice is the variety of life" and such a trip into a different world is a tonic for the soul.

Growing up as a quitter:

The pound is now worth R20. When I was a boy the pound was worth R2. A packet of Simba chips was 5c, now it is about R5. When I was five or six years old, my primary school held a 10km "big walk". The start was at the end of Tafelberg Road. We all walked back to the Lower Cable Station (5km) and then everyone turned around and retraced their footsteps to the start, which was now the end. My mom was waiting for me at the 5km turn-around point. I pretended I had blisters or sore feet or some such weak excuse and was summarily whisked back (by *Volksie*) to the quartered oranges at the end point. Pathetic. But worse still, when I went to collect my sponsorship money (1 and 2c per kilometre) I could only claim for 5km and not 10. "Oh, I got blisters." Quitter!

Some kids are, and some kids aren't. My brother Mick had more tenacity than a bull terrier. He didn't quit. But, sadly and ashamedly, I did.

Recorder lessons, Cubs (dyb, dyb, dyb, dob, dob, dob and all that), guitar lessons, lighting for the primary school play – I could tell a few sad tales. A varsity drop-out. I remember desperately wanting to jump ship in Las Palmas after having sailed all the way from Cape Town – only a few more days to Genova and there would be $3000 each for me and my ex-wife. She made me stay the distance and I am glad I did. And so, in my twenties, I began to learn to be a stayer. To be a stayer and dmb, dmb, dmb better than anyone else. Quitting is sometimes essential for survival, but that is relatively seldom. Staying the distance and doing your best (dyb) is generally the best policy. If a person is not naturally tenacious one has to learn to be a stayer by being forced into it. A boss, a bursary contract, conscription, the fear of DB (detention barracks), a firm hand – that is what is needed. The fear of consequence. A child to provide for.

Postscript

During the last months of the Angolan bush war I was up in Kroonstad. The battle of Cuito Cuanavale raged a few thousand kilometres away while my comrades and I busied ourselves purloining rations and faking weekend passes. There were posters pinned up all over the base. "Winners Never Quit – Quitters Never Win."

Greetings from Planet Earth ...12 June ...What a place!

I have been hard at the coalface. Went for a paddle at 5pm on Friday. When I came back there were people swimming at Bakoven, so warm was the water.

On my 38th birthday I had a cocktail of Red Bull and espresso and ran up Table Mountain in 59 min 50 sec. I was exhausted for the rest of the day – burned out. Yesterday it was nice and cool and I did the same trot in 60 min 20 sec. I even stopped to take pics along the way. My heart was quite calm on reaching the upper station and I carried on with the day, no issues. Even went for a surf at lunchtime. It is good to be a bit fit.

This morning I went up the Head. I had egg and bacon rolls at home with my local friends, a pair of semi-tame gulls and a pair of redwing starlings. Hungry robins and thrushes constantly at my office door requesting cheese.

14 June 2015 ... I am 51 today. Nobody bothering me – it is lovely.
Love

Your Pal – Kalos

Chapter 29

Scatterlings

My friend Lukas Shikufinde came to Cape Town in search of a better life. He is a perfectionist.

"I like to make pofect Mr Karros," he says.

He likes to call me Mr Karros, so I call him Mr Lukey or Mr Lukas.

Shortly before leaving for Canada, Mr Lukas and I were having a bite of lunch together and feeding bits of cheese to the tame redwing starlings flying in and out of my kitchen window, when he asked, "Mr Karros, where are you going overseas?"

Mr Lukey and Mr Karros sharing lunch and a bad-hair-day

So, after our meal, I pulled up a second chair at my desk and opened Google Maps and showed him. We started in my garden before zooming up into the air above Camps Bay. Then, panning slowly northwards, we flew to Oshakati and put down at the Shoprite supermarket and looked around. We took off again, flying low, over the sandy paths that led to Lukas' home. Then, up, up and away, over Angola and Congo and the Med and down to land again right outside our mutual friend Mr George's factory in Switzerland. "Wow, it's a nice factory, Mr Karros!" We look at the snow-capped mountains. I tell him about snow.

Soon Mr Lukey and I were skimming over Norway and Greenland, tracing the route of an Emirates 777 all the way to Pearson International Airport, Toronto … and on by bus to London, Ontario, and Zaan's little house by the park.

Lukas says that he would love to go there but right now he is busy "building a better life" for himself.

Often in the early mornings I am on top of Table Mountain or Lion's Head and meet up with my pal José. José has one gold front tooth and his warm, wide smile flashes back at the rising sun. He overflows with love.

José is my age but unlike me he is heavily muscled, like Mr T. His job is taking care of patrons (call it PR/bouncer) at The Power and The Glory, a bar and restaurant at the lower end of Kloof Nek Road. I couldn't imagine anyone making trouble near José, but I am inquisitive.

"José," I ask him, "do you ever get trouble there?"

"What do you mean?" he asks.

"I mean drunk youngsters and fighting, like we get in Camps Bay."

"Oh no," he laughs, "I just kiss them and all trouble go away."

"Kick them?" I ask, thinking I had misheard him.

"No, no," he says in his Portuguese accent, "I put arm around neck and kiss them."

When José was fifteen, his mother sent him to the market in their village in central Angola to buy ingredients for dinner. While making his purchases, he and some other boys were rounded up and taken away. José never saw his mother again. His mother never heard from her son.

José had been abducted by UNITA soldiers and forced into uniform. From child soldier to adult soldier, he ended up fighting alongside the charismatic rebel leader Jonas Savimbi. He spent many years with Savimbi at Jamba, close to the Namibian border at Caprivi, and left him in Moxico after he fell in 2002 as government troops closed in.

José

After the death of "my general", José walked to Namibia and then carried on all the way down to Cape Town where he has made "a better life". Better than what? Better than landmines and RPGs, certainly.

Another person I meet regularly on my runs is Storm. He trains two hunting pointers on the back of Signal Hill between the old cannons and the kramat. He carries a plastic whistle and the dogs point out the Guineafowl scrabbling around in the bush. Storm misses the shores of Lake Malawi and his family and his home in the hills. But his wife is with him now, as well as a new-born baby he sometimes feels too old for. Storm tells me about the economy in Malawi and that he came to South Africa "you know, to make a better life". Storm tells me that he has not been home for years. I offer to buy him a ticket provided I can come along and stay with him for a week. "We can rent a car," I say. Storm just smiles. I don't think he believes me.

In 1982 Johnny Clegg released a song called *Scatterlings*. It became the painful anthem of my generation as they moved away, one by one, to make new lives for themselves – better lives. Each uprooted one.

In 1987 I lived with an ex-Rhodesian in Vauxhall and drank beer with ex-Rhodesians at a bar in Earl's Court. Displaced young men. Young veterans of a lost war. Young men who had lost not only buddies but their country and homes as well. They were brave men, robust and positive, but behind their beards and bravado, a deep sadness lurked. Each uprooted one.

My mother's partner, Ian McLean, left Rhodesia with his wife and children at the end of the war. Forever a displaced person, longing for the powerful magic of the African bush.

After the war most of the palefaces left Zim while Mugabe and his Zanu-PF undid the economy. There are now between one and three million Zimbabwean nationals living inside South Africa. Scatterlings all, homesick and uprooted, trying to make a better life or even just earn some money to send back home. Malawians, Congolese, Nigerians, Burundians, Mozambicans, Somalians, Zimbabweans … I talk to them all. All homesick.

Here I sit in Canada at my desk overlooking the park. It is raining.

We are the scatterlings of Africa, each uprooted one
On the road to Phelamanga, beneath the copper sun
And I love the scatterlings of Africa, each and every one

25 July 2015   Letter #30

A letter written in modern times.

Today is the 18th of July – I leave for Canada on the 18th of August.

I am very excited.

This evening I Skyped with Zaan.

Alice through the Looking Glass

I have just sat for a nine-and-a-half-hour straight push, detailing up two restaurants in Zimbabwe and one in Joburg.

I craft my drawings on the "Looking Glass" – or is it Orwell's "telescreen"? I have three on my desk arranged before me. The smallest one has an eye. It is my laptop which I use for emails and skyping and such. The big monitor directly in front of me is the workhorse on which I earn my living. The big screen to the right will play me music while I am detailing up easy work, or is used to display reference pdfs or jpegs. It is so sci-fi. Today's work has been tedious but not taxing, so I have eased the process by YouTubing The Killer's **Direct Hits** on the righthand screen. How's that *eksê*?

After Skyping with Zaan, I watched The Killers in concert at the Royal Albert Hall on YouTube. The music of Brandon Flowers. Quite an entertainer! I ate a can of corn kernels, out of the can, with a spoon for supper. What a world!

You know Mr G … I have been "teetering" over the last weeks …

Even if I say so myself, I have been very close to the edge.

My personal edge.

So close that I could feel the pull, but I pulled back, I think just in time.

And now as I work, I'm sitting in my sleeping bag,

I can feel clear water running out under my arms, draining out, and not
because I am hot.
Because I am fucked.

Today is the 24th ... Feeling much better.
At 6pm load-shedding kicked in – plunged into darkness.
Working with laptop and headlamp.
This may seem self-indulgent, but I am going to write it anyway,
Because it is one of life's experiences and I would like to document it.

BURNOUT

For years I have been burning out. Pushing so hard in the service of others.
I have been a slave to my ex-wife for the sake of my daughter
And I have worked and worked and paid and paid.
I have done my duty and sacrificed and paid my dues.
In fact, stealing from Rodriguez, I may have even overpaid them.
I have been worried about my health and stress levels,
Zaan has, Bill has and my mom too, but I got trapped,
I have just gone on and on and on.

Now is the time for change. The die is cast. All things come to an end. The
house at 2 Berkley Road has been sold. The money comes at the end of
August. Soon I will be debt-free. As soon as I have fulfilled my current work
commitments for Simply Asia, I will take my first work-free break since 2007.
I am looking forward to that.

Ian gave me a book on burnout. I find that I am a typical case, one of many.
I have made the decision to save myself now. For years I have been holding out.
This burnout has been held at bay for a long time, but I must watch myself,
now that the end (unbelievable as it may seem) is actually in sight.

I am not anxious in any way, but the slightest work stress can cause a seriously
destabilising reaction. I feel like a twig that could just snap. I manage myself
with great care. I am so volatile. I can suddenly become incredibly impatient and
aggressive for no good reason. Sometimes I feel fine and sometimes I feel on the
verge of tears. Sometimes I cry. Sometimes I feel like toppling over. Sometimes
I feel disjointed, disconnected and distant. I feel like I am in sticky glue – often
working at a reduced pace. I carry on in a slow measured way. Task after task.
Sometimes I cannot seem to be able to take deep breaths.

It becomes so shallow.

I sweat out clean water. I need to navigate carefully. Easy does it, but it is not easy.

Since Zaan left for Canada about 10 weeks ago I have sat and worked in my sleeping bag from before light until way into the night. I take a quick run, ride or paddle almost every day. It is that hour that saves me.

Below is a song by Harry Manx.
It is worth Googling and watching him play his six-stringed banjo.

He looks just like a young version of uncle Bill,
But way less formal, I bet you he's a good guy ...

You jumped the wire and you headed down on old Montgomery Lane
You were half way home to heaven when you heard that voice again

She said, always keep me close even cross a distant sea
One more thing, yeah before I go don't forget to miss me

Trouble came to tear him down and laid his plans to waste
Thoughts of her keep coming strong, like a feeling he could taste

He sent her words as sweet as wine and stars on a full moon night
She sent him kisses soft as rain all bathed in a summer's light

The day drew near when they would meet, she rose two hours 'fore dawn
She tried so hard not to cry but now the tears had come

I miss Zaan like the song.
But that is not what I wish to record here.
Read the last line of the song. I am like that.

C

Afterthought

31 July 2015

Most people in this country never have the pleasure of a hot shower.
I choose not to run a heater, so I sit and work in a cosy sleeping bag if it is cold.
At night I sleep as warm as I wish and do not sit in commuter traffic
to and from work.

I run and ride on the mountain with sunbirds.
Today I saw a young falcon trying to take down a dove.
I am often with the sea.
I am deeply connected to the sea.
Maybe it is not so bad.

Chapter 30

Why do people leave?

In New Zealand, Australia, Italy, Austria and Canada I have spoken to people who have moved away. They all miss South Africa terribly and wouldn't have left if it weren't for the crime, the perceived danger of physical violence and a lack of faith in African governance. Whether it be the owner of a "Seffrican" flag-festooned restaurant in Freemantle or an older couple shopping at the IKEA in Burlington, it is always the same story.

Mike Charles was a mysterious fellow back in 1987. I hope he still is. Some Saturday mornings he would head off in his Rover and return an hour or so later with a box of Castlemain XXXX lagers, a sack of charcoal and a plastic bag containing a few yards of the most excellent *boerewors* I had ever tasted. (Maltahöhe came later.) He never told me where he got it.

Down below our house in Vauxhall there was a rather bleak concrete driveway. A pair of steel gates opened onto the passing traffic of Harleyford Road. In the afternoon we would light a fire in an old wheelbarrow and *braai wors*. Ice-cold Castlemains were opened and, seated like a pair of princes on upturned plastic milk crates, we would chat.

Mike was born and raised in Rhodesia (now Zimbabwe). His dad was the local dentist in the town of Umtali not far from the Mozambican border. During the bush war, Mike had served in PATU (the Police Anti-Terrorist Unit). Like most ex-Rhodies, Mike pined for the bush and a wheelbarrow *braai* with a "slopey" on a Saturday afternoon in London was about as close to it as he could get.

He would tell me about sitting in the entrance of his little tent overlooking the Zambezi River with the smell of the grass and the trees. And the camaraderie. And the haze over Mozambique. And Kariba. And trips down to Beira with his parents and his brother John when they were boys.

He told me of one Saturday afternoon many years earlier when he had developed a craving for a packet of tomato sauce-flavoured crisps. He took orders from the troops in his platoon and then headed out in an army Land Rover on a 30km drive to the nearest village. Bumpy roads, dry heat, dust, dongas and the deafening whir of cicadas. Eventually, he pulled up outside a trading store selling rubber boots, bicycle pumps and patches, cheap sweets in glass jars, mieliemeal, air rifle pellets, cigarettes and tobacco, pocket-knives, *takkies* and *vellies* and, of course, Willards tomato sauce-flavoured chips.

On his way back to camp, Mike was ambushed. Automatic weapons opened fire alongside him as he passed by and his ambushers kept shooting until his Land Rover disappeared in the dust. Unscathed, he kept going until he was safely back among his comrades. They inspected the vehicle. Hundreds of shots had been fired but there was not a single bullet-hole to be found.

After distributing his purchases among the men, Mike went back to the Landy and noticed the single hit that everyone had missed. One round had passed through the driver's flap-down sun-visor, in one edge and out the other, about a foot away from his head. He stared at the visor ... just two tiny holes ... no other damage to the vehicle at all. Mike reflected that if he had left the village shop a fraction of a second later, those two holes would have been on either side of his head.[1]

⁂

The most unfriendly people I have ever met work at Moscow airport.

On two separate occasions, six years apart, Moroccans have cocked and pointed automatic weapons at me.

A pair of communist-era Hungarian border police also left a lot to be desired.

The other side of that coin might well exist in Zimbabwe. One could start with a driver named Lucky, or perhaps, better still, the man who runs a mostly dysfunctional guesthouse in Teviotdale Road, or my fellow guests there: a group of Malawians on a training-week at the nearby Groombridge Spar. How we laughed while we ate a heap of fresh white bread, sliced thick and spread with margarine, along with sausages in chewy, red skins, all washed down with sweet, lukewarm tea.

Not the Ritz, but hey, you could never have so much fun at the Ritz.

You know what? … It hurts us so much to leave.

---

1   In my Introduction I contemplated the "morphing" of memory.

    I recently bumped into Mike Charles at a birthday party and asked him to recount the ambush story. "Which one?" he said. Mike had been a busy chap during his Rhodesian national service with PATU and had been involved in quite a few "contacts". In the updated (2018) version of his story, not very many rounds were fired and only two struck his vehicle, one of them through the sun-visor as described. I had to dig around in my memory until I found the tale which had blended with Mike's 1987 story and combined into my memory's version as written above. Finally I found it.

    In the 1970s one of my dad's colleagues, a fellow by the name of Ben Illeman, was a captain in the Rhodesian army. He had been ambushed as he drove through a donga. About 200 cartridge cases were later picked up at the scene – not one round had hit his vehicle.

30 August 2015   Letter #31

Hi Gareth

A long month coming to a close

**Choose your fights – time of great wrestling coming – but peace now
In Canada**

1 Aug 2015

You can still change the world by dreaming the world,
You can still create the moon from an old bent shoe.
I finished work quite late on Friday evening.
My last intention was to Google the Phoenix, but I forgot.
At my bedside I have a small book of Bushman poems
(Given to me 20 years ago by Billo)
Loosely translated by Stephen Watson
From the /Xam recorded by WH Bleek and Lucy Lloyd
in the second half of the 19th Century.
This morning I opened on a poem that I have not read before.
I have always glossed over it because the content, at first glance,
is not as appealing as the rest.
The poem is about "The Nature of /Kaggen" the mischief maker.
He was captured and thrown into a fire for doing something bad:
Even then old trickster, young trickster, even there in that fire,
Your arms sprouted feathers, you flew out of the flames,
Even then in that heat you conjured feathers amidst fire,
You flew out of its blistering to wet your burnt flesh …

There are such beautiful thoughts there too … there is a poem about a /Xam man dreaming about plucking up the courage to ask his "mistress" (madam) for some thread to sew the beautiful buttons she gave him onto his jacket. //Kabbo's Request for Thread.

The poems about contact with the "white" man are simply heartbreaking. It is worth Googling the poems to look into the souls of the last remnants of that disappearing race, now gone.

⬥

Today is the 1st of August and the sun is shining. I rode on the mountain and stopped to watch a new cable-car cable being pulled up over the rocky precipices. I spoke to an (apparently) elderly man overseeing the work. He was just 52. My age – older by just over half a year. He had grown up in Bo-Kaap about a kilometre from where we grew up as boys. We were separated by a line called the Group Areas Act. His childhood friends and schoolmates were the same young men I did karate with in the 1980s. Suleiman Samaai, Imma, Aubrey, Elias and so on. Both of our school classrooms were filled with the same teargas that came drifting up from the city in June 1976. This is what I thought yesterday:

On Death

One day I will die,
And my bones will lie there, in a heap with my meat.
It might be old meat, or it might be middle-aged meat.
I do not know, because I cannot see around corners.
One thing is for sure, however,
It cannot be young meat any more.

7 Aug 2015

Today I am almost crazy with excitement – holiday time is just around the corner.

I have no client work to do this weekend. It is a very long time since that has happened.

On Monday I meet with DHK Architects to do a week of design/detailing on a project called Amangiri in Utah. I must now, this weekend, get the sold house at 2 Berkley ready for handover to the buyer on Tuesday morning.

A Voice of Reason – some thoughts

Yesterday on the radio they were talking about SANParks and the muggings on Lion's Head.

On Sunday 10 people were mugged on Lion's Head. Five separate couples, apparently by a group of knife-wielding men who sped downhill and away. Easy pickings.

The SANParks ranger at the bottom was so engrossed in his phone that he did not even notice anything was amiss.

When a surfer paddles out into the sea, he knows he might encounter a shark and he makes provision for that in his mind. Or hers. When hikers go onto the mountain they have to do the same. When Simon van der Stel headed out to Stellenbosch in 1690 he knew that he might encounter a lion or a rhino and made provision for that. There are no wild lions and rhino left in the Cape – but there are far more dangerous things. As times change, the nature of danger changes. That is just the way it is. As the human population continues to grow unchecked and there is no will to enforce the law, the pendulum will swing further to the bad side before it starts to swing back. It is mostly a function of competition for resources and we will more than likely not see the pendulum swing back in our lifetimes. For now, we need to focus and survive.

There is a thing that I call "prejudice", or pre-judging a situation. It is about being streetwise.

I have lived and worked in the building and construction sector in South Africa for many years. One gets to know the "types". Our society is hugely diverse. Most people are wonderful. A small percentage is not. Times have definitely changed. I have found the actual "personality" of society has changed.

Ten years ago, I used to pick up any type of hitchhikers and really enjoy the chat. I don't do that any more. I will still stop my *bakkie* on Kloof Nek for three teenage surfers needing a lift to Glen Beach but not for three young men of the Congolese type.

Over the past years, as a member of my neighbourhood watch I have been involved in more arrests and interactions with criminals than I can remember. Every single one of them fits a certain "look and feel" demographic. Sad but true. The daily news tells me more of the same.

In the 1940s young males of the "type" we now fear in the Cape fynbos were not a real threat to my grandfather, but young German males in the Italian Campania were considered a deadly one.

In the late 1950s, when my mom visited Italy, German males were no longer a threat. A few years ago, PAGAD bombs in shopping malls were a real worry – now armed gunmen are. There are no more PAGAD bombs. Suicide bombers did not exist a few years ago, now they are not uncommon ... and so on.

Things change so fast. As Pieter-Dirk Uys said, we must "adapt or die". One must be alert and prepared to identify a potential danger even at risk of being considered prejudiced.

Hypervigilance is needed in South Africa now. If you set your alarm five nights out of 10, you reduce a certain risk element by 50%. If you set your alarm ten nights of ten you reduce that particular risk element by 100%. One must try to compound one's risk reduction strategies by overlapping them.

Don't surf at the river mouth alone at dusk. If you are a vulnerable type, walk where there are other people, carry pepper spray, have it handy and be prepared to use it, test it regularly, replace it regularly, be aware of the wind direction. Practise self-defence training and strategies in your mind.

Train your mind to think like the minds of your warrior ancestors who survived attacks – your existence is proof of that. You have exactly the same genetic capabilities. Train your dog to be a disciplined effective protector, not a stupid fool of an animal. If you see a group of people who look like muggers, they probably are muggers. Do not give them the benefit of the doubt. Turn around.

Step onto higher ground, arm yourself with a rock (a crude but effective tool). Pencil flares make a great defensive weapon … no licence required.

Use the rock after the pepper spray. Do not be attacked by a "wounded lion". Decide in advance whether or not you will defend yourself, i.e. if you can, or whether you will just roll over and be mugged. But whatever you do, do not entertain the notion that there will be some ranger or ready assistant, willing to jump in to the fray and save your bacon.

I went for a bike ride on Table Mountain this morning. I found the rain-soaked contents of a stolen bag: some shorts, many pens, an asthma pump, a tampon tin etc. One should not take things with you that you are not replaceable. Your backpack should be a sacrificial item. Car keys, ID, passports, credit cards and so on must never be in a bag that can be snatched. These items should be attached to the person in concealed pockets.

Another thing I strongly suggest is that people get involved with their Neighbourhood Watch or similar groups. Many "Westernised" people live their lives in a series of bubbles. A cushy office environment, the car, then the mall, then home and TV and video games. People are totally disempowered and out of touch. And as a result, fearful.

A Neighbourhood Watch has something for everyone. Committee-type people can organise patrol rosters. Sociable people can patrol and have contact with a friend while providing a great service. Lone wolves (like me) can ease around the suburb doing ad-hoc patrols keeping their eyes open, a radio call away from backup. Every half-hour spent out there is one half-hour more protection.

We must realise that Pax Romana is over. We now need to revert to frontier-style living. We need to take care of ourselves like our forefathers did. Luckily, we are not up against the hordes of Attila the Hun, but rather a few cowardly individuals who, with collective effort, can easily be defeated. We just need to stand together and put in the time.

Canada

Well, I landed here over a week ago, time flies and time lags.
My dad died on the 19th of August.
After years of incapacitation the end came quickly for him.
I am pleased, for his life as it was, was no life I would wish on anyone.

I was 10 000m up at the time, having just flown over the mountains of
Norway (latitude Bergen) on a clear day … heading for Greenland,
looking down over rivers of ice,
vistas previously only imagined, now real, and yet unreal.
There is whisky and ice on the drinks trolley and brittle plastic glasses.
Read a few more pages, have a pee, pop a Stillnox tablet.
Sleep, wake up, reset the internal time clock.
No jetlag for Mr Scientific.

❦

Zaan is here.

Zaan has been here for some months.

Her little house on Anderson Street, Wortley Village, London, Ontario, is a
paradise. It is not an Atlantic seaboard mansion, or a villa on the Via Castello
where one is served delicacies by scheming Filipino servants. No, it is much
better than that. It is a tranquil hideaway in a park full of trees. Every room
is filled with the essence of calm. Small rooms of perfect proportion and
lovely doors and architraves. The essence of calm flows out of (or in from)
the back door onto the wooden deck recently built by Zaan. Giant trees rise
up all around, creating a world of green and dappled light. Woodpeckers,
orioles, bluejays, humming birds, chickadees, nuthatches and many others
are constantly busy at the bird-feeders and all around. One can usually see
twenty birds at a glance. Chipmunks and squirrels race among the plants in
the garden. Skunks come in the evening.

Zaan has a big silver diesel *bakkie* called a RAM. There are no small
bakkies in Canada. There are no Nissan 1400s or Opel Corsas or Toyota
Hiluxes or Nissan Hardbodies. There are AMCs and RAMs and big Fords
and big Chevrolets. On the roof of Zaan's *bakkie* are a pair of EPIC surf-skis.
The other day we went down to Port Stanley on Lake Erie. We paddled in the
lukewarm water, surfing the onshore chop. It was lovely. Today we rode our
bikes along the riverside trails to Springbank. It is so very peaceful. Canada
geese in V-formation honk overhead. No one causes *kak*. Everywhere you go,
one witnesses the efforts of Northern European types "making nice". Quite
the opposite of Afro-destructiveness. Zuma-ism, Mugabe-ism. We run in the
soft forest too … warm and dappled.

More news will follow. A trip to Toronto in a week's time and maybe a drive to the Algonquin National Park.

Be safe – Take care
Carl

Chapter 31

Hitchhiking in Natal

As a young man I sometimes worked in potentially dangerous areas. When surveying for the civils company I worked for (1983, '84, '85, '86), I carried a .45 pistol concealed on my person. I felt way less vulnerable.

When I was in the army I hitchhiked quite a bit. I always wore my pistol. On arriving at camp I handed the weapon in at the armoury and when I left, I picked it up.

I hitched to Johannesburg and to Bloemfontein. I hitched to Durban to visit my dad. I was dropped by a farmer at a farm gate somewhere near Bethlehem. It was getting dark. I arrived at the railway station in Ladysmith around midnight and sat out the remainder of the night on a wooden bench. And I have to say – the uncomfortable bump of the holster behind my right hip made me feel a lot better about where I was and what I was doing there.

One Sunday morning after visiting my dad, I was hoping for a lift on the side of the N3 in the direction of 'Maritzburg. There was a steep earthen road-cutting opposite and a drop-off behind me, a chain-link fence and then sugar cane. A HiAce minibus went past, then pulled over and stopped about 20m ahead. Two men got out. Five or six men remained in the vehicle. One walked past me and stood about 10m behind me. The other crossed the road and positioned himself opposite me. These were heavy, ominous men. SADF uniforms were not appreciated by that type in those days. Being early on a Sunday morning, cars were few and far between.

Suddenly, up the hill and around the bend, came a pale blue Jumbo Golf. I ran into the road waving my bag and signalling frantically. The Golf stopped and I jumped into the left rear door. I remember it like it was yesterday.

"You're fucking lucky, *boet*," said the driver.

Thirty seconds short of a shooting – saved by three "Dutchmen" heading for Midmar Dam for a day of fun and fishing.

A few months later, back in the navy, a buddy at Waterfall barracks named Mac told me a similar story. He had been on pass to visit his parents in Pietermaritzburg and was hitching down to Durban airport when a minibus pulled up. For him, there was no fence between the verge of the road and the sugarcane field. Mac ran for his life, crashing through the rows of cane and finally lying still until his pursuers lost interest and left.

29 September 2015   Letter #32

Hi Gareth

I hope that you are fine. We leave Canada tomorrow ... back to RSA.

Below are my notes from the month. Maybe you might like to dip into my thoughts and impressions.

Love
C

4 Sept 2015

One day in August a "black southeaster" was blowing with a lot more south in it than usual. It has been a weird winter. I have been running up and around Lion's Head for decades and I thought on that day I would go the back way to avoid the wind. The path runs uphill from a pair of old British guns and then does a few long switchbacks, zigging and zagging toward Bantry Bay and back again. I approached the big granite boulders at the end of the first "zig" and then turned onto the "zag" that leads away from the Fresnaye side (direction Table Mountain) when a whirlwind came barrelling down the mountainside, lifted my 96kg frame off the path and deposited me into the recently burnt, now newly revived bulb plant growth. My light blue CANADA cap went up a hundred metres or so toward the sea, then returned like a boomerang before disappearing into the sky! A second smaller dust devil followed, giving me a Kansas-style dusting.

Off I go to Oz, dear Dorothy! Such is a jet flight – to another hemisphere, another continent, another life-zone.

I landed in Toronto and caught the Robert Q bus down to London, Ontario. After life in South Africa, it is so calm here.

I travel quite a bit in southern Africa. Driving or railing by Gautrain from Johannesburg's Oliver Tambo International Airport towards Sandton is not much different from the outskirts of Toronto. It is the very heart of Economy RSA, and from this perspective, Toronto is not really any smarter. Johannesburg is an impressive machine of a city, make no mistake, but for those in the know, there is a sense of fermenting rot hidden away somewhere behind the warehouses and industrial headquarters, new concrete, massive highways and viaducts. Afro-pessimism – our equilibrium tipped by our daily experiences and the news we are exposed to. News of massive corruption that would not be tolerated in any civilised country. Zuma-pessimism, Malema-pessimism, Mugabe-pessimism. We cast our eyes north, to Sudan, Somalia, Nigeria, Zimbabwe … It seems that the people of Africa simply cannot run a country. We feel free to compare British and German cars, or British and Italian cuisine, or German and Italian soldiers, or British and German humour. We are comfortable with such comparisons of national traits, but heaven forbid if anybody compares Africans to anything. If we do, out comes the howling "Race Card"!

As I watch the country I love and the city I love slowly disintegrating due to unchecked population expansion, urbanisation, corruption, bad governance, cadre deployment, weakness of character and lack of political will, I unreservedly hold the view that if a selected group of German, Swiss, Norwegian or Canadian ex-pats were put in control of the country, it would soon enough be transformed into a going concern. It is not bad luck or bad weather or bad geography that causes the South African economy and the once "mighty" rand to slide terminally southwards. It is the South African. The South African is like the modern Greek – a hopeless basket case in desperate need of help.

I watch the walls and electric fences go up. Homes become fortresses. Alarms puncture our nights and days while dogs bark endlessly. Bad drivers copy other bad drivers and park wherever they wish. Taxi drivers assault their fares and are then surprised that people don't trust taxi drivers anymore. Home invasions occur with greater frequency and greater violence, circling like a dark force out of Tolkien's imagination. Weak Westernised men have become so disempowered that they no longer know how to bear arms and make a stand. It is pathetic. How does one raise children in South Africa?

Over-politicised young South Africans disrupt academic life at our universities. The statue of the great racist-imperialist Cecil John Rhodes is removed from the UCT campus. Removed from view, consciousness and memory.

Where does it stop? Must we tear down the Union Buildings and parliament and replace them with huts in the style of Shaka's uMgungundlovu?

If you think about Rhodes, was he any worse or better than the rapacious predatory genocidal King Shaka, or does his memory just happen to be the colour of the chip on the shoulder of the historically non-lettered young South African?

This is a mixed bag of thoughts all leading to one place, I guess.

In the 1970s when I reached boyhood consciousness, my parents worked in the performing arts. The orchestra was full of eastern European musicians. Many of the opera fans and concert aficionados were Germans and eastern Europeans. Men who had served on the Eastern Front. Women who had escaped from the rubble of Berlin and even Russian captivity. From East Germany, Romania and so on. Greta Weddepohl, Angelica Flegg, Gisela Gustavsson, Wolfgang Fischer, Helmut Klos, Werner Eichler, Zoltan Kovacs, Virgilio Gherasim and Willi Kinsky were some of the many I knew. Then there were others like the numerous enterprising engineering Italians, the Dutch families with all their children and the petit-bourgeois Anglo types from all over the Empire. The memories of the last shells and bullets of The War still cooling only 25 years behind them. As a boy in Belgium after WWII, our neighbour Bertrand dug up WWI shells to sell as scrap metal. Willi Kinsky sometimes talked of the tanks and conflict on the *Ostfront*. It was a devastated Europe that motivated these Europeans to move and settle in South Africa, and they moved to a country of sunshine and seemingly endless opportunity. My own dad came out as a four-year-old in 1938 – my grandparents seeking a brighter future away from the storm-clouds brewing in Europe.

My own dad at 4

Many of South Africa's Jews came from Lithuania. In the late 1970s my high school was 45% Jewish. In the 1980s, like rats on a sinking ship, they began to move. Almost all the Jewish kids in my school left for the USA, Canada, Australia and New Zealand. So clever they were at it … thousands of years of providing stepping stones for one another. Rematerialising all over the globe, thriving, then becoming fearful or persecuted, and moving on again. The organism called the Jewish diaspora. Most of my goy pals went, too.

Where do we go, must we go, can we survive, will it get better? No, of course it won't, but.

Zaan and I are having a splendid holiday here in Canada. It feels seriously weird for me at times, taking it easy for prolonged periods. My mindset is not well geared for kicking back. I had a long holiday in 1993 sailing to Italy and wintering on Capri. Then Capri and Norway again in 2003. And now again in 2015!

There was one or other kind of pressure or work on all the trips I took over those years. Engine rooms and children and being on the schedules of those in charge. Zaan calls it "being on someone else's clock".

Here in Canada, Zaan and I are on our own clock. It is very pleasant, but I keep having to banish the thought that I don't really deserve it. A Calvinist hangover – Northern European workaholism.

Time goes fast and slow. Two weeks in Canada are like soft rubber. It seems like a short time and yet I can barely remember arriving.

It has been a wonderful restful period for me. We exercise every day. An 8km run in a forest on a soft path, or a 10km flat paddle on Fanshawe Lake or surfing the wind chop on Lake Erie, or a 20 to 30km bike ride on forest and riverside pathways. The warm, scented summer air of the bursting Northern Hemisphere meadows and woodlands is unbelievable, triggering memories layered upon memories of places visited over decades and places never even visited but only dreamed of. Goldenrods, cornflowers, white scented meadow blooms, daisies, cat-tails and dappled light.

I have also slept a lot … unbelievable deep, long, untroubled sleeps and afternoon sleeps. No fear of the creeping ones at night. Catching up on sleeps missing from years. Sleeps thick with dreaming. Wonderful movies directed by my own subconscious mind. Dreams that continue all night long, picking up where they left off if I wake up to go for a pee or just wake for the fun of it.

7 September 2015

07h30 … Zaan and I hopped on a VIA Rail train to Toronto. Zaan booked us in for two nights at the Sheraton overlooking the City Hall. Toronto is a big city with many exquisite glass buildings that must kill a lot of birds every year. We walk and walk for three days. The 7th is Labour Day so there is a big air-show with F16s and F18s and even a WW2 Mustang which by comparison is painfully underpowered. An aircraft that, in its day, was a super-high-tech flying dragon – a long-range bomber escort, destroyer of European trains and retreating German columns.

We walk to China Town, Little Italy and Little Portugal, which all seem to have fallen foul of globalisation and lost much of their national identities. We walk to the Distillery district. We spend hours in the AGO (Art Gallery Ontario), Canadian art, Group of Seven, Camera Atomica, Henry Moore. We spend hours in the Royal Ontario Museum … Etruscans, Chinese, Ancient Egypt, Koreans, Mexican fabrics and hundreds of massive dinosaur skeletons … a fabulous submersion in ancient cultures and millions of years of pre-history.

Zaan cleverly upgraded our room to one with a fantastic view and access to the upstairs lounge with unlimited Starbucks coffee, breakfast (eggs, butter, toasted croissants and bagels, cheese, jam, fruit and Bircher Muesli) and an unlimited evening *hors-d'oeuvre* buffet (chicken wings, codfish smackeroos, ranch dressing, salads). Needless to say, I did the business, feasting to the gills.

On Wednesday we were due to leave for London on the 17h30 train, but a bomb scare delayed us for a few hours and we only got in at 11pm … lucky for the unlimited breakfast.

13 September 2015

Last night we left the *bakkie* unlocked and one of the local trolls took the opportunity to steal my Leatherman, my new sunglasses and Zaan's driver's licence. Fools that we were. Apparently there is a lot of that kind of thing about.

On Tuesday 15 Sept, Zaan and I left on a week-long road trip, returning home last evening via the back roads. The London city limits were a culture shock (druggies and a beggar with a rough cardboard sign) after cruising for hours and hours on a perfect late summer's day through the farmlands of

Ontario. Saturated light and bucolic perfection: red barns, horses and cows, neat farmsteads, tall forested areas, rivers and bridges, big shiny pick-up trucks and men in checked shirts, combine harvesters gathering dark brown wheat and maize fields like two-metre-thick carpets squaring off the miles and over the hills.

We left Whitefish Falls at about 10am and drove via Parry Sound where we had intended to paddle and spend one more night, but the driving just took over (our bodies simply too well exercised to contemplate putting the surf-skis on the water).

On the 15th we drove up to the small port town of Tobermory and found a perfect self-catering cabin right on the edge of the lake, complete with a jetty, ducks, seagulls and a view across the sound of the twice-daily ferry docking and departing.

The next morning, we headed off on our skis up the inlet known as Big Tub Harbour, at the top of which are two shipwrecks from the late 1800s. The water is crystal clear and fresh, which feels odd being accustomed to a lifetime of salt water.

So there we were, only just over a week ago, Zaan and I, on the Bruce Peninsula at Tobermory where the sea is fresh (because it is actually Lake Huron). We have Zaan's big RAM *bakkie*, two Epic surf-skis, two Fuji bicycles, an espresso pot and a bag of gear each. We walk in the national park through the forests of birch and cedar. We paddle along the limestone cliffs of Georgian Bay and cycle on the smooth, seldom used roads of a large property development. The bikes are silent, there are few birds, the verge between the edge of the tar and the forest is full of summer growth and wild flowers. The warmth of the days is sublime.

After three nights in Tobermory, we take the big ferry to South Baymouth on Manitoulin Island. It is a day of light squalls. Cool. Being seasonal, most things have already closed down for the winter. We drive all the way up to Meldrum Bay, then back to Lake Wolsley where we hire a rudimentary cabin. Zaan and I paddle a few kilometres and out through a bridge culvert in to larger windy waters of the north channel. Later on, we eat one side of a huge rainbow trout given to us by a couple of fishermen. During the night, rain falls gloriously on the roof of our little cabin. We lie under a pair of smoky old quilts. As the squalls pass, the dripping from the oaks takes over with a heavier but more inconsistent beat.

The next morning we pack up and drive east through Little Current and on to Whitefish Falls where we stop for a late breakfast at the Red River Lodge (just over the Bailey Bridge). We rent a three-bedroom cabin for $90 (Canadian) and feast for $10 a head. That evening we paddle on the lake at Willisville. Big rocks of the Canadian Shield rise out of the water. There are dense forests above. It is extremely beautiful.

20 September 2015

Zaan and I head out early on a long paddle west (into the breeze) into the Bay of Islands. We stop to rest from time to time on warm islands of ice-smoothed igneous rock. The striations of the last ice age are clearly visible everywhere as though the glaciers had only recently melted away. When we finally turn around, the wind has come up and whips us straight back to Whitefish Falls with very little effort required from the paddlers.

21 September 2015

A drive back to London via Espanola and Parry Sound on a perfect late summer's day.

26 September 2015

Saturday … I rode my red bike along the river and up past the green iron bridge, then turned inland and up into the suburbs. The houses are modest but neat. There are no burglar bars. There are few fences of any kind. Most lawns merge into one another. Night-creepers have not really started making *kak* here yet. They already do in the big cities. It is starting in London (Ontario). *Tikkoppe* gain access to unlocked cars at night but seldom smash a window. I rode back down to the big fountain at The Forks, where the two branches of the Thames meet. The Canada Geese are gathering, honking to their comrades as they come in to land. The birds are busy now, as they put the last warm days of this prolonged summer to good use. Soon it will be cold, and then very cold. The first red leaves are showing. In a few days' time Zaan and I fly back to South Africa – Land of Hope and Glory (once) – now Land of Worry and Ingloriousness as the rotten ones ply their trades – their deadly cocktail of corruption and incompetence.

I spent an hour this morning talking to an elderly Canadian Hussar outside the little Hussar's museum near Gibbon's Park. We talked about life and history and travelling in countries that once were Rome. The smells of today's ride have been reminiscent of my short stay in London (England) and subsequent visits to the UK.

Europe – South Africa – Canada

Europe: The last time I travelled in Europe (Norway excluded) was in 2003. That was twelve years ago and it was already crowded. Packed. Great for an historical or cultural holiday, but not a place to live and work. I do pine for Europe, however. For places I have visited like Istanbul, the Wienerwalt and the Mediterranean countries as well as places I have not been to, like Praha and Barcelona. *Gambon* and olive oil, black pepper and red wine. Tio Pepe e *taralli con mandorle. Pasta di crostini di Parmigiano. Pasta di primavera.*

South Africa: Wild and exciting. A place where adventures can be had every day. Perhaps even a little too wild and exciting at times. A place where people are seemingly free to misbehave across the spectrum, from traffic violations to wholesale corruption and even murder.

Canada: Cold in winter, perhaps too cold. A gentle place to be. A place to exist in safety. A comfortable place where people generally behave themselves.

Animals of Ontario seen by me this trip:
Many birds including Canada Geese, woodpecker, nuthatches, orioles, flickers and eagles.
2 Groundhogs
1 Deer
1 Rabbit in the mouth of a red-fox at Meldrum Bay
2 live snakes and 1 dead one on Bruce Peninsula
1 Racoon swimming in the North Channel off Lake Wolseley
1 Big rainbow while paddling on Lake Wolseley
2 Skunks being fed peanuts from Zaan's back deck
2 Chipmunks being fed peanuts in Zaan's garden
100s of DOGS ON LEADS! Why? "Dog on a string," I call them. I can only assume that these people need to have a bit of absurdity in their lives, or maybe they enjoy picking up warm shit in little coloured plastic bags (pervy), or perhaps they need to have something they can order around in the imperative. Just crazy.

Chapter 32

Europa

Fast forward – August 2018.

I spoke to a woman working at Keflavik airport. She had left Kenya 30 years earlier and for the last ten had made her home in Reykjavik.

She told me that she was so distressed about the "black-on-black racism" in South Africa. She talked about the burning and looting of Somalian businesses. "Can I call it racism?" she asked.

I said, "In South Africa they call it *xenophobia* … a euphemism … a rose by any other name."

"I despair of my people," she replied, "and their capacity for corruption and breaking things down. That is why I left."

Iceland is an extremely tough place. Even in midsummer it is very cold. It is almost unimaginable that people settled there over a thousand years ago and not only survived but built a very civilised country. There were not even any trees to chop down for firewood. Hard work and planning prevailed against massive odds. Avarice and war had their day, but now it is a peaceful, liberal and model democracy. I try to imagine what Madagascar or Nigeria might be like if they were governed by Icelanders. Does a warm climate and good weather automatically lead to social malfunction? What is it?

Like the Kenyan woman did three decades earlier, I too have been casting my mind around the globe, wondering where I might relocate in order to spare myself the sadness of witnessing, and living through, the breaking of our beloved South Africa. It is very difficult. Over the years so many of my contemporaries have exiled themselves. They made their calculations and have existed far away, living with decades of longing. Cape Town – what a wonderful place to live. But the Zuma years have exacerbated latent Afro-pessimism.

Zaan and I travelled on a fast train from Munich to Salzburg. At every station I looked for and only managed to spot one piece of litter: an empty plastic bottle lying below a platform just outside Salzburg. The trains are on time and no one sets fire to the carriages. I see no informal settlements beside the tracks. People obey the law. They wait for the little green person to appear before crossing the road. Nobody makes a random U-turn. Through hard work, imagination and planning, a paradise arose in *Mitteleuropa* after the destruction of World War II. Refugees from Syria, Somalia, Afghanistan and elsewhere now clamour for a home there. I had not been to *Mitteleuropa* for twenty-five years and felt the need to revisit the city and the places where my parents courted. A closure of sorts.

<hr />

Through the countryside Zaan and I whizzed in safety and comfort. In 1945, only 73 years earlier, a train ride here would have been perilous. Allied Mustangs and Typhoons scoured the land like fire-dragons, swooping down and firing rockets at anything that moved. The forests were full of routed armies on the run. Snipers sniped and hid themselves away. Hitler's armies fought and fled. Children attacked Russian tanks with *Panzerfäusts* in the streets of Berlin. Twelve-year-old boy soldiers reportedly burst into tears when they were taken prisoner. The hardened Russian invaders found it difficult to shoot them. Thirteen of Gustav Klimt's paintings were apparently destroyed, along with Schloss Immendorf, by retreating German soldiers.

If you take a walk around the picture-postcard streets of Salzburg and spare a moment to look down every now and then, you will notice, set into the sidewalk, at the doorways of homes or shops, 4x4-inch brass squares called *stolpersteine*: the silent, screaming memorials to Nazi victims, human beings who had been dragged from their homes or places of work and transported like animals to face the grossest inhumanity or slaughter. Auschwitz, Dachau, Theresienstadt.

Bend down and read:

HIER WOHNTE
GOTTFRIED NEUNHÄUSERER
DEPORTIERT1941
SCHLOSS HARTHEIM
ERMORDET 8.5.1941

In the 1930s and early 1940s people lined up to join the Nazis.
Enthusiastic crowds filled the streets,
Overjoyed to be part of Adolf Hiltler's "One Thousand Year Reich".
We all know about the devastation that followed.
The Rwandan genocide was no less horrific.

"The ANC will rule until Jesus comes," said Zuma, but still we fear Malema and his red-clad EFF mob for their similarity to Hitler and his Brownshirts. The rising tide of populism.

We know that sooner or later they must fall, the tyrants and the dictators, but the killing and looting and destruction is why civilised people are filled with dread.

History is great in history books and very interesting in museums.

The history of Europe tells us that things can change very radically and very quickly.*

Will the EU empire survive? What about Putin?

The question is … can bad history be dodged?

* Timeline:
476, the fall of Rome, C5 C6 C7 the Germanic invasions, C7 C8 the Muslim/Moorish invasions, C9 C10 the Viking invasions, C11 attack on Muslim Spain begins, C12 Crusades begin, followed by centuries of wars in Europe.

Pre-500 BCE

c. 5000 BCE Talheim Death Pit,
c. 1104–900 BCE Dorian invasion
c. 753–351 BCE Roman–Etruscan Wars
c. 753–494 BCE Roman–Sabine wars
743–724 BCE First Messenian War
710–650 BCE Lelantine War
c. 700–601 BCE Alban war with Rome
685–668 BCE Second Messenian War
669–668 BCE Sparta–Argos War
600–265 BCE Greek–Punic Wars
595–585 BCE First Sacred War
560 BCE Second Arcadian War
540 BCE Battle of Alalia
538–522 BCE Polycrates wars

500–200 BCE

509–396 BCE Early Italian campaigns
500–499 BCE Persian invasion of Naxos
492–490 BCE First Persian invasion of Greece
482–479 BCE Second Persian invasion of Greece
480–307 BCE Sicilian Wars
460–445 BCE First Peloponnesian War
449–448 BCE Second Sacred War
440–439 BCE Samian War
431–404 BCE Second Peloponnesian War
395–387 BCE Corinthian War
390–387 BCE Celtic invasion of Italia
335 BCE Alexander's Balkan campaign
323–322 BCE Lamian War
280–275 BCE Pyrrhic War
267–261 BCE Chremonidean War
264–241 BCE First Punic War
229–228 BCE First Illyrian War
220–219 BCE Second Illyrian War
218–201 BCE Second Punic War
214–205 BCE First Macedonian War

200 BCE onwards

200–197 BCE Second Macedonian War
191–189 BCE Aetolian War
171–168 BCE Third Macedonian War
135–132 BCE First Servile War
113–101 BCE Cimbrian War

113 BCE – CE 439 Germanic Wars
104–100 BCE Second Servile War
91–88 BCE Social War
88–87 BCE Sulla's first civil war
85 BCE Colchis uprising against Pontus
83–72 BCE Sertorian War
82–81 BCE Sulla's second civil war
78 BCE Marcus Aemilius Lepidus
73–71 BCE Third Servile War
73–63 BCE Roman Expansion in Syria and Judea
65–63 BCE Pompey's campaign in Iberia and Albania
63–62 BCE Second Catilinarian conspiracy
55–54 BCE Caesar's invasions of Britain
58–51 BCE Gallic Wars
49–45 BCE Caesar's Civil War
44–36 BCE Sicilian revolt
43 BCE Battle of Mutina
43–42 BCE Liberators' civil war
41–40 BCE Perusine War
32–30 BCE Final War of the Roman Republic

1st–10th century CE

35–41 Iberian-Parthian war
49–96 Roman conquest of Britain
51 Armenian–Iberian war
69 Year of the Four Emperors
69–70 Revolt of the Batavi
193 Year of the Five Emperors
208–210 Roman invasion of Caledoni
238 Year of the Six Emperors
271–278 Colchis–Roman War
284–285 Roman civil war
306–324 Civil wars of the Tetrarchy
350–351 Roman civil war
360–361 Roman civil war
367–368 Great Conspiracy
376–382 Gothic War
387–388 Roman civil war
394 Roman civil war of 394 AD
482–484 Iberian-Persian War
526–532 Iberian War
535–554 Gothic War

541–562 Lazic War
582–602 Maurice's Balkan campaigns
c. 600–793 Frisian–Frankish wars
650–799 Arab–Khazar wars
680–1355 Byzantine–Bulgarian wars
711–718 Umayyad conquest of Hispania
715–718 Frankish Civil War (715–718)
722–1492 Reconquista
735–737 Georgian-Umayyad Caliphate War
772–804 Saxon Wars
c. 800/862–973 Hungarian invasions of Europe
830s Paphlagonian expedition of the Rus'
839–1330 Bulgarian–Serbian Wars
854–1000 Croatian–Bulgarian wars
860 Rus'–Byzantine War
865–878 Invasion of the Great Heathen Army
907 Rus'–Byzantine War
914 Arab-Georgian War
939 Battle of Andernach
941 Rus'–Byzantine War
955 Battle of Recknitz
970–971 Sviatoslav's invasion of Bulgaria
982 Battle of Stilo
983 Great Slav Rising

11th century
1002–1018 German–Polish War
1014–1208 Byzantine–Georgian wars
1015–1016 Pisan–Genoese expeditions to Sardinia
1015–1016 Cnut's invasion of England
1018 Battle of Vlaardingen
1024 Battle of Listven
1024 Rus'–Byzantine War
1043 Rus'–Byzantine War
1044 Battle of Ménfő
1048–1064 Invasion of Denmark
1050–1185 Byzantine–Norman wars
1057 Battle of Petroe
1060 Battle of the Theben Pass
1066 Norwegian invasion of England
1066–1088 Norman conquest of England
1067–1194 Norman invasion of Wales

1067 Battle on the Nemiga River
1068 Battle of the Alta River
1073–1075 Saxon Rebellion
1075 Revolt of the Earls
1077–1088 Great Saxon Revolt
1078 Battle of Kalavrye
1088 Rebellion of 1088
1093 Battle of Schmilau
1093 Battle of the Stugna River
1097 Battle of Gvozd Mountain
1099–1204 Georgian–Seljuk wars

12th century
1109 Battle of Głogów
1115 Battle of Welfesholz
1121 Battle of Didgori
1126 Battle of Chlumec
1130–1240 Civil war era in Norway
1135–54 The Anarchy
1142–1445 Swedish–Novgorodian Wars
1144–1162 Baussenque Wars
1159–1345 Wars of the Guelphs and Ghibellines
1164 Battle of Verchen
1169–1175 Norman invasion of Ireland
1173–1174 Revolt of 1173–74
1185–1204 Uprising of Asen and Peter
1198 Battle of Gisors
1198–1290 Livonian Crusade

13th century
1201 Battle of Stellau
1202 Siege of Zadar
1202–1214 Anglo–French War
1205 Battle of Zawichost
1208–1227 Conquest of Estonia
1209 1229 Albigensian Crusade
1211 Welsh uprising of 1211
1215–1217 First Barons' War
1216–1222 War of Succession of Champagne
1220–1264 Age of the Sturlungs
1223–1241 Mongol invasion of Europe
1223–1480 Tatar raids in Russia
1224 Siege of La Rochelle
1227 Battle of Bornhöved

1231–1233 Friso-Drentic War
1234–1238 Georgian-Molgol War
1239–1245 Teltow War
1242 Saintonge War
1256–1258 War of the Euboeote Succession
1256–1381 Venetian–Genoese Wars
1256–1422 Friso-Hollandic Wars
1260 Battle of Kressenbrunn
1262–1266 Scottish–Norwegian War
1264–1267 Second Barons' War
1265 Battle of Isaszeg
1275–1276 The war against Valdemar
Birgersson
1276–1278 6000-mark war
1276 War of Navarra
1277–1280 Uprising of Ivaylo
1278 Battle on the Marchfeld
1282–1302 War of the Sicilian Vespers
1283–1289 War of the Limburg Succession
1288–1295 War of the Outlaws
1296–1357 Wars of Scottish Independence
1297–1305 Franco-Flemish War
1298 Battle of Göllheim

14th century
1302 Battle of the Golden Spurs
1304–1310 The Swedish brother's feud
1307 Battle of Lucka
1311–1312 Rebellion of mayor Albert
1312 Battle of Rozgony
1321–1322 Despenser War
1321–1328 Byzantine civil war of 1321–28
1322 Battle of Bliska
1323–1328 Peasant revolt in Flanders
1324 War of Saint-Sardos
1326–1332 Polish–Teutonic War
1333–1338 Burke Civil War
1337–1453 Hundred Years' War
1340–1392 Galicia–Volhynia Wars
1340–1396 Bulgarian–Ottoman wars
1341–1347 Byzantine civil war of 1341–47
1342–1350 Zealot's Rebellion
1343–1345 St. George's Night Uprising
1347–1352 Neapolitan campaigns of Louis
the Great

1350–1498 Wars of the Vetkopers and
Schieringers
1350–1490 Hook and Cod wars
1356–1358 Jacquerie
1356–1375 War of the Two Peters
1362 Battle of Helsingborg
1362–1457 War of the Bands
1366–1369 Castilian Civil War
1366–1526 Ottoman–Hungarian Wars
1369–1370 First Fernandine War
1371–1913 Serbian–Ottoman wars
1371 Battle of Baesweiler
1371–1379 War of the Guelderian Succession
1371–1381 War of Chioggia
1372–1373 Second Fernandine War
1373–1379 Byzantine civil war of 1373–79
1375 Gugler War
1375–1378 War of the Eight Saints
1381 Peasants' Revolt
1381–1382 Third Fernandine War
1381–1384 Lithuanian Civil War
(1381–84)
1382 Harelle and Maillotins Revolt
1381–1404 Second Georgian–Mongol War
1389 Battle of Kosovo
1389–1392 Lithuanian Civil War
(1389–92)
1395 Battle of Nicopolis

15th century
1400–1415 Glyndŵr Rising
1401–1429 Appenzell Wars
1407–1468 Georgian-Turkoman War
1409–1411 Polish–Lithuanian–Teutonic
War
1410–1435 War of Slesvig
1414 Hunger War
1419–1434 Hussite Wars
1422 Gollub War
1422 Battle of Arbedo
1425–1454 Wars in Lombardy
1431–1435 Polish–Teutonic War
1434–1436 Engelbrekt rebellion
1437 Budai Nagy Antal revolt

1438–1556 Russo-Kazan Wars
1440–1446 Old Zürich War
1441 Battle of Samobor
1443–1444 Long campaign
1445 First Battle of Olmedo
1447–1448 Albanian–Venetian War
1449–1450 First Margrave War
1449 Battle of Castione
1449–1453 Revolt of Ghent
1450 Jack Cade's Rebellion
1451–1455 Navarrese Civil War
1453–1454 Morea revolt
1454–1466 Thirteen Years' War
1455–1485 Wars of the Roses
1462–1485 Rebellion of the Remences
1462–1472 Catalan Civil War
1463–1479 Ottoman–Venetian War
1465 Battle of Montlhéry
1465–1468 Wars of Liège
1466–1469 Irmandiño Wars
1467 Second Battle of Olmedo
1467–1479 War of the Priests
1468 Waldshut War
1468–1478 Bohemian War
1470–1471 Dano-Swedish War
1470–1474 Anglo-Hanseatic War
1475–1479 War of the Castilian Succession
1477–1488 Austrian–Hungarian War (1477–88)
1478 Carinthian Peasant Revolt
1478 Battle of Giornico
1479 Battle of Guinegate
1482–1484 War of Ferrara
1484 Battle of Lochmaben Fair
1485–1488 Mad War
1487 Battle of Crevola
1487 War of Rovereto
1488 Battle of Sauchieburn
1492–1583 Muscovite–Lithuanian Wars
1493 Battle of Krbava Field
1493–1593 Hundred Years' Croatian–Ottoman War
1494–1498 Italian War of 1494–98
1495–1497 Russo-Swedish War
1497 Cornish Rebellion of 1497

1497 Battle of Rotebro
1499 Swabian War
1499–1504 Italian War of 1499–1504

16th century
c. 1500–1854 Lekianoba
1501-1512 Dano-Swedish War (1501–12)
1502–1543 Guelders Wars
1503–1505 War of the Succession of Landshut
1508–1516 War of the League of Cambrai
1509–1510 Polish–Moldavian War
1514 Poor Conrad's Rebellion
1514 Dózsa rebellion
1514–1517 Saxon feud
1515 Slovene Peasant Revolt
1515–1523 Frisian peasant rebellion
1519–1521 Polish–Teutonic War
1520–1521 Revolt of the Comuneros
1521–1523 Revolt of the Brotherhoods
1521–1523 Swedish War of Liberation
1521–1718 Ottoman–Habsburg wars
1522–1523 Knights' Revolt
1522–1559 Habsburg-Valois Wars
1524–1525 German Peasants' War
1526 Revolt of Espadán
1529 First War of Kappel
1531 Second War of Kappel
1531-1532 War of Two Kings
1534 Silken Thomas Rebellion
1534–1535 Münster Rebellion
1534–1536 Count's Feud
1536-1537 Reformation in Norway
1536–1537 Pilgrimage of Grace
1540 Salt War
1542–1543 Dacke War
1543–1550 Rough Wooing
1546–1547 Schmalkaldic War
1549 Kett's Rebellion
1549 Prayer Book Rebellion
1550 Battle of Sauðafell
1552–1555 Second Margrave War
1554 Wyatt's rebellion
1554–1557 Russo-Swedish War
1558–1583 Livonian War

1560 Siege of Leith
1562–1598 French Wars of Religion
1563–1570 Northern Seven Years' War
1565 Great Siege of Malta
1566 Siege of Szigetvár
1568–1570 Morisco Revolt
1568–1648 Eighty Years' War
1569–1570 Rising of the North
1569–1573 First Desmond Rebellion
1573 Croatian–Slovene Peasant Revolt
1578 Georgian-Ottoman War
1579–1583 Second Desmond Rebellion
1580–1583 War of the Portuguese Succession
1583–1588 Cologne War
1585–1604 Anglo-Spanish War
1588–1654 Dutch–Portuguese War
1587–1588 War of the Polish Succession
1590–1595 Russo-Swedish War
1593 Battle of Sisak
1593–1606 Long Turkish War
1593–1617 Moldavian Magnate Wars
1594–1603 Nine Years' War (Ireland)
1595–1621 Moldavian Magnate Wars
1596–1597 Cudgel War
1598–1599 War against Sigismund

17th century
1600–1629 Polish–Swedish War
1602 Savoyard escalade of Geneva
1605–1618 Polish–Muscovite War
1606–1607 Bolotnikov Rebellion
1606–1608 Zebrzydowski Rebellion
1610–1617 Ingrian War
1611–1613 Kalmar War
1615–1618 Uskok War
1618–1648 Thirty Years' War
1618–1639 Bündner Wirren
1620–1621 Polish–Ottoman War
1625 Zhmaylo Uprising
1627–1629 Anglo-French War
1628–1631 War of the Mantuan Succession
1630 Fedorovych Uprising
1632–1634 Smolensk War
1637 Pavlyuk Uprising

1638 Ostryanyn Uprising
1639–1653 Wars of the Three Kingdoms
1640–1668 Portuguese Restoration War
1648–1657 Khmelnytsky Uprising
1651 Kostka-Napierski Uprising
1651–1986 Three Hundred and Thirty Five Years' War
1652–1674 Anglo-Dutch Wars
1653 Swiss peasant war of 1653
1654 First Bremian War
1654–1667 Russo–Polish War
1655–1660 Second Northern War
1656 War of Villmergen
1663–1664 Austro-Turkish War
1666 Second Bremian War
1666–1671 Polish–Cossack–Tatar War
1667–1668 War of Devolution
1670–1671 Razin's Rebellion
1672 First Kuruc Uprising
1672–1678 Franco-Dutch War
1672–1673 Second Genoese–Savoyard War
1675–1679 Scanian War
1676–1681 Russo-Turkish War
1679 Covenanter Rebellion
1683–1684 War of the Reunions
1683–1699 Great Turkish War
1685 Monmouth Rebellion
1688–1697 Nine Years' War
1689–1692 First Jacobite Rising

18th century
1700 Lithuanian Civil War
1700–1721 Great Northern War
1701–1713 War of the Spanish Succession
1703–1711 Rákóczi's War of Independence
1707–1708 Bulavin Rebellion
1712 Toggenburg War
1714–1718 Ottoman-Venetian War
1715–1716 Jacobite rising of 1715
1716–1718 Austro-Turkish War
1718–1720 War of the Quadruple Alliance
1722–1723 Russo-Persian War
1727–1729 Anglo-Spanish War
1733–1738 War of the Polish Succession
1735–1739 Russo-Turkish War

1737–1739 Austro-Turkish War
1740–1748 War of the Austrian Succession
1740–1763 Silesian Wars
1741–1743 Russo-Swedish War
1745–1746 Jacobite rising of 1745
1756–1763 Seven Years' War
1757 Georgian-Ottoman Battle
1763–1864 Russo-Circassian War
1768–1772 War of the Bar Confederation
1768–1774 Russo–Turkish War
1770 Georgian–Ottoman Battle
1770 Orlov Revolt
1774–1775 Pugachev's Rebellion
1775–1783 American Revolutionary War
1778–1779 War of the Bavarian Succession
1784 Kettle War
1784–1785 Revolt of Horea, Cloşca and Crişan
1785 Battle of the Sunja
1787 Dutch Patriot Revolt
1787–1792 Russo-Turkish War
1788–1791 Austro-Turkish War
1788–1790 Russo-Swedish War
1790 Saxon Peasants' Revolt
1792 Polish–Russian War of 1792
1792–1802 French Revolutionary Wars
1794 Kościuszko Uprising
1795 Battle of Krtsanisi
1798 Irish Rebellion of 1798
1798 Peasants' War

19ᵗʰ century
1803 Souliote War
1803–1815 Napoleonic Wars
1804–1813 First Serbian Uprising
1804–1813 Russo-Persian War
1806–1812 Russo-Turkish War
1808–1809 Finnish War
1809 Polish–Austrian War
1815–1817 Second Serbian Uprising
1817–1864 Russian conquest of the Caucasus
1821–1832 Greek War of Independence
1821 Wallachian uprising
1823 French invasion of Spain

1826–1828 Russo-Persian War
1827 War of the Malcontents
1828–1829 Russo-Turkish War
1828–1834 Liberal Wars
1830 Ten Days' Campaign (following the Belgian Revolution)
1830–1831 November Uprising
1831 Canut revolts
1831–1832 Bosnian Uprising
1831–1836 Tithe War
1832 War in the Vendée and Chouannerie of 1832
1832 June Rebellion
1833–1839 First Carlist War
1833–1839 Albanian Revolts of 1833–39
1843–1844 Albanian Revolt of 1843–44
1846 Galician slaughter
1846–1849 Second Carlist War
1847 Albanian Revolt of 1847
1847 Sonderbund War
1848–1849 Hungarian Revolution and War of Independence
1848–1851 First Schleswig War
1848–1849 First Italian War of Independence
1853–1856 Crimean War
1854 Epirus Revolt of 1854
1858 Mahtra War
1859 Second Italian War of Independence
1861–62 Montenegrin–Ottoman War (1861–62)
1863–1864 January Uprising
1864 Second Schleswig War
1866 Austro-Prussian War
1866–1869 Cretan Revolt
1866 Third Italian War of Independence
1867 Fenian Rising
1870–1871 Franco-Prussian War
1872–1876 Third Carlist War
1873–1874 Cantonal Revolution
1875–77 Herzegovina Uprising (1875–77)
1876–78 Serbian–Ottoman War (1876–78)
1876–78 Montenegrin–Ottoman War (1876–78)
1877–1878 Russo-Turkish War

1878 Epirus Revolt of 1878
1885 Serbo-Bulgarian War
1897 Greco-Turkish War

20th century

The Russian Army's Vostok Battalion in
South Ossetia
1903 Ilinden–Preobrazhenie Uprising
1904–1908 Macedonian Struggle
1904–1905 Russo-Japanese War
1905 Łódź insurrection
1905 Revolution of 1905
1906–1908 Theriso revolt
1907 1907 Romanian Peasants' Revolt
1910 Albanian Revolt of 1910
1910 5 October 1910 revolution
1910 Portuguese Monarchist Civil War
1911 Albanian Revolt of 1911
1911–1912 Italo-Turkish War
1912–1913 Balkan Wars
1912–1913 First Balkan War
1913 Second Balkan War
1913 Tikveš Uprising
1913 Ohrid–Debar Uprising
1914 Peasant Revolt in Albania
1914–1918 World War I
1916 Noemvriana
1917 Toplica Uprising
1918 Judenburg mutiny
1918 Cattaro Mutiny
1918 Aster Revolution
1918 Radomir Rebellion
1918 Finnish Civil War
1916 Easter Rising
1917 Russian Revolution
1917 February Revolution
1917 July Days
1917 Polubotkivtsi uprising
1917 Kornilov affair
1917 October Revolution
1917 Junker mutiny
1917 Kerensky–Krasnov uprising
1917–1921 Russian Civil War
1917–1918 Soviet-Turkish War (1917–
1918)

1917–1921 Ukrainian War of Independence
1917–1921 Ukrainian–Soviet War
1918–1919 Polish–Ukrainian War
1918–1924 Left-wing uprisings against the
Bolsheviks
1918 Left SR uprising
1921 Kronstadt rebellion
1918–1922 Heimosodat
1918 Viena expedition
1918 Aunus expedition
1918–1920 Petsamo expeditions
1918–1920 National revolt of Ingrian Finns
1921–1922 East Karelian Uprising
1918–1920 Estonian War of Independence
1918–1925 Allied intervention in the
Russian Civil War
1918–1920 North Russia Intervention
1918–1922 Siberian Intervention
1918 Georgian–Armenian War
1918–1920 Georgian–Ossetian conflict
(1918–20)
1918–1919 Georgian-Russian conflict over
Sochi
1918–1920 Armenian–Azerbaijani War
1918–1920 Latvian War of Independence
1918–1920 Lithuanian Wars of Independence
1918–1919 Lithuanian–Soviet War
1919 Lithuanian War of Independence (War
against the Bermontians)
1920 Polish–Lithuanian War
1919–1921 Polish–Soviet War
1921 Georgian–Russian War
1924 Georgian Uprising against Soviet
Union
1919–1920 Revolutions and interventions
in Hungary (1918–20)
1918–1919 Hungarian–Romanian War
1919 Sejny Uprising
1919 Khotin Uprising
1918 Georgian–Turkish War
1918–1919 Austro-Slovene conflict in
Carinthia
1918–1958 Polish–Czechoslovak border
conflicts

1919 Polish-Czech war for Teschen Silesia
1918–1919 German Revolution
1918–1919 Greater Poland Uprising
1919–1923 Turkish War of Independence
1919–1922 Greco-Turkish War
1918–1921 Franco-Turkish War
1920 Turkish–Armenian War
1919–1923 Royalist and separatist revolts
1919 Christmas Uprising
1919–1920 Italo-Yugoslav War
1919–1920 Czechoslovakia–Hungary War
1919–1921 Silesian Uprisings
1919 First Silesian Uprising
1920 Second Silesian Uprising
1921 Third Silesian Uprising
1919–1922 Irish War of Independence
1920 Husino rebellion
1920 Vlora War
1920 Kapp Putsch
1920 Ruhr Uprising
1920 Slutsk Defence Action
1920–1924 Biennio Rosso
1921 Uprising in West Hungary
1921 February Uprising
1922–1923 Irish Civil War
1923 Corfu incident
1923 September Uprising
1923 Klaipėda Revolt
1923 Leonardopoulos–Gargalidis coup d'état attempt
1924 1924 Estonian coup d'état attempt
1924 August Uprising
1925 Incident at Petrich
1932 Mäntsälä rebellion
1933 Casas Viejas incident
1933 Anarchist uprising in Spain (1933)
1934 Asturian miners' strike of 1934
1934 Austrian Civil War
1935 1935 Greek coup d'état attempt
1936–1939 Spanish Civil War
1938 1938 Greek coup d'état attempt
1939 Hungarian Invasion of the Carpatho-Ukraine
1939–1965 Spanish Maquis
1939–1945 World War II

1939 Nazi German invasion of Poland
1939 Soviet invasion of Poland
1939–1940 Winter War (Soviet invasion of Finland)
1940 Soviet invasion of the Baltic States
1940–1941 Greco-Italian War
1941–1945 Soviet–German War
1941–1944 Continuation War
1942–1956 Ukrainian Insurgent Army
1944 Slovak National Uprising
1944 Warsaw Uprising
1944–1956 Guerrilla war in the Baltic states
1945–1949 Greek Civil War
1947–1962 Romanian anti-communist resistance movement
1953 Uprising in East Germany
1956 Uprising in Poznań
1956 Hungarian Revolution
1956–1962 Operation Harvest
1958 Opération Corse
1958 First Cod War
1959–2011 Basque conflict
1967 Greek coup d'état
1968 Warsaw Pact invasion of Czechoslovakia
1968–1998 The Troubles
1970–1984 Unrest in Italy
1972 Bugojno group
1972–1973 Second Cod War
1974 Turkish invasion of Cyprus
1974 Carnation Revolution
1975–1976 Third Cod War
1975 Portuguese coup d'état attempt
1976–present Corsican Insurgency
1981 Spanish coup d'état attempt
1988–1994 Nagorno-Karabakh War
1989 Romanian Revolution
1990–1991 Soviet attacks on Lithuanian border posts
1991 January Events
1991 The Barricades
1991 Ten-Day War (Slovenia)
1991–1992 Georgian war against Russo-Ossetian alliance
1991–1993 Georgian Civil War

1991–1995 Croatian War of Independence
1992 Transnistria War
1992 East Prigorodny Conflict
1992–1993 First Georgian war against Russo-Abkhazian alliance
1992–1995 Bosnian War
1993 Cherbourg incident
1993 Russian constitutional crisis
1994–1996 First Chechen War
1995–1996 Imia/Kardak military crisis
1997–1998 Cyprus Missile Crisis
1997 Albanian civil war of 1997
1998–1999 Kosovo War
1998–present Dissident Irish Republican campaign
1998 Second Georgian war against Russian-Abkhazian alliance
1999 War of Dagestan
1999–2009 Second Chechen War
1999–2001 Insurgency in the Preševo Valley

21st century
2001 Insurgency in the Republic of Macedonia
2002 Perejil Island crisis
2004–2013 Unrest in Kosovo
2011–2013 North Kosovo crisis
2004 Georgia, Adjara crisis
2006 Georgia, Kodori crisis
2007–2015 Civil war in Ingushetia
2008 Russia–Georgia war
2009–2017 Insurgency in the North Caucasus
2013–2014 Euromaidan and pro-Russian unrest in Ukraine
2014 Crimean crisis
2014–present War in Donbass
2015 Kumanovo clashes
2016
2017
2018 … and so it goes.

25 October 2015   Letter #33

Hi GR

On the radio a while back (during the winter load-shedding) there was a discussion about saving water and electricity by taking shorter showers and so on. I have only fathered one child. My ex-wife and I therefore have a "breed-out footprint" of 0.5 persons each. In my opinion, that entitles me to longer, hotter showers than those who have "bred out" three, four or even five children. Looking at the exponential knock-on effect down the generational line, I should be entitled to even more benefits along with other single-child parents. There should be tax-cuts, free holidays, more fun et cetera ... I should be second in line only to those who have not "bred out" at all.

I have been in a no-news bubble for over 2 months. Only the odd snippets have managed to sneak through: headlines seen on the newsstand at the supermarket, a comment passed about the European refugee crisis or Oscar Pistorius being released from prison. I have just taken the morning to update myself a little as a result of a pack of about 10 political cartoons emailed to me by a friend. Cartoons featuring Putin, Iranian ayatollahs and nuclear missiles, Obama and Clinton. As I was not in the current news loop, I only understood one of them – the Bill Clinton one.

Okay, so there is a refugee crisis in Europe. 650 000 people have entered Europe this year. The population of Cairo is estimated at 17 million. That would equal about 3.8% of Cairo's population arriving in the whole of Europe. Is that a lot or is it a little? The entire 650 000 would only increase Istanbul's population by 4.6%. Is that a lot or is it a little?

I have two points of view. I naturally align myself with the modern organised European-style countries like Norway, Canada, Austria or New Zealand, and I totally abhor the idea of such "civilised" countries being swamped by masses of humans that so easily become *untermenschen* in the eyes of their reluctant hosts. But, by the same token, I realise that those who have fled their homes would never have done so unless truly horrible things, totally beyond their control, were going on. And just as I find myself powerless against the revolting, corrupt ANC and Zuma, and unable to wish away the likes of Malema, I realise that these refugees are equally powerless to do anything but run away. Their situation has simply become too bad.

Taking it all one step further, I remain amazed at the concept of passport, borders and nationality. Just as Darwin contemplates slavery in his **Voyage of the Beagle**, I contemplate these things.

The second paragraph of the **American Declaration of Independence** starts as follows: "We hold these truths to be self-evident, that all men [sic] are created equal, that they are endowed by their Creator [sic] with certain unalienable Rights, that among these are Life, Liberty and the Pursuit of Happiness. That to secure these rights, Governments are instituted among Men, deriving their just powers from the consent of the governed."

To me it is absurd to be allowed to keep a parrot in a cage or to think of owning a human slave, and it is equally absurd that I must have a document that permits me to travel freely to countries X, Y and Z while another member of my species holds a similar document (issued by a different government) that restricts his or her movement. Of course, I understand the practical necessities for passports and borders just as well as the Southern plantation owners understood that their cotton-based economies would fail without slaves – but it all still remains a great hypocrisy.

For now, Putin will bomb Syria to create refugees, Obama will continue to be a pussy and agendas that we cannot even imagine will play out behind the scenes, making certain entrenched families richer and richer.

Let me go and have another long hot shower and a cup of tea.

C

Chapter 33

Denny and Calvin

Denny is a friend our ours in Canada. He moved from Jamaica as a young man and still returns from time to time to visit family, birdwatch in the highlands and eat breadfruit. Jamaica, it seems, has a fairly high level of crime. Perhaps it is the warm weather/good climate thing. When you don't have to fight against and plan for a cold winter, then there is time for crime and violence. Or excessive breeding, which leads to overpopulation, which in turn leads to antisocial criminality.

When Denny was a teenager, he and his friend Michael crept into the room of a snoozy cousin named Calvin. Calvin was older than them and a little scary, but somehow Denny and Michael thought that giving Calvin a fright might be fun. That's how boys are, given to testing boundaries. So the two little pests crept up behind the sleeping Calvin and at the signal simultaneously shouted, "Boo!" Calvin jumped up at once, whipped a switchblade from under his pillow and gave the two smaller boys a good thumping.

Years later, as a young man, Denny was back in Jamaica for a visit and he thought he would pop in and greet his cousin Calvin. Calvin, by then, owned a restaurant with a house behind it. The restaurant opened in the evening and was still closed when Denny arrived, so he walked around the building and tried the back door. The back door was unlocked and so, not unlike Goldilocks, Denny quietly entered. And there, low and behold, on a divan by the window, lay Calvin, fast asleep, right in the middle of his siesta. Denny once again thought to wake Calvin with a fright. That's how men are, they sometimes have difficulty growing up. But before booing Calvin a second time, he thought he would first check for a switchblade. Stealthily Denny slipped his hand under Calvin's pillow and withdrew, to his surprise, not a knife but a huge chrome automatic pistol. Denny placed the firearm carefully on the dresser a safe distance away and proceeded to wake Calvin gently.

Living with a high level of crime is not fun. Some South Africans like to compare our crime levels with those of Brazil or Venezuela. Or how bad it is in Malmo, Sweden, these days. It makes them feel better.

New York was bad once, but it has improved. One can read Malcom Gladwell's book **Tipping Point** and learn that it was not Bernard Goetz who, in 1984, by shooting four would-be muggers on a New York subway train that turned the situation around. No, it was political will and decisive planned action.

In South Africa, for so long now, there has been little political will for anything other than kleptocracy. And there seems to be very little ability to plan. Too many unskilled cadres holding public office. It seems hopeless.

Calmer times – Denny and Zaan share a picnic

9 December 2015   Letter #34

Hi Gareth

A few months ago, driving up Hospital Bend, a youngster realised that he had forgotten something at home (or perhaps was lost) and tried to U-turn. Four lanes of fast-moving steel ground to a screeching, hooting halt while the little person quavered in his Atos, then headed down the Eastern Boulevard (Nelson Mandela Boulevard) towards the city centre. Fuck! There is suddenly an epidemic of U-turning on our roads. In Zimbabwe I notice they drive rather well, so maybe it is Malawi-style. I have never been there, so I can blame them.

Driving and texting at the same time also. Parking on the wrong side of the road facing oncoming traffic is so commonplace that the traffic cops don't even ticket for it anymore. In fact, they hardly ticket for anything at all and most people don't pay their fines anyway. I ask myself, when did the rot really set in? When did the home invasions and littering out of car windows and dog-crapping and general disregard for the law become totally integrated with normal living? Hmmm …. maybe it is not the Malawians after all, maybe it is just the *zeitgeist*. It has gotten Rotten in Paradise.

On rats and sinking ships

There are white rats and dark rats and multi-coloured rats. There are northern rats and southern rats. There are circus rats and feral rats. You can train rats to behave, but a rat is a rat. Back in RSA after a time in Canada, I see that there are many fewer trained rats around here, and it is getting worse. We live in a country with no law and no consequences for bad behaviour.

I am reading a rather depressing book. It is by RW Johnson and titled **How long will South Africa Survive? The Looming Crisis**. It is about Zuma and the thugs and criminals who are the Natal ANC who now "rule" this beloved land of ours. The criminalisation of the state. It is a difficult book to finish because the content is so sad.

With bad, corrupt, criminal rats in command and undisciplined, poorly trained, stupid rats running riot everywhere, the Titanic is imperilled not by the icebergs without, but by the rodents within. Too far south to jump ship? ... ^I^A ANC[1] ... too busy feasting to care!

Love Carl

---

1   **Added in 2018**
    Q: How bad, corrupt and criminal is a government when the opposition parties bring six votes of no confidence against a patently corrupt president – and everyone knows he is corrupt – and he survives every one?
    A: Very bad.

Chapter 34

Murder

Notes in a Diary   24 October 2014

In the past while, four people within my immediate sphere have been sense-lessly murdered.

The son of the caretaker at the local Shul. My old friend Caspar, broken-hearted.

A policewoman and a policeman down the road in Hout Bay two weeks ago. Senselessly shot while on patrol by a 28-year-old man.

Last weekend Zaan's friend, Alex Otten. A little girl's daddy can never be replaced.

Arrests have been made in all cases.

For starters, the perpetrators should be annihilated.

The mine shafts are empty, the sea is deep.

We are now in September 2018.
The Citizen Newspaper reports:

In the past 10 years, more than 175 000 people have been murdered in South Africa.

That's more people than in the Afghanistan war (about 144 000) or in the atomic bombing of Hiroshima (about 135 000).

Between the beginning of April 1994 and the end of March this year, 485 177 people were murdered.

Soon some poor, as yet unknown, person will have the unhappy distinction of being the half-millionth South African murdered since democracy.

There is more chance of being murdered in South Africa than dying on the road.

And the number of road deaths is insanely high.

Xmas 24 December 2015   Letter #35

Dear Gareth

23 Dec 2015

I wake at 5am, make coffee and then go for a run around Lion's Head. It is a perfect morning. I collect Zaan and we drive down to Bakoven and go for a paddle on a sea with a dying swell. Let us say it is the summer solstice. We meet two species of dolphin today – Heaviside's and Dusky.

In Arctic Norway Dag reports that schools of white-sided Atlantic dolphins and killer whales have been chasing fat herring into his frozen fjord. Yesterday a humpback whale washed up on Strand beach. A few days ago, Zaan and I came across a baby dolphin in Barley Bay, only just born, swimming around with its mother.

I spent today doing nothing too serious, like eating scrambled eggs and smoked salmon with our friends Jules and Mags. This evening at 18h30 I went for a surf down at Glen. There were just a handful of guys out. Maybe five at most. The first hounds of the new swell were running before their master and the waves were excellent. Turquoise-green like old bottle glass. A new swell will come tonight with a light summer rain. When I returned home I jumped into the warm water of the swimming pool followed by a hot shower outside. I cannot ever remember seeing a sunset so vibrant and gorgeous, with such a glorious full moon rising over the right side of Lion's Head. And the small bricks on the house across the road and the yellow and white frangipani. And the sea in metalled grey and black. I cannot ever remember it being so beautiful.

Ophiocordyceps unilateralis is a parasite fungus that "zombiefies" ants. There are many parasitic things in this world (ex-spouses included). I came across a new one the other day. We had prawn-*skottel-braai* evening down at the shed. A guest called Conrad postulated over the concept of "parasitic personalities", i.e. the personality being the parasite driving the body to do its bidding to its own end. A beautiful and novel idea to be toyed with, I thought. Like the concept of a meme – not a thing but rather a thought – and yet able to replicate and spread like a virus. In this case, Conrad's parasitic personality tried to get him to over-capitalise on abundance, willing his body to consume calories and excessive amounts of unhealthy food and drink beyond his needs. He came to the gathering with alcohol-free beer and fought hard to limit his intake as best he could. As the feasting progressed, however, and load after load of garlic peri-peri prawns was delivered to the table, accompanied by toasted baguettes soaked in spicy olive oil, we watched Conrad do battle with this invisible entity which finally won, forcing him to plunge into a massive bowl of ice-cream and hot chocolate sauce. An epic struggle lost and won.

24 Dec 2015

After a morning big eat, I have just been for an hour-long run on mountain tracks to decalorise. No mad dogs, no Englishmen, no one.

I trotted along in the heat, reflecting and laughing – what a treat.

A few weeks ago, after two hours surfing on a perfect bank at Soetwater, Zaan and I arrived hungry at our friend Craig Price's house in Scarborough. During and after a not insubstantial brunch, I managed to consume (noticed neither by myself nor the others present) a 2.5lb Consul Jar of chocolate Maltesers. Because of this, and to my great shame, I have subsequently been called an "Oink" and a "Piggy". (Yesterday Zaan and I had breakfast with a pair of UK lady friends. After breakfast I was appropriately presented with a jar of Melissa's Bacon Jam as a gift.)

At more or less the time of the Malteser episode, I sent out a piece of Zuma hate-mail. It included the Mowgli, Zuma, Louis Prima, Monkey clip.

While trotting along today and laughing and singing the monkey song to myself, I wondered: Could that clip be construed as racist? Would me comparing Zuma to an ape be any more racist than Craig comparing me to a pig?

"He either misunderstood entirely the nature of the machine at his disposal, the machine he was running... ...or he was deliberately closing his eyes... ...or he's a liar."

— Craig Williamson

In the 1980s or '90s I cut out a newspaper cartoon depicting FW de Klerk as the three apes of See No Evil, Speak No Evil, Hear No Evil fame. Is this any less racist than comparing Zuma to an ape? Such are the minefields of P.C.

Hypocrisy, prejudice and multiple moralities

Zaan and I have a friend named Redwan (the wine guy). He was born in France and now lives in Munich working as a top-drawer financial analyst and investment banker. His dad was a Moroccan businessman and even though Redwan is a 100% straight-up Franco/German on the inside, on the outside he looks more like a Libyan. And so, he gets hammered at immigration every time he enters the United States. A chap looking like Anders Breivik, on the other hand, would pass through customs at JFK without receiving a second glance. Redwan would probably be treated with utmost suspicion if he tried to buy a "Second Amendment" firearm over the counter in Oklahoma, but a fellow like Timothy McVeigh would have no problem at all. I would stop my *bakkie* on Kloof Nek and pick up three tow-haired surfers, but not three cannonball-headed Congolese. Because in South Africa, the Congoloid phenotypes might well also be the hijacky types. Call it prejudice if you want. I call it survival.

Humans smile at the keeping of dolphins in tiny Sea World pools or multi-hued jungle birds in cages, but would be horrified at the thought of keeping a chimp locked up in a telephone booth. It is okay to hunt the bluefin tuna or the marlin and hang them up heroically, but not the rhino.

Not anymore.

Ways of seeing and what you choose to see ... The absurdity of it all.

Last week I was filling in (on the screen) my SACAP re-application form for my next five-year cycle as a registered architectural professional. One of the questions concerned my race group. I was offered three options: Black, Coloured or White. If one did not answer all the questions, the form would not submit. At this stage of the game, how on earth am I supposed to know whether I am Black, Coloured or White? It is like asking Religion ... Jew, Christian or Muslim? To me the answer is, of course, "None of the above."

In 2014 I was filling in a form at our local police station in Camps Bay. I was faced with the same question. RACE GROUP? But this time with a caveat: "For statistical purposes only." I took a chance and went for black. The sergeant assisting me checked the form once I had completed it. "But you are not black!" she said. I took her arm and placed mine alongside hers. We were almost exactly the same colour. On the counter was my black leather wallet from which I removed a white till slip. I placed these two items down beside our arms. I was certainly not black, and neither was she. Clearly, according to the till slip, neither of us were white. I then quipped, "Black is not the colour of my skin, it is the colour of my soul." "*Hai, suka* ... you can't say that," she exclaimed in horror. "Why not? Is there a problem with someone having a black soul?" I asked, pointing out of the door toward the parking lot where a black BMW glinted in the sunshine. "Do you see that car?" I said, "That is the colour of my soul."

And so we left it, my firearm licence re-application form says that I am "black" (for statistical purposes only) and a so-called "black" woman and a so-called "white" man with almost identical skin colours parted laughing at the ridiculousness of it all, while sparing a thought for our fellow so-called "blacks" in absentia: Tiger Woods, Barack Obama, Mariah Carey, Bob Marley, Ian Khama, Halle Berry and so on.

The other day I was listening to the radio. The talk show host Redi Thlabi became annoyed with a man who called in and compared the previous regime to the current one. She reminded us of the days when the township streets were full of SADF troops and how she hated that. Well, those troops were mainly conscripted so-called "white" boys of our generation and those troops hated being there as much as their presence was hated. Just ask the fly-boy Ant Allen for starters.

Back then I despised the apes Magnus Malan and PW Botha as much as I do Zuma – it was not racism then as it is not racism now. It is not us, the people, but those in power over us who really do the evil. Hitler, Gaddafi, Stalin, Saddam Hussein, Zuma, Chairman Mao, Kim Jong-il and so on. We are destined to be mere powerless, frustrated, divided, little ants blown along with the sands of time unless we make our stand and stand united.

Love and Xmas greetings – Carl

Chapter 35

Zuma and The Jungle Book

I watched the 1967 Walt Disney, **Jungle Book**, Mowgli, King Louis
video clip on YouTube again the other day.
https://youtu.be/c9cWkUhZ8n4
https://youtu.be/x3W2WbM7J6g

And even if it is full of monkeys and other animals,
one must keep an open mind and not just start crying "foul!"

King Louis is Zuma.
Mowgli represents to Zuma the potential source of unattainable money and power, namely: "Man's Red Fire."

Mowgli is a personification of the Guptas and the bribe-rich arms companies and other corruptible entities like KPMG, Bell Pottinger, McKinsey and SAP.

The little grey-headed trumpeter guy – he might be Julius?

The monkeys in attendance are, well, you know, the populists.

Bagheera and Baloo arriving are Pravin and Cyril or Jacques Pauw and Corruption Watch.

The good guys hoping to stop King Louis and clean things up before it's too late.

But are they?

31 January 2016   Letter #36

Hi my buddy

I jot down notes as I go, during the month.
I compile you some thoughts.
It is so busy again.
Terrible waiting also for my and ex-wife's lawyers ... grind ... hnnn hnnn hnnn – no progress.
I just pay.
One day I will either die or have news.

30 December 2015

And so the year of 2015 draws to a close.
People litter and breed mindlessly.
Misanthropes continue to find their own species appalling in general, and wonderful individually.
The weather in Cape Town has been constantly splendid for holidaymakers for weeks.
Still mornings, white-capped southerlies offshore in the afternoons.
Beach weather deluxe.
Largish swells coming in every few days – not many surfers around, nice waves at Glen Beach.

The hotels are all chock-a-block.
Restaurants are reportedly booked out.
It is hot.

Cape Town has never been better equipped for tourists.

Young people are having a blast in this friendly Afro-European hybrid city of ours.

Cars crawl up Kloof Nek, the Clifton roads are jammed, but everyone seems happy.

Camps Bay beach is a happy place – a relaxed hubbub drifts up to our quiet abode.

Along with the sound of a busking saxophone, played badly but persistently.

This morning Zaan and I ran the loop around Lion's Head in a superb perspiring heat.

Then we paddled in a very cold sea.

A young seal tried to eat a live medium-sized crayfish right next to my ski.

Not an easy meal for an animal with no hands.

The other day my friend Grant Williams and I went out for a surf at Glen.

There were about 4 or 5 guys out. Fun, snappy, small summer surf.

All of a sudden, I noticed a crowd of people on the rocks, waving and cheering.

Feeling like a surf celebrity I waved back and paddled for an oncoming peak.

Grant took the wave as I saw the small inflatable Camps Bay rescue boat arrive, and then pull aboard the stiff mutton carcase of a drowned woman floating just behind the break line.

The crowd immediately dispersed.

Perhaps they were not waving and cheering for us after all.

Such is life … as you well know … hanging by a thread.

1368 road deaths in the 2014 festive season …

500 already this year by 20 December.

Zuma the Zulu has made so much *KAK* this year in RSA,

I wish that it were rather he than any one of the 500.

New Year's Eve Zaan and I were asleep by 21h30.

New Year's Day we ran the loop and then up to the top of the Lion's Head.

Then I went surfing at Glen for the second low tide in a row.

3 January 2016

Zaan turned 46 yesterday – another perfect day – and we paddled out in the morning. She saw three penguins. Whale Rock is packed with two species of tern as well as many cormorants. I watched a long string of cormorants come in to dock. The leaders over-flew the LZ while the trailing 75% landed. The leaders then circled back and dropped down among their pals. The sea is warm and full of fish. Today when we arrived at Bakoven, about a kilometre out to sea, a huge white-bellied whale (southern right?) breached over and over again. It was clearly smashing up a shoal of fish as terns and cormorants wheeled and splashed into the churned water in a frenzy of feasting. The big jumping whale bellowed its hollow whale noise and also repeatedly slapped its tail onto the surface of the water with a loud smack, the reports of which took a few seconds to reach us over the calm water. A second smaller whale blew from time to time, but far less frequently than the big crasher. We paddled out and saw some dolphins who are Zaan's friends. Cape dusky dolphins, not the shy Heaviside's that have been around Whale Rock recently. It was all so nice that we decided to have Zaan's birthday again today.

⬥

Soon after New Year some injudicious fool named Penny Sparrow tweeted or facebooked something about so-called "black" people on the beaches behaving like monkeys. MELTDOWN!! The whole country went ape. News, radio, TV … geez man.

I hear the government convened a board of enquiry to investigate and establish why there seems to be so much new racism in the country. Apparently there is a groundswell return to a pre-post-apartheid racist mindset.

Well, I don't need an enquiry board – to me it is quite simple.

In 1994 when the ANC came into power with Nelson Mandela at the helm, there was hope. If, after two decades of ANC governance, crime was under control, the criminal justice system was running like a Swiss clock, SAA was operating at a profit, Eskom was delivering with no load-shedding or selling surplus power to our neighbours, the other parastatals were not failing and there was little corruption and cronyism, there would be far less racism in South Africa.

But as the palefaces and a large percentage of the not-so-palefaces watch in horror as Zoomababoona etc. drive the country to the edge of the abyss, there is knee-jerk racism and I suspect that it comes from the same place and is a very similar emotion to that which was felt by the more liberal Euro-South Africans (like me) when PW Bothababoona and Magnus Malanbaboona were doing their worst. And I remember, while conscripted in the SADF, (racist) words like: Dutchman, Rockspider, Rocks, Boer and Bonehead. Same place, same thing.

Not the product of proper thought – only base emotion.

When are they going to let you out?

Love
C

Chapter 36

Hotel Bottles

In the 1970s the Camps Bay strip was an unsophisticated place. At the far end, the Alvin Cinema played **Zorro** and **The Lone Ranger** to sun-browned kids on Saturdays. At the near end, surfers pulled on their wetsuits and paddled out at Glen. The Atlantic was just as icy as it is today, and the white sandy beach just as white and sandy. The same road ran north to south, lined with the same scraggy palms. But everything else has changed. Filly the horse is no more, along with the upturned dinghies under which we, as little boys, played. We would burrow under a boat and use it like an igloo. They were so warm inside after the cold, cold sea. I remember my first can of Coke and my first Liqui-Fruit inside an upturned boat on Camps Bay beach, sitting with Robby and Mick, using the underside of the thwart as a table.

Camps Bay – as snapped by Ant Allen from his paraglider

As bigger boys, walking home from school, we would pass the Wimpy and a restaurant called The Pink Geranium and three or four cafés (Lincoln, Sher's and Sakkies, all selling the same chips, cokes, smokes, pies and little bamboo-handled fishing nets for children). These have all been replaced by nightclubs and restaurants. And the benign pedestrians of my youth have made way for drug dealers and a roving gang of delinquent teenagers ready to steal anything that is not bolted down or watched like a hawk.

At some point the iconic but seedy Rotunda Hotel metamorphosed into The Bay, a generic, smart, international style, beach holiday establishment. Blue pool, loungers with rolled-up yellow towels, rooms and suites, restaurants and bars, smart brunches *al fresco* and cocktails at sunset. Back then, it was a place where teenage boys could sit and watch TV, gloriously smoking and drinking beer out of "hotel" bottles.

The "hotel" bottles were made from thick brown glass worn to a rough whiteness at the shoulder and foot. The French doors all stood wide open, curtains billowing in the warm summer breeze. Anyone could walk in or out. We sat at sticky little tables, Magnum PI or The A Team playing on a fuzzy television set. We collected our drinks from the Men's Bar which was connected to the TV lounge by a short passage. The alcoholics and local drunks welcomed us boys as potential future recruits to their ranks. There didn't seem to be an age restriction.

Once or twice I remember some of our school teachers arriving. "Chips, here comes Sir!" Alan Clegg called out as John Donald, Tucker and Robbins strolled up the drive. Boys would disperse, leaving unfinished beers on the tables and cigs smoking in the ashtrays. We would all crowd around the Pac-Man machines in the foyer and slowly drift away. Ravenscroft and I would filter into the Ladies Bar – the teachers didn't go there. I don't think anybody did. There certainly weren't any ladies.

There is a period in the lives of male humans, between childhood and maturity, when they are given to stupid things. This can be quite a long period, much longer than one might think. Often aided and abetted by the consumption of alcohol.

One Friday break at school, Ravenscroft and I and two other boys planned a beach party. It would be held at the beautiful Bakoven inlet at the southern end of Camps Bay. We would each bring a bottle. Even though it was mid-winter and nightfall was at about five-thirty, our juvenile imaginations managed to conjure a tropical sunset scene replete with willing girls desirous of our debonair company.

After class Ravenscroft and I walked to the local off-sales and each purchased a 750ml bottle of Vin Coco (which, for those who don't remember, was nothing more than low-grade cane spirit mixed with a liberal dash of coconut-flavoured suntan lotion). We hung around at my house, preening, and at the appointed time walked down to meet the others at the beach. The four of us were the only people around. The sun set behind thick dark cloud. I sat on a clammy rock, sipping away, watching an already skulled pal running and jumping and generally going berserk. The remaining three of us were sombre. There were no girls.

I do not remember leaving the party or how I navigated myself homeward, but I do remember the headlights of the car that nearly killed me as I crossed the road below my mother's house. I crept into the garden and up to the living-room window. Bill, Mick and my mom were watching Magnum on TV. It must have been between 7.30 and 8pm. I waited for a few miserable, poisoned hours before letting myself in. I woke up the next morning in a bed full of dried black vomit. I was terribly ill, but nobody seemed to notice. It was very strange.

It wasn't only me. We were all at it. Drinking at the Rotunda, the Hout Bay Hotel, the Kings and the Liz. Walking miles and miles through the night. Plunkett trying to cut our feet off with his father's electric lawnmower as we lay down in hope of sleep on the spinning floor of the Plunkett garage. It was all rather close a bit too often.

One of my naughtier friends was down at the Rotunda on a Friday night. He was standing at the counter of the Men's Bar waiting to be served another beer when he spied an Avis keyring with a set of car keys attached.

Later he was arrested in Bellville more than 30km away, trying to break into another car. He spent the rest of the weekend in a police cell full of fleas and gangsters and stabbers and bad men. It was only in extreme cases like this that parents got involved.

It was a youth of too much freedom.

28 February 2016   Letter #37

Last year while Zaan was in Canada, a black southeaster blew two fledgling thrushes out of their nest and to my office door. They could not yet fly but greedily ate the grated cheese I offered them. They grew up in the thick vegetation outside my "coalface". Soon enough they were airborne and moved camp to the bushy thicket down near the pool. A few times a day they would come for cheese and soon became the resident pair of Cape olive thrushes at number 10.

Three days ago, something killed one of them. All that was left was feathers and the lower beak. The remaining bird has filled the air with unremitting thrush-song for three days now. A complex series of varied calls with gaps only long enough to draw breath. To some it might sound joyful, but I know that it is not. It is the language of sorrow.

When we were kids in the 1970s we often spent our Saturday mornings at the Kinekor Kiddies Club. Free Perk's Pies were handed out at the door. A lucky few might get a Roger Moore James Bond 007 poster. Or a seven-single of the latest pop song as a prize for disco dancing.

We would get 50c pocket money (7 cents bus fare each way, 35c entry fee, 1 cent over for three pink Star sweets). We walked down to the city and kept the bus fare. Sometimes we went shoplifting for little toys at Jack Lemkus or Garlicks. We did not shoplift at Stuttafords because Robby Kinsky's mother worked there at a cosmetics counter on the ground floor next to the escalator. A nine-to-five standing up job. Her feet hurt like hell by the time she stepped off the bus every evening and on Saturday afternoons. She would sit on the couch in the lounge of their Kloof Nek flat, kick off her low-heeled navy-blue court shoes (huge bunions were visible through her nylon stockings) and smoke. Her feet would be up at last. Robby and I would be building a puzzle.

Robby's parents were divorced. Robby's dad Willi moved from one home to another. Gardens, Fresnaye, Tamboerskloof … He was an entrepreneur. Willi had fought on the Russian *Ostfront*. From time to time he would tell us about the cold and the tanks.

"Adolf Hitler would have known exactly what to do with you," he would say to me, setting up yet another Gross Deutschland-style task for us two teenage boys. Like his ex-wife Val, Willi would also come in exhausted wearing a pair of small '70s denim shorts and long, lace-up, Afrika Korps desert boots. A very tall, lean, roguish figure. He would sit down in his old chair and, like his ex-wife, put up his tired feet, smoke and fall asleep. His Romeo y Julietta cigar would drop to the floor and leave another black scar on the wood before smouldering out. We collected the beautiful cigar boxes. Robby had Durex condoms in one of them, ready for some hopeful future day. But when he did eventually need one, it was still in his cigar box and so he impregnated his young girlfriend. She was a priest's daughter and it was a very depressing teenage wedding. It is also a loving marriage that has outlasted almost everyone else's.

⸺⸺

Back to Kinekor Kiddies Klub. We watched British and Australian kiddie movies and shorts. The Australian ones featured lifeguards and lifeguard-surf-boats and tough bronzed youngsters. There was bad stuff like hulls being sabotaged in the dead of night. The British ones usually starred a gang of crime-busting kids who always got the bad guys before the cops could. There were great sound effects. When Inspector so-and-so and the Scotland Yard flatfoots finally arrived in their siren-blaring Rovers, the baddies were already trussed and bound.

The other day I remembered a film called **Trouble with 2B**. I Googled it and revisited this classic from the early 1970s in the comfort of my own office. Every character and sound effect was stored, ready for instant recognition, somewhere in my brain cells (even the handcuffs, the science lab noises and the wasp). Memories that lay unaccessed for about 40 years.

14 February 2016

Today is St Valentine's Day. The remaining thrush began "singing" at the top of its voice around 03h00. It was still dark and raining. The poor thing piped down at 7am. It must be exhausted. Zaan and I paddled our surf-skis on a dark sea in the rain. A kilometre or so out, a whale sent up a high column of spray from time to time. The other day I saw seven Heaviside's with a baby. When we returned from paddling, the beach was foot-printed only by raindrops. It was quite warm, so we stood and watched the wagtails catching flies, and then swam.

There is a lot of aggression in South African society. There is road rage and police violence. One notices this after returning from a country like Canada. There is aggression from owners of dogs. There is aggression if you point out to someone that they are behaving in an anti-social manner. I think perhaps this aggression stems from frustration. People are frustrated by the systems that no longer work. If the law worked and there were real consequences for transgressors, people would break the law less often and so there would be less reason for law-abiding citizens to become frustrated and aggressive.

Sunday 21 February 2016

A week of sun and rain. Twice up Table Mountain in the cool of morning. On Tuesday we paddled at 06h30. We found a school of Cape dusky dolphins in the kelp just outside the Camps Bay tidal pool. They came to meet me and Zaan. For at least an hour they jumped and spun and splashed. Groups of three, four and five in the air together. Juveniles and adults. The next day I remembered my camera. I found only two dolphins, but there was a humpback whale.

A few mornings ago, Zaan and I came across a large Mola mola in Barley Bay. Amazingly it had three fins in the air at the same time. At first I couldn't quite make it out. Then its head kept popping out, eyes and all. Mouth chomping.

I said to Zaan, "What's it doing?"

She answered, "Going for a swim."

Hmm. It was, in fact, gobbling up small rugby ball-shaped jellyfish with luminous lines on their sides.

Friday 26 February 2016

I ran/walked up Table Mountain, starting in a thick mist. Lower cable station to the upper station in 62 minutes. Cool air, no stress at all. The ex-wife saga drags on. The lonely Thrush has a new mate.

Two birds on Saturday morning.

Onwards my friend.
Chaz

Chapter 37

Dag's Paper Round

I sometimes wonder why certain people are successful in business – why they are such good salespeople and seem to make money almost without effort. How they see opportunities or gaps in the market and exploit them.

From a very early age, Gordon was attempting one business venture after another. Taking photographs of his school chums and selling the prints long before the average Camps Bay resident even owned a camera. Diving for and selling rock lobsters to the neighbours. Having towels and gear monogrammed with his university residence's logo and selling them to his fellow students for a tidy profit. Was it because of his businessman dad or did it simply come from within?

Or what about the Jewish kids who grew up immersed in it? Business was talked about at table, while walking to shul … a family business … lucky/unlucky? The chains that bind us, the chains that set us free.

Or a South African millionaire who, as a boy, in the days before recycling, collected the newspaper overruns at the town printing press and supplied the local take-aways with wrapping for their fish and chips.

I wish I had it in a greater measure.

A lovely story was told to me by Dag. Growing up in Norway, in the West Coast town of Bergen, Dag took on not one, but three paper rounds. Two in the early morning and one in the late afternoon. If you have ever been there, you will know that Bergen is very wet and very hilly. And that it would be physically impossible for one boy, even a tough one, to manage more than a single paper round, let alone three. Unless, of course, that boy knew how to delegate.

Dag tells me that he would collect his newspapers from the lorry on the main street above his home on Jægerbakken. He would then pile them on his cart and proceed downhill. At every intersection another boy would be waiting to receive his share of the papers for delivery up his designated side street.

"In payment," says Dag, "each boy would receive a sweet-mint."

"Sometimes the boys would rebel or become mutinous, saying the pay was too little or the work too much. Then I would just punch them on the arm, Kallemann. Hard, like this!" And he showed me.

Life was tough in Norway in 1970. A long time would pass before flabby teenagers could order pizza online in midwinter Narvik to be delivered to their door in black Lada Nivas, still hot, through rain and icy sleet.

Vision and entrepreneurship, those are key.
To see the gap and go for it!
And not to be lazy.

Imagine the gold in the sea.
Lying there for centuries, waiting for treasure-hunters with their aqualungs.
Imagine a flat world waiting to be deemed spherical.
Imagine all that oil, hidden for so long, under the ground.
The first taste of it, seeping out free of charge, in Tajikistan and Pennsylvania.
Finally, after years of persecution, Melville's sperm whales get their reprieve.
Unimaginable communications, like WhatsApp.
Free videophone conversations around the world, in an instant!
Imagine what unimaginable technologies and advances and ways of seeing await,
just around the corner.

A madman sees things that don't exist.
A visionary sees things that do not exist, yet.
We live in the time of visionaries and fast-paced change.
We are indeed lucky to live in these times.

I remember at twelve years old being hopelessly in love with a girl in Welkom and walking down to the post office, writing out a telegram and paying a rand or two to send it. My childish handwriting – telegraphed away in Morse code.

Telegraph machines printed out long, thin strips of paper. These were then torn into appropriate lengths and glued onto the pink telegram slip. The enveloped telegrams were placed in small leather saddle-bags suspended under the seats of thick-tired bicycles and delivered to homes and offices by lanky telegram-boys. Some brought bad news. Mine didn't. It was so short, it probably didn't even need to be torn.

DEAR LYNETTE = I MISS YOU VERY MUCH STOP = LOVE CARLOS

1970s telegram
1980s fax
1990s email
2000s Skype
2010s WhatsApp
2018 Quo Vadis?

I still remember when my dad booked trunk calls.

⁓

I recently chatted to a Canadian couple who have, for the past twenty years,
lived in China. They are in stem cell research … curing cancer.
They choose to live away from the interference of religious groups
and people who,
when they hear the words "stem cell", see dead babies.
These two people have harvested their own stem cells via liposuction
and grow them in a culture.
They introduce billions of fresh stem cells into their own bodies regularly.
They are like Tolkien's elves.

4 April 2016   Letter #38

Hi Gareth

March flew by ... a rollercoaster of ups and downs.
One day I will be able to share with you the ex-wife crap I am dealing with, but not now.
I re-read what I wrote this month ... it is pretty dark.

7 March 2016

Such is the dark hour of the soul.
I have just been out to run the loop around Lion's Head.
An easy run normally ... today not 200m without my mind stopping my body for a chat.
I am careworn and preoccupied.
These stones of my simple childhood.
I sit finally on one of the two old British naval guns near the kramat.
Cannons of my childhood – 1713 – cannons of many childhoods.
A cool iron morning seat.
See the *rooivalk* floating overhead
And the sun as it catches the tablecloth in a full blaze of colour.
Where I sit, in the shadow, it is sepia-toned like an old photograph.

My imagination ties a rope around my neck and hangs me from one of the big pines.

My walks and runs are filled with gibbet fantasies.

I have been here at this place many times before.

Many times in this life of bondage.

I believe that some people don't mind it much and for others it is torture.

For creative persons trapped in humdrum.

For free-spirited people chained to the ever-boring.

To a life of service.

At the exit of sleep and the threshold of waking I pass through the hate.

I hate my ex-wife and I long for the peace of death.

I know it is always darkest just before dawn.

And there is Allegra and the possibility of a good life with Zaan.

I long for freedom but I must wait.

I am now terribly impatient.

There comes a dreadful time after boyhood when a man can no longer call out,

"Mom, help!" That time has come and gone. We are alone now.

Beyond mother's help.

I am terribly bad at waiting.

Zaan says: "But you agreed to it, you signed ..."

And I think of all those boys and men who volunteered for Parabats or Recces or to fight in WWII

Who later regretted volunteering. "Ah, but you agreed to it, you signed up …"

"Ah, but I had no idea that it would play out like this."

"How the hell was I to know?"

Outside last evening the **11ᵗʰ of March 2016** the sky was full of swallows and their kin.

Two kinds of those and others, like gulls and ibises, returning home.

The sun is setting more north now as summer cracks off.

A crescent moon and a soft blue sky and the swallows.

Down below it is howling at the beach, stinging sand and veils of spray.

But we – Zaan and I – sit in warm still air behind the wind-shear.

These past few days have been a time of anger and reflection for many in Cape Town.

A 16-year-old girl was raped and murdered in Tokai.

While out jogging, a young life so violated, then snuffed out.

Three men appeared before the magistrate for rape and murder.

A fourth for possession of her mobile phone and some jewellery.

Such is the reality of the dread of the South African parent.

And such is the reality of what might happen to one's beloved child.

Last evening I heard the story reported again on the radio. With all due gravity. Then the talk-show host promptly went on to extol the virtues of a novel he had just read. It featured a group of American itinerants who take pleasure in their spree of killing as they travel the country.

I was reminded of a Jack Johnson song lyrics:

Why don't the newscasters cry when they read about people who die,
At least they could be decent enough to put just a tear in their eyes.

There have been four rapes of young women near UCT. They were held captive, too. The last one for over 24 hours. They finally got the guy.

Does it help?

I just don't know what to say … it is all so terrible.

One thing for sure: I cannot imagine why anyone would wish to breed in these times.

28 March 2016

So down at heart,
Not to mention the work strain.
Perhaps we meet again under a lighter sky.
On this plunging ball thru' space,
How we bog ourselves down,
With the most mundane things.
We have had the first rains.
Easter has passed,
Perhaps April will bring.

Love to you my brother
C

Chapter 38

On Killing

I was speaking to a doctor a year or so ago and he said, "Yes, people become enraged and murder each other and people die." I listened carefully as I was asking for advice (he has experience in these matters). "Be careful," he said.

In Cape Town, one of our most celebrated musicians, Taliep Petersen, was murdered by two hitmen paid for by his wife. Our once-famous South African sports star, Oscar the Blade Runner, in a moment of jealous rage, shot and killed his girlfriend Reeva.

I have contemplated death and killing for as long as I have contemplated life and living.

People die as a result of old age, physical malfunction, illness, accident, euthanasia, fighting, murder and war. As my philosophy evolved, I could only imagine killing a human being in an act of self-defence or while defending someone from an attacker. Or causing a death through euthanasia or suicide.

One day my ex-father-in-law had the insufferable gall to phone my brother Bill and accuse me of firearm negligence. I was deeply insulted and infuriated. I wrote to him as follows:

*I write this on the first day of **16 Days of Activism Against Violence Toward Women and Children**.*

My brother Bill has called me to tell me you phoned him to say that:

(1) You feel that I might be a threat to the physical safety of your daughter and your granddaughter Allegra.

(2) I have guns lying around the house.

No parent should have to worry about these things. So, for the record:

My father was raised with a .22 rifle as his companion and later served in the police in Kenya during the Mau Mau war. He introduced my brothers and I to firearms when we were boys in the early 1970s.

My Grandmother taught us to use her Arminius revolver and use, strip and clean her Walther semi-automatic pistol in the early 1970s. She had been taught how to use firearms by her father who rode with the Texas Rangers. They all knew "the drill".

I carried a side-arm when I was working under sometimes fairly threatening circumstances in the "townships" and "informal settlements" throughout the years 1982 to 1986.

I was trained and drilled in the use of semi-automatic pistols and LAR's (FN, R4 and G3) in the South African Navy and in the Army during a 2-year national service in 1988 and 1989.

In all of this time, I have never, not on one single day, had one or more "guns lying around the house".

I have extreme respect for and am quite comfortable with firearms.

Carl and Bill 1976

I wrote further that through all the years of his daughter's shenanigans, "I never once used loud or abusive language. I never raised a hand to her. And I have never once been violent towards her."

So, as I re-read my last letter to Gareth, I contemplate what a person imagines and what a person might actually do. What lies purely in the realm of fantasy and how that fantasy might evolve into real action. I think of

Anders Breivik and Timothy McVeigh and the September 11 plane flyers. At what point did their warped fantasies become real possibilities and then actual actions?

I think that my ex-father-in-law's concerned call to Bill had an unexpected consequence in that it opened my mind to a possibility that I had not ever even dreamed of before. Namely to harm the mother of my child, or my own child, or to harm a member of my family. It was like seeing a repulsive pornographic image – once seen, it could never be unseen.

The very idea of violating a cast-in-stone taboo!

I told him not to measure me with the same yardstick he uses to measure himself.

27 April 2016   Letter #39

Hi Gareth

Today here in RSA it is Freedom Day ... the day we voted.

This letter might jolt you a bit at the end ... but here we are, from a cool Cape Town.

Krinkel-klonkie waarvandaan kom jy hierso gou-gou aan? Van die sterre, van die maan?

About a quarter of a century ago, when we still lived up in my mom's big house against the mountain on the windy side of Camps Bay, there was an alcoholic bushman who regularly came to our door. He carried with him a four-stringed *ramkiekie* which he played rather beautifully. Mournful tunes of some lost Karoo. His instrument was homemade: a five-litre Castrol oil can, a greasy plank for a neck, his strings were fishing line and each soulful fret made of copper wire. I gave him a real guitar once, which he quickly pawned to buy liquor. He lived in the bush down near the Symmonds Field. One day he knocked on our front door one time too often and I became irritated. I went outside and picked him up by the back of his trousers and carried him up the twenty stairs using only one hand. He was so light that his bones must have been made of paper. He was not an old man. Maybe 30 or 40 pounds. He was starving of course. I felt so sad at my action, so lacking in humanity, and I still do today. My hands still remember, as if it were yesterday, the feel of that broad belt and the heavy denim of his pants. I have not done many wilfully unkind things to innocent creatures in my life. I think I can remember them all.

Yesterday was Friday 15 April.

I used to love surfing so much, but now it is so crowded most of the time.

Even in the early morning, Glen Beach is packed with school *liteys*. I decided to take the day off. So I waited for the *liteys* to go to school, put on my wetsuit and ran down for a surf. I paddled out. The waves were so *kak* (big close-outs) that I surfed one back to shore and ran home. "Derdesteen," I thought. In the *bakkie* and away.

And so I arrive in the parking lot at paradise. Only a few cars. Dog walkers and delivery vans. Warm late summer air. *Weskus*. Perfect waves. No-one out. Two guys putting on wetsuits, but they walk about 300m south and paddle out there. I negotiate the shore break right in front of the car park and out to sea. How can it be like this? Every other surfer in Cape Town is somewhere else, busy with something else.

It is indescribable, but let me try. Warm water, no side current to speak of. Perfect large peaks with easy channels for paddling out again. Easy running take-offs, hardly any stroke is needed. I call my grandmother to see this. She flies past in the form of a grey gannet and is gone. For an hour-and-a-half I surf alone. Waves for jam. Then one guy from Richards Bay paddles out, followed by a drone flown from the beach. A gyrocopter flies past low. The wind starts to push SW and I am out. Through the shore break and back on the sand. Ha! What a phenomenal time. Utterly relaxed. No other guys hustling and paddling around. Pure Zen, my China. Sliding down those deep smooth drops. Hearing the crash behind and the tapping of the front underside of the board as it tickles its way down the face.

When I was in yacht-building we'd discuss a triangle – there was a word at each apex: Time, Quality and Cost. If you wanted a quick boat build it would cost more and quality may be compromised. If you wanted a quality product it would cost more and take a longer time to produce etc.

The other day I was telling Zaan's son Nicholas about surfing and contemplating humans. I told him that I am a co-operative person. I like to share the waves and we can all have fun. Take pleasure from others having a good ride. I told him about a guy I know named Justin. Asking him once why he is such a greedy pig in the water, he responded, "Surfing is like chess to me. I take as many waves as I can – that is how I win." People like that make me very aggressive and I want to hit them, but of course I am not allowed to.

Grant Williams conjures up an imaginary trial for me:

"Imagine yourself before the magistrate," Grant says:

"Why did you punch Mr S in the face?"

"Well, he paddled on my inside Your Worship."

"You do realise that assault with intent to do grievous bodily harm is a serious offence?"

"Yes, Your Worship, but he was dropping in on everybody and generally being a pig in the water."

And so on and so forth – no good.

So back to the triangle. People are like this: Draw a triangle and place the words Competitive, Co-operative and Anarchist (either they simply don't care, or they are ignorant) – one at each corner. A person can only be at one point on that triangle. I am a very co-operative person. Public spirited, involved in community, and the most disappointed by those who don't care.

We see them in the house rental business. Some leave a place so clean and tidy you wouldn't even know there had been guests to stay. Others just wreck a house. It can be really disheartening. Some people drive co-operatively. Others race their Harleys or Maseratis through the neighbourhood. Not a care for pedestrians or intersections. Or at 3am no thought for those asleep. Then I can hate.

OK, so I am basically non-competitive. I never liked games because I couldn't care about who wins. I get very aggressive with non-co-operative people and I am hellish impatient (Tom Petty's **The Waiting is the Hardest Part**). My ex-wife saga is all about waiting. Gareth, I do not know how you cope with that. Waiting causes impatient types like me to secrete anti-dopamine depression chemicals right into the core of my limbic system … you know, the hypothalamus, the fornix, hippocampus, cingulate gyrus, amygdala, the parahippocampal gyrus, and some parts of the thalamus. That is why I am always busy, I suppose – to fight depression.

"Was it you or I who stumbled first? … It does not matter …
The one of us who finds the strength to get up first, must help the other."

⁂

Sometimes I talk to my ancestors. Especially when I am out in nature. My grandmother comes as a grey or tawny bird of prey. A ruffled steppe buzzard with odd coloured feathers, an unusually large and incorrectly coloured *rooivalk*, a dark gannet. Yesterday, on Table Mountain, she was a grey-headed red-wing starling. It is fun.

❦

This writing thing began in 1987 when my mom bought me two small red silk-covered books at Liberty in Regent Street, London. The border of each page had cherry blossoms on it. During the surfing years before, and the years after, I was pretty diligent with my camera.

I now have crates of journals and photo albums. Ekhart Tolle says that both the past and the future do not exist – there is only the "now". I did understand the concept, but I was not able to assimilate it. I am starting to get it now. I am starting now at 51 to get that lesson.

Sometimes I dip into my boxes of journals with interest and wonderment, because so much of the detail has been forgotten. Why do I love to write? Because it is my means of trapping the past, snaring it if you like, so that it does not simply slip away into totally pointless nothingness.

Today I feed on that fruit, I plunge my hand into that box of chocolates.

This is a memory of a two-year-old story told to me, by you, in 1982. I put it to paper in one of my notebooks eight years later in 1990. Let's see how accurate it is and how much of it is the creation of my mind. Operation Sceptic … June 1980 … Angola … you called it "Operation Septic".

Hot air, dust and diesel smoke. Angolan bush fell before the mighty six-wheel-drive 61 Mech. Ratels. Small antelope and birds flushed from their peaceful livings, dashed and flew before the roaring beasts, screeching warning cries as they went.

Yesterday had been a great day. The six-vehicle patrol had stumbled on a SWAPO depot in the flat grass and thorn-bush savannah. The group of Kalashnikov-toting men guarding the rude station ran like the wind as the "friendly" supply trucks they had been expecting, turned out to be SADF armour. The Ratels' 20-millimetre cannon strafed the little camp while the SADF soldiers in the backs of the vehicles stuck their torsos out of the top hatches and fired with automatic rifles dropping the enemy as he ran.

"It was like rabbit shooting," you said, as we sat on the Technikon steps soaking up the winter sun. "Our rifles sounded like pop-guns as we hung out of the hatches mowing down the terrs. It was all so easy and clean. We swept in like big bullies and never even had a shot fired at us in return."

The base the South Africans were looking for was still some kilometres to the north-east and the next morning, euphoric and victorious, the long brown six-wheelers broke laager and set off to seek fresh quarry. Reconnaissance information had located and coordinated a smallish terrorist encampment consisting mainly of well-camouflaged dugouts in a patch of thick bush. The squadron of six potent SADF Ratels and the soldiers packed inside them were considered to be more than sufficient fire-power to "sort out" this cluster of undesirables and it probably would have been, if not for those unexpected, hidden, Russian anti-aircraft guns which lay in wait.

The encounter was bitter. Armour-piercing rounds from the low limbered AA guns tore through metal the South African *troopies* had been led to believe was impenetrable. One Ratel was knocked out cold, while two others stood burning. Gareth and his surviving mates charged down the centre aisle of their flaming vehicle. Gareth cleared out the uninjured men. Do I remember him telling me that as one of his comrades crouched to jump from the dead machine, an incoming round (from some munitions plant in mother Russia) clawed its burning way through the Ratel's armour-plate and then through the man who landed dead, chest-down in the sand? I think I do.

Gareth unthinkingly side-stepped his ex-comrade and re-entered the smoky hulk. He returned dragging a bleeding helmeted figure and the first-aid case. "I felt no pain, just a numb automatic drive. I watched myself as if in a dream, as I patched the driver's mutilated body with compresses and bandages. I remember the spatting of incoming 7.62 AK fire as it smacked into the steel above my head. I remember thinking I must fix the driver or we'll never get out of here."

Gareth then closed the case and dashed over the veld towards the knocked out Ratel. The tearing noise of supersonic ammunition filled his ringing ears as he dived for cover behind the big steel dinosaur which had ground to a halt, side-on to the anti-aircraft gunfire. Small arms volleys and bursts raked in from all angles as SWAPO soldiers fleeing the three surviving Ratels (which had flanked and turned on the SWAPO camp) stopped and fired wherever they could find cover. The three Ratels, one to the left and two to the right of the original formation, had not taken a single round of enemy fire. In constant contact with one another, the cool-headed navigators and drivers turned and came in diagonally from the rear, thus protecting each other and their halted comrades from being hit by friendly fire. Soon enough the two Soviet guns had been silenced and dead and dying bodies littered the bush.

"Yesterday's rabbit hunt had gone all wrong" and the eventual victors
(who had paid so dearly in terms of men and machines)
now took their savage retribution on the corpses of their vanquished foe.

Gareth, the self-styled medic, bandaged and packed the wounds of the injured and the dying as the dull thudding of SAAF Puma helicopters filtered into the sound mix. Low they came. As they landed air crew booted boxes of fresh supplies out of their doors. The crews of the doomed Ratels (dead, wounded and alive) were whisked away to the morgue, hospital and T-bone steaks of the big base camp back in South West Africa.

On another day Gareth, I remember you telling me about being sent all over the "Republic" with another survivor to visit the moms of the boys you had seen die. No counselling, just a young boy yourself, really.

What a life we had and continue to have.

During our high school years in the "Republic" the thought of conscription hung heavy over all of us. All so called "white" male South African citizens had to register in their standard nine year at school. Thereafter the dreaded registered letters came twice a year. On the back of the envelope a blue five-pointed fortress, on the inside … a two-year SADF call-up, destination 8 SAI Upington, 2 SAI Walvis Bay, Discobolus Kimberley, School of

Engineers Kroonstad, 1 SAI Tempe Bloemfontein, Bethlehem … or, if you were the luckiest son-of-a-bitch alive, Saldanha Bay. Non-citizens like my brothers and I stood nervously on the side-lines like impala sniffing the air, sensing lion in the long grass. Rumour had it that our turn would come, and it did come.

At that time, I was very interested in finding out as much as I could. I soon realised that ninety percent of the guys in our class at Tech had been in the defence force. Many had been involved in fire-fights. Some in battles like yourself. A guy called Barry Smith had matching machine gun bullet entry/exit wound scars on his torso, front and back. He told us of his spiral *Flossie* flight up out of the war. I was amazed that many of the sloppy looking civil engineering students sharing desks with me had been lieutenants and corporals the year before. One guy had been a grader driver building roads for Jonas Savimbi in Jamba. Another had been a marine *killick* (leading seaman) in inflatable craft on the Kunene. There we sat in a class full of veterans behaving like unruly schoolboys. It became abundantly clear to me then that two years in the SADF did not necessarily make a man out of you.

One could postpone the draft by staying enrolled at a place of tertiary education. Conscientious objectors like our friend Gustav were sentenced to four years in jail. Two years in a civilian jail like Pollsmoor and two more in military detention – in a blue overall – being called a "*fokken blou-job*". Jehovah's Witnesses like Bill's diving buddy Mark Scott got four years inside. For the time being I stayed enrolled. My brother Bill, who was working at the SA Museum at the time, got two weeks to pack up and leave the country or "serve". Bill went to California and lived in a basement full of old furniture and slept on a deflating air mattress.

Today Allegra and I went for a run in light drizzle up on Table Mountain. What a different world it is for her and your Michael's generation.

Better and worse in some ways.
Too many people.
The elephant in the room.

Signing off – PIP PIP – Cheerio.

Kalleee

Chapter 39

The Mark of Cain

We have learned from war, that peace is preferable.

We have learned from humankind, that humankind cannot realistically
learn from history.

We have learned from Jon Ronson and Robert Hare that about 1% of adult
male humans are psychopaths and about 10%, sociopaths.
And we notice that the majority of the population are essentially
dull "herd animals" – passive if content and content to be passive,
but easily roused into a mob.

We have learned from watching the history of humankind,
that the "herd majority" of humans are willing to be led by leaders
who are psychopaths and sociopaths:
Hitler, Stalin, Putin, Amin, Gaddafi, Obote, Genghis, Pot,
Mao Zedong, Trump and so on and on.

We have learned from the study of social anthropology
that during our evolution as a species,
the more aggressive/warlike groups of humans
were more successful than the peaceful,
and thus, the genes for cattle-raiding and slave-taking,
in the human collective, prevail.

We have learned, therefore, that human populations,
led by a psychopath or a sociopath, will make war.

War is the inevitable consequence of being human.

It is the mark of Cain.

4 June 2016   Letter #40

Flying Mr G

4 June 2016

There is some kind of joy in the country because we were not downgraded to
JUNK STATUS.
With the ZAR at 17 to the EU and 15.6 to the US$ and 22 to the GBP.
Cold comfort.
We watch the govt. and their ongoing destructive activities.
So hopeless and rotten they are.

1 June 2016

A cold front pushing quite hard.
Big cloud on Lion's Head.
As I trot down just near the paraglider launch pad, a black eagle passes close by.
I see its full adult plumage and back markings.
No rain comes … only a southeaster.

May has been utmost temperate

The deplorable shenanigans of the ruling party continue.
It is all there to read in the **Mail & Guardian**.
A peregrine falcon whizzed by, between me and a rock face.
It is the second time, that peregrine.
My Granny Dinny, I think, simply commandeers the birds to show herself.
We go up Table Mountain often.
On these warm May mornings in the crags, there are small pockets of cool air.

One can almost taste the nip of the Arctic summer.

Documents are finally signed.

The house at number 12 will be sold and my ex-wife paid her millions,

Then she will go.

Gareth, we share this planet with pigs.

They are worse than pigs … (Quote: Robert Mugabe)

They are worse than animals … (Quote: Manny Pacquiao)

That is so absurd … why are pigs and animals the benchmarks for badness?

We Homo sapiens should be the benchmark for badness.

Some individuals, do, however, touch greatness.

I almost touch greatness sometimes … or taste it.

I do not aspire to be a great, I never have.

But I love to taste or touch it.

Hungarian salami and buttered Hungarian rolls in the Hungarian hills.

That would be great.

Or to walk into the Pantheon again or to see the Farnese Marbles in Naples.

Or to see Praha, or Wien.

To expect humanity from human beings is like expecting compassion from a crocodile. To expect anything other than dishonesty from the Zuma group, the same. Humans evolved over thousands of generations as a brutal thieving species. That is what we are.

We first banded together for protection. Small defensive groups evolved into larger bands and soon enough went on to attack, rape, pillage and lay waste. Empires were conquered.

An African friend of mine, a house painter from the Eastern Cape, tells me that there is a special African gene in the African male – a gene for laying waste to things. He says that his people will destroy anyone's successful enterprise out of jealousy – his own spaza shop, for instance. If he says it, then it is not racist. Being a so-called "black" person, he is exempt from being racist.

I tell him about Hitler and the Third Reich. I fly him to Europe on Google Earth and call up pictures of Dresden and the Blitz. "Europeans can also do a pretty good job of destroying things, no?" He thinks a while and replies, "Maybe the African man lacks the something needed for fixing again that which has been broken."

My friend Rolf Kirsten owned a farm in Namibia just outside Maltahöhe. Some of the camps had cattle in them, some were game camps. Other camps were left unoccupied so that the grazing animals could be rotated and thus not overgraze the farm between rainy seasons. The baboons figured out how to open the gate catches and special baboon-proof catches had to be fitted. Zuma and his band of pirates are like the baboons on Rolf Kirsten's farm. They would tip over the half-drums of the coarse salt cattle lick to search for the few maize kernels that might be in the salt. Sometimes Rolf would allow passing herders to corral their goats on the farm overnight. The baboons would tear the unweaned kids in two in order to get at the curdled milk in their stomachs. The baboons would open gates and leave them open – cattle would wander out, game would wander in and it would take days to sort out the chaos. Those destructive baboons were simply unable to see the bigger picture because they were baboons.

I was present at the 100th birthday of this Chicago Aeromotor.
100 years of constant operation.
A few years ago, Rolf Kirsten was forced to sell his beautiful dry farm to the government.

The land his family had painstakingly husbanded for over 100 years.
The Farm Daweb is now laid waste.

Yesterday I spoke to Gordon who is visiting the Island of Capri. My old stamping ground.

I longed for a walk down to Punta Tragara and a gin and tonic at Piccolo Bar in the Piazzetta. Dinner with Mario Coppola at The Faraglioni. My time there is long gone.

In my life I have had quite a number of those painful "last night of the holidays" experiences, starting in Welkom in 1976 with Lynette Stewart and ending one stinger of a night in Capri in 2001 or 2002. My marriage was already, I guess, pretty heavily on the rocks. My then dear but deceitful friend Jacques, by now, well ensconced as paramour. He had weaselled her head and turned her heart.

Carlos, Phillip Kantor and Jacq the Knife

My then-wife and I were on the isle for a short vacation, staying in the small apartment below the Villa of our friend, the Prince. The state of our union might have looked okay from the outside, but from the inside it felt confused and awful.

Out early one evening, my then-wife, our daughter Allegra, Alfredo, Antigone, me and some others were out having drinks in the Piazzetta. It was warm, balmy, tranquil.

I turned towards the church and, seated at the next piazza bar, were two young women, one of whom was looking at me. She was elegant and long of limb. Clear blue glass beads hung around her neck. She had on a sleeveless halter-neck pullover and was, to my eyes, absolutely exquisite. And by the way of that rare electric magic, we were both instantly in love. But I was trapped with my party and all the incumbent responsibilities. She just looked and smiled.

Later, after some muddled excuses about not wanting to go to the restaurant, wife and Allegra were escorted to our apartment and I said I needed a walk.

I walked down to the Piazzetta, radar on... down to The Qvisisana, along the strip, past the restaurants, up to Punta Tragara and now ... losing heart ... back up the back way to Via de la Botege... and there, finally, at a sidewalk restaurant opposite the shop where I bought a copy of a Pompeiian ring some years earlier, I found the two of them eating dinner.

She smiled and I pulled up a chair. We started talking about their trip through Europe, ending tomorrow ... back to Pennsylvania. We were so in love ... the second girl so painfully in the way ... three being the proverbial crowd.

After some hours I walked them up to their accommodation somewhere near Croce and returned home, feeling soulful, to a loveless wife in a quiet apartment at 2am.

I went to bed and couldn't sleep for that exquisite pain of love lost and the knowledge that, if circumstances had been different, things would have been different too.

❧

Some years back I was sitting, kind of blue,
down at our little boatshed at Bakoven.
Suddenly a wonderfully built woman dashed down to the water and dived in.
"That's the one for me!" I said out loud.

It was one of those rare electric moments.
The Cupid arrow,
or the flower drops in the Midsummer Night's Dream.

It was Zaan.

We had bumped into one another a few times before.

2016 – Cupid's barb holds firm

All best Old Pal
C

Chapter 40

A Fork in the Road

I touched on this in my second letter way back in 2013.

In 1993 Clea and Uwe and Michel Personic and I sailed a 70-foot yacht from Cape Town to Genova. Aga Jari had been built by Uwe at the Southern Wind Shipyard and was due to be shown at the Genova Boat Show. We sailed via St Helena and Gran Canaria while Yeltsin took over from Gorbachev.

Aga Jari moored off St Helena

It was autumn. Clea and I left the boat and were exhausted by the time we arrived in Capri. I went straight to bed and woke up two days later. Capri – what a place in 1993. And there we were, a novelty couple, trim and tanned as one is after a few months at sea, young and beautiful, among friends and glamorous high society. It was a magical time. Back and back we went, year after year, until 2003 when it was not so magical any more. By then, my wife had been having an affair with my best pal and surfing buddy and I was trying to fix our marriage for the sake of our daughter. Clea was not interested. I never went back again.

Capri is all tall limestone and grottos and pine trees. Cyclamen in the springtime. Roman history, pre-Roman history. The hotel at Punta Tragara was the HQ of Churchill and Eisenhower in WWII. British secret agents roomed at the Qvisisana. The humid air is scented richly with the essences of verdant growth. Ocean salt and pine are, without doubt, an extremely powerful elixir of love. Capri is a very sexually charged place.

I remember one night on that first visit an incident that is still hard for me to believe. I do believe it happened, I remember it clearly, but I cannot believe it.

We were invited to the Villa of a very wealthy couple. He was a little older, she was about my age and elegantly groomed with an air of sophisticated casualness. There were a few small children, servants and an au pair or two.

After dinner, before camomile tea was served on the terrace, she invited me for a tour of the house. Much of it was medieval and very interesting to me. At some point she stopped with the history and said something like, "If you leave your girlfriend, I will leave my husband and we can be together, you and I." Then the tour continued. It was a fork in the road.

I didn't leave my girlfriend, but I often wonder what would have happened if I had. The sophisticated woman divorced her husband and remarried soon after. It could have been me, but it would not have worked out. Her society was high society, mine was camping out of the back of a *bakkie* in Namibia. Over the years I watched from a distance. We were never invited to her villa again.

26 June 2016   Letter #41

Hi Gar.

On the morning of the longest night.
Up Table Mountain I went.
Crisp and clear and wet.
Much damage to the path from rockfalls after the rain.
Some wise person said:

Don't wait for the storm to pass in anticipation of the sunshine to come.
Learn rather to dance in the rain.

What set of trip switches need to be tripped to turn a good day into a bummer day?
Accounts need to be paid.
More than 10k to the tax consultant for doing the books and 18k to the ex.
Pool pump at No. 12 burned-out next door.
Selling my house next door to pay her out.
Uncertainty.
Ek verlang na my liefling … Zaan in Canada.

OK … upward and onward … rain dance.

Brother Mick is kiteboarding with his wife Brenda and 21-year old twins Mikaela and Keanu in Mauritius. They are all really good.
It was Mick's 50th birthday on the 19th of May. We had a good laugh. He invited all the old buddies from the '80s and '90s. As a gift, I gave him an Opinel filleting knife which I bought in Canada last year. I remember

an evening some birthdays back, maybe 2012: Brother Mick brings out something called his "last man turns out the lights bag". It is a kind of desert rucksack crafted by Mick-Man himself. Attached to the bag is a quiver of maybe 50 hunting arrows and a very fancy white collapsible fibreglass hunting bow. The kind of bow one would buy at a store which stocks gadgets and gifts for the urban male. Stores called Toys for Boys and such. I remember that the world was due to end soon (according to the Mayan Calendar) so yup, it was 2012.

Anyhow, Mick was a few drinks in and ready to lecture the gathering on some of the finer points of post-apocalyptic survival. In a trice Mick had the bag all laid out, the bow was strung and an arrow notched. He drew back. Perhaps in China where that type of equipment is manufactured they don't have men with Mick's strength to test them. There was an explosion as the bow shattered. Both he and I were sprayed with a shrapnel of fine white fibre-glass spicules. It took at least a week for the itching to subside.

In November we were again gathered at Mick's house. I enquired about the bag and it was summarily fetched, wrapped in a blue kikoi, along with a new (superior) bow and a quiver of maybe 60 arrows. He buys one or two whenever he passes that kind of shop. This time the bow was not strung but a piece of wood drilled with small black holes was withdrawn from the depths of his bag's dark and mysterious interior. Soon enough, a pointed dowel and some kapok were added to the mix and, like a huge bear of a shaman, Mick began to make fire right in the middle of his dining room table. Rubbing those hardened palms, spinning the dowel with its point wedged into one of the little holes, until … pop … there it was … a flame. A not insubstantial effort was required to bring that small flame to life, but once it was there it was time to further explore the contents of the small rucksack that would provide Mick and his family with a competitive edge while out foraging with the other five million inhabitants of greater Cape Town – or those of them surviving.

For obvious reasons, some of the trade secrets cannot be revealed, but notably there were 14 pairs of spectacles in there. Those cheap "readers" that one can purchase at Clicks for R120 a pair. Like Noah's Ark, Mick's specs were strength graded two by two. 1.50 and 1.50 … 2.00 and 2.00 … 2.50 and 2.50 and so on right up to 4.00 and 4.50. I guess he figured that once his eyes were at 4.50, he would be out of arrows or something.

Well, have fun in Mauritius Mr Mick and family – good on ya for keeping it all together. I hope that *Opinel Efile* is there too, or at very least down with the "fire-sticks" in the "last-man bag".

⚜

Some time ago I wrote about life in the RSA being akin to being aboard a once-fine passenger liner with the wheelhouse locked from the inside. "Monkeys in the wheelhouse, Pirates at the helm". A tragic ageing pale estate agent from Natal named Penny Sparrow tweeted something on twitter about South Africans behaving like monkeys on the Durban beaches over the festive season. She has been fined R150 000 plus costs.

You should see what's going on the country at present. Tshwane (Pretoria), the SABC, the EFF, the ANC. Wasn't there a song once? … **You ANC Nothing Yet.**

Well, there won't be much left when they're finished with this place.

Love – C

Chapter 41

All's Well in Kuwait Central

June 2016 … A letter from Gareth forwarded to me by a person at the British Embassy:

"All fine thanks. The fire was in block four down the passage 50 metres from my block 8.

We were unaware of the incident until afterwards when the inmates not dead or being treated in hospital were bundled black and soot covered into our block and others.

We gave them clean clothes and let them shower and eat.

Police managers came from all over to check on the situation.

As it turns out, the cause of the fire was a faulty air conditioner which the inmates had tampered with in efforts to keep it running.

It shorted out and caught fire, cutting all the power out.

The plastic casing burnt and spread to the bedding as the cell occupants unsuccessfully doused it with water as they yelled for help through the locked door.

As it happens, cry wolf, that block scream and yell all day and night for no good reasons anyway and so were largely ignored until the power had gone out and the extractor fans in every room stopped drawing the fumes out.

In the pitch darkness the smoke built up and the smoke poured into the main block as the cell occupants lay dying in agony.

The calls by the block bosses to the security on duty outside were similarly ignored for the same reasons until the smoke started reaching the neighbouring block five.

By which time the cell occupants were dead and still locked in … and the smoke levels in the main area had reached unbearable critical levels.

Finally I gather from them, as the nearly 200 occupants cowered in the suffocatingly acrid toxic smoke billowing everywhere, the outer door was opened, but still without permission to allow such a mass exodus of terrified panicked and asphyxiating inmates.

The police and security took ages to get instructions and backup staff to handle the hundreds of inmates that were dying behind the grille door to the block.

Even the police wardens were at pains to get to the locks as the smoke engulfed the areas outside the main door and screaming, groaning, suffocating blackened inmates panicked helplessly to a desperate degree.

I could hear a helicopter circling above for around an hour as police feared a breakout or lapse of security.

I heard the fire engines which were prevented from entering and all came to the wrong location.

I had no idea what all the commotion was until I had a call from London to say there was a fire fifty metres away and spreading and that there had been deaths and casualties.

All the surviving inmates are housed on top of us in high density as we wait for their block to be cleaned and the aircons replaced.

I am fine here and gave away clean tee shirts, towels and pyjama pants to the afflicted visitors.

All seems to have settled down as the inmates returning from the hospital are sent back in small groups.

This incident will have drawn attention to a more efficient fire response procedure, I am sure. But exactly what I have not yet heard.

We were hoping they would buck up with the promised Amiri release program.

I wish you or Matthew would make an appeal on my behalf based on my outstanding behaviour and prolonged mental trauma.

He must surely know of an unofficial ear to whisper into?

My dad is getting very frail I fear.

Anwar as far as I can gather was also far away on the opposite side of the fire and quite safe.

Thanks to Sahar too for phoning. I saw the call but had no idea who it was from.

I also mailed you a brief heads-up to let you know that we were fine."

24 July 2016   Letter #42

Hi Gareth

My old surfing pal Grant rocked up between jobs … leaving Dubai and starting in Bahrain on 1 August. He was due to start a 10-day cruise in the Seychelles last Sunday, but his friend phoned to say the boat needed repair work done in Mahe … trip cancelled.

I can handle a house-guest for a few days but not too long.

What a good guy he is – courteous, helpful, tidy and clean. Every day he tries to take me for breakfast or dinner or a movie, but I am like a *perlemoen*. I love my cave. The other evening I gave in and off we went to a bar/restaurant called Hudson's in Kloof Street for an early burger. All I wanted to do was get into bed with my book (**Mr Nice** at present). After that, a bad sleep. I woke over and over, anxiety attacks and heart palpitations like I have not had for a long time. From now on the answer is NO.

Last evening Grant and I *braaied boerewors and choppies* and this morning surfed excellent waves at Glen. Just the two of us out on a Sunday morning! Light offshore breeze, warmish water and lovely.

13 July 2016

Dinny's 113th Birthday – Zaan and my 9th anniversary.

This morning I was up before the sun. Bike ride on Table Mountain followed by a paddle on the smooth dawny sea. I watched the sun rise for a second time on my surf-ski off Glen beach. The waves were small but okay. At 09h30 I was back home in my wetsuit and off down to Glen for some longboard riding. Now I feel better.

Fear of Going Surfing

Today is the 10th of July.
Cape Town basks in a warm beautiful NE day.
The sea is gorgeous.
I find that I have developed a fear of going surfing.
I am not afraid of the water but of meeting too many people in the water.
I love surfing on weekday mornings when few others can.
But I am afraid of driving all the way there and the waves are *kak* with an onshore breeze.
Or the tide is too high, or the swell too small.
And then having to turn back and head home and get caught in the traffic.
Mainly I really hate crowds.
I cannot bear feeding from the communal bowl.

I do not, as a rule, surf on weekends.
But today I made an exception because it was such an exceptional day.
On almost empty dawn roads I drove past Paarden Eiland and through Milnerton.
Past the flamingo-filled lagoon and on to Derdesteen.
I was suited up at the water's edge as the sun came up.
Two guys had beaten me to it.

The morning was the tail-end of a dropping swell.
Tide still a bit high but by 11am low tide, the swell would be gone and the sea packed.
The larger sets rose and broke on the outer banks before fading away and reforming closer to shore.
The surfing was technical – one had to pick and choose lest you land hard and smash.
I had a couple of good rides and no bad ones.
Funny concept: Rides.

By the time I allowed myself to wash ashore there were maybe 20 cars in the carpark.
The waves were gone.
The water was getting packed.

I drove back to Camps Bay.
A *bakkie* like mine had just ripped through the double fence at Milnerton High.

It lay there on its side in the freshly ploughed earth.
A fire engine had arrived on the scene.
Too fast and carelessly, the humans, they drive.

The P-Eiland flea market was filling up with grungy types.
Baggy synthetic jerseys and tight jeans and cheap boots.

I collected Allegra and her boyfriend Leo freshly returned from three weeks in Mozambique. They had a great time.

Thankfully not needed, I went on down to Bakoven and paddled on the uncrowded but less exciting wide blue yonder.

I sit now drinking tea.
The entire house is open … warm air wafts through.
A pair of humpbacked whales moves towards Llandudno.

The other day on the radio I heard a woman talking about how UNICEF needed to urgently save 65 million children facing imminent death due to ignorance and chaos.
I turned it off.
These people are so stupid.
Why urgently save 65 million to breed out 130 million more unwanted?
If you don't need them, don't breed them.
If you can't feed them, don't breed them!
But sadly, stupidly, unconsciously, ignorantly they do. And UNICEF and OXFAM and their sisters and brothers keep feeding and inoculating the babies.
Will the tide of human population ever turn?
Will it turn before it is irrevocably too late?
Is it already too late?

What a world our single children will inherit from our generation!

Carl

Chapter 42

Via Zaris

A brand-new night, same old moon.
Somewhere I read that you shouldn't believe everything you read.
Sometimes you read stuff that kills you, a little bit.
And the stuff I read kills me a little bit every day.

I had found a shoebox full of copies of my ex-wife's love letters to her lover.
I read them.
I drove up to Namibia with a broken heart.

There are 220km of nothing fit for human habitation between Keetman-shoop and Mariental. Somewhere between the two, I saw a thin man walking towards me. He wore a crazy, vacant expression on his face ... I tore past at 140 km/h ... all tweaked for driving long distance ... optimum warmth, optimum blood-sugar, caffeine level: high, optimum music.

And him? ... Optimum nothing ... Just a worn-out man in worn-out gear.
What does he think as he walks along?
Where does his mind go?

At night I camp. Sleeping in the back of the open *bakkie*.
In the cool morning, I head off for a long walk ... been here before ...
this lovely place.
But this time the red rocks are mostly concealed by tall golden grass.
It is so beautiful, and not a breath of wind.

As I walk through the grass, I try to analyse my emotions:
Happy? – No
Sad? – No
Depressed? – No

Excited? – Not.
Then what?

It is time to stop tilling the same old ground, I think.
I long for new experiences.
I fear a day when I take stock and say: "So where did my life go?"
Allegra is still small … it will be years of parenting.
I am trapped. My situation is not good.

The desert air is so still. Windmills stand high and motionless above the tamarisk and the old stone basins. Small birds – plenty of small birds – all telling their stories to an otherwise quiet world. Rosy-faced lovebirds race by. The sky is milky.

Then on to the Naukluft, where I spend a night … what a sunset, so brutally sudden … under the stars … and then another … same nights, different stars, maybe?

A genet wakes me. The night air is cold on my face.

I walk far into the mountains and listen to the quietness and swim in the pools.

Then I pack up and drive to Maltahöhe, via Zaris. I will visit the Kirstens.

It is so spectacular out here – so golden and layered and so big that it cannot be photographed with any success. Mountains and plains stacked into infinity. Southern Namibia must be visited to be believed.

Along the wide gravel road I travel, feeling empty … bobbing along … like a cake with a missing slice. Why did she do this to me? And she will not tell me with who. Cruelty.

I need new, good thoughts. Everything is all I think of, so what can they be? I have thought all I know, over and over again. And so I arrive at the foot of the Zarishoogte pass. And there I see, sitting at the roadside, a little man with a bicycle. The bicycle has a flat tyre. Flat tyre or not, the Zarishoogte pass is not the place for going up on a bicycle. I lift the bike onto the *bakkie* and seat the little fellow beside me. Quite by chance, I have a puncture kit in my console. I hand it to my passenger. He accepts my gift gladly and smiles his crumpled face but seems unable to do more than mumble.

Ant Allen has provided me with a dozen or so Red Bulls for my trip. Which, with coffee, make for great solo driving. I reach into the glove box and hand him one. He is a Nama man, a small exhausted man of this hard desert land. He has never tasted anything like this before. Fizzy, warm, berry-sweet. And certainly, never so much caffeine. If the perfect advert for Red Bull should ever be made, this would be it. He was soon talking 24 to the dozen. Telling me all the intrigue and scandal of the district, and that Rolfie Kirsten is a very good man. But that much I already know. I deliver the man and his bicycle to the township behind the town and double back to Daweb.

I stay with the Kirstens on Daweb for a few days. It will be the last time. Daweb will soon be bought (expropriated) by the Namibian government and destroyed as a communal goat ranch. But we do not know this yet. We are happy. After some days I leave. The medicine of these good friends begins to work once more. I drive down through the pale Vloere. The road to Helmeringhausen is fine dusty sand and constantly falling away, ever downward, towards the river, towards the sea. It feels like flying.

Alongside the Orange River it is all flowers,
one must try to make oneself better.

… and one does …

From the depths of despair, only two years later

Zaan and I travelled the same way, in joyful fun.

25 August 2016   Letter #43

Hi Gareth

I wish I could wave a wand and get you out of that place.
And I know that you do too.
It is desperate.
I think of you so often.
Loss of liberty.

Zaan and I are off to the USA tomorrow. I have never been there before. Zaan was an AFS exchange student as a teenager in Oxford, Ohio. We will go and visit her host-parents Barb and Hardy and stay there for the long weekend until Tuesday.

Here is some news from my last month.

31 July 2016

Gisela, the widow of my dad Øystein, died of liver cancer on Friday 23 July.
Just under a year after my dad.
Her life started in Berlin ... great air battles were fought overhead.
One night a massive aircraft wing landed in their garden.
It stood like a tree, right in front of their front door.
She and her sister were taken onto the trains returning from the *Ostfront*.
To comfort the wounded and dying men.
A little later Russian soldiers occupied their childhood home.
What changes the world has seen since then!
And now to die in a faraway country in a faraway time.

She was a dancer. They said she could fly through the air.

She was strikingly beautiful but insane.

A product, no doubt, of the privations and stresses of that great destructive war.

From day-one of our years knowing her, she gave Øystein's sons no joy.

Every visit was a trial.

A couple of days spent with Ø and G in their apartment in Durban was a horrible experience.

All of Øystein's friends were, one by one, alienated and replaced with hers.

She alienated Øystein's sons and grandchildren.

After a few visits, they did not want to go there anymore.

My mood would steadily deteriorate as a visit day approached.

A euphoric feeling of liberation would fill me when I left and drove home.

In 2010 Øystein was made to sign a will against his will.

He begged me to secretly bring him his old will to re-sign in 2011.

In short, a lousy soap opera in which my brothers and I were each forced to play a part.

What a horrible business.

Dirty and trashy.

And now we must go through the last chapter ... the final episode.

And try not to get injured in the crossfire and fallout.

This last week has been a horrid week.

BUT

One of the beautiful things about being human is that you can choose what you think about. On Friday afternoon, after returning from Stellenbosch, I went for a paddle. I came home cleansed by the sea. I revisit now only for the sake of documentation.

The other day I went for a morning surf down at Glen. I was singing to myself the funny Madness song **Night Boat to Cairo**.

Perhaps 20 hours later I awake from a most stressful dream: On a square plinth of stone in the middle of a fast-flowing green river, in a chasm of Imperial Porphyry, stood three columns set on the right angle. The forth column was snapped off leaving only a jagged stump of rock. On top of the three columns was placed a square capital. The columns were about 6 feet tall and I was trapped on this hard-carved island. The columns were quite slender and I could just push through between them, but I could not stand up straight. Nor could I sit down on the jagged stump of the missing fourth column. The fast-flowing water hosted unknown but very real and lurking dangers. Beyond, perhaps 50 metres away, were sheer red cliffs. I could not see from where the water came nor where it went. After a prolonged period of acute discomfort, up the gorge, against the current, came an elegant pharaonic barge … much like the Khufu ship. There were many oarsmen. The blade of each oar was made of green jade, carved like a Maori war club. As the vessel rounded my imprisonment, I saw the delicate fashioning of the steering oar, as it felt the current and turned the ship around and away. Back from whence it had come.

Returning to the real world:

Allegra told me that her friend Lena would not be joining them at the dance. "Why?" I asked. Lena's boyfriend Bob had cheated on her and they broke up. "Ah," I said. "That's humans for you. That is what we do – humans cheat, raid, exploit and make war. Unfortunately that is the nature of our species, my love."

"Imagine a crocodile," I continued. "Imagine scolding a crocodile like this: you naughty beast, look what you have done. You dragged a young impala into the water and drowned it and then you ate it!"

"Yes," replies the reptile, "and the day before yesterday, too, and I will do it again. I am a crocodile, and that is my nature."

⚓

All my life I have admired adventurous people. I am sad to say that I am not an adventurous person. I have read with great enthusiasm the works of Melville and Nansen and Gavin Mortimer and Giles Milton. Biographies and autobiographies. Vicarious forays into the lives of people who love adventure. And even though I am a big guy, I most often feel like AA Milne's tiny character Piglet. So onward I push into the world of travel like a salmon swimming against the stream. All my memories tell me that it is very worthwhile, but it would be so much easier just to go the other way.

10 August 2016

After months and weeks of approaching, the 9th of August dawns and I am suddenly in the funnel's vortex. It is time to go.

Emirates Airlines now flies three times a day from Cape Town to Dubai (i.e. 21 Boeing 777 flights per week). The flight is only 30% full and I have three emergency exit seats to myself. I read until dinner, drink beer, go for a pee, put on my eye flaps, insert my ear plugs, pop a Stilnox sleeping tablet chased by a watered-down whisky and away I go into dreamland with the small (thoughtfully provided) luminous "wake for food" sticker stuck to my right eye flap. The flight from CT to Dubai is about 12 hours long. Maybe 7 hours after popping my pill I am awakened for breakfast. Eat, read, land and transit to flight EK 241 headed for Toronto. That was nice 'n' easy.

Flight EK 241 is chock-a-block. The aircraft is a double decker Airbus A380 – there must be 700 passengers aboard. All but a very few are Eastern, Arabic and Indian types returning from visits to their native lands. Many are first-timers to Canada. There is some mistake with my requested emergency exit seat and I am plonked in a no-legroom seat next to a loudly protesting Muslim woman who refuses to sit next to any male passenger. Oh boy!

Some tactful manoeuvring fixes the problem and I get swapped with a tiny white-swaddled Indian woman, who's feet probably didn't even touch the ground below the aft emergency exit seat in which she had been placed. Lordy alone help her if she had to try and open the emergency door.

And so, finally, I hunker down to my usual routine ending with the "wake for food" sticker on my eye flap and the Stilnox down the hatch and the expectation of a lovely sleep right up until a late afternoon luncheon ahead of a gentle touchdown in Canada. I wake an hour later. The sleeping pill must have been faulty … under-spec … and so starts a very long day of bobbing 10km above Romania, Northern Europe, Norway, the Atlantic, Greenland, more Atlantic, some Canada and finally Toronto.

Why they do not "potty train" all people properly remains a mystery to me! Maybe they do not have potties and are simply permitted to piss all over the place in Jalalabad and on Mecca.

Once landed in Toronto we wait half an hour before we are permitted to disembark (disembowel). The Pearson Airport arrivals terminal is apparently full to capacity. It must be allowed to clear a little before we are allowed off. I am at the back of the plane so I am one of the last out. The mess is indescribable. It looks as though a large troop of chimpanzees has been having a party over and under the seats. Every here and there an elderly person sits. Once out of the plane door, I pass at least 30 wheelchairs and wheelchair attendants lined up ready to go in to collect the aged. The pair of escalators directly ahead are not functioning and many of my fellow passengers struggle to pull themselves up the slightly larger than average sized steps. It is truly pathetic to see young, weak, overweight people so horribly at odds with this very mild obstacle.

Next, we arrive at the immigration hall … aaargh!
I arrive in London after a two-hour bus ride on the Robert Q.
I am collected at the bus depot by Zaan.
Zaan and I love each other very much.

---

21 August 2016

We ride our bikes up the riverside path

Like Stellenbosch when we were kids … staying with Dinny … on holiday!
The smell of the river.
The smell of growing green.
I stop by the green painted iron bridge at Meadowlilly.
Zaan races up the hill for a bit of extra exercise.
My body is tired from carpentry … Zaan and I have just built new front steps.
It is a windless summer's day.
It is a most glorious warm day.

Yesterday we drove down to Port Stanley to paddle on Lake Erie.
Zaan's big RAM *bakkie* is like a boat.
Ehh putt-putt along … automatic … the world is so neat and tidy around here.
Neat homesteads, neatly mown lawns.
Order for my order-loving eye (*Alles in Ordnung*).

I wonder what it is that makes my Third World brethren tend toward disorder and chaos? Surely Canada with its freezing winters is every bit more difficult to be prosperous in than sunny and rainy Zimbabwe? Can we fairly blame it on the massively disruptive effects of the slave trade over the centuries? Perhaps, perhaps not.

Down on the lake it is like being at the seaside, but the water is saltlessly fresh. We paddle out into the light onshore breeze and run back with the small swell.

Piglet seems to enjoy this type of holiday.

There is no pressure.

The years and years of surf trips sure had their excitement, but it was stressful too:

Will it be onshore tomorrow?

Will there be waves at Gerickes Point or Jongensfontein?

Should we drive to Jeffrey's Bay?

Where will we camp?

Will the seals at Outer Pool bite me?

Are there sharks?

Over here there are no sharks or whales and if the wind blows onshore or offshore it does not really matter, because you just do something else.

Like going for a run this morning in the soft sandy trailed Komoka forest.

We trot a 9km loop.

Greens upon greens under greens.

Greens to black in the deep shade.

Greens to gold above where the sun hits.

Blue sky and white cloud.

This is the summer.

The winter is on the flip-side.

The other side which I have not seen myself.

Neither here, nor in Arctic Norway.

Sunny-side UP.

Working hard too ... lots of new stores being designed from my office up in the trees.

And peace and companionship and love and much joy.

Love, Carlos

Chapter 43

The New Will

Our dad never fully recovered from the venal thrombosis, or whatever it was, that knocked him down in 1988 (refer Chapter 12). He learned to walk again but his sense of balance was gone so he relied on vision to keep himself vertical. The back/front aspect of having no balance betrayed him though, and he fell fairly often. Dad went in for surgery time after time, and his leg bones and hips were cobbled together with steel and titanium. It was a vicious circle. The more he fell, the more afraid he became of standing up. The more he sat, the weaker and heavier he became. All the while his bones lost density, causing them to break more easily.

In about 1990 Øystein and his long-time partner Gisela were married. Gisela, a child of WWII Berlin, was nuts. As a young woman she slipped out of *Deutschland* and rematerialised in Stellenbosch – and it was to this town that Gisela and our dad moved to live out the final chapters of their lives.

A German control-freak hoarder, seriously traumatised by the Russian counter-invasion and occupation, Gisela would not permit so much as a biscuit to be passed to our dad without intercepting it and handing it to him personally. And there was simply no possibility of a private conversation. If I wheelchaired him up to the local coffee shop, she would be sure to follow with her pissy dog a minute or two behind. The crosses we must bear.

One day in 2011 Øystein and I had a very rare moment alone together (i.e. without Gisela present). He was lying in hospital once again, awaiting his second leg amputation, when I popped in unannounced to see him. Realising that we could talk without being overheard, he told me that he had been pressurised, against his wishes, into signing a new will, and that we, his sons, had been removed as heirs.

He told me that Gisela and some friends wanted to rob us of our inheritance. He was also unhappy that the bank had been appointed as his executor. He asked me to please arrange for him to re-sign his old or previous will. He asked me to keep it confidential and away from Gisela until after his death.

I had been party to the drawing up of our dad's old will. It was an uncomplicated one-page document giving Gisela usufruct of everything until her death – thereafter the residue of his estate would devolve, in equal portion, to his sons. It was simple enough and fair. Gisela had no children of her own and had come into their relationship without material assets other than some household effects.

I had an MS Word copy of the document on my PC, so I quickly drove back to Cape Town and printed off a couple of copies. I drove back to the hospital and within two hours, dad's old will was once again current. For over 18 months he had not had a chance to tell any of his boys about his wife's sneaky trick.

I gave one copy to brother Bill, filed the other and left it at that.

In August 2015, after a few years in a Stellenbosch old age home, Øystein finally died.

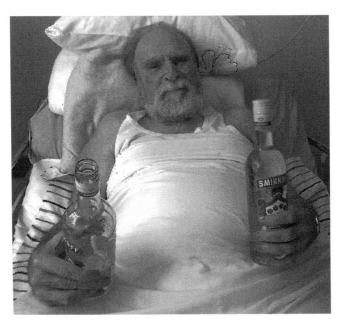

Cheerful to the end, loving a meat pie and a Pepsi, or a good slug of voddies.
Everyone was sad but also relieved – the poor man had suffered too long.

Soon enough, Gisela scuttled off to her attorneys and proceeded with the execution of our dad's estate as she had planned, smug with her 2010 will – a small triumph for her and her conspiratorial pals.

When I produced my dad's later dated testament,
Gisela and her conspirators were horrified.
She died within a year. It might have been the shock.
It was like one of those Grimm fairy tales.
It was not the spinning of Rumpelstiltskin, or pockets of coal turned to gold,
But it was something.
Not to be defrauded thus.
A small triumph.
But it left us feeling tainted – it was not the way our family behaved.

Letter #44

The wind splashed in my face
I can smell a trace
Of thunder

For 1970s/80s South African Anglophone lads,
Rodriguez, like Pink Floyd, was a keystone in our rites of passage,
We all had a copy of his **Cold Fact** album.
With abstract images
And the tantalisingly obscure phrases that peppered his songs,
They were a feast for young minds,
Boys to men: Angola in Ratels, or on the beach at Plett, or surfing at Jeffreys.
Or in Joburg, or in the SADF … Upington, Bethlehem, Kroonstad,
Influencing our lives in the keenest way,
And Sixto Rodriguez, living in Detroit, didn't even know.
The rumour was that he had committed suicide on stage, but he hadn't.
In Detroit he lived and laboured on,
Unaware that on the other side of the world,
he had achieved some sort of cult status,
While another grew fat on his royalties.

30 August 2016

We crossed the big latticed suspension bridge over the Detroit River,
Zaan and I.
Slipping through Immigration, out of the USA and back into Canada.
After the intensity of the I-75 (Dixie Highway) Northbound through Toledo

up towards Detroit, Canada's 401 seemed like a country lane,
quiet dusky green fields on either side of the road.

Where was Rodriguez as I passed over the bridge? The old man.
I know, most intimately, every song he released ... every word, every note.
I am sure that he was only a few miles away.
We must have almost touched.

Well, that was a weekend out of Canada and into the United States of America.
My first weekend in that country of so much influence.
Music, World War winners, Cowboys and Indians, Clint Eastwood movies
and Presidents.
Kennedy, Nixon, Lincoln and Jefferson.
Moon walkers, Chicago gangsters, the Cold War, the Vietnam War,
the American Civil War,
the invasions of ...

This past weekend was the first time I spent a US dollar in the US.
I have spent dollars in Indonesia, Greece and Italy.
I once paid with a ten-dollar bill for a room for one night in Kusadasi.
Last year I spent $4 on two meat pies in Zimbabwe.
That was my supper, in a Harare parking lot ...
The pies were hard, crusty and dry.

On Friday morning Zaan drove us, in her big RAM van, down from London,
Ontario, over the Ambassador Bridge and into the USA. It was a long day. An
hour spent with Immigration. Then tough traffic, fast trucks and plenty of
them. We finally broke off the I-75 Interstate and found our way via a small
ice-cream shop in Pandora to the tidy, red brick, green-lawned university
town of Oxford, Ohio. Thirty years earlier, Zaan left high school half way
through matric to go to the USA as an AFS exchange scholar. Possibly the
best year of her life up till then ... time spent with wonderful, intelligent,
informed and loving people who not only provided a safe and nurturing
environment, but also took her sailing and snorkelling in the Caribbean,
and skiing in Montana. We were with the Eshbaughs again and I now had a
chance to get to know them.

We cut our way through tall maize and soya-bean fields.

And small towns, more-or-less as one would expect from Ohio

And some unsettling signage.

As we drove down into Ohio, I noticed a nearby city on the map called India-napolis. Indy 500. Indiana Jones. Did my old school pal Andrew Hopson still live there? As emails would have it, he did – and on Sunday he drove down to Oxford. After an interlude of 35 years, we spent the better part of a day together. Thirty-five years of friendship, undented. After 30 years, Zaan's AFS host-parents' love untarnished. Aren't humans wonderful?

If you don't know the story of Sixto Rodriguez, watch **Searching for Sugarman**.

17 September 2016

I leave Canada in just over a week.
My workload had become extreme again,
but we made a one-night dash for Niagara Falls.
There were about 40 emails waiting for me when we returned.
They sit in the pit of my stomach and make me feel nauseous until I have gone through them all.
A sort of Calvinist punishment for taking a day off.
It is now 19h30 … work stops … been at it solidly since 08h30.

Yesterday Zaan and I paddled up the mouth of the Niagara River.
It was sunny and warm and windless.
The water clear and warm – taste, no salt in it!
We took some snaps with my small waterproof camera.

In some of the photos of this phase of my life, there are traces of youth.
Some show an old man … yesterday, in horror, I deleted one instantly.
Too much beer and *braai* on the back terrace.

My brother Bill emailed me some pics the other day,
Showing Mick placing Dad's ashes in the Eerste River,
just below his former home.
Mick looks up … our paternal grandfather Rolf looks up.
And so we leave the middle-age that crept up on us,
So unnoticed as we watched over our little children.
And so begins our old-age …
Do Not Go Gentle … he says with some desperation.
We are powerless to resist.

In the park next to Zaan's house there are many trees,
a huge lawn and a round sandpit.
In the centre of the sandpit are three red slides and climbing bars,
Two large plastic crates with blue lids – full of toys left there by some kind
person –
Are unpacked, played with and packed away again,
A few times every day, by orderly disciplined people.
Sometimes they are left lying around but,
The lovely yellow trucks and other items are not wrecked or stolen.
Boys and girls play as we did while their parents watch.
In just over a decade the little boys will be men.
In a short fifteen years they may be fighting in armies far away.
There are Boer War memorials all over Canada: Pretoria, Modderfontein.
Above us fly two slate grey fighter jets.
I Google them … they are F35s … The latest!
The "entry level" version costs US$148-million,
The "navy" version US$337-million.
Let us take an average of 200 million US dollars apiece.
You can buy a house in Camps Bay for 1 million US.
Those two young pilots up there had, strapped to their backs,
A pair of winged dragon suits worth 400 Camps Bay homes.
Strap on that dragon suit my boy, and learn to fly in the soft blue Canadian sky
So that one day you can come screaming down
Over some future Syria
And unleash your hell.

In the quiet of the late afternoon,
A needy young man on a bike freewheeled down to the play boxes,
And pinched a stainless-steel cooking pot.
I talked to him, he was so polite and broke.

Zaan and I ride along the riverbank past goldenrod and daisies.
The first trees begin to show their autumn colours.
This is such a precious time.
None to waste.

26 September 2016

I am sitting airside at Pearson International Airport in Toronto,
Drinking a Muskoga Mad Tom.
The first one is for me, the next for you, my friend.
I have just finished a fantastic book called **Sapiens** by Yuval Harari.
There is hope after all.
I am heading home after seven heavenly weeks with my love and best buddy
Zaan.
I cannot believe that I could have been this lucky.
I used to struggle with the meaninglessness of life.
I do not any more.
Adding value to Zaan's life and Allegra's life gives me all the meaning I need.

29 September 2016

Home Jerome – Surreal, Depressing, Exhilarating, Glorious.

Chapter 44

The Smell of Bacon

Not long ago, but for a very long time before that, there lived on an island in the Bering Sea a race of giant sea cows. These huge, gentle mammals grew up to 9m metres in length and chewed their diet of kelp without the help of true teeth.

They were first discovered by human beings in 1741 when a Russian expeditionary ship ran aground on their island. One of the ship's complement, a German naturalist named Georg Steller, observed the 8 to 10-ton animals to be monogamous, living and raising their young in small family groups while communicating with sighs and snorting sounds. Just lovely.

Within 27 years of their discovery by Europeans, the slow-moving and easily caught mammal was hunted into extinction for its meat, fat, and hide.

That is the sad story of **The Humans Meet Steller's Sea Cow**.

It was different with the humans and the pig.

⚓

In the early 1920s, my grandmother Dinny was in her late teens. The spectacular R44 scenic drive linking Gordon's Bay and Rooi Els had not yet been constructed, so, in order for her and her brothers Bill and Jack to go camping at Pringle Bay, they needed to go by sea. Dinny's father (Daddy Shaw) knew a man with a fishing boat who, for a small fee, would transport the three youngsters along the False Bay coast and drop them off on the south end of the beach where the waves were small enough to put a skiff ashore. After wading to land, the three Winshaw adventurers would lug their tents and fishing rods and other equipment all the way to the lagoon at the north end of the beach, set up camp and cut loose for a couple of weeks.

They would spear soles in the shallow water and catch *biskop* off the rocks. Large *kreef* (rock lobsters) would be flicked out of the rock pools, boiled and fed to their two dogs. There were no houses anywhere along that coast in those days. In the event of an emergency, they would have had to walk about 10km on a sandy track to the whaling station at Betty's Bay. One can only imagine what it must have been like – not one house!

Dinny told us wonderful stories of adventures in a pre-modern world. Of passages to Southampton by liner, or at age fourteen being her father's driver, chauffeuring him over the Cape's gravel-surfaced mountain passes in a Model T Ford. And of frying bacon with her dad by the side of the road on a wind-stoked fire of twigs overlooking a spectacular valley, with a bubbling pot of coffee in the hot ash slightly to one side. We could almost smell the sizzling! Or marketing wine in Mauritius, or five days travelling to England in a Solent Flying Boat with overnight stops at Victoria Falls, Kampala, Luxor and Sicily. My younger brother Mick and I longed for the possibility of one day being able to match her exploits, but somehow we felt we never would. We were wrong.

In the 1980s, Mark van Kets and I would pack our diving gear and sleeping bags into the boot of my Mazda and drive to Pringle Bay in an hour and a half. There was so much more convenience in our time. We did not need to organise a fishing boat. It took us five minutes to decide, 15 minutes to pack and in 20 we were off. We would dive for *kreef* and abalone and spear fish in the kelp forests. We would sleep on the dunes or in any one of many half-built houses in the rapidly expanding seaside town. In later years we would surf there and everywhere else. We were free to move. Our adventures were many, quickly executed and by comparison, very easy.

With new roads, cars, jet planes flying nonstop to the other side of the world and cheaper airfares, soon enough, between my brothers and me, we had out-travelled and out-adventured our magical granny: San Francisco, Tahiti, Bora Bora, Morocco, the Basque coast, Norway, Europe, St Helena, the Canaries, New Zealand, Indonesia, the Whitsundays, Madagascar, the Comoros … and I had fried, thanks to Dag, my bacon on a wind-flared fire of twigs in a small iron pan below a glacier on the edge of a steep mountain drop-off overlooking a deep fjord – and had smelt the sizzling.

"Where to next?" I often think.
Dinny went from mule carts to passenger planes in her lifetime.
Will we go virtual on all this? ... Yes, I think we will.

Sometimes when my old mom comes to visit we open Google Maps – Satellite on my large monitor. Off to Salzburg and Wien we fly. We pop in at her favourite shops and restaurants and churches. We Google any information we desire as we move from place to place. We look at rotating street views of Nova Scotia and Yalta. I am able to track Wilfred Thesiger's thirsty trip across Arabia's Empty Quarter, skimming low over the dunes while seated at my desk sipping a cup of tea. I sometimes visit bays on the distant islands where we have previously dropped anchor. The technology is still comparatively basic, but more is coming.

Yesterday I hovered over Rome, a city I visited often over a ten-year period from 1993 to 2003.

We stayed with a friend in a palace near the top of Via del Plebiscito. We would come and go, walking to the Capitoline Museum or the Pantheon or Piazza Navona. The green wooden gates were open by day and, at night, a knock would get us in. I have just Googled my way to the entrance of the

Palazzo Grazioli. Outside stand two men in camouflage fatigues. They have truncheons hanging from their belts and automatic rifles in their hands.

Zaan spent a few weeks in Paris towards the end of 2017. I asked her how Paris had changed in comparison to her previous visits there. Impressions? "Security," was her answer, "uniformed men with guns … groups of eight or ten." She told me of security checks and bag searches at the entrance to almost every store. Of security at the metro and the airport. And the smell of urine in the streets.

Soon enough, I believe, there will be virtual tours, purchasable (piratable?) to anywhere.

Shortcomings there will be for sure, such as not being able to see the exact texture of van Gogh's brushstrokes, but hey, we are not all that particular.

The advantages would be multifarious: price, convenience, no crowds. No men with guns. No smell of urine. A long trip could be broken up into episodes, no need to take leave from work. Venice could be visited in winter without the fear of wet feet. Cairo without the heat, the flies and the bothersome touts in the marketplace. Or how about a journey down to the Titanic without even pulling on a wetsuit! Admittedly, there might not be the smell of sizzling bacon, but halfway through you could always press the pause button, waddle off to the kitchen, fill the kettle and pull out a frying pan.

Perhaps one day there will be booths, like olden-day public phone boxes: in you step, insert your card or finger or eyeball … type an address and instantly materialise at your desired destination … teleported!

No more treacherous boat trips for refugees.

30 October 2016   Letter #45

Hi Gareth

This being a short one.
Such a month since my return to RSA.
Such intensity of work and herding of cats.
Such a period of unimaginable politics that I cannot even begin to describe.
The daily radio news plays like a soap opera of unbelievable convolution.
And exhaustion at the end of the working day, which is usually a bit late in the evening.

On **8 October 2016** I wrote:

While out running on the mountain early this morning,
I saw, in the bay below, a ship pulling some funny manoeuvres.
I was reminded of this:
In 1989 I sailed into Port Louis harbour – Mauritius.
Just to the right of the harbour mouth lay a large rusting tanker with its bow about 100m up the beach. The captain, entering the port at night, had not paid close enough attention to the leading lights and ran his ship aground. He had become confused and dazzled by the many red and green lights in the city. I have entered ports such as Las Palmas, Noumea and Genova at night … identifying the leading lights is not always easy.

Returning to RSA and reflecting … I am dazzled by the magnificence of our environment, but deeply troubled by the politics of the country.

One might ask: Are the rumblings louder than usual?

More thoughts:

Allegra has missed six weeks of UCT lectures because of protests.
She should have started exams two weeks ago and will now only start in a week's time.
Look on Google and see Cape Town on Thursday afternoon.
Fees Must Fall is the big issue, but the more interesting sideshow is the call for decolonisation.
The world is globalised … or globalising fast.
No one can call for this process to be reversed.
Rhodes must fall.

And science must fall!

I watched a YouTube clip on Science Must Fall …
https://youtu.be/C9SiRNibD14
… as argued by a UCT student trying to explain lightning and Newton's observations regarding gravity and falling apples in a decolonised African context. The UCT student will no doubt be a Nobel Laureate soon enough. If not, at the very least an ANC cabinet minister.

Too tired now to write more.
Love C

Chapter 45

Shoulder Chips

I am so tired of all the shoulder chips.

I accept that people have them for historical reasons.

The functions of oppression and persecution.

I know that it hurts brown people to be called *monkey* or *nigger* or *kaffir*, or Jews to be called *Jew-bugs* or *kikes* or *schnorrers*.

They say you can commiserate with people but you cannot feel their pain … I get it.

Being lucky enough not to be burdened thus is a real blessing … not having the baggage of those tiresome shoulder chips!

You can call me *multiple cuckold* or *asshole Norsky* or *Langeraad* or *paleface* or *kaffir* or *whitey* or *Jew-bug* for that matter and I simply could not care less – but I admit that I was not pogromed by Nazis or quirted and teargassed and persecuted by the old NP SAP. Strangely enough, I do not like being called *white*.

We had a friend named Jeremy Tyfield aka Tyfie. He was a Jewish lawyer with no chips and a great sense of humour. Tyfie fought hard battles in court, a prize-fighter, no holds barred. A man with great compassion and his own private pain. And a man who was not afraid to call a *c u next time* a cunt.

He grew up in Camps Bay and schooled at SACS. We loved his smoky, rough and tumble stories. We loved his tales. Here is one that brought tears of mirth to his own eyes:

Tyfie had been fighting a tough settlement – the matter had not been taken to court, but the aggrieved parties had instead agreed to spare themselves the expense of litigation by going the arbitration route.

At the end of it all, Tyfie stood in the centre of the ring, his gloves held high, 12 rounds and his opponent soundly beaten. The documents were signed, and lawyers, advocates and paralegals were packing up their papers and folders and pens, when the opposing client, a grey-haired and somewhat austere German man, leaned over and asked Tyfie for his card.

Tyfie recalled that he was not a little surprised, but he smiled his crooked Tyfie smile, opened his wallet and with a flourish handed one over.

"You neffer know," said the old German, "ven you might need a vize und cleffer Chew."

What a great guy! Tyfie taught us how to be light.

Like religion, shoulder chips are heavy burdens.

Sadly, we lost Tyfie due to his insatiable appetite for tobacco.

He is sorely missed.

4 December 2016   Letter #46

Hi Gareth

On Allegra's 19th birthday (17 November 2016) I received the following from your friend Shireen:

Hi there

Just to let you know that I received a message from the British Embassy that Gareth's phone has been confiscated. As such out of contact.

Kind regards
Shireen

October was a terribly busy month for me and I did not write you a good letter.
Perhaps the YouTube link added value?
November, I thought that I might not be able to send you one at all.
But yesterday I received a message from you confirming that you can receive a pdf via a friend's phone. So here goes.

I have taken the hurried letter of October and fleshed it out properly. Added some meat and carrots and onions to the stew, so to speak:

The weather here at the Cape is becoming drier, hotter and windier.
There is a drought and too little water in the dams.
Or, looking at it another way, there are too many people.
Like jobs, classrooms and state medical facilities, there is actually no shortage
– just too many people.

Strict water restrictions were put in place from the 1st of November: watering by bucket only.

I am sad about the water situation, but I must say that I am really enjoying the bucket challenge. My garden is not large by comparison to some of those around me. Over the years, I have planted "water-wise" plants, but still, I was running my irrigation sprayers for 20 minutes twice or three times a week in mid-summer. The micro-jet system is a very impersonal way of watering a garden. Using a bucket is lovely. I have selected those triangular builders' buckets because they pour accurately. I have made little dams around my selected plants and they get a couple of litres each by hand.

Before dawn now, in the cool quiet air with the early scolding thrushes, I am so much more involved with the garden. Not just a case of turn on the tap, wait for the sprinklers to hiss into action, go back to the computer for 20 minutes then up and turn off the tap again.

In 2012 I built an outside shower. We shower outside standing in a large plastic crate fitted with a hose which runs out onto the lawn. Splash-water is caught in buckets. The lawn has been reduced in area by the insertion of flagstones. It is pretty like this and requires much less water.

All our roof rainwater either ends up in two JoJo tanks or has been diverted into the garden. I have installed a Slimline JoJo tank with two taps for pool backwashing. No more water wastage there. One of the taps is at the base of the tank, the other about a quarter of the way up. The tank is kept full of water. Once in a while, the upper three-quarters of the tank is run out into the pool. The pool is then backwashed back into the tank until full. Between backwashes, the backwashed material settles at the bottom of the tank. Twice a year that sludge is run off into the drain. I have stopped using the pool chlorinator as splashed salt water kills lawn and plants and fresh water must be used to try to un-salt the salted. Dishwashing is done in a plastic tub in the sink – gazanias love dishwater.

The past while has allowed me to listen to the radio while working on detailing and driving around. What a fascinating patch of history, both local and international, we are currently living through. Zuma, the Guptas and Thuli Madonsela's "State of Capture" report. Water-saving ideas. The ANC. Hillary Clinton vs Donald Duck … and then Donald Duck for President! Brian Molefe resigns but is so wealthy by now that he does not need a job any way? And Penny Sparrow's "monkeys" vs Julius Malema's "We are not calling for the slaughter of white people, at least for now... The rightful owners of the land are black people. No white person is a rightful owner of the land here in SA and whole of the African continent." There is so much racism on the radio it is insane. So much "black" this and "white" that.

First off, I find the labelling of people "white" and "black" to be ridiculous. There is so much of it in South Africa that it has become a theme in itself.
Obama – the first "black" president in the White House.
Black golfer – Tiger Woods.
Black activist – Walter Sisulu.
Black actress – Halle Berry.

Why does the so-called "black" parent seemingly cancel the paler one?

Black/White/Black/White/Coloured/Orange!

Trump – the first orange president in the White House. How about that?
We all remember when, during apartheid, boys were boys and men were also boys?
"The garden boy ..."
Is Zaan, my 47-year-old girlfriend, a girl?
Am I white?

Just like "Christian Name" made way for "First Name" on forms. Surely, we can think of something better, if we even need a colour reference at all?
  Then we have had tension at our universities. Rhodes Must Fall, Fees Must Fall, Science Must Fall! Why must everything fall, I ask myself? Did Berlin have to fall in order for it to be built up again? Did Stalingrad? Why not rather just build up, or must humans also destroy? Is it an unavoidable facet of human nature? I think it is.
  Allegra missed weeks of UCT lectures as a result of the protest action. She thankfully managed to complete her exams and is in Vietnam now with her boyfriend, Leo. There was an uneasy truce on campus during the exam period. Who knows what will happen next year?
  Trotting alongside the main "Must Fall" theme over the past couple of months, we have had a growing commotion around "decolonisation". This is a most interesting subject for me. I have read quite widely on the subjects

of science, history, social observation and social anthropology – Diamond, Dawkins, Darwin, Nansen, Kapuscinski, Pinker, Sajer, Olusoga and Erichsen etc ... all the way through to Rudolf Höss. I recently completed the very accessible **Sapiens: A Brief History of Mankind** by Yuval Noah Harari. I am currently reading **King Leopold's Ghost** by Adam Hochschild. These two books together provide an interesting insight into the horror and agony of being colonised as well as highlighting the unstoppable inevitability of it all. There have been recent suggestions that there might be some kind of "nationalist pushback" against globalisation, but having been otherwise convinced by Harari's arguments, I wonder.

Looking at the broader picture, we have all simply been invaded and colonised over and over again. Homo sapiens cannot go back to living in small, independent, hunter-gatherer groups. That point of no return was reached thousands of years ago. My Viking forebears were ultimately colonised by Christians. Our old Nordic religions are lost. We cannot cry about that now. Our southern European and British forebears were thoroughly colonised by the Romans. Their languages and cultures are all lost. Before that, our Neanderthal ancestors were so heavily colonised that only about 2 or 3% of their genes remain in our bodies. I could blame this on Africans as it was African Homo sapiens who colonised Europe and wiped out our Neanderthal ancestors who were, way back, of African origin themselves. And similarly, going forward, it was Africans who ultimately became the Roman Empire that colonised and evolved into the Europe that in turn conquered and colonised Africa.

Meanwhile, in Central and Sub-Saharan Africa, the Bantu tribes showed each other little mercy. The people of Kongo were already slaving when the first Portuguese arrived. They also overran, enslaved and bred with the Khoi and San people of the South, and thus we had the lighter-skinned clicking Nelson Mandela with his Khoi mitochondrial DNA. And hybrid steatopygia in Xhosa women.

No, we cannot go back, as painful as it must sometimes be and as painful as the histories are, we are now in the time of globalisation. And until we humans face a global cataclysm which scatters us into small bands of post-apocalyptic survivors, we are all colonised and will become even more so.

We Homo sapiens, who all pretty much drive the same cars, fly in the same planes, drink the same drinks, use the same devices, share a common global economic system and wear the same clothes, have all bought in. Let anyone try to buck the system and they will simply fall by the wayside.

My message to those who really believe in decolonisation would be: Discard your shoes and your jeans. Live in a hut and be happy with your hut. Do not aspire to having a house or a car or a new device. Throw away your current device. Get your education in a university with no elegant plumb and square ivy-clad buildings. A university with no degrees, no library, no lavatories, no books, no paper, no maths, no written word, no English with which to communicate your pain over the airwaves and of course, no airwaves! No fuel with which to fill Molotov cocktails and not even any half bricks to hurl or windows to smash. No football, no more ice-cold beer, no Nik-Naks, no maize meal even! ... and no chicken.

Looking it straight in the eye, there are simply two choices: walk barefoot backwards into folklore and illiteracy or lose the chip on the shoulder, admit that overpopulation and global warming are problems of our own making and move forward, trying every day, as hard as we can, to help all living species survive the massive challenges that our own species has created on this fragile planet. There will be two billion more of us by 2050, they say.

Last week we heard that State Security Minister David Mahlobo has allegedly been hanging out with a Chinese organised crime figure who traffics rhino horn and openly brags about bribing our justice and immigration officials. Bunch of cunts.

Government organisations and parastatals like Eskom, Transnet, SAA, SABC and SANParks have been looted and are still being looted.

National and provincial government departments have accumulated R46-billion in irregular expenditure. Auditor general Kimi Makwetu said the Passenger Rail Agency of South Africa (PRASA) contributed R13.9-billion in irregular expenditure. Makwetu released the auditor general's report on national and provincial audit outcomes for the 2015-2016 year on Wednesday. He said that the irregular expenditure in 2015-2016 had increased by 80% since the previous financial year when national and provincial government departments had incurred R25.7-billion in irregular expenditure. Along with PRASA, the health departments in KwaZulu-Natal and Mpumalanga, the department of water and sanitation, and Gauteng's road and transport and human settlements departments are responsible for 50% of the R46-billion uncovered in Makwetu's report.

The people in command have enormous arrogance, little integrity, negligible honesty and few skills. SADF soldiers are being sent home because there is no food.

Soon I may feel the need to go away.

⌘

The Dalai Lama says that one should not judge oneself
by comparing oneself to others.
I try not to.
I am grateful that I do not commute daily, or work down a coal mine,
and I do know that I enjoy the very best of the best of the fruits of life.
Sadly, I feel the work I do to be a complete waste of time.
A waste of my life.

When I was a young man my grandmother Dinny often said to me: "Do not allow yourself to be put upon by others." She said this frequently with regard to my pre-wife who became my wife and then my ex-wife. I would look at her blankly. I had absolutely no idea what she meant. But she did.

I live carrying the burden of having been hugely untrue to myself, with the excruciating knowledge that I can never fix it. We have only one life, you see, and when we are young we are stupid … some of us are, at least.

Life is a rollercoaster. And I do long for a time when I will not have to deal with floods of emails and the constant needs of others – a time when my body does not vibrate or tingle ever so slightly against the hard edge of stress. A time when I can relax and chat with a friend for as many hours as I like without needing to go and attend to some or other project that feeds off my soul like a thirsty infant. I know exactly where my existential crisis comes from. As Zaan has taught me:

Not everything works out as we planned it.
There comes a time to move on and align our dreams with our actions.
Because that is what we did not know to do when we were young.
Maybe we did not know what our dreams were back then.
But we must do it now, for time is running out fast.
Align our dreams with our actions.
Maybe some of us did, but not me. Not really.

26 November 2016

Among the white horses of the light southeaster,
Last evening at sunset there must have been 100 whales off Camps Bay.
At any one time about 15 to 20 plumes of white mist stood,
Illuminated by the rays of the setting sun.

This morning I needed to go to the city early.
At about 08h30, as I came over Kloof Nek, I saw a white sheet in the sea.
It looked like the dorsal fin of a giant sailfish.
I thought it might be spray or mist thrown up by a navy submarine.
I raced home, grabbed my binoculars, and saw a long row of whales,
Head to tail,
All spouting at fast pace, as if to deliberately create this effect.
And all around, the ocean was filled with more whales.
I believe they are gathering before heading off towards their Antarctic summer
feeding grounds.

3 December 2016

Towards the end of the paddle,
About eight dolphins arrived,
With a couple of little ones amongst them.
The water was very cold and clear.
Zaan and I slowed right down.
The dolphins were particularly relaxed
and swam with us for about twenty minutes.
Gliding upside down a foot or two below the surface.
Showing their white bellies and genital slit.
Surfacing alongside, almost touching our boats.
No breeze, cool air.
I said to Zaan, "You know, this is as good as it gets."

Best greetings
Carlos

Chapter 46

Why?

I sometimes wonder about what people take for granted in this life. Why, for instance, are there no instructions on a corked wine bottle or a can of peaches? How would you open these things if you did not know? Or what would you do with a packet of cigarettes or even toilet rolls?

Or this intriguing steel object seen not infrequently in Canada?

When I was a young man and there were referendums and things,
I thought about simply not knowing what other cultures don't like about each other.
About being unaware.
Why was there all this enmity?
What was it the ex-Europs were so scared of that made them resist dismantling apartheid?

What is it exactly that Zulus and Xhosas don't like about each other – or the English and the French? Why, when I was in the army, did the *souties* and the *Dutchmen* always end up fighting?

In South Africa, with its heavy racial biases, such knowledge would be a great tool.

I would have liked to – and still would like to – do the following exercise:

1. Figure out the major ethnic/population types in the country. Say: (so-called) Black, White, Coloured, Indian etc.
2. Get 1000 volunteers from each group to write down five reasons they dislike or fear members of the other groups and provide five reasons they like or admire them.
3. Put the data into a computer for distillation and correlation.

The end result would be the five most common reasons why:

So-called "black" people are mistrustful of/dislike so-called "white" people.
So-called "black" people admire/like so-called "white" people.
So-called "black" people are mistrustful of/dislike so-called "Indians".
So-called "black" people admire/like so-called "Indians".
So-called "Indians" people are mistrustful of/dislike so-called "black" people.
So-called "Indians" admire/like so-called "black" people.
And so on …

Then, if a so-called "white" person, who is truly committed to fighting racism in the country, wanted to know how to "live the change", he or she could just check the list.

"Oh," he or she might say, "the so-called 'black' people don't like us palefaces because they perceive us to be mean-spirited, cold and inhumane," or whatever the case may be. Or so-called "Indians" might discover that they are mistrusted because they are too shrewd in business. Or so-called "blacks" are disliked/feared because they protest in an undisciplined and anarchic way. Then we could all work on improving ourselves in ways that steer away from the negative stereotype. And on the flip side, so-called "black" people could feel happy and proud that they are admired for their warmth, humanity and laughter – and the palefaces for their inventions.

26 December 2016   Letter #47

Zaan and I paddled from Bakoven to Hottentots Huisie this morning. We saw a sunfish. The sea was flat. No wind. Seals like giant maggots twisting and squirming on the big granite boulders just off the hotel. A most perfect day. Thousands of Capetonians spent it at Camps Bay. They used to call it Boxing Day. I have just completed my 2016 CPD credit input for SACAP. That done, I turn to focus my gunsights on GR.

Dear Gareth

Thank you for the email. Yes, I did get your two emails regarding "the prisoner transfer agreement". Like you, I do not know and cannot imagine how this whole horrible business will work itself out. All I know is that we do not have time to throw away.

A rebel without a clue, take 3:

Not everything works out as we planned it.
There comes a time to move on and align our dreams with our actions.
Because that is what we did not know to do when we were young.
Maybe we did not know what our dreams were back then.
But we must do it now, for time is running out fast.
Align our dreams with our actions.
Maybe some of us did, but not me. Not really.

I keep coming back to this.
I know that I must align my dreams with my actions.

But I do not really know what my dreams are.

I do not seem to have any concrete dreams.

All I want is freedom, and the freedom that I already have is massive when compared with yours.

And the freedom I have is huge when compared with most other humans on the planet.

But I want more freedom.

I do not have any other tangible dreams.

Only the desire for companionship, good health, financial wellbeing,

peace and freedom,

Before I am too old …

I suppose those are fine enough dreams to have?

Maybe it is a hell of a BIG ask!?

I do not (nor ever did) want to be a famous artist, or a professional musician, or a *maingat* architect, or a top lawyer or a director of a construction company.

Just to be off the rat-wheel with enough money to live comfortably.

And to be apart from Homo sapiens at large.

I do like to read and write.

I drew a new cartoon strip the other day … like "so what already". BTDT.

I took my mom to radiation therapy on Friday. She is eighty-three.

It is the last day of her third week – six weeks will complete the course.

She feels sick, her mouth is dry,

Her throat does not want to swallow.

She has lost many kilograms.

My mom's mind is clear but her body hurts. She has had so many operations.

There is bad arthritis in her bones.

She tells me that she does not want to live through five more years like the five just past.

She would love a painless exit,

And fears a lengthy degenerating bedridden slide to her end.

Virginia has, by global standards, had a long and good life.

She has never gone hungry, never been bombed, jailed, conscripted or suffered occupation by invasion.

She has had hot showers every day and has three sons and three grandchildren who live nearby.

But she is getting tired of her continued pain and physical decline.

I am a person supportive of suicide if life becomes intolerable, so we talk very freely.

But it is difficult for a younger person like me, with so much energy and who lives so intensely with running and paddling and bike riding and working, to judge what makes life worth living.

Would the occasional visit from your grandchildren and sons be enough?

How long would you, my friend, sit to be free for one day, to drink tea and dip biscuits under the pine trees looking up at the mighty Twelve Apostles and down over the broad Atlantic?

Or have a month to do as you please?

24 December 2016

The traditional evening of feasting where we come from. My mom's partner Ian McLean made the feast. Two types of ham, two types of Brussels sprouts (one with walnuts), a roast fillet in some delicious reduction, a platter of sliced duck breasts on *rucola*, tongue laid out in a mustard sauce, haricot beans, crispy roasted potatoes, chicken liver pâté, thinly sliced baguette, a dish of carrots and small beetroot, some sweet potatoes too, all set on a beautiful embroidered cloth with a bunch of mom's garden flowers in a vase flanked by two candles in silver candlesticks. Plus plenty of beer and wine. My mom and Ian were the hosts. Brother Bill and his partner Tess were there. Zaan's son Nicholas arrived before Zaan and me, with five jars of French jam. Ian's daughter Suzanne brought her son Orion. And so we were *en famille* at 6 Chas Booth Ave. Allegra and her friend Leo are on a two-month backpacking expedition in Vietnam.

Lucky we are. Very.

One wonders how many more of these we'll all have together.

I see the value and I do appreciate the effort, but I become detached and struggle to extract the essence of what others across the globe seem to get out of it.

It feels like I'm missing something fundamental!

Love
C

Chapter 47

Marriage

To me, marriage is an anachronism.

An archaic social convention.

Like wearing powdered wigs, or riding a horse, or wearing a sword – things from bygone eras.

I ask people, "What is it you are after exactly? The blessing of an imaginary god or the blessing of a lawless gangster state?"

Rather take responsibility for your own actions!

My old friend and lawyer Myer Orman advised me not to marry. "All you need is a contract of relationship, my boy. I will help you." Stupidly, I did not listen.

Unfortunately Myer was gone before I could ask him for help with my divorce.

My advice for anyone embarking on a relationship is this: make sure that your dreams and those of your partner are aligned. If you are a serious, contemplative man with scant need of restaurants and society, do not tie your life to that of a woman who craves a house full of friends and babies and friends' babies and parties. And if you want to build a yacht and sail around the world, find a partner who wants to build a yacht and sail around the world. Don't choose someone who desires a little boy to fuss over and a little sister for the little boy and two golden retrievers and a big house and an SUV. Because if you do, you are done for.

DONE FOR

Early February 2017   Letter #48

Hi Gareth

January 2017 … A better year? … Let us hope that Zuma falls.
Let us hope that GR gets out.

The mind can never stop thinking,
On and on … reassessing the variables.
Reassessing the constants … recalculating the equations.
Constant dissatisfaction even when it is so close to perfect.

Oh, how we complain.

The sin of remaining silent when we should voice our protest is what makes
people cowards.

What is it that makes men fearful?
Do they fear confrontation?
Or a beating?
Or do they fear being disliked?
Or is it the uncertainty of the outcome?

Every shot that you do not take will not strike a target.

A crying child is carried past, the sun is too hot.
The tide is high.
Cool water laps up against the boatshed steps.

Returning to my thoughts:
Surely we were not fools enough to make plans for this life and expect life

to fall in and accommodate our plans? To expect a mind not to return to its thoughts would be like expecting the sea not to return with the tide.

In the distance now, I hear the crying child.
I hear the parent trying to pacify the child.
I cannot imagine why, in modern times, we still have them, but we do.

My mom likes to talk a lot.
Sometimes jumping from one subject to the next, sentence for sentence.
Not always easy for the male brain.

She told me the other day that her friend's daughter, aged 42, had a baby.
Both mother and baby almost died during the process, but they didn't.
My mom's friend is off abroad to visit them.
There is no dad … only an anonymous sperm donor.
But she wanted a baby so badly!
I could just puke.

In my mind's eye I see some neurotic pre-middle-aged woman who is unable (or unwilling) to maintain a stable relationship with anyone, taking it upon herself to disturb the slumber of the uncreated and deliver the poor thing into this pig-iron world. I consider this to be an act of supreme selfishness.

From time to time I interrogate myself on breeding in modern times.
You cannot not want those already born, your friends, and those you love.
But you can let sleeping dogs lie.
You do not need to wake the unborn, the sleeping souls in their darkness of Nirvana.
You can simply leave them be.
We were/are the first generation to really have that power.

Humans … once you see them for what they are … gee whizz … you can never close that can of worms again.

I see them walking their dogs on strings.

It is like a spaghetti bomb.

Like Pogo, I have seen the enemy and he is us.

I pull on a wetsuit on these calm days. The sea is cool, not its usual icy self. I put on my old weight belt with all its dented lead. I spit in my mask and swim out to sea. I do not wear gloves or booties or fins.

I pull myself down the long kelp stems.
Down to the bottom of the sea.
There are no people there.

16 January 2017

I went to see an old friend, Craig Price, in McGregor on Friday. He knows your brother Tammy. I returned on Saturday morning and fell into a pit of anxiety and depression such as I have not experienced for many years. Lying there, drifting in and out of the sleep zone, wishing more than anything to be magically removed from life. It was like first day back at school in 1977, Standard 6. It happens when too many triggers fire simultaneously. The work to come. The responsibility to come. Another year on the rat-wheel. The difficulty in selling the property next door. The having to give my ex-wife all those millions as a settlement. Having to drive to Calitzdorp. The property in NZ and what to do with it. Reading about Burchell's travels in the early 1800s. Corruption, the political situation and degeneration in South Africa. Global overpopulation. Human stupidity. My dad and his widow's estate. Organising, organising, organising … It all compounds and the hyena comes to feast.

This is a state one has to pass through and out of.

Like a mist, it suddenly clears.

26 January 2017

In times past, great schools of basking sharks were seen off the Cape coast.
Herds of around one hundred animals off Maiden's Cove.
All the same gender, apparently.
After the war, old man Smorenburg, the self-appointed sheriff of Clifton,
used to shoot at them
with his .303.
He said they were "man-eaters".

In the late 1960s and early 1970s, the Paarman, Van Geems and Moon children would row out to smaller groups of the animals, then jump overboard and try to grab onto their fins and great gentle backs.

When I was at high school, there were only a few left. The Bakoven boys would report seeing them in twos and threes, swimming close inshore.

Mick, Alan, Uwe and I met up with the last lonely one in Barley Bay in the 1990s.

Then, like the ancients, they were gone.

Love
Carl

Chapter 48

Fiki and his Mom

Brighton Court is situated on a busy intersection at the southern end of the Camps Bay strip. In the late '90s my mom and I owned four bachelor flats there, two each. I served on the body corporate. If I remember correctly, there were 38 units in total: some were owned by absentee landlords, some were rentals, others housed permanent occupants. We ran ours as holiday rentals, long before the advent of Airbnb. It was a period before Camps Bay became a sought-after destination. Websites were in their infancy and the internet still sounded like elastic bands: "boing-boing."

A live music venue called Dizzy's Jazz Cafe opened opposite, causing considerable late-night mayhem. Another nearby noisy anti-social establishment was co-owned by the infamous Belgrade mobster Goran Bojovic. His dodgy pals were shareholders. When we complained, Doug Cleland and I were surrounded and threatened by a group of Slavic men, each with his hand on a holstered pistol. Life became rather scary and I carried a gun full-time. Fortunately for us, Bojovic was shot and wounded at La Med the night after Christmas. He vanished from his hospital ward and turned up dead not long after. It was all a bit much and we sold our flats.

During that time a feral woman moved into the triangular space below one of the staircases at Brighton Court. She could seemingly speak only one word – the name of her little boy "Fiki". Perhaps it was Vicky. I don't know.

Fiki's mother seemed to be perpetually coated in dust. She wore ash coloured rags and her hair was grey and matted. She reminded me of a prehistoric woman I had seen in a Sterkfontein diorama as a boy.

From time to time she and Fiki would walk down to Bakoven and use the shower on the beach. She and Fiki would strip off and lather up under the cold water, then wash and wash and wash. Afterwards, they'd dry off on the sunny slipway before getting dressed and moving on.

The residents of Brighton Court did not know how to deal with what was effectively a cave-woman and her cub living in a cave beneath the stairs. Their humanity was not tooled-up to deal with her humanity. Social workers were called in and Fiki was taken away. No longer needing a home for her cub, she moved out shortly thereafter.

For months afterwards I would see Fiki's mom wandering along the Llandudno road looking tragic, until one day she was gone.

I often think of Fiki and his mom, sleeping curled up with nothing more than a few scraps of cardboard between them and the cold granolithic floor, covered with a few greasy blankets they kept hidden behind the bins. And the residents of Brighton Court in their apartments above, with full bellies and heaters and TVs.

Back then, at closing time, Blues restaurant stuffed its plate-scrapings and food waste into clear plastic bags which were stacked in the alleyway behind the Camps Bay library. That is where Fiki and his mother ate. She never begged for anything.

Sunday 26 February 2017

A Letter from the Outside #49

Dear Gareth

Just another day of life (to borrow from Ryszard Kapuściński).
The wind blew in the night and pulled back with the sunrise.
White caps turned into scrubbed scuff and the scuff into a sheet of glass all the way to the horizon,
where the ships are full size and there is a little kink as the Earth turns downward towards Antarctica.
This morning Zaan and I did not get up early.
We talked and laughed and drank coffee and made love.
We sat at the old teak table on the verandah and breakfasted on an omelette with melted cheese on the outside and green pepper, mushroom, onion, chorizo sausage and more cheese on the inside.
We had more coffee and mango juice.
Zaan and I are beyond lucky for having each other and we know it.
The birds flew in for breakfast.
We have a seagull, a pair of redwings and their chick, a few olive thrushes, robins, doves and a rock pigeon … all regular eaters, having trained us well.
The seagull and the male redwing will eat out of our hands.
They all love puppy-pellets except for the little robins.
The robins, who are the favourites because they are small and exquisite, get fragments of cheese.
Cheese is the preferred food of all birds.
I clean up their shit gladly.

Tomorrow marks the start of another week on the racetrack.
Yesterday I paid all my bills and my provisional tax.
It is the end of Feb.
R18 900 to my ex-wife every month until the house is finally sold,
And she gets her millions.
But I am not murdering myself now as I was then.
I am never so very tired.
Once I have paid my tax, my ex-wife gets half of what I earn.
Two weeks out of every four … five hours out of every ten.
And the taxman gets his share, leaving little over for me.
I was such a sucker, but nothing can be done about that now.

Talking about the future?
This is the future!

When we were boys there were infinite days ahead.
Infinity = incomprehensible.

As young men, we surfed.
We went on surfing weekends.
There was no thought that this would not go on forever.
Then one day, forever came.

One night, a decade ago, Gordon and I stood on the deck of **Seacomber**.
Teak beneath our naked feet, watching the full moon rise,

Over the low hill between the sea and the lagoon at Whangamumu, North Island, New Zealand.
The whole world sparkled.

Gordon, who was 69 at the time, said: "I wonder how many more times I will watch the full moon rise from this deck? Not that many, maybe ten."

A year or two later we were moored in the Baie de Kuto, Isle of Pines, New Caledonia, and watched the full moon rise. It was utterly exquisite. The whole world sparkled.
Gordon asked the question again.

I wonder if I will ever stand barefoot on a teak deck again,
Soft white cotton trouser legs flapping in the Pacific evening breeze.
A safe anchorage, the lapping sea,
The slap and ting of the rigging.
All's well and temperate.
I do certainly miss that, for all the stresses and strains of yachting.

But back to the future. I took our 83-year-old mom down to the boatshed the other day. In 30 years that's about how old I will be. The physical degradation of the next 30 years is not something to look forward to. At 52, I am fitter and stronger than I was at 18 or 19. On the mountain Zaan and I still charge past slack-bodied 20-year-olds waddling like penguins.

Recently we have had just the bests of days. Early mornings up Table Mountain or paddling along the coast or riding our bikes.

These days have the flavour of something rare and ephemeral.
Especially now that December and January and February are gone.
How do we clutch onto them as they speed by?
We cannot.
But we try to know their value for they, like our lives, are also slipping by.
Star light, star bright.

C

Chapter 49

Living with an Artist

Among other things, Zaan paints and sculpts ... **www.zaan.co.za**

People sometimes ask me, what is it like to live with an artist?

In the dying years of my marriage, I bumped into Zaan on the mountain every now and then. I was running away my pain and she was busy finding her feet after returning to Cape Town after years of living in Canada, Ireland and Saipan. I would greet her politely, chat for a moment and then trot off. For the sake of our daughter Allegra, I was still hoping to save my little family unit from destruction.

This July, Zaan and I will have been together for eleven years.
So, what is it like to live with an artist?

One afternoon, a year or two later, I sat at the little green boatshed looking out to sea contemplating the now utterly wrecked state of my once healthy conjugal union. There were a few people on the beach, but not many. It was one of those glorious June days when the weather turns summery and continuous south-westerly breezes push warm water in from the east. Suddenly, an athletic woman dashed down to the water's edge and dived into the sea.

"That's the one for me!" I said out loud, and stood up, squinting into the glare. I remember walking down onto the sand to get a better look. Cupid's arrow had been let loose and found its target. I was very surprised to see who it was.

The artist I live with is a person of heightened senses. On our first walks we took together, she would point out tiny flowers and details that others would miss by miles. A reflection of clouds in a muddy puddle. Fresh magic dropped into my known world. The flip-side of heightened senses is, of course, that the persistent yapping of a neighbour's doggy is much worse. Loud voices are louder, bright lights are brighter. A person needs to get used to hypersensitivity.

Sometimes Zaan paints late into the night. One of my favourite things to do then, is to come into the studio with a bottle of red wine or a beer and sit and watch. To watch the creative process, to observe the work unfold and reveal itself, as a blank canvas goes through its metamorphosis via the tip of a brush.

We do not have a television, so this is like a show in slow-mo … **In the Studio – with the Artist** … in real time.

Sometimes I will sit and read a book like Hemingway's **A Moveable Feast.** I look up every now and then, from art to art.

Zaan and I trail-run together, surf together, paddle together and sleep together.

!!! Just fantastic !!!

31 March 2017   Letter #50

Hello my friend

30 March 2017 ... today I wrote this to my ex-wife ... I am so upset:

It is said that forgiveness does not excuse the behaviour of someone who has wronged you, but rather prevents their behaviour from destroying your own heart.

The problem is that I not only have a problem with forgiving those who have wronged me, but most of all, I am unable to forgive myself for being so stupid as to have allowed it to happen in the first place. It is also said that you should forgive yourself for not knowing what you did not know. I cannot forgive, but I will hopefully be able to slowly let it go once I stop being bled through the neck.

We signed a final settlement in May 2016. Ten months have passed and we have not sold the house which needs to be sold so that you can be paid your settlement. During this time I have paid you R188 500 in alimony, which equates to at least a quarter of a million before tax. Today I must drive all the way up to Calitzdorp to measure up on a job to earn your alimony for next month.

Can you imagine doing that? All that driving and work, just to give it all away to someone you utterly resent.

Yesterday at Ahmed Kathrada's funeral, Kgalema Motlanthe once again asked Zuma to do the right thing and step down. Only Zuma can do it, but he will not because he has no integrity and is totally corrupt. One day he will be gone and we all long for that day.

You too can do the right thing: free me — only you can do it.

SMAK!

On Friday (17th) afternoon I went for my favourite kind of paddle.

Autumn sun, cool sea (not cold), a playful swell and a light North Westerly breeze to blow me home.

Afterwards I sat on the step in the warmth, feeling the silver light bounce off the water, through my closed eyelids and through my skin of my body. A man walked past, muttered a greeting and jerked me from my reverie. I sat there, looking about, contemplating my swim when a barefooted fellow in shorts, a green shirt and a camouflage hat came down over the greensward (stage right) towards the deserted beach. In each hand he carried a red cool-box. He looked at me, then appraised the beach's emptiness, before calling out hopefully, "Ice-cream lollies" just because he was there and it had been a long walk.

Cool water lapped over my feet as the man's call was instantly answered by three dogs as they shot out of their house barking wildly. Around and around the ice-cream seller they ran, determined to chase him away. It was his dark skin, you see. I watched the ice-cream seller calmly accept the tirade and walk away, back from whence he had come.

"So unempowered or so Zen?" thought I.

My aggressive nature would never have tolerated that.

I sat and watched and thought: How far had he walked on those hardened feet?

And had he sold any ice-cream lollies?

⟨⟨⟩⟩

And so a time came to pass when there were too many people on the planet and their heat caused the ice caps to start melting. A tipping point was reached and the roads became choked with cars. The big cities ran out of water and fires burned on the mountains and through the informal settlements. But very few acknowledged that there were too many people – so they just kept on breeding.

And Europe, led by Germans riddled with post-Nazi guilt, and kind, naive Scandinavians, allowed themselves to be invaded by the shrapnel of the Middle East and there is tension – but the Western men have grown too soft to push back.

And Europe (and the West) gave away technological secrets in exchange for cheap goods. "We still have the ideas," the Europeans say tentatively, while the Far East produces the hardware and tourists queue to see the wonders created by the forefathers of the current Europeans: Florence, Paris, Barcelona, Roma, Venice. Just look in wonder. Ozymandias.

We in South Africa watch while the parasitic Zuma regime unashamedly indulges itself in an orgy of looting. The media makes its noise and we hope like mad, but we know what happens in Africa so we don't really have much hope. And yet we keep hoping.

In the USA Trump trumps, while in the UK they worry that Brexit will cause the pound to fall, threatening their holidays in Spain.

Back in South Africa one of our friends feels a failure and is depressed.
So, I asked Zaan, how does one deal with his kind of depression?
She replied without hesitation:

Go ride around town on your back wheel,
Go get another tattoo, or maybe a piercing,
Go to the bar and have a drink,
Or buy a bottle of Captain Morgan.
And have a jolly good time!

So I just laughed and sang a little song, first heard in a fragment sung by Theo Kotze one evening sitting in a soupy sea on the sharky reef at Ding Dang. Three young men out at sunset with a large but infrequent swell coming down into the bay, all the way from the lighthouse, past the harbour and through to Voorbaai. It goes like this:

(1ˢᵗ part sung to the tune of **Hoe Ry Die Boere**)
Hoe ry die boere, drie op n drol, vinger in die hol, bles poephol,
Hoe ry die boere, drie op n drol, bles poephol – Hoera!

(2nd part sung to the tune of Jingle Bells)

Bles Poephol, Bles Poephol, Bles Poephol – Hoera !!!

Tingalingaling my poepol sing, Bles Poephol – Hoera !!!

Then there are some lost lines followed by:

En die jongste een se ma sê "trek my tiet, dan kom ek weer".

Ha, ha, ha.

Beste Kalleee

Chapter 50

Mentorship

An 8km run is not much these days when compared to the 400m extra lap,
As ordered by John Donald back in 1978.

Zaan and I trotted an 8K this morning, up at Cains Forest, honking
Canada geese and all.

I smiled as I thought of Donald's: "Litvett, when you going on a diet?"

Constructive criticism *à la* Donald,
a question offered for me to contemplate.

Mentorship should not necessarily be wrapped in cotton-candy kindness,
a little bit of stressor can go a long way.

❦

Once I was with John Whitmore on his farm at Elands Bay. I was friendly with his daughter Sian and we went there for weekends. He asked me to go and fetch some firewood and pointed to an old farm tractor with a four-wheeled trailer hitched behind it. I had no idea how to start, let alone drive, a tractor. John started it and said, "Off you go." And off I went, alone on a tractor into the duney landscape. I returned a few hours later, the trailer piled with sandy stumps and fallen gumtree branches. That simple experience was a rite of passage moment. A seventeen-year-old boy pushed out of his comfort zone by an older man.

My mentor over decades, Gordon Verhoef, has set me tasks designing houses and buildings and projects that I would never have imagined myself capable of. If I did not have the imagination or belief in myself, he certainly did. "My boy," he would say, "If I didn't think you could do it, I wouldn't ask you."

During basics in the navy we were also pushed out of our comfort zones. Our instructors first seemed like monsters to us, but we grew to be very fond of most of them: Sydow and Lubbe and Cooke – but not the sadists.

One Saturday morning, Robby Kinsky and I walked over Signal Hill to his father's hillside home in Fresnaye. Two little-big guys, eleven or twelve, going walkabout, turning rocks and looking for scorpions as we went – talking about his grandmother's baking and the treats that were sure to be waiting for us: *streuselkuchen, mohnkuchen, pflaumenkuchen* and so on. But his dad Willi had other ideas (later for cake) and he presented us with a five-litre can of bitumen and some paintbrushes and put us to work painting the roof of the tar-papered gazebo in the back garden.

We found a ladder and Robby and I climbed onto the roof. One of us held the can while the other painted, starting at the top and working our way down. It was tough, messy going, particularly once we had reached the edge and the "tin-boy" could no longer sit on the roof and had to position himself on the ladder below the "brush-boy". Thick blobs of goopy bitumen fell down onto the "tin-boy" and soon we were both as black as Sambo.

Eventually the job was done and Willi was called to inspect.

"Good," he said, "and now you boys get clean." But we did not know how.

Willi provided us with a short syphon hose, a flat pan, (the type one uses to drain the oil from a car) and some rags. We siphoned petrol from his VW Combi and washed our sticky bodies. We were stained grey for a week or two and our shorts went into the bin, but we discovered what we were capable of. One more feather in each of our caps.

Later that evening we rode around the suburb on an old Vespa, Robby at the handlebars, me riding pillion behind him. Boys to men.

Apart from our defence force instructors, the John Whitmores, Donalds and Willi Kinskys of this world also helped to toughen us up. It is vital for youngsters to have wise, caring, firm and pragmatic mentors to guide them and shine a light into the darkness that confronts all young people from time to time.

Rolf Kirsten

As a young man, I adopted some of my parent's friends as mentors: Friedel Sellschop: diamond and neutrino physicist, Gerry Milsom: East Anglian entrepreneur and hotelier, Danie Bosman: Royal College of Surgeons, Eric Rosochacki: Businessman and thinker, and, of course, Hannes Fagan, Rolf Kirsten and Granny Dinny. I have been fortunate indeed to have known people like these, for they have made an enormous difference in my life.

I think, though, that the best mentors would be one's parents
for the simple reason that nobody cares more than they do.
Or so they should, anyway.

29 April 2017   Letter #51

I was working in the garden this afternoon,
Digging up my compost heap,
Spreading the good stuff around.
Swimming under the pool cover like a leopard seal.
And waiting for rain.

I stopped in at my office and Googled the SA Weather synoptic chart.
That beautiful long cold front reaching almost to Luanda just vanished!
Sucked into a massive high-pressure system.
I had been counting on a lovely big soaking for Sunday.
It is so hot and dry today that my eyeballs are burning.
Fuck it!

Hi Gareth

At the beginning of the month,
I had to drive to Calitzdorp to measure up a house.
I hate driving long distances.
It scares me rather badly.
This last Easter weekend in RSA there were 235 road fatalities.
Last year around 150.
As I drive imaginary crash and burn scenarios play out before my eyes.
A few days ago, 20 school kids died and burnt in a taxi/truck head-on collision in Gauteng.

In earlier times, as sail gave way to steam, clumsy sail-assisted steamships like the Birkenhead made their ways across the oceans. Sometimes they never made it. Soon enough, steam left sail behind and, in turn, steam made way for oil-powered ships. These days we watch as hybrid cars make way for fully electric cars. Elon Musk. Where did all the horses go? It is just an extension of the same process really. They call it the advance of technology and I wait for this dream:

One day, bright old father sun will be in the harness.
Highly efficient solar panels will convert sunshine into bulk electricity.
Desalination technology will have improved dramatically.
Sea water will be converted into fresh water by cheap solar power.
Sunny countries will pour this water onto new farmlands.
Deserts will burst into GM croplands.

⚜

We have had a warm and windless period with a flat sea.
It is called an Indian summer.
In Cape Town we wait impatiently for rain.
Great shoals of anchovies can be seen in the evening and early morning.
Dolphins charge in and out, feeding till they are stuffed.
Sometime a week or so ago, as the sun set, Zaan and I saw a number of Bryde's whales.
Blowing and puffing and showing their tails and backs and fins.
As they scooped up their shining glittering feasts.

⚜

I spoke to a Swede this morning.
He said that one should view politics as entertainment.
Easy for a Swede to say.
I remember as a teenage boy, a slow-motion bicycle crash.
Bouncing off a car, then bouncing off the kerb, then getting hurt.
Or those slow-motion sticky nightmares where you careen from one obstacle to the next,
Helpless, towards the cliff.
We have all had them in one form or another.

Living under Zuma has been like that.

The utter helplessness of it.

This cunning wolf in a clown suit.

⚜

Zaan and I have booked for Canada. We will be gone for just over two months. We leave on 11 June and return to RSA on 18 August. There is a lighthouse on the horizon. We are very excited. It has been a long season. My last rental vacated last weekend. I have one more Wellness Warehouse to do. I am working on a big Motorcycle Pub in Niseko Japan – The House of Machines – and two small projects for GV … then it all calms down. I am truly looking forward to that.

Love to you there in Kuwait

C

Chapter 51

1980s Surf Parties

In the '80s of the last century there were things called "surf parties"… maybe there still are. Our surf parties were, without a doubt, the most exciting and interesting surf parties ever. Everyone was invited. Surf parties were held at the Llandudno Surf Lifesaving Club and at the Clifton Surf Lifesaving Club, the OPBC at Granger Bay and at private homes – seldom on the beach. They were held at the Santos Hotel in Mossel Bay on New Year's Eve and at rented houses in St Francis Bay and Jeffrey's.

For about a decade, a spontaneous surf party ran at the Kings Hotel every Friday and Saturday night and thereafter at the Camps Bay Bowling Club for another ten or twenty years.

Sometimes a kid whose parents were away had the family home invaded by loutish gate-crashers who flung sofas into swimming pools and armchairs into rivers and danced broken glass into highly polished parquet floors. They abused the bedrooms and drank beer out of silver heirloom trophies won at some bygone event. Sometimes surf parties were an excuse to raise cash by selling alcohol, but mostly they were just for fun. We all knew each other – a large, loose social group of a couple of hundred kids.

⚜

The excitement was palpable as we arrived. Speedy, Gibbons, Uwe, Mike, Alan, Craig and girls. The steep streets were jammed with VW Combis, Toyota panel vans and rusting, sticker-festooned Datsuns and other surfmobiles.

Music would be pumping. Bob Marley, LKJ, Van Halen – **Jump** … it all kind of blends … It was late 1984, Alphaville's song **Forever Young**: the late-night theme tune.

There was dancing in the playroom – the ping-pong table had been folded away.

At a trestle table bar, with a wet newsprint sheet serving as a tablecloth, the pretty mom and her assistants were selling beer (and sweet Esprit alcopops for the girls). There was an oval galvanised-steel tub with chunks of ice and bottles. Plastic crates stood against the wall. Trade was very brisk.

The house stood on tall concrete pillars and underneath there was a paved entertainment area which led onto a broad terrace which in turn folded out into a magical garden … that's how I remember it, anyway.

There were no mobile phones in those days, let alone any of the other social networking tools we have today, but the news would get around that *so-and-so* was having a party on *such-and-such* a night and the crowds would gather. The kids would drink way too much and drive home totally plastered.

Late on that particular evening, as partygoers began to drift away, I went back for one last visit to the bar. I asked for a whisky as I had had quite enough beer. "That you will only find upstairs," said the mom. I looked at her blankly. "Come," she said, and I followed her obediently up the steps and

~ 421 ~

around the house to the back door. I was led into the kitchen and the door was locked behind us. The boy-trap/man-trap had been sprung.

In 1986 as Halley's Comet left us, headed back into deep space, I gave up promiscuity, but that is another story.

Many years later, I bumped into the whisky mom.
She had become an alcoholic and seemed down and out.
I know that it wasn't, but I felt that somehow it was my fault.
I guess it wasn't all good.

20 May 2017   Letter #52

Take responsibility for what you communicate with others.
If we can, avoid doing violence to the minds of unseen others.

Hi Gareth

13 May 2017

Cape Town is hot and sunny … we wait for rain … proper rain … not the five minutes once a week that we have been getting over the past while, as cold front after cold front just touches the southern tip of Africa before being pushed away by the ever-present South Atlantic high-pressure system. I watch it here …
http://www.weathersa.co.za//media/data/observation/synoptic/ma_sy.gif
You will remember that when we were boys, the rain set in at Easter.

And as we wait for rain, we ride the horrible political rollercoaster,
That comes with life in South Africa and has been horrible for as long as I can remember.
As people, we live well in a beautiful environment,
With our front eyes wide open,
And eyes open in the backs of our heads.
I have probably never felt completely at ease to fully put down roots.

I read this in a book the other day by a fellow named Tim Snyder, about Donald Trump, called **ON TYRANNY**:

Since the crisis is permanent
The sense of emergency is always present

Planning for the future seems impossible (or even disloyal)
How can we think of reform when the enemy is always at the gate?

Apart from the **disloyal** part … this is pretty much the agitated sense I have had during my life here in RSA … while others have calmly built empires and careers and shopping malls.

Shopping malls is where I work and, boy oh boy, they are putting them up in South Africa at an amazing rate (throughout Africa too … Botswana, Kenya, Angola, Ghana, you name it).

In the past while, among other projects, I have done ten new stores for Wellness Warehouse. My work is the exact opposite of building the pyramids I suppose, or something like that. Here today, gone tomorrow. Quick in and out, transient. But I work from home and if one has to work, that is the best way to do it. Zaan and I have fabulous fun. We trot up Table Mountain regularly, run on the trails, paddle on the ocean and stop our bicycles at the end of Table Mountain road as the rising sun touches us and we look down across the broad sweep of the bay. Below us, thousands and thousands of commuters inch their way into the city. Cars, buses, taxis and 3rd world trains … ouch … hours and hours of gridlock every day. Horrible.

Zaan and I will fly over to her house in Canada for two months (mid-June to mid-August). We are lucky indeed. I do work from there, but it is a very pleasant change of scene.

⬥

May 12, 2017 – Today marks the 24th day since the body of the boy, allegedly killed by two farmers, was discovered. … "Coligny locked in protest violence after child killed" …

The guys could be telling the truth that the boy jumped off the bakkie while they were driving him to the police station. The child pinched a few sunflowers.

The town of Coligny in the north has gone crazy because of this "racist" action. Shops are being looted, houses are being burned.

My friend Alfredo Pesce once told me that, as a boy, just before the war, he went to steal peaches from an orchard in the Campania outside Naples. He did not see the *contadino* with a sickle harvesting long dry grass among the trees. The man stood up and threw the sickle (like a boomerang) at Alfredo, the spinning blade narrowly missing his head. Alfredo, the little peach thief, came back that night and set fire to the grass in revenge. The orchard was badly damaged.

These two incidents, 80 years apart, are almost identical:
1. boy steals something that is growing.
2. adult/s overreact.
3. there is destruction.

Why is the one incident labeled "racist" and the other not? Why when "township" residents beat a thief to death in what is called "mob justice", is it not described as a racist incident?

Many years ago, long before the formation of the neighbourhood watch, I apprehended a housebreaker in Camps Bay. With the assistance of another man, we took him to the police station in the back of my *bakkie*. I sat on my prisoner as the other man drove the *bakkie* down Geneva Drive. The prisoner wriggled and tried to escape and it was tense. His sweating body was like spring-wire. He could have fought me and jumped and broken his neck. I could have fallen off the *bakkie* and broken my neck. There was nothing racist about the action at all.

It seems that these days the "race card" must be played at every turn. I know I have said this before, but it really gets my goat: Why is Obama with his paleface mom and nut-brown dad a "black" man? Why on earth are Mariah Carey, Tiger Woods, Lenny Kravitz and Halle Berry "black"? Why is "black" the default category for a child of a union of this nature? It drives me nuts. Why is anyone for that matter? It is such a misnomer. Why does racism sit in the front pew?

To quote the Ray Bradbury novel **Fahrenheit 451**:
"Those who don't build must burn."
It's as old as history …. and as juvenile delinquents … for whatever reason.

❧

They love to litter.
They love to steal.
Ho-Ro, Ho-Ro.
They love to rape
Ha Ha, Ho-Ho

Humans! South Africans!

Our news is just poison.

But I regularly tune in – always hoping to hear of Zuma's demise,

Or Brian Molefe's nose being rubbed in the mud,

Or a consequence for some corruption … but it never happens.

It just gets worse.

The shit piles up so fast over here that the bottom of the pile is swiftly buried.

An unseasonal southeaster blew so strong that scaffold boards flew around like match sticks up near my mom's house. Trees were blown down. Our home was bombarded with molecules– attacked and buffeted and shaken by horrible molecules tearing down from the mountains.

The very air we breathe attacked us.

14 May 2017

Zaan and I paddled over a clear sea towards Hottentots' Huisie. Floating on an invisible mattress of water molecules and salt. The molecules of the air were still at last.

We were at brother Mick's house later that evening, laughing and drinking beer and karate-water. His son Keanu called to say that he and a girl (fellow student) were renting a room at the university so that they could study undisturbed for the upcoming exams.

After Mick hung up he laughed, "If it had been me," Mick said, "I would just be *schlonting*."

Whatever that might mean!

"Schlonting," indeed.

Some of us live like princes, some of us live like queens
Most of us live just like me, we don't know what it means
To take our place in one world, to make our peace in one world
To make our way in one world, to have our say in one world
No use crying, there's been no crime
I say it's just the way the wind blows

15 May 2017

Perfect days in May … My workload has suddenly diminished.
Make hay, so up Table Mountain Zaan and I did scurry.
The air was so warm and dry, reminders of my time in Namibia in 1993.

In '93 the black hyena came to call. I cancelled my work obligations and drove my bakkie up to the farm of my friends Rolf and Rosemarie Kirsten. 18 000 hectares bordering the small town of Maltahöhe. For weeks I walked that farm, removing snares from the bush. At night I drew. Daweb is a huge farm, at that time divided into many camps. Some were called game camps and were inhabited by springbok, kudu and gemsbok and one or two ostriches as well as wild cats and bat-eared jackals and ordinary jackals, barking geckos and many other beautiful creatures, along with a magnificent assortment of birds. At first the farm seemed like the great wilds of semi-desert Africa, but later I realised that most of the animals were as good as trapped in their pens.

The farm had been worked and husbanded by the Kirsten family for just over 100 years. Money had been made in the 1970s from the pelts of new born karakul lambs, but that business died with the arrival of awareness – "Beauty Without Cruelty". Rolf now ran a couple of herds of hardy small Bonsmara cattle. The work was tough but good. Beautiful Land Cruisers, long grass, rocky ground, generators and inverters, boreholes, windmills and round reservoirs. Diesel, spanners and sockets and a big night sky with all the mysteries of space hidden behind the intensely bright firmament of stars. The southern sky at night.

Carly and Uwe on Daweb

Rolf had two assistants on the farm – Albertus, a Hottentot-type Nama, and James, a San-type Nama. James was the real deal with folded back lips and a buttery skin of indescribable hue. They spoke in clicks. I wonder what became of them?

A year later I was back there, in the nearby Naukluft mountains, 100 years to the day after the Germans defeated the Witbooi Namas in 1894. We always went up there in July or August. In the short months between we had sailed to Italy via St Helena and the Canary Islands. Travelled all over Europe, enjoyed snow in Norway and Christmas and New Year on the Island of Capri. Wow, what a time we had. Days of real life.

I was at Daweb again a few years later when a Chicago Aeromotor windpump turned 100. One hundred years of non-stop pumping. I liked that.

A few more years passed quickly by and then one day the Namibian government informed Rolf that he was selling Daweb and how much he would get for it. The farm was dealt out between about 20 local families and a piece was added to the existing "*dorpsgrond*".

Daweb is now a dust bowl.

There are no more wild animals.

Everything is broken.

No windmills work.

There is no water.

Goats have ruined the grazing forever.

It is finished.

Doing my sums now,
I can't believe that 1993 trip to Maltahohe was a quarter of a century ago.
Boys turned swiftly to middle-aged men ...
my middle-aged mom to my old mom.
I was a boy and then became an older boy – but I never felt like a man.
I never referred to myself as a man.
I do now ... I am a middle-aged man.

To me, my mom has always been a middle-aged woman ...
even when she was young, I suppose.
She is now 83 and shakes badly.

And your Suzie ... beyond.

***

Today is **20 May** ... still no rain. Perfect weather.
Beautiful paddles and mornings down at the boatshed.
Soft warm sun, fried eggs for breakfast.
Swimming in the sea.
There are whales already ...
Sea Point, Muizenberg and Gordon's Bay all report sightings.
Trump is dancing with the Saudis.
The ZUMANC is pure corrupt evil crap.

My workload came back on full burner
Just as I was easing into a relaxish mode.
Back to the coalface tomorrow.

Love and Be Strong ... C

Chapter 52

On Memory

My family left Pretoria at the end of 1969. I was five-and-a-half years old.
We lived in Stellenbosch for a short while when I was three.
I know when my earliest memories were laid down.

My first clear memory is that of falling into the Eerste River at Karindal. My parents and their friends were swimming at the concrete weir and I toddled in. I clearly remember the golden light and the bubbles, a momentary slow swirl, maybe half a revolution, and then being yanked out by an adult. There was no coughing or spluttering. There was no fright. I just remember it as very serene and very beautiful. I suppose there must have been some reason for this moment to be imprinted – perhaps there was a lot of parental alarm and scolding afterwards. I was three.

Many years later I was held down by big surf in Barley Bay, running out of oxygen. It felt exactly the same.

My next two memories involve bigger boys being horrid.

Still three years old at Stellenbosch, playing in the white sand below a swing, a bigger boy pulled the swing back and let it go. The well-aimed pendulum struck my head hard and I was taken indoors to my mother, bleeding and shocked.

In Pretoria at the age of four, I was tricked by the sons of a family friend into showing them my teeth. I was a trusting boy so I lay back, closed my eyes and opened wide. Suddenly there was a fizzing explosion inside my cranium as an entire can of Andrew's Liver Salts was dumped into my little mouth. I think it was Mussolini who said, "It is good to trust others, but much better not to do so." That would have been a good lesson for me to learn, but sadly I didn't.

I do not remember the arrival of Mick,
because I was only two, but Bill does.

My fourth and fifth years yield well-populated memories. I clearly remember the Apollo 11 countdown, "Ten, nine, eight, seven, six" … coming out of my dad's radio in the house in Pretoria. I can even remember the "wilie" (short for wireless) as I heard the words emerge from the little punched-out holes in the radio's faux-leather cover: "And here is the news read by Michael Todd."

I remember opening a kiddies skin-diver set the night before departing for Durban, lying on the floor breathing through the mask-snorkel-ping-pong-ball-combo and kicking my little fins in an imitation of what frogmen do. And the free gifts in cereal boxes opened upside down because the toys were at the bottom (and learning how to read upside down because of it) and brother Bill always claiming them. And the brown honey-coloured varnish inside the boxes in the time before cereal was packaged in plastic bags. And the petrol companies incentivising us with Galoops and space-rocket stamps and treasure.

A few days after receiving the skin-diver set, I remember a real skin-diver, with a speargun, wading backwards out of the water at Umdloti and selling us a freshly shot garrick.

I remember a whipping from my grandmother after she spotted me imitating other boys throwing gravel at a passer-by. And another for calling a skinny-legged boy "chicken bones" at my elder brother's bidding.

Many of those early memories feature either punishment or reward. Functions of learning. Cause and effect.

I wonder why we cannot, in general, remember incidents from our lives when we were younger than three? I wonder if six-year-olds can remember incidents from their second year the way I can remember my teens?

In my life I have not really exposed myself to hallucinogenics, so I have no memories of any Ayahuasca or acid trips. I recently watched some movies and documentaries on LSD (and others) featuring users like The Grateful Dead and samplers like Paul McCartney and Steve Jobs.

A friend in Canada and a sangoma friend in Cape Town have both invited me to carbon copy induced experiences: "You will be able to see the ancestors sitting alongside you, right there. You will be able to talk to them." Truth be told, I am afraid of my own mind.

On a New Year's Day afternoon, some years back, I was visiting a friend in Noordhoek. He is a great confectioner and on display, near the kitchen, were some fudge-like, toffy-iced, nut-topped, triangular treats. I popped one into my mouth and heard my friend say, "Only one now, Carlos!"

My capacity for feeding being rather well known, I assumed the limit of "only one" was so that there would be enough for everyone else. FHB. Looking around to see that I was not being observed, I snuck another, had a few beers and left. Bye-bye and thank you, Happy New Year etc …

Heading past the Noordhoek Farm Village, the entire road suddenly whiplashed like a giant rollercoaster. I slowed down to a crawl. Over and over, in the manner of a rug being shaken, the road surface came towards me in waves. By the time I got onto the Blue Route highway, I must have been travelling very slowly indeed. Incredibly tall white-stemmed palm trees bent down and swayed above me as tiny Matchbox cars whizzed past. I remember looking down at them as they overtook me, focusing on the single, central pin holding their wheels on.

When we were boys, the pump attendants at the Camps Bay Shell garage sold dope to the school kids and petrol to our parents. A *stop* (stick) cost one rand. A *stop* was a carefully folded square of newspaper containing some sticky *dagga-koppe* (cannabis heads) and lots of *pitjies* (seeds).

A German friend of ours was about to turn 21 and his parents were throwing a big party at their holiday home in Hermanus on Saturday evening. We were all invited, so, on Friday evening, Mark and I drove to the garage and spent the eight rand I had in my pocket. We took the eight *stoppe* home and, using my mom's coffee grinder, ground the contents into a fine green powder, *pitjies* and all. Next, we mixed the fine green powder with the contents of two chocolate Royal Cake Mix packets, threw in some eggs and milk etc, and set about a-baking.

The next afternoon we arrived at Rolf's parents' holiday home.
Every traditional German stop had been pulled out:
Wein und Bier, Dekorationen, Tische mit Fleisch und Wurst und Brot und Kuchen und Salate, Jungen und Mädchen. Wunderschön! The whole nine metres.
Word spread quickly as to what Mark and I had, concealed, in the back of my car.
The cakes were thinly sliced and passed around.
Some of the guests were in, some were out.
The majority were in.

When the time came for Rolf to make his speech, he could do nothing more than pour the contents of his beer glass into his mouth and then let it trickle slowly back into the glass. His mother and father were horrified. Virtually none of the painstakingly prepared food or drink was consumed. Our friend Alan's skeleton turned to jelly and Mick and I had to drag him around like a giant rubber chicken. He thought he was going to die. Mick and I fell asleep outside on some brick paving. Mark crept under the staircase inside the house. From time to time Mick and I would wake up and talk to Mark through an open but oddly located window, at floor-level, right next to where we lay. The following morning the window was no longer there. But we found Mark in his little hideout, right behind where the window had appeared a few hours earlier.

Late on Sunday afternoon, brother Bill found Mick and me in our mother's garden, lying on the patio flat on our backs, fast asleep, eyes wide open, staring at the sky. He says we looked as if we had been brushed with glue.

⌁

In our little house in Canada, after dinner, I say to Zaan:
"You go up and work on your painting, don't worry, the goblins will
do the dishes."

But instead of washing up, the goblins take the chocolate and sit on
the back deck and gobble it. They like the quiet of the evening and the
crunchy almonds.

They like to sit there and remember things and think of stories.

I am the goblins.

I think I know why I cannot remember the future.

25 June 2017   Letter #53

Hi Gareth

Today is the 20th of June 2017 … Zaan and I have been in Canada a week.

During the night it rained
We ran 9km in the Komoka forest this morning
Golden sunlight on the leaves
Silver drops drifting down, shaken free by the breeze
Easy running on soft springy earth

The air cool, flavoured with pine and broadleaf woodland fragrances
Happy memories triggered of Northern hemisphere travels or holidays:
Norway, Austria and Capri.
Or is this ancient genetic memory?
Whatever it is, there is a grounded sense of wellbeing in the early summer
forest.

A person can always find reasons to be unhappy in a place.
Some, of course, do have good reason.
A person might go to Capri and find the crowds of tourists to be too much.
Or the smell of dog shit in the narrow lanes or the black blobs of spat-out
chewing gum,
Or the Mediterranean empty of everything except salt water,
Or hundreds of boats below the Punta Tragara, where you would prefer
none but your own.

A person might go to Capri and find beautiful cyclamens popping up
on Monte Solara,
Or smell the exquisite mix of deciduous trees and conifers on the
warm moist air.
Or wander up Via delle Botteghe entranced by everything, headed for the
salumeria at Croce,
And buy panini, mozzarella, tomatoes and cold meats for lunch,
And picnic on a flat red-tiled roof among the pines and almond trees.
When we arrive in Canada, Zaan loves it immediately.

She says "it is like landing in cotton-wool" … and so it is.
For me, all my life I have suffered from a feeling of homesickness.
That is a kind of depression caused by a sudden uprooting
or change of scene.
Even on the best surf trips as a young man, that sadness would be
present for a while.
This time the least so, because I am now used to it here.

A person coming here to London, Ontario, might find a lack of
cultural depth,
There are no ancient Etruscan grave sites to visit or a Pantheon or an
Altstadt Mit Domkirche.

But it is deeply peaceful, that is the first thing that strikes us.
There are no tourist crowds,
The dogs are well behaved, on leashes, and the dog shit is picked up.
Crime is not really a factor,
And there is none of that African cliff-hanging wildcard craziness
that constantly buzzes in Cape Town.
It is also unbelievable not to be working for a change.
To sit and eat an omelette after a run in the forest,
And then sit and sip coffee slowly,
And just breathe in the air and watch slow white puffs drift down from
the trees.

And be embraced by the soft air laden with birdsong
and then just sit some more.
And then when sat enough, get out some tools and do some woodwork,
Or read a book or make a cup of tea.
Just lovely.

***

The actual act of travelling here is quite a shock, I suppose.

As easy and luxurious as it is, I do not like being so close to the species.

Big jet liners: Nine hours to Dubai in a Boeing 777, followed by 13 hours in the double decker Airbus A380 whizzing up from Dubai over Tehran, the Caspian Sea, Norway, Iceland, Greenland and finally dropping down at Toronto. 850 passengers on board.

I do not like watching movies on the plane, so I read, eat, drink whisky and beer, pop a sleeping pill, sleep for four hours, read, eat, doze and so on.

One of my on-board books this time was **Songlines** by Bruce Chatwin. It discusses the Australian Aboriginal culture and their system of mapping their entire continent into a massive web of pathways or routes by way of songs memorised and passed down through the generations. As the second flight dragged on and my eyes tired, I began to fiddle with the in-flight entertainment touchscreen. I found a section containing numerous music albums from the days of my youth: Pink Floyd, Genesis, Fleetwood Mac, Tracey Chapman, Mike Oldfield and so on.

I kept my eye-flaps on and listened to the music of the late 1970s and 1980s. Every note and nuance still stored and instantly accessible somewhere in my brain. The listening and recognition happening in three distinct stages separated by split seconds: (1) anticipation of the sound fragment, (2) hearing the sound fragment, (3) recognition of the sound fragment. Why does one remember hundreds of songs so easily but not maths formulae or history?

Maybe that is why we have such big brains: to remember before we could write all the stuff down: The Lore, The Way and The **Songlines**.

Today – 25 June 2017

Just come in from packing away my tools.
It has been a woodwork day.
I have been making cedar cladding for the portico.
I will send pics.

Love C

Chapter 53

Spooks

I am not a person with much experience of the paranormal.

I believe that we can sit down and talk to our ancestors because Brian and Julia have both told me so. I have spoken to a friend through a window that was no longer there in the morning.

Twice I have watched Craig Priceless crawl across a wall just like Spiderman. Once, to gain entry to Uwe's apartment through the open bathroom window, which he did.

And again, down off the crowded upper balcony of a home in Llandudno where a surf party was being held. The closest thing I have seen since was Gollum in the movie **The Lord of the Rings.**

❦

The Fagans own an old fishing cottage at Witsand at the mouth of the Breede River. They have had it since we were all grasshoppers. Uncle Hannes taught us to sail dinghies there. We would go up for long weekends of windsurfing and fun. I do not know what it is like these days. Certain improvements would have been made I expect, but when we went there as youngsters there was no electricity, no running water and no flush toilets. We cooked on gas and lit glass-fluted paraffin lamps at night. Rainwater was collected in a large asbestos tank along with dead birds, which we dutifully fished out as soon as we arrived – then drank the water. In the early hours of the morning, maybe twice a week, Isaak, the driver of the "night soil" wagon would collect our buckets of poo and toilet paper and replace them with emptied ones (not clean ones). We would hear the chains and clatter of his donkey cart. There were no showers or anything like that.

The central component of the house was a large dining room and open-plan kitchen with a sandy cement-screed floor. There were two sash windows and two long benches against the wall below them. A pair of wooden, turned-leg tables and perhaps eight or ten green painted bentwood chairs looked onto the kitchen. There was an alcove containing some games, a few books and magazines, a rusted iron trivet, a couple of dried porcupine fish and a pansy shell or two. A couple of soft sprung beds served as divans. One door led outside, the other into an array of bedrooms and sleeping places. When we were boys, these were the accommodations of the adults. The children slept in an attic above the eating room on one of the ten to fifteen gritty old mattresses that lived up there. It was a lovely place which, while the Fagan boys were growing up, could accommodate a holiday crowd of at least twenty people.

One weekend in 1982, four couples went up to Witsand for a few days. My girlfriend Nicola was with me. Mick and Francois were also there, but I cannot remember who the others were.

After unpacking we selected our rooms in the "adult accommodation" areas, rolled out our sleeping bags and prepared our nests. A perfect evening

– eight young adults being good and behaving responsibly. The next morning we rose early and breakfasted together, nobody having slept at all well as a result of strange noises during the night. All couples were suspects and all denied any noisemaking.

We spent the morning sailing but in the afternoon the weather became cloudy and cold with a spattering of rain, so we returned to the cottage to read and relax. After a while, I realised that Nicola was missing from the group. We searched and called and ran out over the dunes to look for her. In the distance we spotted her returning from the beach down at the river mouth. As she approached we saw that she was crying and very upset. She told us that she had felt a powerful need to go and walk there. As she strolled alone in the stiff breeze, her recently deceased grandfather approached her, wearing his usual dark brown tweeds. The gap between them reduced until he was only a few metres away. She reached out to him and he vanished.

We were all unnerved and again discussed the strange scraping noises of the night before. Again, we all denied responsibility. As bedtime approached, we shoved our sleeping bags and bedding up through the trapdoor and into the attic. We were spooked.

After supper the kitchen was tidied, dishes were washed and everything was set to rights down below. Teeth were brushed and one by one up we went into the loft, where we felt we would be safe.

The last one up hauled in the ladder and laid it over the trapdoor opening with a mattress on top of that. And so, like the little girls under the care of Miss Clavel, we went to bed.

All night we lay there unable to sleep. Listening. Scrape, scrape, scrape … scrape, scrape, scrape. Hot followed by cold, cold followed by hot.

The next morning the mattress was pulled away from the trapdoor opening and we looked down. The green painted bentwood chairs had been dragged into every corner of the room. We quickly packed up and left.

Mick and I still talk about that night sometimes. It was truly scary.

<hr>

On a Friday evening in August 2018, I stood alone on the bridge which spans the Wienfluss at its confluence with the Donaukanal. It was hot and cars and cyclists passed by. I was watching Zaan down below as she photographed reflections in the water. Suddenly the scent of my father encircled me. I felt his presence strongly. He said quietly but clearly, "My Carly, don't say bad things about me any more." And the presence was gone.

25 July 2017   Letter #54

Hi Gareth

Just before setting out for the European continent in 1987, I saw something written in thick koki pen on one of those curved posters on the other side of the tracks in a London underground station: *"Travel narrows the mind, as it limits one's point of view to the extent of one's own experience."*

I have recently finished reading **Songlines**: a truly excellent book by Bruce Chatwin, published in 1987. It is a book about travelling, wanderlust, the unsettled nature of mankind, territorial aggression, nomads and much more. Chatwin's point of view is contradictory to that of the subway graffito: *"Travel does not merely broaden the mind, it makes the mind."*

21 June 2017

Today Zaan and I drove two hours to Long Point, Ontario.
We travelled as if in a dream, on perfect roads,
Past farms and homesteads so beautifully neat.
Organised people settled here and bent the countryside to their will.
Their work ethic and sense of order made manifest.
Zimbabwe could look just as good and be run just as well.

Human life in South Africa has become harsh.
The mountains and the salty sea remain ostensibly the same, so we hang on.
We find the beauty and we feel the pain.
We know that the time of the paleface in Africa is drawing to a close.
The continent now heads toward an age of exploitation, suffering and stagnation.

As much as I love the spirit and *vivre* of the people,
I sure could live without the chaos

Yesterday was 1 July 2017

It was also the 150th anniversary of Canada as an independent state.
I think that in the 1970s and '80s in RSA we had too much bad nationalism.
Republic Day … short-panted Voortrekkers parading with their flag standards.
Our neighbours' sons returning home from school in cadet uniforms.
Die Vlaglied.
Cradled in Beauty.
Die Rooi Gevaar.
Conscription.

Ringing out from our blue heavens, From our deep seas breaking round;
Over everlasting mountains, Where the echoing crags resound;
From our plains where creaking wagons, Cut their trails into the earth
Calls the spirit of our Country, Of the land that gave us birth.
At thy call we shall not falter, Firm and steadfast we shall stand.
At thy will to live or perish, O South Africa, dear land.

Ratel, Ratel …Ha, Ha, Ha … Magnus Malan … You know the story.
Zaan and I rode our bikes in the morning – stalls of all kinds were being set up and the early-birds were already milling around in their red and white outfits. Types no worse than those at the Milnerton flea market, I suppose.

A vintage field gun.
Soft men in historical "redcoat" uniforms … play actors.
Proxy aggression.
Monkey see, monkey do.
No thought applied.
How about monkey do not?

To steal a little more from Chatwin's book:
There is no such thing as war crime … all war is crime!
Do not ask the Bengal tiger to chew the cud.
Do not ask the crocodile to leave alone the antelope and eat the grass.
This is what I have taught Allegra.
Human nature, long wrought.

Work with it, work around it, because you will not change it.

Have you read Konrad Lorenz, **On Aggression**?

The army was there, just like in the RSA back then.
MAGs and BRENs and LMGs to fire up the imaginations of young and old boys alike.

Back home the garden is full of birds ... golden oriole, grackles, woodpeckers, creepers, nuthatch, wren, robins, chickadees, hummingbirds and more. The back deck is like a constant viewing platform with rabbits and chipmunks below. Squeeze the juice dripping from the days.

The rain came to tease and then left, leaving the brilliant night open for a glorious fireworks display of utter wastefulness. Mr Killjoy here does not really like fireworks that much, but the children do. And I guess some adults do. I suppose I just don't get it. Never did, really. Don't like the crowds. Hated sports day at school.

3 July 2017

For three days I have been a bit sleepy and dull.
I fear laziness.
It is a horror.
I have just been up in the attic measuring for new window frames.
Hanging out two storeys up.
That shook out the dullness – now I can't wait for more woodwork.

This morning we rode in a somnambulist state up the Thames and back.
About twenty-two easy kilometres.
Perfect early summer.
The air thick with the elixir that changes day into gold.
High above fleecy sheep floating like clouds.
The markers of the pacific trades.
For a moment a breeze in my helmet sounded exactly like the rigging of Seacomber,
Headed south-east from Noumea to the Isle of Pines.

In the **Descent of Man**, Darwin notes that in certain bird species, the migratory impulse is stronger than the maternal. A mother will abandon her fledglings in the nest rather than miss her appointment with the long journey south. Darwin quotes the example of John Audubon's goose, which, deprived of its pinion feathers, began the journey on foot.

⚓

When in South Africa, I long to go to Canada.
Once in Canada, I long for the calm water and fjords of Arctic Norway and Italy and anywhere else.

I long for the Pacific and the mast and deck timber and rigging,

But I do not think that I have ever been really at my ease and happy while
under sail.
Old men remember a war with fondness as the best days of their lives.
Time filters out the stress, the hardships and the dangers.
Good memories remain.

I must thank those who took me there, or invited me, or pushed me, for I
would otherwise not have gone. I would have stayed at home. That is my
story. A lifelong battle between an over developed sense of responsibility,
restlessness and fear.

On 5 July 2017 Donald Trump said *"the defence of the West ultimately rests
not only on means but also on the will of its people to prevail. The fundamental
question of our time is whether the West has the will to survive".*

Is the current nuclear standoff with Kim Jong-un, North Korea's boy
leader, more serious than the Cuban missile crisis of 1962?

I see soft people here. Western people. Fat women focusing on their hair,
nails, lipstick and lashes while their Eastern counterparts herd ducks through
rice paddies in conical hats. Or do they?

8 July 2017

A few days ago, Zaan and I drove through the placid, tamed countryside and sleeping towns to Port Franks (Lake Huron) and took a 17km paddle on the gentle Ausable River. We returned through the bucolic countryside and sleeping towns into the London city limits around 16h30, small-city rush hour. There my mind locked into a kind of culture shock. Good people, hideous people, extrapolating into too many people, of whom, we two, of course, were two.

Could we live here like two salmon in the wrong river?

I am happy enough here on vacation but have been programmed in life by *"Die Protestantische Ethik"* or "The Euro/Calvinist Work Ethic" so every now and then a kind of weirdness grabs me.

For some reason I do not feel that I have the right to free time …
time off … time out.
Fill that unforgiving hour with sixty minutes' worth of distance run.
We still have over five weeks here!
Why must I chase my tail to get something done?
I have already done so much.

It is the first time in four visits to Canada that I am not in a race against the Earth's rotation to get work delivered on time. My sleep is filled with detailed, enjoyable but rather abstract dreams. Yesterday afternoon as we sat in the warm sun watching the birds and chipmunks, Zaan commented that she was struggling to find meaning. I said to Zaan that we must go and buy canvas so that she can start painting her new commission. She agreed. We did.

As the sun sank down to the west, the sky darkened,
and thunder rumbled far away, moving closer.
Then a storm began to develop overhead.
Lightning flashes, loud peals of thunder,
small hailstones followed by large hail and very cold air.
Then came the rain, really heavy rain pelting down,
flooding the road and the park.

By nine-thirty it was mostly over.
Not quite dark, with a few soft drops still falling.

All of a sudden, the garden and the park and the neighbours' gardens twinkled with fireflies.

We rushed outside to see them.

It was like something from **Peter Pan**.

Tiny flying lights,

On and off, here and there, ephemeral, intangible.

For some, pondering the colour of a firefly's light would provide sufficient meaning.

Today it is fresh, cool and bright.

We rode 20km on the bike path up the River Thames, past the iron bridge at Meadowlilly.

Thick patches of purple paste on the asphalt mark the mulberry trees above.

Under every bridge we pass, a troll mess.

Fragments of burnt wood and plastic,

An empty Pringles tube,

A torn discarded rucksack,

A Tim Hortons cup, some filthy rags, a smashed trolley.

Today we only see three trolls: one sleeping on a bench in the sun, one sitting on a piece of cardboard in the same place he sat on Wednesday and a feral matted female. "Where are all the other trolls today?" you may well ask. Probably down at one of the 15 (or so) free methadone clinics in the city. Apart from free methadone, the city of London hands out over 2.5 million free needles to drug users every year.

That is looking down … let us look up … this is what Elon Musk says:

I think there are really two fundamental paths. History is going to bifurcate along two directions. One path is we stay on Earth forever, and then there will be some eventual extinction event. I do not have an immediate doomsday prophecy, but eventually, history suggests, there will be some doomsday event. The alternative is to become a space-bearing civilization and a multi-planetary species, which I hope you would agree is the right way to go. So how do we figure out how to take you to Mars and create a self-sustaining city – a city that is not merely an outpost, but which can become a planet in its own right, allowing us to become a truly multi-planetary species?

In former times, Europeans would send out their sailing ships in search of wealth and conquest. Far away continents such as Africa and the America were in many ways not unlike distant planets: full of unknowns. Elon Musk is thinking in a way similar to those Europeans, but not in the same way. He is not after wealth. He already has it. But much like our European forefathers did not stop to consider whether the New World was really theirs to invade and own, Musk does not stop to consider whether we have the right to colonise Mars. And there are people who do not even stop to consider whether they have the right to torment a fish on the end of their line. It is all in the thinking. The ways of seeing.

10 July 2017

We read that evolution probably happened in short sharp jolts rather than smoothly over a prolonged period. When everything is ticking over smoothly in an optimum climate and habitat, there is no reason for anything to change. Earthquakes, volcanoes, meteorites, cataclysm, mass extinction … these are the things that propel evolution. Small remnant survivor populations kicking off anew in a changed set of circumstances. Adapting.

I am fascinated by the people I see over here. Many typical Northern Europeans … red Irish, heavy Poles, quite a few Italians and Romanians, some Middle Eastern types, Indians, some Asians, a few Jews and a few Afro-Americans. Except for the descendants of slaves, all of them left their homelands in search of a perceived better life.

Tom the Vietnamese gas technician told me this: "I come from a small town 200km south of the capital Hanoi. I left 20 years ago with nothing. I still have nothing."

In years gone by, our people left the "Old Countries" of Europe in search of better lives. Exoduses after famines, wars, pogroms and oppression. At different times there were different choices and different people preferred different places. Canada, South Africa, Australia for the Anglos. The USA for the Italians and the Irish. Some people chose Patagonia. Nazis: Argentina and Brazil. Jews go everywhere, constantly moving, as is their nomadic wont.

I think that those people who chose South Africa had the best time to begin with. Many willing brown hands to help for scant recompense. But now the tables have turned. To quote the dreaded Coachman in our childhood film, **Pinocchio**: "You boys have had your fun, now pay for it!"

Today we rode our bikes 20km down through Springbank Park. It began to rain. Not heavy rain but largish drops. We rode, others rode, other others walked and jogged. It was not cold, it was lovely. One young couple took shelter with their bicycles beneath a low tree. Why, when no-one else did?

Many years before, somewhere in the Operational Area, an officer came across a drunk soldier. "*Troep, hoekom is jy so dronk?*" he asked. "*Want ek verlang, Kaptein,*" came the response.

Two totally unrelated incidents linked at that moment only by the chemical processes inside my head.

Yesterday was Sunday. A set of triggers released certain chemicals into my brain. I wouldn't say the result was depression or sadness, but rather a dullness or numbness and a sense of longing for the "Old Countries" that made me stupid. And in my fumbling attempts to keep working, I cut the main burglar alarm cable with my pliers. I should never have even been up a ladder. Luckily, I did not fall off the roof.

What was it on that Sunday? My biological clock reaching the end of its seven-day cycle? My frantic need to do everything at once? Norsk and Italian language research for Allegra and me? The building at 4 Chas Booth? Marco Simal's new project? Yes, all of these. And I have been paging through Zaan's big Taschen sculpture book. It makes me pine for that which I once so loved. I think of the Farnese marbles. The worked stone of the European cities. The rows of bronze cannon lying outside Les Invalides. The hill towns of Umbria. The walled carless town of Korčula. The Mediterranean. *La Mer*.

12 July 2017

Tomorrow it will be Zaan and my ten-year anniversary of being together.
Two people being kind and caring towards one another can make life a heaven.
Two people being unkind and harsh to each other can make life a hell.
It will also be the anniversary of the birth of our family's prima matriarch.
Virginia "Dinny" Winshaw … born 1903.
We have bought some cedar planks.
I will set up my saw and do woodwork.

14 July 2017

This morning Zaan took us on a long bike ride. When out running, we do about double the distance in Canada than Cape Town. The terrain for running is very gentle. There are no rocks and the paths are springy so there is a lot less stress on knees and feet. When paddling one does not have to work against swell and chop. We ride bikes on asphalt tracks specially tarred and maintained for recreational exercise. There is no worry about being wiped out by a minibus taxi. Dogs are leashed and under control. The cycle paths run along the river, past sports fields or through forests and meadows of summer bloom. It is rather nice.

Last evening after I packed away my tools, Zaan and I went out for an early supper and some India Pale Ale for me. Then we saw a movie called **The Gardener** about a Canadian horticulturalist named Frank Cabot. He inherited a farm near Quebec and turned it into a most gorgeous place. But the lesson to be learned is not to complicate life with fuss, grandification and pretentiousness. Those guys can keep it. A simple life is best.

16 July 2017

Two years ago, a kind person came down to the park and dropped off two black plastic crates or "totes" as they are called in Canada. They were filled with toys. Lovely yellow bulldozers and loaders and diggers and trucks and John Deere green tractors. There were also spoons and pans and stainless-steel mixing bowls for making mud-pies and other such childhood delights. Last year some trolls came at night and took the kitchen utensils. Then they came for the totes. This year all the toy trucks and earthmoving equipment lay strewn across the 15m-diameter sandpit in which the neighbourhood children love to play. So I took some wood and screwed together a 2ft × 4ft wooden frame with no bottom and rope handles at each end. I placed my wooden frame in front of one of the benches where the moms and dads sit while they watch their offspring play, and packed all the toys into it. I look at the park, so neat and carefully tended, and the houses too. Why should all the toys be strewn about?

I have a view of the sandpit from my office window. We can also see it from the deck. Not once in a month has my toy-box been used for its designed purpose. Instead, it gets dragged around. Twice we have found it 100m away standing upright in a corner of the park like a portal into another dimension. It is often used as a doorway into some imaginary room, which worried me as it would crack the skull of any child onto who's head it might fall.

Late yesterday afternoon, Zaan and I were sitting reading on the park-side deck when along came a scraggly little guy on his bike. He clearly had a plan, and we watched him like a pair of spies.

In the centre of the sandpit is a jungle-gym type construction with a big red slide, a medium sized slide and two little slides for tots. It has steps up to the little slides and an elevated yellow plastic tunnel linking the large slides to the two little slides. There is also a climbing spiral and a curved ladder and a pair of swings alongside.

With great effort, the scraggly kid manhandled my wooden frame up the steps. Then, with even more effort, got the frame up onto the top of the yellow plastic tunnel. He did this because the frame was too large to pass through the tunnel. He then shot through the tunnel, back and forth like a hamster, pulling and pushing until he finally managed to get the heavy wooden frame over the top of the tunnel and poised at the top of the large slide ready to go. Then he did a very interesting thing. The little boy went around the sandpit and collected every single toy, large and small, without missing one, and packed them with great care at the bottom of the large slide to be smashed to smithereens by his impending deed.

At that moment his slightly larger brother arrived and dropped his bike on the pathway. "Look what I have done, I have got them all, you go up and push it," said the scraggly boy. The brother shook his head, so the scraggly boy began to climb the ladder, at which point I gently interceded and removed my wooden toybox from the equation.

"There must be a lesson in this somewhere," I said to Zaan as I returned.

We ride to and beyond the green iron bridge on this calm Sunday. Along the river, up through the forests and back down past some kids playing baseball on a sand diamond in a green field.

"Litvett!!" as I was called at PT, was never any good at baseball. "Strike one! Strike two! Strike three!" boomed Mr Donald. All the boys shouted together: "RUN!!! RUN!!!" And so I began to run … "DROP THE BAT" … and I flung the bat away from me as I ran … "OUT!!!" The ball always arrived at first base long before I did. I don't think I ever actually hit a baseball. No Babe Ruth.

Cricket was much worse. "BUTTERFINGERS!!!" Boys are unkind.

I have grown up with not an iota of interest in ballgames. I have never had any interest in balls or cards or Monopoly or winning at games. Just couldn't see the point.

25 July 2017

On Saturday I could sense the dark hyena creeping about. On Sunday I woke deeply depressed after a troubled sleep … firmly in its jaws. On 13 July we were asked to go and measure up some old buildings in Yalta. An old client of mine, and a few others, are thinking of developing a hotel there, just behind the famous Livadia palace. Ten days of uncertainty and worry, trying to get a brief, changing flights etc. It all simply chewed me up. Poor sleep didn't help. On Monday I finally got hold of the main client's representative in Moscow and the air was cleared.

Today is a lovely summer's day.
Zaan and I are happy.
Allegra has flown off to visit her godmother in Italy.
All is well.

Fall in love with uncertainty and she will never cause you harm.
Resist her, and you will be tossed and turned in her waters until you can no longer breathe.

Easier said than done. Uncertainty is what I hate most in the world.

All Best
Carl

Chapter 54

The Shark Killer

Zaan and I were down at the lake the other day where we met a couple of construction workers taking a break. They looked at the surf-skis on our roof-racks and struck up conversation. One of them said that only this morning he had been telling his buddy, on the way to work, about his absolute fear of sharks and how he wanted to be a "shark killer".

We laughed and joked and chatted about him working as a rough labourer by day and a drummer in a band by night and the complexities of fusion jazz syncopation. Know what I mean? Me neither. But on further reflection, I thought how strange it was that a man who lived in a Canadian city, surrounded by freshwater lakes, should be afraid of sharks and want to kill them. I wondered if he had ever been anywhere.

<hr/>

As I paddled, I reminisced about a time in 2003 when I travelled to visit Dag in Arctic Norway. I was designing the houses for his company and we had projects in various stages of completion, from Mo-i-Rana (on the Arctic Circle) to Narvik to Tromsø to Alta. We took a long drive in his Volvo … summertime, the midnight sun. The Lofoten Islands passed us by to the right, soaring peaks rising from the sea. Small painted villages. Few people about. Every now and then a car or a Dutch mobile home (the Dutch seem to like it up there).

Arctic Norway is particularly beautiful in the hours when the sun drops to the horizon but never quite sets. It becomes very still and quiet. Muted. Reindeer pass silently by the houses. The fjords are mirrors. The air is so crisp.

After thousands of kilometres on the road, we finally arrive at the

Gjerstad home. We unpack and eat boiled eggs and butter on homemade bread. Sweet black tea in stainless mugs. It is time for some leg-stretching.

Provisions and sleeping bags are packed into packsacks. Bo the pointer wears one too. He is used to carrying ammunition and hunting gear, but this time his panniers contain raisins and cheese and chocolate and a few cans of herring to leave in the *hytter* – the Norwegian mountain huts. High in the mountains, built and maintained in winter by men on snowmobiles. Inaccessible in summer other than by foot.

Hours spent walking up. All clothes must be removed before picking your way across the larger of the icy fast-flowing rivers that bar the route. Some might question why a person would want to. The answer is because it is so very good and invigorating beyond belief. There is no doubt about one's being alive up there. ALIVE!!! With loons in the high lakelets and arctic char.

In the evening, let's say around midnight, after maybe six to eight hours of trekking, we arrive at a small wooden cabin. We have followed no path. The moss and crunchy ice is steep but mostly easy to walk on. Dag has unfailingly led us to a cabin of interlocking logs, painted light grey. There are a few small windows, a door and a small verandah. Steel cables span from the roof to steel poles driven into the rocky ground to prevent winter storms from blowing it away. For now, it is as peaceful as peace itself. As if in a dream, half a dozen reindeer drift silently by. A low mist diffuses the sunlight.

Inside, the hut consists of two compact rooms: four bunk beds in the back one and kitchen arrangements in the front. A table and a few chairs, a cast iron stove, a kettle, a few pots and pans hanging from nails hammered into the walls. A two-ring gas cooker and a massive stainless-steel cauldron filled with chopped kindling. Open shelves packed with victuals fill every other available bit of wall space: a bottle of brandy (half full), some tins of mackerel, matches, oil, soap, sticking-plasters, coffee, candles, *tobak*. Every visitor leaves something behind and every visitor is free to take what he or she might need. We sit in the late-night sunshine and discuss days recently past and days to come.

In the morning we spin for arctic char, a salmonish/troutish fish that somehow miraculously populates the high lakelets or tarns. They live under a thick layer of ice for much of the year. Their flesh is bright orange and unfortunately for them, very tasty. We have a few for breakfast.

The best days of your life:
when they arrive, are often so few,
that you can count them on one hand.

An hour or two later, after Zaan and I had paddled our fill and packed up our boats, we headed for home. We drove by a building site on a corner, a dusty place with men in hard hats and wheelbarrows and two-by-fours and things. One of the men looked up, cupped his hands around his mouth and hollered:

"Don't forget to tell other people about me okay!"
It was the wannabe shark killer.

I sent an email to Peter Gibbons the other day,
with some photos of me surfing my longboard,
out alone, in perfect surf, at Mossel Bay.
"Those were the days!" Pete replied, and they were!
If we cannot relive them, with what can we at least replace them?

9 August 2017   Letter #55

Hi Gareth

We arrived in Canada on the 12th of June. The fields were ploughed and sown. Brown furrowed earth.

Soon a hint of green appeared.

Now the maize stands 2m tall.

We leave in one week's time.

Then off to Yalta to go and measure up a big old building for a possible hotel project.

Plans need to be ready for a meeting in Singapore in the first week in September.

When the Yalta project came up I spoke to Dag.

He travels extensively, keeps abreast of world developments and knows a lot. He said: "Yes Kallemann, you must go there."

30 July 2017

Dag sent me two book titles:

The Strange Death of Europe – Douglas Murray.

The End of Europe: Dictators, Demagogues, and the Coming Dark Age – James Kirchick.

Kirchick's book is most interesting. I travelled a lot in Europe between 1987 and 2003 … then I stopped going there. And I stopped paying close attention, too. Things have certainly changed since then. I read this book with avid interest … discounting 5 to 10% for Judeo-Yankee bias. I look forward to Murray's book.

In Canada I am completely baffled by the keeping of dogs in the urban environment. Why do they want them? So many people seem to be nothing more than a life support system for a dog or two. Globally (w.r.t. Kirchick's book) I am equally baffled by the persistence of Religion and Nationalism.

Today we rode 33km through Gibbons Park and out along the paths.
There were so few people around that it became a bit freaky.
Like on Rugby World Cup day.
I wondered where everyone was.
Maybe glued to their TV sets watching some global horror unfolding?

The flowers and trees reminded me so much of Klimt's summer landscapes painted at Attersee.
When I was a boy we holidayed at Witsand at the mouth of the Breede River.
The afternoons were warm and windy.
I would walk alone over the dunes, down the long beach and around the point where it was always deserted and lovely.
Today I was reminded of those days as I rode, the warm air in my ears.

Coming back into town:
A group of joyful children in the play pool,
being sprayed by a giant overhead shower.
Two teenage girls talking, laughing on a bench.
A young man flying his racing drones over a football field.
A man in a wheelchair and his wife sitting reading, smoking in the shade of a tree.
An elderly couple standing bent, looking down at a commemorative brass plaque.
An old friend perhaps?
Another day of Life.

Maybe looking at the human condition too closely is like looking for bullets down the barrel of a gun.

I am trying a new trick.
Every evening I try to remember all the good things that happened during the day.
To be conscious and appreciative of our good fortune.

Why all this interest in Europe all of a sudden?
Well, Allegra flew off to Rome, Naples and Capri where she is at present.
It is her first trip overseas solo at 19.
Previously five weeks backpacking in Thailand with two classmates and
nine weeks in Vietnam and Cambodia with her ex-boyfriend Leo.
I long for Italy sometimes.

But mainly because of our trip via Moscow to Yalta in the Crimea.
My most recent travels have been to Canada over the past four years,
And Norway and Arctic Norway, and that is not really mainstream EU.
I admit that Zuma and the Guptas have been grabbing my attention,
More than Putin and Merkel for the past while.

4 August 2017

I have put Kirchick down midway and am halfway through Murray. In order
to know the world, I must read the work of fascists and Nazis and right-
wingers and pro-US types as well as the others. And talk to everyone I meet,
whenever I can. And hopefully get a balanced view of all the confusion.
For what?

If we ever do go for a bite out in Canada, we go for Shawarmas around the
corner at a little joint owned by a Lebanese version of Fagin.
There is a constant turnover of food prep. staff ... "falafel flippers".
Some speak poor English, but I always try to communicate.
For what it's worth, their English is better than my Syro-Lebanese.
Tonight, a 60ish Syrian woman and a young Iraqi man were front of house.
The relief of a safe job in a safe place!
Previously a young Iranian woman, a qualified chemist, was stuffing and
folding pitas,
While her young husband completes his pharmacy degree here.

My dad put on operas every year for Kapuściński's Shah of Shahs until 1978.
He was very fond of the Iranians and even had a permanent "girlfriend" in
Tehran,
As did his own father in Odessa.
Believe it or not, quite a few Iranians I have spoken to in Canada have a:
"Come back Shah, all is forgiven" attitude.

This evening we ate alongside a Somalian man and boys.
With them was a caucasian boy who spoke their strange sounding dialect fluently.
What a world!

According to my family history, I am an immigrant ... born in Spain.
Great grandfather from the USA of Irish and German immigrant parentage.
Great grandmother from England
My mother's South African family on her father's side: Dutch Oosthuizens and French Malherbes.
My grandfather on my father's side, from Norway.

These are my views:

Human nature is what it is. We have to work around it and work with it.

Guilt is an unhealthy emotion. A national guilt syndrome is a very bad thing. The descendants of long-dead colonisers or Nazis cannot endlessly apologise to the descendants of long-dead victims. We can only actively do right things now with the awareness we now have (no-one ever apologises to me that I have only between 2 and 4% of my Neanderthal genes left).

Ignorance and unchecked human population growth are very bad things.

Tolerant societies are foolish to tolerate intolerant immigrant minority groups. (Ref: Kirchick pg 109 – quote: Karl Popper)

I am against the religions and ideologies that divide humanity.

8 August 2017

In RSA ... a parliamentary vote of no confidence: Zuma the great cockroach stays.

177 voted him out
198 voted him to stay
9   cowards abstained
16 never pitched up

After a hopeful start, the result of today's Zuma vote has left me numb and physically nauseous.

I feel like puking.
Nothing has affected me this badly in a long time.
I do not know how to internalise it.

Big Love – C

Chapter 55

On Religion

In today's world, I think I feel most sorry for the Jehovah's Witnesses. Traipsing around in their crimplene suits on hot sunny days, carrying briefcases and wasting their precious time in service of an imaginary god. I was brought the latest edition of AWAKE! a few days ago (No.2 2018). I see the illustrations have become more ... more ... less ... er ... imaginative?

We live near the local shul and sometimes have a rabbi in our guest apartment.

Last time it was a ginger-haired rabbi and his twin-like pregnant wife and their beautiful curly topped delicate little daughter Avigail (her father's joy).

I wonder if it is the same god who called the rabbi to become a rabbi, and who called Yianni to become the good Christian that he is, and who called my old bricklayer friend Boeta-Yu's son to give up bricklaying and become an imam?

They call him Jehovah, YHWH, Allah, G_d.

He allows some to pray using a rosary and some not.

And when you pray, do not keep on babbling like pagans, for they think they will be heard because of their many words. Do not be like them, for your Father knows what you need before you ask him. Matthew 6:7.

He is the god of Moses and he is a jealous god ... and he creates such opportunity for it.

The young ginger rabbi is such a likeable and respectful guy, but during the holy weekend of Pesach he may not use any electric remote device or light switch or vehicle or even tear up his own toilet paper. It is incredible to me. He even showed me an amazing invention in which a light bulb is set in two rotating slotted cardboard sleeves. When the slots are aligned, light comes out, when they are rotated through some degrees, it is dark. No need to switch a switch! The rabbis bring their own lights with them.

A god

Zaan and I visited Bali once. It is the last bastion of Hinduism in the fast Muslimising Indonesian archipelago. Hindus traditionally allow themselves four children per family (three too many, as far as I am concerned) while the Muslims breed unchecked – "Inshalla" – they say, it is God's will. To the Muslim, everything is God's will and they therefore take no responsibility for their own actions. The Hindu women spend all their free time making little votive offerings and flags and rattles to scare off the evil spirits.

I write this passage as a result of a few lines in an email letter from Yianni (the bit about the babbling pagans above). It triggered my thoughts which stick like a burr in my brain-wool and go round 'n round in my head until I formulate them by writing them down. That is what I do. Then I can put the matter to bed, in peace, knowing full well that it will not make the slightest bit of difference.

I am just so thankful that after tens of thousands of years believing in some or other pagan pantheon or animist belief system, and then a short period of European Christianity, my family managed to shake off the shackles of religion and I walk light and free. I am as convinced of my atheism as Yianni is of his Christianity and the Rabbi is of his orthodoxy. And as the Imam is of Allah and as the Catholics were convinced about savagely sacking Constantinople in 1204, destroying Byzantium and leaving the doors wide open for the expansion of Islam. What more can I say?

Well I could say this: I was most amused by a video clip in which atheist comedian Ricky Gervais was talking to some TV guy about god. This is how I remember the conversation:

RG: So, you actually believe in god?

TV Guy: Well, er, yes ...

RG: In one god?

TV Guy: Well, yes, but in three persons.

RG: So you have chosen one god out of the approximately three thousand currently in use?

TV Guy: Well, yes ... er ... I have done some reading ...

RG: So you believe in one god and not the 2999 other ones?

TV Guy: Well, er, yes.

RG: So why do you have a problem with me? I believe in only one less god than you do.

TV Guy: Well, I need someone, er, something to focus my gratitude on.

Oh please! for god's sake.

25 September 2017   Letter #56

Hi Gareth

London, Ontario: 16 August 2016

I was called on 13 July about a project in Yalta.

Since then it has caused me a lot of stress.

I really do not want to go, while those I tell say: "Wow, amazing!" It has filled my dreams with hanging nooses on spring pulleys and high-speed reverse car crashes and every other sort of adrenaline-fuelled unpleasantness. That is how I always react. And then when I am on the adventure, I love it. My logical neocortex brain says, "How amazing to see Moscow and the Crimea, stay in top end hotels, and all of it paid for." My reptilian base overrides that with worry and fear, squirting out chemicals, causing my delicate limbic balance to go awry like Humpty Dumpty.

30 August 2017

Last evening, I emailed the Russia clients my completed work – job done, for now at least.

I have spent the day in a state of utmost sadness, a sticky glue-like fog. The return from a trip away and all the escapism that goes with it. Now to face again the realities of my ex-wife and alimony, trying to sell the house and pay her, family, ageing mom, work, earning a living, paying tax et cetera. Much the same problems as everyone else, I suppose.

Today is Sunday 03 September 2017

I have dealt with many of my work and return issues. I had a meeting with an employer this morning, then came down to our boatshed and cleaned it for about six hours, washing away the damage from the big smashing storm of early June.

The doors had not been opened since I locked up and left for Canada. It was quite a damp affair with rat shit and dried green slime everywhere. Since the water had come up to the roof eaves, even the plates and cups in the top cupboards had been slimed. But now, as I write, I am in the shed sitting in front of my laptop at a clean table after having dined on eggs and toast and coffee. The sea is cranking away outside and the light, a bit too bright for my eyes, is the light of a glorious spring day at the Cape.

But dam levels are perilously low and the politics as terrible as ever. Taxi drivers drive so badly. A police vehicle parks on the red line below a no-stopping sign opposite Pick n Pay and an obese "play-play" policewoman runs over the road to buy more "*slap* chips" and a "two-litre Jive". The anti-social and lawless behaviour of our people really scares me because it is like cancer … it spreads … and cannot be eradicated without a radical intervention that will never come. We live, I am afraid to say, in an unsurpassably beautiful country with a terminal disease. What a tragic truth to face as Namaqualand bursts into bloom.

I came down to the shed today to make breakfast and write my Russia story before it faded. But I have digressed and must digress more before I can begin.

Zaan has gone to Paris for two weeks with her Mom. Zaan and I have been together for ten years and we are now like a pair of Konrad's Greylag geese. It is wonderful. Before she left we did a few runs on Lion's Head. At my age now, fitness is quite quickly lost and must be fought for hard. I went down for a surf at Glen Beach on Friday morning. There were only two other guys out. The waves were fast and tricky, but I like to surf my longboard these days. I was out for about 45 minutes – it was exhausting, my arms felt like cooked spaghetti – but I got two waves and surfed them well and did not take a single wipe-out or suck-back or any other bad thing except a bit of a sore rib. So yes, I was pleased indeed.

Today I went for an early bike ride on the gravel track below Tafelberg Road. As I crawled up one of the steeper looser sections my chain snapped, so I dismounted and began to push my bike. Within a few seconds another rider (an expert sort of guy) pulled up, removed a link, and fixed the chain.

Within three or four minutes, I was on my way again, no worse for my trouble. What luck!

Okay ... now to Russia:

Zaan and I did a whizz trip down to Yalta and back to Moscow. It was too fast and hurried for me to write down anything other than that which was work related. Like all times of much action, there is little time to write and record. This is a pity because those times are the most important.

The Plan:

Zaan and I were due to fly back to RSA from Canada, via Dubai, on 16 August 2017, but we were asked by an old client of mine to divert and please go to Yalta in the Crimea to measure up an old palace building for his Muscovite friend, the investor. The building would be restored and, in conjunction with a hotelier friend from the east, converted into a boutique hotel.

The Reality:

For a month, I chased information. I was given incorrect information regarding the client by incompetent PAs. One client was on a yacht somewhere, out of range, out of comms. The other was simply not responding. FlyDubai tickets to Moscow were booked for us, even though I had requested Emirates flights. A person in Moscow booked us Aeroflot tickets to Simferpol in the Crimea. We would meet the Russian investor in Yalta. He would contact us once we got there. A hotel reservation was made for us in Yalta and a driver would transfer us from Simferpol airport to the four-and-a-half-star luxury "Imperial 2011".

We spent the night of 17 August at the Terminal 3 transfer hotel in Dubai which has, by now, become a home from home. In the early morning we bused over to Terminal 2, from where the low-cost airlines operate, taking the bottom 12% of the flying hordes and their horrible children to places like Kabul, Cairo, Kandahar, Yerevan and Baku. Mostly Arab types whom I disrespect immensely for their revolting toilet manners. It is said that a civilisation may be judged by the way it treats its animals. I say that a civilisation may be judged by the way it uses the lavatory. Swimming with piss, great globs of toilet paper in every urinal, and a crowd of ball-scratching men in floor-length shirts queueing for the stalls. Allah alone knows what they do in there.

After a three hour wait, we depart. A planeload of human "cockroaches" plus Zaan and I. Five or six hours to Moscow – FlyDubai – screaming kicking kids with totally hopeless parents. Luckily we bought emergency aisle seats for 700 ZAR each, for nothing larger than a human cockroach can fit into the crammed seating of a FlyDubai aircraft. Snacks, drinks and water bottles were hawked up and down the aisles by the poor cousins of real air stewards and stewardesses, at sky-high prices. There were no cushions or coverlets, not even any chair-back pouches to put one's book into. Just crap.

We arrived in Moscow, cleared the frigidly unsmiling customs and immigration, collected our bags and transferred to our flight back over Ukraine to Simferpol in Crimea. We arrived at Simferpol on a dark and rainy night and a bumpy half-hour bus ride finally brought us across runways and fields to the airport building. I think we landed on the runway of the new airport (currently under construction) and then had to be shuttled to the old airport building (still in use). Our bags turned up a little later and we went to find our driver who was standing dutifully with a foolscap sheet reading LILTVED. He spoke no English and we no Russian. We were taken to his low-slung black VW sedan and raced off into the night. After about half an hour of high-speed terror, with our driver showing no signs of understanding my pleas for him to slow down, Zaan saw a sign saying Yalta 80km. It was sheer hell, with our driver switching his attention from the road, to his tablet, to his music system, to his phone calls, to some verbal translator app and back to the road. We could not get him to stop and allow us to jump out as our bags were in the trunk and we did not know where on earth we were. Zaan and I fell into that state which falls somewhere between hate and resignation (a state felt quite often in the SADF). Onward and downward, we passed one accident or breakdown after another: a pool of light, a halo of raindrops, a broken car, a few wet and bemused people, slick black tarmac.

Finally, around 11pm, stinking of dried adrenaline, we checked in at Hotel Imperial 2011 and were taken upstairs by Vitaly, the pencil-thin greenish-coloured night porter, day porter and generally never-off-duty guy.

The room was gaudy and had one sheet and one towel. We were not impressed but soon enough learned to love our spacious new home. In the morning we got sheets and towels and as the cleaning staff got to know us better, small items such as a shoe brush or drinking glasses would appear in the room. It was rather touching. I set up my desk and PC and got a lot of work done there.

The day after arriving in Yalta – Saturday 19 August – our interpreter Victoria arrived at our hotel at 10h00 and we caught a taxi to the Livadia Palace where we met the investor, an EU-sanctioned billionaire pal of Putin, and his brother. Utterly charming, very nice guys. Provided you are on their team, no doubt.

At the meeting it was explained to us that the building originally earmarked for the hotel would now be restored using "federal funds" and would become a museum. It was no longer part of the project. The brief had changed.

A new hotel and townhouse complex was now envisaged to be built on the property directly above the Livadia palace, currently operating as the Livadia Sanatorium Big Yalta. The existing "Club House" which housed the massive dining hall for the entire sanatorium would be demolished along with all but three of the existing buildings. The proposed hotel would have 50 rooms (70sqm each) and 50 townhouses of about 140sqm each. All in the Neo Renaissance style of Krasnov. Gyms, pools, treatment rooms, ballroom, rooftop gourmet restaurant and so on... What did we think?

Well, let us just say it was a "**big ask**" – the kind of challenge South Africans supposedly thrive on. Zaan and I were indeed challenged during our week in Crimea and day in Moscow. It was certainly no holiday.

There were no drawings to speak of. We had to pull rabbits out of hats. We used every trick in the bookski, but I think we did okay in the end. We met with the investor brothers at their luxury villa on the Crimea Breeze

Estate and dined on tasty num-nums. We photographed and measured at Livadia. We met the investors again at the small Ai Todor Palace (of the sister of Tsar Nicholas II) which they wanted to renovate. Again, what did we think? How should they renovate? A country club, villas in the forest or a private residence? We measured and took photos and walked the grounds. We observed the children and staff and absorbed a lot of the pre-soviet, soviet and post-soviet vibe ... as well as the Crimea vibe. We spent the next day photographing all of the Nikolay Krasnov buildings in Yalta. We went to the seamlessly style blended Vorontsov palace and even walked down to the promenade for a Crimean shawarma. A blur of acid light and shops and unfamiliar goods and happy people. The Black Sea bashing the sea wall. No English spoken. No foreigners at all.

At 6.30am on 24 August we left our Yalta hotel. The hotel driver handed us our packed breakfasts as we hopped into his big black Audi SUV. Five days later, we rewound the mind-bending night trip of what seemed like a lifetime before. At a conservative pace we retraced our way back up to Simferpol. Fresh accidents, a car and a bus, some views of the Black Sea, some views of Crimea.

We had not had enough time to see Balaclava or Sebastopol. But we had seen a lot. The underbelly, the resurgence of the Orthodox Church, Putinists, Stalinists, Monarchists, the sanatoria and the hard concrete and rebar edges of recent times.

We landed in Moscow and were collected by a man called Vladimir holding up a foolscap sheet in a plastic sheath saying LILTVED. We baled into his black Lexus and started out for a 380-bed hotel belonging to the investors, about an hour and a half's drive south of Moscow on the banks of the River Oka. By this time I was feverish with a flu virus that had invaded my system so Zaan took the "fly by your pantski" pilot's seat.

How should we renovate, what should we do? What do you think of these drawings and this and that? What do you think about building a new (1 000-bed) hotel up here on this field next to our organic farm with its free-range chickens and 1 500 Aberdeen Angus cattle?

It was fast approaching sunset with rain and rainbows as Vladimir pointed his black Lexus northwards and began the trip to our Hotel National on Red Square. Sitting in the back, my head swam as Zaan questioned him on all things from his childhood under the Soviets, being a member of the "Children of the October Revolution" and later "The Pioneers". To modern

Russia, to life under boozy Yelsin and the gangster period, to Gorby the "sell-out", to travels in the world and a naked man in Ethiopia wearing only a Kalashnikov rifle. It was all really enlightening. One fresh car crash after the next until gridlock in the city. Just unbelievable. A vibe you cannot get by Googling. What a life. In the end we got there.

What a great pity that we only had one night at the Hotel National. Now that is the style of things I prefer. Like a key that fits the lock. I am truly to that manner born. How about a week at the National, strolling past the Kremlin and Saint Basil's Cathedral to some or other museum, plus a good plug of voddies straight out of the bottle? Lovely.

The next morning we took a tobacco-stinky taxi to Moscow's VKO airport (we were almost, but not quite, used to the *en route* crashes) and suffered the indignity of a FlyDubai aircraft back to Terminal 2.

I have a mental snapshot of three toy guns lying confiscated in a box next to the airport security x-ray machines … fucking idiots to allow their kids to bring toy guns on a plane.

By 10pm Zaan and I were snug in the Dubai Terminal 3 Transit Hotel with only the 10-hour flip back to Cape Town still on our itinerary.

As I complete this passage, I have been back for two weeks. Zaan has been away in Paris with her mom for a week. The clients and investors have their detailed reports and more. I have drawn and delivered the drawings for a complete restaurant in Niseko, Japan (my second one there) and I have prepared "as builts" for yet another new store, this time in Sea Point. I have done much admin and tax prep too.

From time to time, I stop to think: The clients are currently in Russia with the investor brothers. I sure hope that whatever they decide to do, it does not involve me …

In Life, one should try to figure out what you can eat
and what will eat you …
then steer your course between the two.

Cape Town. The last rain has caused Table Mountain to explode with gorgeous gushing water. The city seems clean and quiet after Russia. I had my bike serviced and a new chain fitted, but the new chain slips. I have been up Lion's Head a few times and my rib still hurts.

24 September 2017

A month ago we checked out of our Yalta hotel.
A month that seems like a year or a week.
Zaan was in Paris for two weeks in that month.
She has already been back a week.

Yesterday morning there were loud bangs and thumps on our roof, followed by the incredible and continuous honking of a pair of Egyptian Geese. They then moved on and honked from every neighbouring rooftop for a couple of hours.

Last evening as Zaan and I sat on the terrace, we heard a terrific screaming up in the sky.
A pair of Peregrines or Lanner Falcons pulled out of their dive maybe two or three metres above us.
Their bulging eyes and fish-like faces flashed past in a split second.
Within a thousand swift wing-beats they were way over the other side of Camps Bay before turning out towards the setting sun.

Such is life ... the long and the short of it ... C

Chapter 56

Die Rooi Gevaar

In Moscow we had a driver named Vladimir Orlov, who, with incredible patience, steered his ageing black Lexus though the purgatory that is his livelihood. Hours and hours of it we shared with him. He does it every day. What a life! Better than Stalin's gulags though, and better than down Zasyadko.

While driving, or rather crawling along, Vladimir told Zaan and me tales of growing up in the Soviet Union. Of, at a young age, becoming a member of the **Little Octoberists** and getting a red star badge. Like all Russian kids, as he grew older he became a red-neckerchief wearing **Young Pioneer,** and finally, pride of prides, a member of the **Komsomol**. He told us of wonderful camps with apples and kind teachers and swimming in rivers and the joy of living in a great nation. **An Empire!**

As a youth, he had heard of the evil apartheid system and was glad that his USSR and Cuba were helping with its undoing. He told us of the terrible gangster period between the fall of the USSR and the emergence of a free market economy. Of crime bosses and ex-Afghan war veterans selling their services as hitmen and security. And of the rise of the Russian Orthodox Church and the new Stalin cult and life under Putin. But Vladimir told us nothing of the Russian obsession with salami. That, I had to find out about elsewhere.

⌐⊸⊶⊶⊷⌐

Die Rooi Gevaar (The Red Danger).

As boys in the early 1970s, we were really worried about a possible Russian invasion.

Communist sponsored and trained liberation armies were actively infiltrating from the north. Russian spy trawlers crawled up and down the Skeleton Coast. The ANC was secretly at work undermining with communist help. It was scary.

When I was about twelve years old, a possible seaborne Russian invasion became a topic of much anxious discussion in the school playground. Some of the boys did not worry because they had been told that the whole of Table Mountain had been secretly hollowed out and was full of jets. At a moment's notice, thin walls of rock could be pushed away and the hidden jets would swoop down and save the day. This possibility relieved our troubled minds a little, but when playing on Camps Bay beach I would often stop what I was doing and peer out over the breakers to check that there wasn't a periscope, or a conning tower, or a whole sub with a deckload of Ruski commandos getting ready to storm ashore.

We did not understand at the time why the Russians wanted to invade us. One of our friends, Helge Schutz, postulated that it was because they needed our sportsmen. Gary Player and Jody Scheckter were two examples and, of course, the entire Springbok rugby team! We had watched films of the Munich Olympics and now Montreal was coming up – they needed our sportsmen!

My dad would occasionally take us to visit his friend Milly who lived in a large stone house on the cliff above Barley Bay. Mick and I would quickly say hello, avoid Milly's very smelly dogs, and slip away down the steps, over

~ 476 ~

Victoria Road, and to the secret cove all set about with granite boulders and bamboo. We would lie on our tummies, peering into the crystal water and try to *angel* (foul hook) the big *kreef* that crawled there, on the sandy sea-bed.

One day, as we crossed the road, hooks and lines ready for action, we were intercepted by Milly's next-door neighbour, Mr Drunky. On our arrival perhaps ten minutes earlier, Mick and I had noticed Mr Drunky leaning against the sidewalk railing intently studying the sea through a pair of binoculars. Now, with us, he could share his surreal fears. "Russian frogmen!" he said, "Look!" As he pointed toward the thick black low-tide kelp bed. "Hundreds of them!" And, for him, there they were – stealthily swimming ashore. For us it was just kelp.

After giving Mr Drunky the slip, Mick and I lay on our favourite rock, arms dangling, our treble-hooks baited with limpet meat as the lobsters began putting out their feelers. But suddenly I felt an urgent need to sit up, just to check, just to make sure, that no wetsuit-clad, submachine-gun toting, amphibious Russian was creeping up on us, James Bond style, where we lay.

Years later, in 1989, as we docked Voortrekker II in Port Louis, Mauritius, our skipper (submarine-driver Lt Cdr Hanno Teuteberg) pointed at two nearby vessels with the dreaded hammer and sickle emblem on their funnels. We all looked, chastened.

❦

I have just finished reading a book called **Iron Fist From The Sea**. One hell of a title, but a really fascinating and well-constructed piece of work, all about the South African Recces (Special Forces) and their clandestine, amphibious, often submarine-borne, operations of sabotage and destruction into Angola, Tanzania and Mozambique. I realise now that it was really the South Africans who were doing all the seaborne raiding and invading at that time. As it turns out I knew, had met, or sailed with, quite a number people featured in the book. One would never have guessed.

24 October 2017   Letter #57

Black widow spiders and killer bees,
There ain't no shade, there ain't no trees.
Hot desert heat, polluted air,
And traffic jams beyond compare.
That's all I got to warn ya 'bout Mexico and California.

There are photos of Rincon Point and Malibu.
A few guys out with longboards.
Take a look at it now.
It is those kinds of days and places we searched for and found too.
Jongensfontein, Elandsbaai, Still Bay, Mossels.

When I was a young man I always had a camera.
I used the film sparingly and took pictures of us in our time.

These days, young people take selfies.
They go home and Google themselves.
It is a different world.
When we were young in apartheid South Africa, it was a very unsettled time.
Many of us did not have a good sense of what a positive future outlook could be,
So we abstracted ourselves in the moment.
Squeezing the juice out of the days: unable to visualise our adulthood.
We did not apply ourselves as we might have done.
The Jewish kids in my class did.
They knew that they would just "keep on trucking" as part of their diaspora.
That is their tradition.

Mick and Alan Best

Now that there is globalisation, I think our kids have a better sense of their place in a unified world. They also have a much more comprehensive under-standing of the fragility of the planet. The tentativeness of it all as our species stampedes towards the edge of the precipice which is the end. But as ever before, it is always important to do one's best (with what one has). Opportu-nities passed by are seldom offered to us a second time. Not doing one's best at school might leave one unable to pass at a top university that one only just managed to squeeze into (or not get into a good university in the first place). Not doing one's very best at university might lead to failures ... and then a dropping out. And dropping out might lead to a step down to a second-tier establishment of tertiary education, at which one will always feel that one has short-changed oneself. A second-tier qualification (or none) might lead to ... Well, who knows? But always, I think that not doing one's best leads to sub-optimal outcomes. It is therefore always the right time to start doing one's very best.

The intelligent man who chose not to do his best now has the fairly responsible job of packing the weekly medications for the sick and elderly at an old age home in London.
It is a job he has held for as long as I have known him.
The dispensary is in the basement.
There are no windows.
The walls are painted green.
The temperature is always the same in there.
There is a constant buzz of fluorescent tubes.
One yellow, 2 red, one white and a green x 7 days.
Placed accurately into their small plastic container.
A different set for every customer.
Hydrocodone, Zocor, Lisinopril, Zithromax, Prilosec, Hydrochlorothiazide.
The intelligent man lives with anger at himself and anger at the world.
And because he is nobody, it is ANGER he has to internalise!

15 October 2017

When I get out of bed in the morning,
I can almost hear the devil say: "Oh crap, he's up."
And I go out into the world and try to do good things.
Good Things.

Apart from the work and being caring towards people, there are good things like a springtime evening run around Lion's Head with Allegra. What a wonderful young woman.

Or a surf at Glen Beach in the morning. Just Patrick the chiropractor and me. And a pair of Heaviside's dolphins appearing and disappearing every now and then. Then Patrick goes off to work and Bruce Tedder paddles out. That's the way it should be – not crowded and crazy as it is so often these days. A person can get uncrowded by going for a surf-ski paddle in the south-wester.

On Wednesday evening a fire started along the coast road near the kramat. There are some informal settlements in the bush nearby. The SW breeze fanned the flames up into the crags of the Twelve Apostles before swinging to a raging SE. Soon enough the mountain was burning almost all the way to Llandudno. A strong pre-frontal NW then pushed the fire over into Hout Bay and towards Oranjekloof. Choppers in the smoke dropping their water bombs. Heavy cloud. Now rain.

22 October 2017

So where did the year go?
The next door property finally sold for R11.5-million.
The house was on the market since May 2016.
It did not sell quickly because I insisted that no purchaser may build forward of the existing structure.
Clea will get a R10m settlement and be gone from my life.
She moves out in early December.

And so my empire of three houses side-by-side in the Camps Bay Glen is whittled down to one.
Had my ex-wife not preferred the others, I would have been a wealthy man stuck in a desperately unhappy marriage.
I suppose I got off lucky.
At the end of this month I pay my final R18 900 alimony.

I am going to take it a bit easy now ... until year end ... been hectic weeks ... Love C

Chapter 57

Hall of Fame, Wall of Shame

Allegra matriculated from Camps Bay High School at the end of 2015. Thirty-four years after Ravenscroft and me. I went back as a parent. A lot had changed in those three decades. Apartheid had fallen. The school had a totally mixed racial demography as well as an economic one. Of the 45% Jews, these days there are almost none. The school's focus had moved away from cricket and rugby and towards the arts, drama, music, dancing, the steel band, the *marimba* band, debating, social involvement and, of course, academic achievement. The last of the Victorian-era hangover had been swept out. There were no more canings and even the horrible old bottle-green and khaki uniform had been replaced with a slightly more acceptable one.

Allegra was a hardworking, diligent and motivated student going for Gladwell's 10 000 hours in as many pursuits as possible. I would go up to the school for the annual Camps Bay Celebration and prize-giving ceremony. As part of the programme, Allegra would perform one of her songs to all the kids and parents. A little later she would be up on stage with the school's boffins collecting a pile of certificates and class awards. Proud moments.

Before the event, I would wander around the same passages I had wandered around as a boy. Touch the same door handles and bricks. All still there. In the time between, someone had collected all the Camps Bay High School group photographs ever shot, framed them and hung them on the ground-storey passage walls. There are hundreds of them and room for hundreds more. Every team and every group. The 1963 Table Tennis Team, 1972 1ˢᵗ Cricket 11, 1981 Synchronised Swimming starring Susan Meltzer, 1997 Rugby U16A, 2005 Interact Society … you name it, the lot. I look for a picture of myself. There isn't one. Simon Wood, Stephen Brand, Alan Clegg, Bayley, Deirdre

Richman and Gunner Way are all present and accounted for – also Ravenscroft, year after year, over and over, cricket and squash. The headmaster John Ince, John Donald, Terry "The Cane" Marsh, Gregor Leigh and Miss Walther, our teachers, all so young. But "Litvett" is nowhere to be found.

Allegra has more than made up for that.

3 December 2017   Letter #58

Hi Gareth

I hope that you are fine … please find below the notes I write to you.

25 November 2017

It is a balmy Saturday.
A badly busked saxophone drifts up above the rest of the beach noise.
The sea is flat and pale under chalky high cloud.
Next door, my ex-wife and her boyfriend John are packing up the house.
She moves out on Monday … that is in two days' time.
It was strangely easy to make the multi-million-rand transfer.
What a situation I got myself into!
But it is over now and I feel elated.
Liberated and free to proceed without the burden of my ex-wife and her interminable alimony.

03 December 2017

This morning at 05h45 I woke to the sound of good rain.
I got up, pulled out the cars and washed them.
Pool overflowing with diverted roof gutter water.
It rained and rained until about 9am … I washed everything.
Ex moved out six days ago.
It feels like a rock has been taken off my head.
Joyful.

A week or two ago, I was talking to two of my "learned friends". One had just returned from a court case in Johannesburg dealing with a man who had been dismissed from his job for saying the following: "Tell that black man to get his car out of my parking place." At the same firm, so-called "black" men are given jobs in preference to so-called "white" men by way of "Affirmative Action". So-called "black" women are given jobs in preference to so-called "black" men and so on. I call it selective discrimination. I work with LD, a Fire and Mechanical Engineering professional. He is a light-skinned so-called "coloured", yet he promotes his business as being "100% black-owned". LD and Son. LD is no blacker than I.

When it comes to me and Lukas, we sit and eat our chicken with our fingers and we couldn't give a shit. Him from somewhere in the bush near Oshikango to the north of Ondangwa, but closer to Oshakati, and me, well, my most recent gene pool is European: Norway, Sweden, Denmark, Germany, the north of France, Ireland, England and Holland. All known ancestors are of the Euro-paleface (Red Planet) type. But then, like most of the people I deal with here in RSA, Lukie and I don't have chips on our shoulders and that is lovely. And when I have been to Zimbabwe or Botswana and Namibia, I don't sense the chips. It is like "paleface" and "brownface" … so what … we don't even notice it. But in the South African political and media arenas it remains a crushing issue that rises above day-to-day interpersonal relations. A political crowbar, a scab to worry at, the "race card" … the card to play when all else has failed.

Why do so many people enjoy watching sports or violent action movies?
So often I ask this but only ever get tangled unconvincing answers.
That is, until I read Konrad Lorenz' **On Aggression** earlier this year.
Now I know!
It is called "ritualised aggression".
Very important to keep the peace.
Panem et Circenses.

Thanks to Lorenz, I also now know why I never liked to compete in sports or competitions or even play games. I used to think that I just found them pointless and boring, but now I think I am simply too aggressive. It is better for me to remain placid until, from time to time, there is "work" to be done.

You get three kinds of dogs: New dogs, Big dogs and Old dogs. Getting older now … heading for the third stage.

Along with the sports issue, another question has bothered me: Why the continued media/political cultivation of the "black" shoulder chip?

Of course there is "black" pain, just as there is and has been Nazi slave state pain and Holocaust pain and Pogrom pain and Stalin pain and Genghis Khan pain and Hutu and Tutsi pain, Khoi extinction pain and King Shaka the Conqueror pain – but we live in a globalising world now where people mostly aspire to northern hemisphere stuff like cars, devices, smart TVs, clothes, shoes, single malt whisky, houses, mortgages, education, liberty and democracy and so on. In my opinion, pain cannot be allowed to convert into a malignant shoulder chip.

We know that the Africans did not build ships and go and colonise Europe[1] and that there was no wheel or written word south of the Tropic of Cancer. And we know that Eurasia runs East/West and Africa orientates North/South. And that the rigors of cold winters demanded the development of planning skills, as did the seasonal flooding of the Nile, Tigris and Euphrates, but we should leave it now. United we must stand or divided we will fall.

22 November 2017

Yesterday Mugabe resigned.
The good people of Zimbabwe are rejoicing.
Everyone is overjoyed that the old tyrant will finally be gone.
Too long it took because of **the fear.**
I hope that **the fear** will go now, and those good people can fix things up, straighten the lampposts, trim the verges and get the economy going again.
Zaan and I celebrated by pouring dark Zambezi honey on our porridge.
But we know deep down that it will only be a change of hogs at the trough.

Last night it rained and rained.
Zaan and I went down to Bakoven this morning to exercise in the shed.
A woman came down with her dog.

---

1   They did successfully invade Europe at least twice before (on foot). The first time they encountered only animals and became Neanderthals. The second time they encountered both animals and Neanderthals.

In one hand a cup of coffee, in the other, a plastic bag full of dog shit.
Like those people who take their sandwiches to the toilet, says Zaan, disgusting.
If I were king, all urban dogs would be shot.
And made into dog food,
And fed to the farm dogs.

But, sadly, I am not king.
Muhammed Ali was king: "Don't count the days, make the days count."

24 October 2017

Last evening Zaan said, "Sometimes one has an overwhelming sense of being defeated, even when one has not really been defeated."

I looked at her and said, "That's exactly how I feel."

This morning I was out on the Tafelberg Road riding my bike. It had rained lightly in the early hours. Keurbooms in full bloom, the moist air most heavenly scented. Far below, those less free than me inched along in the traffic tailbacks on the N1 and the other roads leading into the city.

Another day of life.

I have mentioned one of my hero characters to you before – the WWII Stuka pilot Hans-Ulrich Rudel. My hero not for what he did, but for the bravery with which he did it. "You are not lost until you have given yourself up as lost."

My American great-grandfather WC Winshaw adopted his motto from Virgil: "*Ne Cede Malis*" (yield not to misfortune). He made his fortune and lost it 4 or 5 times in his long career. The family was plunged into penury over and over again, and yet he persisted, trying one entrepreneurial scheme after another until finally, at the age of sixty, he started the winery called SFW.

I have read about so many dogged heroes.
Wilfred Thesiger being the most recent.
Nansen being one of the best.
Odd people but tenacious, determined and steadfast.
Good things to aspire to, if one manages to vanquish the quailing heart.

Our Western society creates whinging people, myself included, I am afraid to say. We struggle for leisure time where our forebears struggled for survival.

Just over a century ago, a wagon trip to South West Africa could have foundered in the waterless wastes north of the Orange River. Now we would be greatly inconvenienced by a blown radiator and a night spent waiting at Grunau. We must really stop whinging and focus on the good. Like a slow night spent at Grunau, beneath the broad and starry heavens, listening to the crickets and geckos.

We have food and houses.
We have some money in the bank.
It is not Dresden, 1945.
Charlie Brown to Snoopy: "One day we will die."
Snoopy: "But on all the other days we will not."

A bad fault of mine is the difficulty I have in truly enjoying the present. I struggle to enjoy the warm downwind sailing because my mind is already worrying about the next mechanical failure in the engine room.

I study a photo of tiny Allegra, maybe two and a half or three, sitting on the edge of a bathtub. Her feet are in warm water. There is a whimsical expression on her face. I so struggled to enjoy my young child because of the nagging weight of all the responsibility and care and possible outcomes. Dread. Anxiety. Fear.

I sometimes see people losing themselves in the joy of their children or dogs. I could not own an animal. Sooner or later we will all have a very bad day or a very sad day. How does a person remain buoyant and light and rise above it all? Enjoy the days before the inevitable downfall. It is so disheartening to live in this beloved South Africa with a government which we taxpayers pay to improve but instead ruin it by incompetence and looting. Perhaps people have, more often than not, lived under terrible regimes and flattening wars. The Catholic Church, Talat Pasha, feudal lords, Pol Pot, the Tsars, the Taliban, the Shah, Stalin, Hitler, Nero, Commodus. Even under the worst emperors Rome continued to function.

What was the secret to keeping chipper during the Blitz, or laughing in the face of adversity?

Did the Roman peasant manage to smile as he bit into a ripe fig or a piece of cheese?

Life was much harder then.

And people took more pleasure from much less.

"We are all doomed," said Marc Faber,
"But that doesn't mean that we can't make money in the meantime".
To which the Rabbi Lapin replied:
"Let us then produce bricks!"
…. Or something like that ….

14 November 2017

Last week Zaan and I paddled on a flat sea headed south.
As always, my eyes scanned the water.
Suddenly, maybe 30m away, just ahead, a humpback whale surfaced to breathe.
It showed its head a second time as it passed close by us and was gone.

Yesterday and this morning I surfed at Glen with one other.
In both cases with fit, young, energised men.
Today a pair of Heaviside's dolphins patrolled the backline.
Sheets of light grey rain fell on the breeze.
Tall mountains shrouded in languid cloud.
What fun.

18 November 2017

Look what is happening in Zimbabwe.

Like a dam wall, it happens so quickly when it finally breaks.

But the wait is so interminably long.

Can you imagine the sense of floating unreality?

Can you imagine the joy in the streets of Harare?

Why are they being so merciful to the old tyrant?

Perhaps bloodshed only begets bloodshed.

I wouldn't have the discipline.

I cannot wait for the day when Jacob Zuma gets his turn.

We all feel like that.

The country hates him, but just like the Zimbabweans, we abide by the law out of fear.

We are trapped by a captured state.

All of us, little insects, ensnared in a huge three-dimensional web of corruption and political patronage.

Lorded over by evil spiders all compromised at one level or another.

The tyrant of Zimbabwe will be allowed to go.

His ill-gotten loot will go with him.

My ex-wife too.

Soon she will be gone – with my irreplaceable capital.

Interesting psychological dispositions.

That blithe combination of entitlement and arrogance.

King Leopold of Belgium was the same.

My mistake with my ex-wife, like the people of Zim and RSA,

Was to allow it to happen in the first place.

My psychology screams.

I am no Buddhist … I cannot bury my guns.

Love C

Chapter 58

The importance of Carping the Diem

What a beautiful day,
Green, with flowers everywhere

We all have two lives
The one we make for ourselves
And the one dictated to us by the decisions and actions of others.

No matter how you try to stack the deck to your best advantage,
You never know how the cards will be dealt.

Just when you think you're at the top of the pile,
A jet turbine could come baling through your 93rd floor office fax machine
And take you with it.
9/11

Or your currency could go through the floor,
Or you could get shot down over Ukraine *en route* to Kuala Lumpur
Flight MH17
The Dutch, innocent bystanders, high above the Battle of Shakhtarsk,
And what about those on the ground, innocent too,
Homes reduced to twisted steel and brick and concrete rubble.

That's why, when one can,
One must try to live a little.

My new wetsuit has been hanging in the garage for over a month now.
Today I took it surfing.

Derdesteen all to myself.
Big peaks.
A fashion shoot on the beach.
Table Mountain rising above a lumpy sea.

23 December 2017   Letter #59

Hi Gareth

This is the year I have been most free of Christmas (99.3% free) and am overjoyed.
Sadly, we are not free of the desiccating southeaster, corruption or drought.
On the 9th it started howling (like never before) and ripping off roof sheets for about a week or more.

Luckily on the 8th, having consulted Windguru, I took the day off.
Zaan and I paddled through to Clifton and went ashore.
The City's 05h00 to 13h00 cleansing shift was there
(the second shift runs 13h00 to 20h00).
They had already filled 100 large blue garbage bags
and had radioed in for more.
Only three-quarters of Fourth Beach had been cleaned so far.
The remaining quarter was still a mess of bottles,
chip packets and empty cartons.
It was not like this in the 1970s and '80s when I was a boy.

And it certainly was not like that just after the last war
with Old Man Smorenburg,
The self-appointed sheriff of Clifton, walking around with a .303 rifle.
People obeyed the laws and order was kept.
The .303 was a hangover from the time of the absurd notion of a possible Japanese or Nazi invasion.
He shot at the fins of the herds of basking shark which are now locally extinct.

Mitch Brown will tell you about this and about Old Man Wrankmore who stomped the Sea Point seabed in lead boots with a copper helmet on his head, Prying off thousands and thousands of abalone with his wrecking bar.
Old Man Paarman did the same at Bakoven with his tokkie-boat.
They did not get rich from it, but only bred out lots of children.
Now scurvy poachers from Hangberg and Hawston take what little remains and sell it to the ever-hungry Chinese.

I am currently reading the new biography of the Romanov dynasty.
In the 1600s, 93% of the Russian population were tyrannised serfs.
Beheadings, the steel-tipped cat and forced labour were the prices paid for even petty transgressions.
Our lives are better now.

I have just read WG Sebald's beautiful novel **Austerlitz**:
In the 1920s the big disused holes at Kimberly were not fenced.
Anyone could venture right up to the edge and look down to a depth of several thousand feet. A visitor at that time wrote that "it was truly terrifying to see such emptiness open up, a foot away from firm ground, and to realize that there was no transition, only this dividing line, with ordinary life on the one side and its **unimaginable opposite** on the other".
That is the way we live every day.
Skating carelessly along the edge of the "unimaginable opposite".
Gareth, that is what you did too much of.

Last Wednesday I went down to check the surf at Glen: lovely small waves coming in, ice blue water, some white horses whipping around out towards Bakoven. Standing elevated on the viewing platform I watched a labourer loading junk into an open lorry. A carved Indonesian gate-post, rotted at one end, once belonging to a pair of gorgeous doors or gates, no doubt. The labourer touched the intricate relief carving. I saw the flicker of something register on his face before he threw it into the lorry with a clang. The second post followed, passed up by a person on the sidewalk below, hidden from view. Next came an old broken pool filter. Paleface cargo. A group of horrible, loud AC Cobras blasted by. More paleface cargo. I ran up home to pull on my wetsuit and collect my board. Within a few minutes I paddled out into a truly freezing sea and had one nice wave before the southeaster came howling in, changing a tourist brochure day into a maelstrom of blinding spray.

This morning is the 23rd of December. I went out for a paddle and saw my first penguin in some years. They used to be quite common. Maybe more in the winter when Zaan and I go over to Canada? Out and about were perhaps a dozen dolphins with their small-finned young pups.

I am currently reading a book called **Anti-Fragile** by Nassim Taleb … now this is a fascinating read! Published in 2012, so not hot off the press, but incredibly insightful. **Anti-fragile** and Konrad Lorenz's **On Aggression** have given me new perspective, now here are a few lines from the prologue of **Anti-Fragile:**

If you see fraud and do not say fraud, you are a fraud … Just as being nice to the arrogant is not better than being arrogant toward the nice, being accommodating to anyone committing a nefarious action condones it. Compromising is condoning. The only modern dictum I follow is one by **George Santayana:** *A man is morally free when … he judges the world, and judges other men, with uncompromising sincerity.*

And that means himself in with the rest.
I am not nearly there, but I like the sound of this stuff … let's see how it goes.
Until then, I must live with my own carefully considered truths …
I think I get the next one right most of the time:
Do not do unto others as you would not have done unto yourself.
And this is what I have been working on more recently,
but have not been 100% successful:
Do not be untrue to thyself.
And maybe one day, I will be able to get this one right:
Ne cede malis … but I can't quite manage it yet.

Big love to you my friend … I am sure that this is the hardest time for you.
Wishing for that day when you can see your Mikey again.
And when you can join us down at Bakoven.

May it be soon.
Carl

p.s. Sorry about the short letter. This period has been so crammed, I have not had much time for reflection.

Chapter 59

Unwelcome Visitors

Notes in a diary:

9 December 2012

I miss my Zaan a lot, in faraway Canada where it is cold and snowy.
She tells that she had serious jet-lag.
I think maybe we both had some sleeping sickness.
The entire weekend past, I was finished.

11 December 2012

Last night cousin Øystein and I did a quiet patrol from 21–23h00 on a very windy night. I was back home and asleep at 23h30pm when my CERT[1] radio went off.

Armed robbery at 10 Chilworth Road … only a few doors from our house.

The same group broke in at 14 Atholl Road 20 min later.

After months of peace.

We pursued them until 4am, first sighting the four male suspects on Camps Bay Drive as they tried to head over to the city. A group of us chased them and got them in some thick bush near the start of the pipe track, but they broke cover and jumped over the cliff edge sliding back down to Camps Bay Drive and over the road into the Big Glen.

They dropped a lot of their loot at that point, which we recovered.

---

1   CERT: Civilian Emergency Response Team

The dog squad finally arrived with about 15 to 20 dogs. Too late.

What a night!

I am swimming in fatigue now.

⚜

By the time the 2010 FIFA World Cup Tournament came to Cape Town, our neighbourhood watch was already pretty geared up. A team of CERT volunteers slept with radios at their bedsides and patrol gear at the ready. Our intelligence gatherers made note of certain patterns and we knew, with semi-certainty, that our most wanted housebreaker (at that time), John Mthambo, would be paying the suburb a visit in the early hours of a certain morning. All CERT members were asked to be up and in their cars by 03h00, with lights off and ready. I found myself slowly moving up Central Drive, heading north, when a pearlescent object appeared to be floating in the darkness just ahead of me. It was midwinter and midwinter at that time of morning can be inky. As I drew alongside the pale object I could make out that it was, in fact, a white Apple laptop computer under the arm of a dark man in a dark outfit, the face of whom I knew well enough. Instantly I radioed for backup and instantly thirty neighbourhood CERTs headed for the scene. When he saw my radio, the suspect broke into a run and ducked up an alley that shortcuts up to Tree Road. But I was faster in my *bakkie* than he was on foot and I intercepted him at the top of the stairs which lead from the alleyway. He broke and ran with me in pursuit, down Tree Road, towards a townhouse development known as The Retreat. By then the first of my fellow CERT members had arrived and there were headlights ablaze. The suspect scaled the garden wall of one of the units and disappeared. Within seconds we had the complex completely surrounded. A selected group entered the commonage of The Retreat. I shouted at the top of my voice, calling for all residents to wake up and look down into their gardens. And one by one they did. After a few minutes, one man, with his small daughter beside him, began to signal that he could see the suspect hiding in a concealed place below. Mthambo was nailed.

For months, Mthambo had been carefully removing glass panes from Camps Bay windows. With great stealth he would enter homes and steal valuable items such as iPhones, wallets and laptop computers. We arrested him with the razor-sharp chisel that he used to ply his craft. Over the next hour, on searching the gardens along his route through The Retreat, we recovered the laptop and a number of iPhones, chargers and other items. Each hidden, for later recovery. Quite a disciplined man. His intention was clearly to escape and return.

Soon after Mthambo's arrest, the balance of the story filtered through. He had robbed, at chisel-point, a number of US soccer fans coming home very late. I do not know if he was inside their rented accommodation when they returned, or if he accosted them as they got back.

We saw him at the Regional Court a few days later.
He was sentenced to 15 years behind bars and would appear on other charges thereafter.
But like cockroaches, his kind appear faster than they can be put away.
The effort and energy required to catch and convict a man like Mthambo are beyond belief.

Letter #60

… coincides with the New Year … I truly hope you get out this year.

1 January 2018

Hi Gareth

This morning is New Year's Day.
Last evening I woke to the loud sound of rain on the roof.
At midnight I woke again to the thunderous reports of fireworks down at Maiden's Cove.
At dawn Zaan and I went down to exercise at the shed.
We then cooked eggs and mushrooms and sausages,
Eaten with hot buttered wholewheat toast and coffee.
It is important in life to appreciate one's luck or good fortune.
Good luck versus bad luck in life is not a 50/50 heads or tails business.
It is a one in ten-thousand chance or maybe even more.

I think about those who have not had my good fortune.
The alternatives being Khayelitsha, Delft, the slums of Mumbai or the Grodno Ghetto in Bialystok, Somalia, Eritrea, Bangladesh, Ethiopia, Kolyma.
One must have humility at one's good fortune and appreciate the boatshed and the sea,
With its crashing waves and the cool SW breeze, and a whale blowing as it passes by, heading north.

Down to the beach a woman comes with two dogs and a fat husband.
Imperatives: Come here! No! Tammy, no no! Good girl! No! No!

What a fuckup.

I am so happy that I have had the good luck not to need to keep a pet.

Or simply to be able to see it for what it is.

I watch a man clasping an infant to his chest as the mother wades in, up to her ankles.

She squeaks and makes some or other comment about the temperature of the water.

The baby is a pupa-like bundle in its father's arms. It makes me sad.

I am sad when I see babies and pregnant women,

Mainly because I have powerful compassion for what that new person will have to experience in its life.

I cannot comprehend the utter selfishness of creating a human life for one's own personal fulfilment.

I do not know why people keep pets or breed.

That is what sets me apart from people, I suppose.

All of the 7 billion people on Earth who are capable of reflection have a view on the world.

My brother Bill and I have, in general, very similar views, and yet very different in some areas.

My brother Mick and I, again similar, but more different.

And that goes through all people close and then further until far removed,

At last you get those with a massively different mindset.

Such as a rapacious Chinese industrialist, or an Imperialist Russian Oligarch, or Zuma, or a Muslim.

I say: "One child per adult."

"It is God's will," says the Muslim.

In my pragmatic way, I consider my approach to be as close to correct as a human's can be:

Do not do unto others as you would not have done unto thyself.

Take responsibility for one's own actions.

Have no faith in god.

One child per adult.

Be a conservator.

Don't be a faddist, eat a balanced diet as per the dictates of grandmother.

Live an orderly life.

Moderation in all things.

Work hand in glove with science, but do not rule out mystery and wonder.

I wonder If I am right.

I know that people such as myself cannot comprehend the workings of the minds of the morons I hear racing their cars and motorbikes at night.

I see the smashed stop signs and guard-rail barriers

and bits of fender on street corners.

I see a bench in a beautiful forested place surrounded by litter.

The handiwork of *skrælings* no doubt.

I consider the world views of Zuma, Gupta, Islamists, Christians, Jews, rhino murderers and parrot cagers.

I had an interesting chat with my mom the other day about having children. She talked about the biological urge of women to procreate being so strong, and the biological urge of men to penetrate women being so strong, and I said: "Well, yes, there are urges, but in order to save the species from its horrible self, taboos are set against men having sex with their own close family members. There are anti-base-urge-taboos."

"There are laws that prevent men from taking murderous revenge: **Anti-base-urge-laws** which protected some of my ex-friends from having their bellies slit by me and so they still walk and talk and soil this planet today. Now that we have enough people on the planet, I think that laws/taboos should be set in place to limit overbreeding ... **One Child Per Adult**".

25 December 2017

Last night, just before sleep time, I knocked over my bedside lamp.

The bulb no longer worked after that.

As I lay in thoughtful hypnagogia, I wondered:

How are lightbulbs manufactured?

By what wonderful processes?

I tried to imagine the minds that actually contemplated electrical currents in copper wires.

I tried to think of any technologies from the southern hemisphere.

I tried to think of any major inventions from below the Tropic of Cancer

This morning when I woke up: Pratley Putty, the Kreepy Krauly and the Dolos were waiting in my inbox.

We who live down in the southern countries should spare a moment and give thanks to the globalising forces that have allowed us to share the liberal arts and technologies of the north – technologies that have provided ice blocks and whisky, wheeled and winged transport, antibiotics, antiretrovirals, universities, democracy, vacuum cleaners and trousers. And letters with which to write, and computers with which to send messages like this, because life would be pretty *kak* without them.

⁘

Many of the problems we have in this world are because we apply linear thought processes to non-linear situations. Say, for instance, a couple of acquaintances go for a 5km morning run. They start off together and arrive back at the carpark together. But one of the two is fitter so he runs faster and stops to wait for his pal from time to time. The fitter of the pair therefore has rest periods allowing him to catch his breath while the less fit friend is forced to cover the entire distance without a break.

A typical linear question might be: who benefitted more (exercise-wise) from the run?

The answer is actually very complex and would need a number of super-imposed three-dimensional graphs to cover the numerous variables.

One of the pair is larger and heavier, but he is also the fitter of the two. He is an "endurance athlete" who possesses a muscle type that does not respond well to stop/go activity as his muscles quickly stiffen after stopping. His cardiovascular fitness is, however, positively affected by breaking his usual continuous 5km trot into a number of shorter semi-sprint runs. His slower, less fit, running partner (who normally plays squash) strains his heart muscle from the sustained 40-minute effort and never properly recovers. What seems like a fairly uncomplicated question has, in fact, numerous possible answers and we have not even gone into metabolism here, or the effects of running with a hangover, the effects of pushing a system overstimulated by caffeine, or the use of anti-inflammatories to mask potential pain in order to show off a better performance.

⁘

I have been listening to some 1980s and 1990s songs on YouTube.

I realise now how close we were to greatness.

We jumped on sailing boats and sailed halfway around the globe like it was no big deal.

But then got bogged down in the humdrum.

We espoused the humdrum because we knew no better.

We scythed ourselves off at the knees.

David Bowie was only 25 years old when he released Ziggy Stardust.

<hr>

I had a thought driving through Sea Point the other day: How cool it would be if all car hooters were replaced with farm animal sound simulators. The horrible taxi hooting would become a symphony of cattle lowing, pigs grunting, sheep baaing and roosters crowing. In Joburg they could use wild animal sounds.

<hr>

The Birkenhead Drill – Women and Children First

I know a young dentist who practices in a small town near Kirkenes, population 7 to 8 000.

There is state care.

The vulnerable members of the community (i.e. women and children) get priority.

But there is not sufficient capacity for everyone, so the local Norwegian men must pay private rates to see their own dentists, in the evening, working overtime, renting the state facility that should be for them anyway!

Why this? … because the system is jammed up with Somalis.

Somali women and children who have never been to a dentist and have no concept of dental hygiene.

I ask the dentist … she says that she is not a racist.

I ask the dentist's boyfriend (a tough outdoorsy 28-year-old Norwegian salmon breeder).

He says: "I guess we must help them."

I ask him why.

He says that he would prefer it if they were helped in their own country.

I asked him why Norway should feel obliged to help the Somalis at all.
He did not know.
I told him that I was territorially aggressive – he said that he was, too.

Who would have imagined, such a story from Vadso?

The histories tell us that about 1 000 years ago
Norwegians like him arrived in large numbers
In other countries
Where they were not exactly welcome
And they did not ask for their teeth to be fixed
They say: "The wheel turns."

9 January 2018

I rode my bike on Table Mountain … it was wet and warm.
Groups of 20 to 30 redwing starlings feasting on termites
released by the night rain.
Riding into termites was like riding into rain itself.
When Casanova was imprisoned in Venice in 1755,
he began to contemplate sanity.
He likened a lucid mind to a glass which does not break of its own accord,
yet how easily it is shattered.

First Nation People

Again I notch this arrow to my bow:

I look with interest at current South African politics.
The government does not want the *Khoisan* people to be declared as the
"*First Nation*".
Also "Black First Land First" noise.

The USA, Canadians and Australians have recognised their "*First Nation*"
people, but it is not so easy for Europeans like me and you. I grew a reddish
beard for a few weeks as a young man of 24 (that was the last time I tried)
so I know that I am one. But our Neanderthal ancestors were so massively
invaded that only about 2 or 3% of their genes remain in our bodies. We
could blame this on Africans as it was African Homo sapiens who colonised

Europe and wiped out our Neanderthal ancestors, but way back they were, of course, of African origin themselves.

At any rate, I have drawn a circle from inside of which all my recent ancestors originate. The compass point is placed somewhere in the middle of the North Sea:
My great-grandfather WC Winshaw had a German mother and an Irish dad.
My great grandmother Ada Charlotte Day was from Fareham, Hampshire.
On my mother's side the Oosthuizens came from Holland
and the Malherbes from France.
My dad's grandad Petter Rasmussen (Liltved) moved to Norway from Denmark.
My paternal grandmother, Birgit Vivienne Solberg, was born in Ørebro, Sweden.

Maybe we Neanderthals could apply for financial compensation in Euros for our displacement. It would be a great class action suit on which to retire!

Big bucks!!!

Has anyone tried this angle before, I wonder?

---

7 Burglaries in ten days and another 3 attempted in that same period equate to an attempt at burglary every day in Camps Bay

This ever-present threat of crime is bad news to all of us who crave civilised socially responsible living. It is never solvable, of course, without a massive shift in the whole country and Sub-Saharan Africa. Economics and Education … as well as … Serious Consequences for Anti-Social Behaviour. Not in our lifetimes and not with the population we have and the incredible incompetence of those in command. There will always be poor (and sometimes violent) opportunists who will take the gap or make the gap. People with very little to lose.

It is like the joke about the lion and the running shoes:
All we can do is try to out-perform our neighbours and neighbouring suburbs, i.e. make it less attractive for the "bad guys" to go for us.

When I look around and see the incredible effort and cost that go into fortifying our homes: cameras, steel palisades, high walls, barbed wire, electric wire, alarm systems, patrol cars, security personnel, numberplate recognition, ADT, BAY, CBCSI ... Surely it costs tens if not hundreds of times more than the stuff that is stolen.

It is insane ... just to keep a handful of skinny, half-starved, often desperate humans out of our homes (humans who live in a lawless parallel world much like the Proles in Orwell's **1984**). And to keep our loved ones safe and our vital PCs where they belong, on our desks.

This morning we ran on the mountain and paddled with dolphins.

There really are two sides to this coin.

https://www.youtube.com/watch?v=I1wg1DNHbNU

There is water at the bottom of the ocean.

You may ask yourself, what is that beautiful house?
You may ask yourself, where does that highway lead to?
You may ask yourself, am I right, am I wrong?
You may say to yourself, my god, what have I done?
Letting the days go by, let the water hold me down
Letting the days go by, water flowing underground
Into the blue again, after the money's gone
Once in a lifetime, water flowing underground
Into the blue again, into silent water
Under the rocks and stones, there is water underground
Letting the days go by, into silent water
Once in a lifetime, water flowing underground
Same as it ever was, same as it ever was, same as it ever was, same as it ever was
Same as it ever was, same as it ever was, same as it ever was, same as it ever was

Time isn't holding us, time isn't after us
Time isn't holding us, time doesn't hold you back
Time isn't holding us, time isn't after us
Time isn't holding us ...
Letting the days go by, letting the days go by, letting the days go by, once in a lifetime.

An unlucky day at the boatshed.

A lucky one!

Be well my friend ... Love C

Chapter 60

The Crime and the Punishment

As little boys Mick and his best pal Francois headed off down the street to buy some sweets at Mr Kapdi's tiny general dealer store in Brownlow Road. Gates have recently been fitted, but back then a boy could either walk via the conventional sidewalk route or nip through an exciting narrow service lane which exited directly opposite the Kapdi store. Service lanes were cool and contained dirt bins and tomato boxes and an assortment of discarded items, the type of which are of interest to six-year-old lads. On this particular day, where the lane takes a ninety degree bend, they found a rotten cabbage and a rusty saw. Next to them was a low masonry wall raised a little higher by way of a wooden fence. Over this barrier lay the garden of two boys named Vimmy and Sam Steenkamp. Mick and Francois thought it would be a great idea to lob the rotten cabbage into Vimmy and Sam's father's flowerbed, thus getting the Steenkamp boys into trouble. They inserted the saw blade into the oozing smelly vegetable and somehow managed to flick it over the wooden fence. The soggy cabbage fell with a thud, followed by cursing and the immense rising head and shoulders of Mr Steenkamp who had been on his hands and knees, planting, on the other side. Mick and Francois did not look back. They fled as fast as their little legs could carry them (sweets forgotten) back to the Fagan home and down into the cellar. There they hid themselves, in self-imposed imprisonment, on the cold cement floor, under a pile of old pine ceiling planks for the rest of the day. Self-punished.

❦

In the SADF there were many punishments, but for most it was a punishment just being there.

Soldiers at Kroonstad, being taught how to drive big SAMIL trucks and Buffels, were simply chucked out of the vehicle if they made one mistake too many and were ordered to walk back to camp. The camp was about 20km from the bushy weapons-testing and vehicle-training area, so they would return exhausted, one by one, late into the night. For minor offences there were large concrete chunks called "marbles" which had to be carried around. For more serious misdemeanours, the *kas* (detention barracks).

Those caught for AWOL went to the *kas*. Some of our HQ troops were MPs. So it was usually their bungalow mates who were caught for AWOL. It was therefore with great hilarity that we not infrequently witnessed our white-holstered MPs doubling their pals from the *kas* to the mess at mealtimes. The prisoners had to mark time by running on the spot while they ate, with drawn pistols in the smalls of their backs. The prisoners wore bright pink *doibies* or *mosdops* on their heads. These dayglo helmet linings would, in theory, make them easier to identify and shoot at in the event of an attempted escape. At mealtimes like these, I sat as far away from the action as possible, ready to dive for cover.

After his three months of navy basic training, Ingram was sent up to Walvis Bay. There was a terrible infantry camp there as well as a navy base. Ingram was stationed at the latter. At that time, Walvis Bay was a small enclave of the Republic of South Africa, situated halfway up the coast of what is now Namibia and what was then South West Africa. The naval base at Walvis was used as a replenishment port for South African submarines and strike-craft on their covert missions to Angola. (An extremely interesting read on this subject is **Iron Fist from the Sea** by Arné Söderland and Douw Stein.)

After a few weeks Ingram was given a pass to go into town for the evening. While sitting at the bar looking out to sea, Ingram was joined by a friendly man just a little older than himself. They began talking about ships and shipping and soon the man began probing Ingram on his knowledge of Russian spy trawlers operating up and down the coast. At that stage of the game, we had all heard about Russian spy trawlers, so Ingram strung the man along for a bit of a laugh. Later, after a good many beers, Ingram made it home to his barracks, never once suspecting that the young man he had been teasing was in fact a super-keen but largely unloved fellow navy man named De Nobrega (aka Nobby the Knob).

At around four in the morning a group of MPs charged into Ingram's dormitory: "*Is jy Ingram? Jy's in diep kak!*" (Are you Ingram? You're in deep shit!) Ingram, still quite tipsy, was arrested, made to dress in a hurry and taken to the combined navy/army detention barracks at the dreaded 2 SAI (2 South African Infantry) base, where he was thrown into a cell and smartly relieved of his belt and shoelaces.

Ingram tells of three days seated on a flip-down cot in a cell with a barred door at one end and a lidless toilet at the other. Opposite the barred end was a brick wall. There were similar cells to the left and right of him, but no talking was permitted. Outside in the yard, he could hear endless sessions of punishment PT. He was terrified. From time to time, a guard or a member of the military would walk past and say, "Ingram, *jy's in diep kak!*" Ingram had no idea why.

At about midnight on the night of the third day, Ingram was brought before a panel of interrogators who had been specially flown up from Naval Headquarters Silvermine in Cape Town. He was seated at a table covered in an army blanket with half a dozen spotlights pointed at his face. Only when he was told that he was being held under suspicion of being a Russian spy did he put two and two together, remembering the beer-soused conversation about Russian trawlers at a local pub.

Ingram was questioned for some hours until the panel finally gave up and sent him back to his cell, realising that Ingram was more of a clown than a threat to national security.

The next morning Ingram was led out into the bright sunlight of the prison yard. Sunburned, hardened men were being made to suffer by merciless corporals. "Drink some water," he was told as his escort pointed towards a dripping brass faucet. Imagining that he was to join the ranks of those being punished, Ingram began to vomit.

Ingram was driven back to the navy base and nothing more was said of the incident. His mind, however, was seriously disturbed and one day he crept out of the base to a civilian telephone box and called his mom. He asked Mrs Ingram to contact our local MP Colin Eglin and ask for help, which she did.

Eglin (the same man who organised navy call-ups for my brother and me) made sparks and within a few days Ingram was flown back to Cape Town where he was brought on orders before the brass at Naval Headquarters Silvermine.

One of the brass opened Ingram's file, "You are a troublemaker young man, calling in your MP like that. There is nothing about any of this in your file! For the rest of your two years you will stay here and mow lawns." And so he did.

⬥

Once, many years ago, Mick and I were on a bus in downtown Lisbon. We were making our way to the railway station to catch a train to Peniche where, we had been told, there were great waves to be had. We each had a backpack on our back and a surfboard under the left arm. The hand of the other arm held tightly onto the overhead rail as the crowded bus jolted along in the morning rush hour traffic. Looking down for a moment, I noticed a hand that did not belong to me feeling its way down into my pants pocket. The bus was so full of people that, at first, I didn't connect the dots. Then my rail-holding hand let go and shot down to deal with the interloper. "Pickpocket!" I shouted to Mick, who was also wedged between the passengers. Looking down, he found that an old man had carefully lifted his shirt, unzipped his money-belt, and was busy removing his wallet and passport. I felt the bones in my pick-pocket's naughty fingers crack as he yelped in pain. The bus stopped at a red light and the pair were off the bus and gone. We watched them as they scurried away through the mass of pedestrians. It had been quick and close. One needed to be vigilant.

For a week or so, we surfed at Peniche's now famous breaks at Baleal and Supertubos before catching a train to Malaga, the city of my birth.

After this period of intense exercise, Mick and I semi-dozed in the warmth, entranced by the hypnotic clickety-clack of the train as it passed through a beautiful hilly country covered in cork-oaks. Every now and then the train would stop at a village, whistles would blow, passengers would get on and off.

Somewhere between Badajoz and Seville, the train drew to a halt at a small station and a group of what appeared to be circus people climbed aboard. They were swarthy gypsy types, all dressed in grubby white, a mixture of children and adults with a few trunks and cases and what appeared to be old-fashioned hatboxes.

We continued rolling on our way for a while, when all of a sudden the carriage was filled with a loud buzzing, like the sound of many large wasps. Up jumped the gypsies, one roguish fellow holding a large glass jar in his one hand and its lid in the other. There was a tremendous commotion inside the

~ 511 ~

coach as the entire grouped swarmed about, the children climbing over seated passengers, all frantically swatting at the escaped insects with bandanas and magazines and the palms of their hands. During the commotion the train slowed down and pulled in to the next village station and as it stopped, the gypsies stopped too, along with the buzzing. They quickly left the carriage, cases, hat-boxes and all. We all watched them, stunned, as they marched off the platform and away.

It was only as the train departed that the occupants of the carriage began to realise that they had been robbed. Handbags looted, pockets picked. The wasp sound must have been a recording or an instrument of some kind. Perhaps something like a soccer rattle. It was a truly amazing performance. Mick and I, with our money-belts well concealed, were lucky.

That was the crime of the Iberian Peninsula back in the 1980s. We were told to carefully bury our shorts, slip-slops and room keys under the sand when we went surfing, or else they would be gone when we got out of the water. At every other bus stop, some seedy individual would open his hand and flash a brown lump at us, "Chocolate … Gasha, Gasha," (hashish) he would say.

It all seems so harmless compared to the home invasions and rape and hijackings and cash-in-transit robberies that we live with in South Africa these days.

2 March 2018   Letter #61

Hello my friend.

How are you?
Have you any news from Mikey?
Have you heard any news from the prison authorities re your release?

I bumped into Yianni the other day at an architectural conference in Cape Town.
He did not have much to say other than that he was working hard on some massive refinery project.

Some rare days, like today, flat sea, no wind.
Horrible dog barking.
I wish I had a James Bond licence to walk around with a silenced Walther PPK and pop them.

February 2018 has been and gone.
Year ends and tax … (bad words left out).
Let us say it has been an intense and fractured month.
On 14 February 2018 Zuma was finally toppled … we are overjoyed.
Will South Africans get the justice they crave?

⌒⋆⋆⋆⌒

Jacob Zuma has always been a profoundly religious man. In a 2006 interview he stated: "*I start from basic Christian principles. Christianity is part of what I am; in a way it was the foundation for all my political beliefs.*" And so, with the other part of what he is – a freewheeling heathen with the mother of Hlaudi Motsoeneng reportedly as his personal sangoma – it was not easy to unseat him.

But it has been done, despite a moronic (crony) ANC majority voting for him to stay on in multiple parliamentary votes of no confidence. The mind simply boggles.

Many of us had a hand in it, tiny hands, hands holding up placards in the "Zuma Must Fall" crowd. But it does all add up … the contempt … the "pin-sticking" … the emails … the social media … the undermining of the mighty by ridicule and dissent.[1]

Zumpty Dumpty …

But we were not the big heroes.
I would like a team photo of the **BIG HEROES:** The person who leaked the "GuptaLeaks" emails,
Jacques Pauw, Thuli Madonsela, the free press media people,
Pravin Gordhan, the fearless radio voices, Zapiro,
the whistleblowers, the Paul O'Sullivans, the brave.

Now moving on. The country's eyes are peeled – looking for Ajay, Atul and Duduzane Zuma. Warrants have been issued and Interpol is now involved. Internationally wanted criminals. And if these guys end up finding sanctuary in Dubai, I would like to mobilise all South Africans to completely boycott Emirates Airlines and Dubai trips. Until they are returned to face the music.

---

1   As predicted by Korad Lorenz – **On Aggression**: pages 286 and 287

How is it then about the pain?

I hear much talk about "Black Pain".

Apartheid pain and slavery pain.

Chain immigrants.

I am personally with the Neanderthal pain thing.

The pain of their destruction over many thousands of years.

My 2.5%.

I feel so much pain for the Finnmark Norwegians I never knew, almost all dead and gone by now. People who had their rugged northern homeland ravaged by the retreating German army at the end of WWII.

I feel the pain of the Boer farmers who had their farmsteads burnt and families imprisoned by Kitchener's English. And the pain of the Jews when reading Pivnik or Höss or Sebald.

Or those who fell foul of Stalin, or Genghis Khan, or Napoleon.

Or women trapped in marriages to cruel men.

And the pain of GR, incarcerated.

Mankind, master of pain.

Man, there has been a lot of it!

Man who maketh beautiful things and beautiful music:

Bach ... Air on a G String, Flora da Luna, Europa, Michelangelo, Clementi.

Beethoven's Moonlight Sonata.

The wonderful books I read.

Mankind can be so base, but is also capable of rising to such heights:

Paintings by the Romantic Movement.

Paintings by the Canadian Group of 7.

A poem by Shelley ... Stanzas Written in Dejection Near Naples.

Full Fathom Five.

Most appreciate so little of the beauty ... they espouse low things.

Violent games on their computer screens.

War games ... games in which they can kill but cannot get hurt themselves.

What a miserable state of being.

Relatively few are like us with our eyes open.

Wondering at towering snow-capped mountains over fjords.
Coral reefs and banded sea snakes.
Forests and rivers.
The Cederberg and its streams and red rocks.
The love of beautiful things.

So many years I have spent working for others and doing things for others,
And I crave to do my own things for myself,
But now when I get the opportunity, I do not really know what it is that I want to do anymore.
I don't really want to go surfing because the sun burns me
And there are too many people in the water.
And too much traffic
But I do long for surfing.
And I do not really feel like flying all the way to Sumatra
to find uncrowded surf.

In Steinbeck's **East of Eden** there is a police chief.
He longs for his retirement.
He dreams of a time in the future when he can go camping and canoeing again.
When he turns 65 and the day comes ... he is too old.
He does not want to sleep in a tent anymore.

What is the peace I crave?
I simply do not know.

My brothers and I spent the 1970s growing up in Tamboerskloof.
By then, many of the old Victorian homes had been torn down to make way for blocks of flats.
We went to school at Tamboerskloof Primary.
Every year, as we went along, every term or so, a few new kids would arrive at our school.
Many of these children were the fall-out from recent divorces.
Moms with one or two or three children would move into flats near the school.
Graham Smith, Petter and Bradley Boye-Thorsen, Monica Human, Robert and Alan Clegg, Derek Bosman, Bernard, Marlis and Robert Kinsky.

It was rather sad.
Working moms with latchkey kids.
Yale keys on knotted strings around their necks.
Strings with spitty chewed ends.

This is what I really worked hard to avoid when my marriage hit the rocks.
The dads, I suppose, like the helicopter pilot Mr Clegg, kept the house and remarried, paying minimal child support and raising a brood of half-siblings to our classmates. (Some of the dads, perhaps, lost everything, I don't know.) There were other families in the neighbourhood that managed to stay together. Most barely (like the Lendrums) and a few rather well (like the Fagans). Many of the families that kept it together fell apart a few years later, once one or more of the children had finished school.

Allegra is at UCT doing her 3rd year BSc … Oceanography and Geology.
She is gravitating towards Oceanography now.
She is just fabulous … full of enthusiasm and happy energy.
Going to gym, running, playing and singing in a band.
I am glad to have been able to provide as I have.
And so we go, passing the best we have to the ones that are of us.

A short letter, late too … but sent with LOVE

C

Chapter 61

The Organist's Diatribe

In 1994 a movie was released called **Bad Boy Bubby**. I went to see it at Cape Town's Labia Theatre. Like **Brazil,** Bad Boy Bubby was not for everyone, but it certainly was for me: marginally distasteful, but very, very true.

I went back a second time with a piece of paper and pen to copy down the anti-god diatribe by the church organist. I lifted it as best I could:

The Organist's Diatribe

There is no god of this earth, we are alone.

We do not live: we are all just a complex arrangement of atoms and subatomic particles, but our atoms do move about in such a way as to give us identity and consciousness.

We don't die, our atoms just rearrange themselves into other, perhaps less ordered, states.

There is no god, there can be no god, it is ridiculous to think in terms of a superior being.

There should be no acceptance of the concept of a superior being, we arrange our lives creating more order and harmony than a supposed god ever arranged on earth.

We measure, we plot, we create wonderful music.

We are the architects of our own existence!

What a lunatic concept to bow down before a god who slaughters millions of innocent children, who slowly and agonisingly starves them to death, beats them, tortures them. Rejects them.

What superior being would let his children die in their millions, slowly suffering?

If anything, we should harbour the concept of god as an inferior being.
We should think him out of existence, we should think away god.
It is the duty of all human beings to think god out of existence, so that we may
bear the full responsibility of our actions.
So that we may take responsibility for who we are.

⁕

As with Rabbi Hillel's Golden Rule, I have taken on board two important lessons from the organist:

1   To think away god
2   To humbly take responsibility for who I am.

27 March 2018   Letter #62

Hi Gareth

I hope that you are okay that side ... warmer there ... **18 March 2018** ... our days get cooler.

As I paddled off Clifton early this morning, I noticed a certain winteriness. Dark water, *duikers* in groups of 10 to 15 flying about. The refreshing outside cold showers (taken quickly, as drought dictates, no time to wait for the water to warm up) are now bracing and not altogether pleasant. The house opposite is now not always fully booked. Zaan and I can therefore have our morning coffee in bed with the sliding door wide open without feeling that we are going to be peered at by the guests across the road. The cool brings smells that remind me of surf missions up the coast. Good memories. But it also brings a restlessness at the change of season. A time to plan trips.

The Grey Matter of the Mouse

In the opening pages of **Antifragile** by Nassim Taleb, he observes the following:

"While in the past people of rank or status were those and only those who took risks, who had the downside for their actions ... now the exact reverse is taking place ... At no point in history have so many non-risk takers, that is, those with no personal exposure, exerted so much control."

My subconscious mind extrapolated as follows:
Stress is a function of uncertainty.
Anxiety and fear cause stress, they are both functions of uncertainty.

In former times, when we had real "skin in the game" we could more realistically fear being physically hurt. These days, we fear and are anxious of outcomes such as failure or humiliation and ridicule. One might be given a stressful job or assignment and fear that one is not equal to the task, or that the client might not be sufficiently pleased with the outcome, or that one might lose money.

For me one of the most stressful aspects of anything is simply the period between agreeing to do something and getting it done. Some people call this "commitment anxiety". This can even be something as apparently trivial as the three weeks between accepting a party invitation and the event, or, as Zaan and I experienced last year, the month between agreeing to go to Yalta and actually going there. Once we were there and doing the tasks at hand, all my stress evaporated. I have had the same experience out at sea while waiting for big storms to hit. We know that they are inevitable, lurking somewhere over the horizon and on the way, and that can chew away at a person like me. One is then unable to relax and enjoy the majesty of the ocean and the albatrosses and the seething swells and the sailing. But when the storm hits and there is real work to be done on the foredeck, there is no stress or fear – just a calm oneness with the task. For me, fights and confrontations have been the same.

I can only imagine what it must have been like during WWI ... the nail-biting wait, knowing that sooner or later you would be ordered over the top. If the machine guns and shells don't get you, the stress alone will have an effect on your body and its nervous system. But everyone reacts differently to stress.

I try to avoid stress by never procrastinating. I always try to get things done as soon as I can.

Not doing a task as soon as possible leaves time for stress to ferment.

27 March 2018
2.5m swell, no wind, possibly light NE until 11h00.
Low tide pushing to high at 12h00.
I haven't done it for a long time, but this morning's conditions were perfect.
I am waiting on two new Wellness Warehouse stores, a Kauai and another FFMM.
I get the Wellness briefs tomorrow.
As I drive along Sea Point's Beach Road, I see maybe 100 dolphins.
Close inshore, heading towards Putt-Putt ... no-one else seems to notice them.

The people are so oblivious to anything that is not on a lead or on the screen of a phone.

Hopeless humanity.

In the 1980s and early 1990s it was all scrub covered dune out there.
The West Coast, that is.
Uwe, Mike Mater, Alan Best and my brother Mick would be the only ones out at Derdesteen.
I don't think anyone else really surfed there (or at 365).
Today, a Tuesday, I imagine four or five cars and maybe 8 to 10 guys in the water spread over multiple peaks.
I pull in at about 08h30 … full house … cars even parked along the road.
No rusty Datsuns, all top-end shiny and new … maybe 35 cars.

Plenty of waves though. What a great place.
Smooth water, peaks and Table Mountain.
Nice guys too. No hustling. Just too many of them.
It is difficult not to find a person on your inside.
Many of them pull back, wasting good waves.
I have my boards in my garage.
Mick and I sometimes trot down for a surf at Glen.

I often wonder when I will stop surfing.
One loses fitness and Derdesteen is a long drive with dense traffic – always at
risk of a sub-optimal result.
And my home break is mostly *kak*.

Last week there were many whales passing off Bakoven.
The next day I paddled in the morning with maybe 50 dolphins and 25 seals.
They thought I was a kind of messiah and followed me back and forth,
Hoping that I would lead them to some holy bait-ball, but I could not.
Eventually I had to cut and run for home.
I felt that I had let them all down.

The next day there were three Heaviside's and a few Duskys about.
They paid little attention to me.

⁕⁂⁕

Zaan and I are planning a trip to Austria in August,
to coincide with Gordon's 80th.
Planning stages yet.

Best Greetings and Big Love ... C

Chapter 62

It is Time

There are a couple of young *kokerbome*,
Standing in pots on a Bree Street sidewalk.
It is raining heavily and they don't know what the hell is going on.
They will never make it back to Namaqualand.

Some time ago it used to rain in winter,
Then it didn't,
Now it does again.
Real rain has fallen this winter and for now the drought is broken.
Where does the rain come from, where does it go?

Due to an espresso at eight in the evening,
I couldn't sleep, time on my hands,
And at 2am I was going through my mind,
When I stopped and began to ponder time.
And the lesson I had given to Allegra and Ella in the Company Gardens all those years ago.

Is time, into which we travel, the 4ᵗʰ dimension? Yes.

I define time as "how long it takes" but cannot define "long" or "takes".
Does time seem to speed up as one grows older because of:
1 The physical size of the individual passing through time?
2 The repetitious nature of adult life?
3 The absence of a steep "learning curve" or "mental stimulation gradient"?

Steven Hawkings wrote about time, but now he has gone.

Time is merciless.
Time waits for no man or woman, ageing is merciless.
Time is vast and tiny and probably not linear in nature.

A time will come when everything as we know it will no longer exist,
Not one atom of Michelangelo's David or the Earth,
Or anything else that we hold dear,
Will remain attached to the atoms they are currently attached to.

If you are looking for a god, how about **Time**?

Time is the Almighty One.

Time giveth and time taketh away.

27 April 2018   Letter #63

Hi Gareth

I hope that you are fine.

27 April 2018

Today is Freedom Day.
I went with Zaan to Hout Bay to upgrade her phone.
The Riverside Mall, a sortie into the human condition.
Battered antipodean palefaces, so unglamorous.
Poor half-starved Sub-Saharan men, begging for jobs at the traffic lights.
Victims of chaos and failed states.

There is such humanity in the people I talk to, and I am deeply compassionate.
But I feel absolutely disparate, like they are a different species.
A species that I do not want to be part of … both the palefaces and the browns.

Pensive, I watch:
Suburban fathers pushing prams … the horror.
Sun-damaged middle-aged women, fake lashes, scuffed heels,
tight jeans with knee-tears.
Lives wasted? … No freedom.
Hog-tied and buttfucked in cages of their own making.

The end of a long dayski earning the daily crust.
Time is the only thing money cannot buy.
(Health can be assisted by money, but not bought.)

(Yet time and health are the two most squandered elements of human life.)
We waste our days earning money with which we cannot buy back our time.

I am about halfway through **Second Hand Time** by Svetlana Alexievich.
I find reading about the Russians utterly fascinating
(including/especially the Russian love of salami).
And the communists' relationship with money and poetry
And how all that changed with the onset of capitalism.
What chaos and devastating instant change!
(I am reading about Yeltsin and Gorbachev on the side.)
I wish I had known about all that when Zaan and I were over there last year.
All that stuff happened, and I was totally unaware.
1990–1993 … a completely different reality.

I bought three of her books, recommended, as usual, by the advocate.
I have 2½ of her books left to go.
I do not know what I will do when I have no more of her books to read.
I felt just the same way while I was reading the Sebalds, the Fermors, the Thesigers and the Kapuscinskis.

I worry about what I will read when I am old.
Should worst come to worst, I guess I will just re-read them all.
Could be worse.
I am not looking forward to old age.

Winter is coming.
On Wednesday night it rained and poured.
Mosquito time is over.
In some parts of the world, the rainy season means mosquitoes.
It is autumn now and the iris bulbs push up.
In Canada and Europe it is springtime and the bulbs push up too.
In the morning, while out running on the cool moist mountain,
I heard a noise like a tarpaulin flapping in a gale.
I looked up to see rocks half the size of cars falling from the cloud.
They had dislodged from the rock face high above.
And were checked by the trees and other rocks previously fallen.

I had the Lion's Head almost to myself.
The path that was overgrown,
The one that runs up the front, past the old lookout post,
Looks like a buffalo-trail now.
Sometimes a hundred cars are parked there in the morning.
Headlamps light up the peak at night like so many creeping glow-worms.
This morning at 06h30 again … trail runners … early-uppers.
I pick up empty plastic bottles and Red Bull cans.
Hannes Fagan taught us to do this as boys.
There are people who litter and people who pick up.
I imagine the litterers are a bunch of cunts similar to a group of destructive crap goblins.

If you call someone a *poes* or a cunt, it is not a sex thing.
I have been told that black does not actually mean black when referring to a so-called "black" person,
Just like cunt does not actually mean cunt.

C U Next Time.

C

Chapter 63

BUVLOG

On a late-winter's morning in 1988, Seaman Paris Zannos, Seaman John White, Seaman Peter Gibbons and Seaman Carlos Liltved appeared before the Master at Arms, at BUVLOG, as the accused in a summary trial. They had been caught, by Commander Rawsthorne, with a bottle of sherry in a tea urn with the "probable intention of drinking while on watch".

At the main entrance gate to BUVLOG stood a small brick box of a building with a concrete roof. On the left it had a bulletproof window and a bullet-proof door to the right. Outside there was a small terrace accessed by four or five steps. It measured about 4m × 4m × 4m externally, but only 3m ×

3m × 3m inside. The walls were oppressively thick. It contained a sticky linoleum-covered desk and two sticky chairs. A G3 rifle rested in the aft righthand corner, and a small sticky fridge at left. On a sugary table, below the bulletproof window, stood an electric hot water urn which bubbled away day and night. Pilfered milk was kept in the fridge. A twin fluorescent light burned white from dusk to dawn. It was our "Duty Room" and for all I know, it is still there.

Years of smoking had changed the colour of the Duty Room's ceiling from white to a sepia brown. That is where we passed our shifts.

In summer it was hot and in winter, cold. There were port-watches and starboard-watches and dog-watches and flag-raising at eight-bells and flag-lowerings at sunset. We blew bosun's pipes and pretended to look for bombs under vehicles with mirrors on long poles. I do not remember any more how it all worked, but sleeping and "gypo-ing" took priority.

A shift or two before the sherry bottle incident, John White and I had decided to make it rain in the Duty Room. We opened the lid of the tea urn and switched on a small heater. Outside, the weather was wintery and miserable with rain steeping down, but inside we wanted things tropical. After about an hour, orange drops began to fall from the ceiling. Three hours after that, at 04h00, the next watch arrived and were horrified to find John and me sitting on the table laughing in nothing but nicotine-coloured underpants, soaked yellow.

In retrospect, I don't think we really bought into the whole communist-threat ideology.

On other nights, the fuses of large red "Widow-Maker" or "Cobra" firecrackers were inserted into little holes just forward of the filters of burning cigarettes. This was done just moments before a change of watch. The booby-trapped cigs were then concealed in a cardboard carton or behind the rifle and the fridge. The cigarettes would burn down over a couple of minutes until "BANG! BANG! BANG!" The new watch thought they were under attack.

What motivated Commander Rawsthorne to leave his Clovelly home on a cold wintery Saturday evening, around 10pm, and drive through to Simon's Town to catch the Duty Watch up to no good, remains a mystery. But Zannos and White and Gibbons and Liltved were most certainly laughing and fooling around when he suddenly appeared at the chained gate, demanding to be let in.

Rather than hassle with a 9mm pistol, I would often stand duty with my water-UZZI replica sub-machine gun. It looked just like the real thing but "shot" water and was superbly efficient at extinguishing cigarettes. Being non-standard weaponry, Rawsthorne eyed it suspiciously but said nothing, probably not wanting to expose his own ignorance in these matters.

He climbed the steps and entered the Duty Room, making a withering comment on the state of our uniforms, before paging through the duty book with its rows of fictitious rounds. He stepped outside for a breath of fresh air, then came back in. He heard a sound. "Clonk, clonk, bubble, bubble." He cocked his head, lifted the lid of the urn and, aaah, at last, something.

"So what is this?" he asked, "Take it out please." He left triumphantly with our bottle of sherry.

On Monday morning after tea, Zannos, Gibbons, White and Liltved were lined up before the Master at Arms. We were very neat in our black uniforms with shiny brass buttons, black ties and polished shoes. The grey-bearded Master lounged low in an old swivel-chair behind his desk. A few Chiefs and POs stood by.

"Which one of you is the owner of this?" asked the Master, pointing over his shoulder in the general direction of a display cabinet.

There was no response from the men.

"The bottle of sherry," he growled.

"The bottle of sherry is mine, Master," Zannos replied politely.

"Why do you think Commander Rawsthorne would feel the need to come around here at ten o'clock on a Saturday night and check on the duty-watch?"

"Because he is a cunt, Master."

The Master at Arms eyed Zannos for a moment or two, then began to laugh. The NCOs laughed too. "Get out," he said, "the lot of you."

"May I have my bottle of sherry back?" asked Zannos.

The Master shook his head. "No, just go."

<hr />

We had a fellow on our duty-watch named Laban. He was a Pioneer. Pioneers were employed by the navy to stand guard. Pioneers wore navy uniform but had no rank, badges or training.

When not on guard duty, the members of the duty-watch slept and rested in a lovely old stone building with a steeply inclined, white wooden ceiling. One morning, while Laban was still asleep, we took one of his boots and, using a long pole, hung it by its laces from an old lamp-hook at the apex of the roof.

Shortly before eight-bells, Laban became frantic. He knew that one of us had pinched his boot, but he didn't know who had done it or where it was. With one socked foot, he burst into the Duty Room and drew his pistol. A round went off. The small space was crammed with men and it was fortunate that the bullet missed them all. It left a gouge in the lino floor, a nick in the wall next to the fridge and a chip in the ceiling above their heads.

Hanging Laban's boot up there, hidden in plain sight, was also a **cuntish** thing to do.

27 May 2018   Letter #64

Hi Gareth

A month, gone in a flash, but seems like an eternity.

Hope that you are okay, my friend.

A short letter because this month has been so busy with work and prep for Canada and getting Zaan's house ready for long-term tenants. I have been working on a new factory in Paarden Eiland, two new Wellness Stores and a tented camp in Serengeti.

I went out for a paddle this morning at 07h00. Call it first light. Off Glen Beach I could see a small fire burning in one of the inhabited caves. Cave dwellers burning plastic for a little warmth. In the light offshore breeze, it smells really toxic. Imagine the life that goes with it.

My muscles are a bit sore after a day of building furniture and gardening, so I do not paddle far. (After too much computer work, I need to do some physical hand-work or I go a bit moggy. Back to the Serengeti project today.)

As I paddle back with the dawn, I am downwind of the bakery. Croissants and fresh rolls. And I think of those poor, cold, plastic-burners in their damp little cave with their damp blankets and the damp earth under their backs.

Beautiful days we are having between the rains. Big rain again tomorrow. Below is a tale of two otters.

4 May 2018

When we were boys, the mere sight of an otter was like gold.

It made us feel rich, enriched.

I remember a fleeting glimpse of one down at Betty's Bay when I was about 10.

This morning I went paddling while it was still dark. Sea so warm. Big kelp gulls sitting on the water in Camps Bay, feasting on something. I returned into the Bakoven inlet at about 07h45. Little goblin heads popping out all around me. I stopped my boat, otters everywhere … or so it seemed. I soon worked out that there were only two, but they are so fast and inquisitive that it seemed like an entire family.

One left after a few minutes and the other stayed, the next hour was the treat of a lifetime.

The otter approached then darted off, only to return, each time a little closer. Soon it was climbing onto the bow of the surf-ski and flopping off, or managing to run towards me before losing balance and falling back into the water. Then it would climb up on the stern, with more success, and be there for a while. It hung onto my paddle and sniffed my toes … I was a little worried that my toes might look tasty. Little round ears and a cute face. Hard, rasping breathing.

After some time I paddled back to shore with the otter following me, bouncing and jumping playfully. I went back into the shallow water and held my ski for it to climb onto. It swam between my calves and snuffled my legs.

We went out into the channel again. The otter came up with a large kelp-coloured *klipvis* which it crunched up right alongside me, obviously showing off.

Ah, the sun appears and it is time for man and otter to part ways.

***

Interacting with people and seeing how they drive and park and litter and spray paint BIAFRA in red, green and yellow on Table Mountain, and reading about the corruption and badness, I realise more and more that we must never make the mistake of assuming that others share the same or even a similar moral compass or awareness. Most people are just oblivious.

Love
C

Chapter 64

Allegra

Yesterday, at 6am, my daughter Allegra and I ran along Tafelberg Road.
It was dark and starry with warm pockets of air every now and then.
We chatted and laughed as we trotted along.
In a few months she will have completed her BSc in Oceanography and Geology.
She works hard and is kind and humble.
She writes songs and plays the guitar and sings beautifully.
Soon she will be twenty-one.
She keeps fit.
She is pure sunshine.

If I were given the chance to rewind my life to the age of fifteen or sixteen, I would take my own daughter as my role model.

Like Allegra, I would work intelligently and diligently in appreciation of the incredible opportunities I have been afforded. I would take pride in doing all my projects as well as I could. I would see things through and not be a quitter.

I would leave that dreadful can of worms labelled "cynicism" tightly sealed,
And rather take pleasure in living life. One might as well.
Every hour spent anxious or angry or unhappy is an hour of happiness lost.

I would embrace more and reject less.

And learn about boundaries and how to say "No" as she has.
And not allow others to parasite me.
And not always feel the need to please.

I would hopefully laugh and smile more and have fewer harsh opinions.

I would listen carefully to those older and wiser than myself, and deconstruct their wisdom:
Down to first principles as Allegra does and I do now.

As much fun as it was to misspend that part of my youth,
I would not head out with Ravenscroft nearly as often as I did.
The closing of doors in one's own face is such a stupid thing to do.

26 June 2018   Letter #65

Dear Gareth

Cape Town ... 4 June 2018

The rain is over for now.
A warm NE breeze has started to do its work.
I have just been for a bike ride up on Table Mountain.
Water is running everywhere.
Down below, the bay shimmers in the early sunshine.
This city I love so much.
Off to Canada soon – I am due to leave on the 10th.
I am looking forward to being with Zaan again, but I hate the zone immediately before and after travelling.
The actual trip is a variable.

Ever since I was a boy, any change of environment would upset me.
Kindergarten in Pretoria, then Sub A at Tamboerskloof Primary.
My first week at high school, or even a wedding.
Or arriving at Mossels or Seal Point on a wonderful surf trip with my pals.
I know now, cerebrally, that I must force myself to pass through it.
Allow the fire to run its course, burn itself out, and pass away.

You see, travel has so enriched my life:
diving with manta rays and walking up to Komodo dragons,
Europa, New Zealand, Indonesia,

And sailing on yachts!

I remember so well the sickness and culture shock of my first few days in London back in 1987.

It is a part of who I am, like the monkey on the old man's back in the tale of Sinbad.

How dark and negative I must have been during the initial stages of every amazing trip my ex-wife organised. Yes, I know what it is now. I try to hide it and show a positive smiling face until it goes away.

I arrive in Canada and every fibre of my being screams. I want to go straight back home. I feel sick in my guts, my fingers tingle, my chest vibrates, it is so very unpleasant. I am fighting an angry nervous tension that feels like a faulty sweating detonator. To my eyes, the people around me are hideous. I wonder if I manage to hide it – or can the excited, loving Zaan see? I cannot let on. Fuck, it is a battle. I cannot spoil things by letting the cat out, the monkey out. I think she knows. Zaan is not stupid. I am a big boy now. I will be fifty-four in a few days' time – a big baby.

When I was younger I would sometimes just cut and run. I ran from Plett once. I made Zaan leave Mossel Bay once, on a perfect sunny uncrowded surf day. We had only just arrived. I ran away from my first sleepover at the Fagan home and hid under the bed in our spare room while the two families searched for me. I simply had to escape. This is part of me. And it has been for as long as I have known myself. "Know thyself!" commands the Delphic aphorism. I try. And I do know that after a day or three, I will be as happy here as I have been anywhere else, like a snuffling pig in the thick leaves of an oak forest floor. The trick is getting through the relocation, the uprooting.

⌖

The trip – now that is another tale. A nine-hour flight to Dubai in absolute comfort on a three-quarter full aircraft. Drifting in and out of sleep, lounging against the emergency exit door with plenty of legroom, assisted by a sleeping pill and a few glasses of red wine. Then a three-hour layover in the massive sci-fi humanity-infested airport and onto a chock-full A600 double decker for the thirteen-hour flight over Norway and Greenland to Toronto. No emergency exit seats! Emirates is selling them now for a few Judas coins to men with short legs and feet that barely touch the ground. I squeeze into my little seat. A tall man with no wiggle-room.

Apart from myself, there were four other Caucasian adults at the boarding gate. Two diminutive elderly Italian women (who I ended up sitting next to) and a young Canadian couple. With the exception of one or two Africans, all the rest are from countries like Pakistan, Indonesia, India, Saudi Arabia, the UAE, Syria, Kazakhstan, Kyrgyzstan, Libya and Egypt. Countries where (as can be witnessed at Dubai Airport Terminal 2) men are not toilet trained and babies are permitted to scream non-stop. Makes you hate, but it goes away later.

The Italian women prove to be fabulous onboard companions and I walk away with a head-load of 1950s Calabria and a recipe for *parmigiana di melanzane* scribbled on my boarding pass.

⌖

Back in Canada … I have been here for a week … working and riding my bike up and down the riverside trails. I have bought a skateboard too. Bicycles and skateboards, the toys of childhood. The smell of the trees and leaves no longer reminds me of Europe and other places. They now remind me of here. It is my fifth consecutive summer in Ontario.

The citizens of London do not know how very lucky they are. They complicate their relatively easy lives by keeping dogs which they lead around on strings morning, noon and evening, picking up the dog shit in little plastic bags. The stinking bin at the entrance to our park contains many packets of dog shit. Flies zoom in and out (and flies land on our meals). The poo-bin is emptied every so often by a pair of young female garbage collectors. There are similar green drums at all park and greenbelt entrances and exits. Big plastic bin-liners containing little bags of dog shit – where do they take them all? Most of these people have no clue about the real world. They live in a tolerant, liberal cocoon.

I wrote to you before about visiting Rolf Kirsten's 18 000 ha farm just outside Maltahöhe, Namibia. At first glance, a seemingly endless unknown wilderness, but once thoroughly walked and driven over a number of years, it became a familiar entity. Mapped in the mind. At times, it became a claustrophobic system of fenced camps. Then a person does not go there again. Maybe that is happening here now.

I took Zaan's truck and moved the poo-bin to the end of the street, away from the park and away from the houses. It was like hitting an ant nest with a club. The people milled around, dog leash in one hand, poo bag in the other, dithering, angry and confused. "Where must we put our poop now?" Take it home! "We could never do that." Why not? "Because we have picked it up already." Oh boy!

So I brought the bin back and put up a sign.

After much reflection, I believe that I suffer from a certain type of PTSD. When I see prams and babies I get extremely anxious and stressed. The nature of our suburb here is changing,

The lovely older people are moving away and younger ones are moving in. With them come more dogs and more baby carriages.

Maybe it is time to relocate to a farm in the country, on a lake shore.

23 June 2018

This morning I rode out after the rain, along the river, by the fields, through the forest and up on a new cycle path over a bridge on a railway line. A killdeer plover has laid three eggs in a scrape on a field. I stopped to watch two little girls build a crude wigwam of sticks to protect the nest. Hundreds of thousands of small winged ants had emerged after the rainy night. Redwing blackbirds and robins and sparrows feasted. From the bridge at the top of the hill, you can watch and feel as massive double-coupled diesel locomotives pass just beneath your feet, pulling their trains behind them. Carriages marked Santa Fe, Union Pacific and Kansas City Southern de Mexico. Box cars and open trucks with every kind of load imaginable. It is magnificent stuff.

Canada is not really a holiday as much as a change of scenery. It is my 5th year in a row. It is not necessarily my first choice, not really being the place I would want to live. I miss the ocean too much. I have an office set up here and I always work on Vida coffee shops or Simply Asias or Wellness Warehouses or other projects. This time, however, I am trying to work on a project of my own (I will tell you about it soon), but I am also waiting for two new store briefs. I feel relief every day the briefs do not arrive because it means I can get on with my own work. But every morning I spend 2 or 3 hours dealing with plan submissions, fire-chief requirements, changes to a factory roof designs, emails, insurance, paying accounts, etc. Admin. You know the drill. There are "crocs and sharks" waiting in my inbox every day – no big deal, but not relaxing. To free up time for myself, I have recently turned down three not insignificant jobs: a house in Franschhoek, a large restaurant in Cape Town and more tented camp work in Serengeti.

26 June 2018

I have been in Canada for two weeks now. One slowly forgets one's own home and plants and garden. I am finally used to it here. Last night I dreamed a continuous South African nightmare. It started with mindless U-turns and the breakdown in RSA driving style. Then cash-in-transit heists, degraded schools, the looting of shops and stupid politicians driven only by their lust for money and power. Men and women prepared to destroy that which has been built over decades for the sake of a quick and criminal buck. Absolutely no capacity for planning or seeing the bigger picture. Politicians robbing the people and the people robbing themselves. Ignorance and incompetence. A dream of sadness and loss. Why the need to break?

Cry the Beloved Country.

And what I have on offer in Canada is so much more than the wildest expectations of all those clambering immigrants from Somalia or Syria. I suppose it is just that Cape Town is such a wonderful place and we experienced it at its very best.

Where will you make your future?
Carl

Chapter 65

The Winds of the World

Early in the morning, along the river paths, I run or ride. Homeless people, men mainly, sleep rough. Today I found one lying face down, flat on the concrete, wet, under a bridge. I could follow the trail of debris and the soggy marks of his blanket from the bench on which he had slept until the dew became too heavy. Another sleeps with his legs protruding from a tiny, red and white plastic kiddy play-tent. Yet another is under a nylon flysheet supported by a shopping trolley, sodden clothes strewn about. And another and another and another. Some are up already, smoking, the early birds. All are surrounded by the shrapnel of litter. Like a bad parent, London Ontario is a city unable to confront its problems. More than two million free needles are handed out to drug users every year. And free methadone to fentanyl addicts. An expanding crisis of addiction. Our friend Lou sells used cars and runs a car repair business on Dundas Street. He can no longer leave his vehicles outside at night. "Drug addicts," he says. His glass shopfronts have been shot at. He is thinking of selling up. Lou is despondent. Up on the East Side and down by the river, you can see them everywhere. The biggest component of Lou's business these days is replacing side windows. "The addicts will smash your window for anything. Don't leave a thing in your car." (Sounds like home, I thought.) "It's not like it used to be around here," sighs Lou.

I was asking friends up in Antigonish about leaving properties unoccupied over the winter (this is a town in Nova Scotia, one must remember). "No," they said, "you can't any more … drug addicts will break in. We're twenty minutes out of town. It is no longer safe."

When we were kids in Cape Town, we would sometimes sleep with the front door wide open on warm summer nights. In about 1973, I remember my dad asking me one evening to close and lock the doors. I was surprised and not a little scared. The first sniff of the winds of change.

On Friday evenings at 7.30pm, we would lie in bed listening to our favourite radio program Squad Cars:

"They prowl the empty streets at night, waiting in fast cars and on foot,
living with crime and violence,
these men are on duty twenty-four hours out of every twenty-four,
they face dangers at every turn, expecting nothing less!
They protect the people of South Africa, these are the men of Squad Cars!"

Their reality became our reality when they lost the capacity to protect us. I think of New York at the time Bernie Goetz shot his four would-be muggers on the subway, and how, slowly, the crime situation was turned around for the better. It is possible, but there must be the will. People cannot simply say, "Oh, that's the way it is, we cannot do anything about it … 'twas ever thus."

Please raise your hands, those of you who sense a future which is an improvement on the present.

No hands?

The winds of the world

⟨◦⟩

The day after the rainy day, I rode my bicycle up to see the trains but there were none. The wigwam of twigs was no longer there. A baseball game was in progress where it had stood. The killdeer had lost her clutch. She had laid her eggs badly and will have to try again. Hopefully it is not too late in the season.

As I passed the game, a man wearing dark tracksuit trousers and luminous sneakers performed a jerky dance to trash-can music. His back was covered in tattoos and it looked as if he was trying to dry the ink.

⟨◦⟩

If every one of the hundreds of people who use the paths every day, including the dancing man, had to bend down and pick up just one piece of litter, there would be none. I pick up ten. In general, Canadians, like South Africans, simply don't bother. Somebody else will come along and do it.

- 545 -

The other day the troll-litter was particularly bad
And I was at the point of giving up,
When suddenly I spied two pieces of paper lying on the mown grass,
some distance away from the path.
The memory of Hannes Fagan forced me to pick them up.

Printed on each were the words:

BE THE CHANGE

31 July 2018   Letter #66

Dear Gareth

I have talked to quite a few older people while in Canada this year.

I greet them along the way, and then when I hear an ex-European accent, I home in.

Mostly they have been Italians, around seventy and even older, from Calabria, having come out to the Toronto area after the war. Mostly during the 1950s. Typically, the father would come first with an older sister. They would lay down some sort of foundation and the rest of the family would follow in dribs and drabs over the next few years.

Today I met and talked to Nicola (Nick) D'Ascanio who was born in 1940 in Abruzzo, Italy. His father had been captured by the British, in North Africa, before his birth. Nick's dad was held as a POW in Australia, only returning to his wife and children in 1946. Nick still runs marathons at 78.

I asked him if he misses Italy. "I was fifteen when I come out here," he said, "It was tough, I don't remember much."

"It was tough in Italy too," he added. "You know, the Germans destroy everything when they retreat."

Their accents remain, but they do not "*verlang*" because of the time passed and the raising of their children and grandchildren. They have had good lives here in Canada, away from the ravaged motherland. The land of sunshine and figs. "Canada is our home now," they say.

I ask them all, because I miss home. I ask them because I am sad about the country I am away from. The beloved country in the process of being destroyed. Consuming, cancerous politics ruining what could be a paradise.

I try to get into the headspace of people who have successfully broken those ties.

Zygmunt Gorski: 63 years old, was five when he came to London from a Polish town close to the Ukraine border. He has worked in forensics for 37 years, reconstructing road accidents. His father was 17 at the outbreak of WWII … his father's brother was murdered but his father survived.

His mother and many of her family were arrested and sent to Siberia. Zygmunt never saw his mother again. His dad, with four children, successfully gapped it for Canada.

By building my houses, furniture, gardens and pools myself – by being so personally involved with the sea and the mountains and the community – I think my roots are deeper than those who pass the time between meals watching Grand Prix on their big TVs or playing PlayStation or walking the malls.

9th of July 2018 – STOP PRESS:

I am sitting at my desk in Canada overlooking the park.
I am writing about early memory.
News fresh in.
I have just heard via WhatsApp that it's official.
Gareth has been notified by his embassy that he will be released
on the 17th of September 2018.
Ten years have been stolen from his life.

Over the years people have asked me, "But don't you think, maybe, possibly, that Gareth could, actually, be guilty?"

I reply: "Could you be a drug smuggler? I know I couldn't."
And they back off.

Do you remember where you were when you heard about 9/11 or when you listened on the radio to Apollo 11 blasting off, destination the moon? I do! And for me this moment will be one of those. A momentous piece of news for those who love the man.

⚜

Zaan and I have been up in Nova Scotia. We stayed a few days with Barb and Hardy, her AFS host parents (30 years later) in an 1860s home at Waternish

(45 minutes' drive from Antigonish). It was like being in a time capsule. Not a single piece of furniture is less than a hundred years old. The 168 acres on which the house stands, as well as the river running through it, has been declared a nature reserve by them. They have convinced other owners upstream and downstream to do the same. This means safe swimming for the trout and salmon, and safe snuffling for the bears. Lovely, humid and rather buggy inland in high summer. Foggy and cool down at the seaside. Cold, they say, in winter. Very.

We drove down the coast towards Halifax, passing many abandoned homes, curtains in shreds, peeling shingles, patched roofs. Some even with a car or two, tyres flat, decaying in the meadow where the driveway once was.

We stopped at a lovely seaside town called Musquodoboit Harbour. Surfers were longboarding at a long sandy beach named Martinique. As in many parts of Canada, the old railroad has been cleared of its tracks and sleepers and now serves as a winding, almost flat, hiking and biking trail. So beautiful, with lakes and rivers and mountains to the left and right. Trees, birds, deer and (once dynamited) rocky cuttings and mozzies, of course. But Gareth, the light intensity is right for the northern European gene.

We passed through Halifax and drove on to Mahone Bay and Lunenberg. Fjord and island coast much like parts of southern Norway. Some houses are similar to Norwegian homes while others are more like those you will find in New Zealand. Ultimately, it all came from the same place.

There are many properties on the market here and reasonably priced, too. In a lot of cases, the grandparents are deceased and their grandchildren, now in their 30s and 40s, dispersed to the cities a decade or two ago. The in-between generation … 70+ "baby boomers" … are currently packing up and leaving in their numbers (scaling down) or have already left for retirement villages in Toronto or Ottawa.

It is a quiet place with none of the drug problems of cities like Halifax and Antigonish. I know that it is really tough there in winter, but imagine a life with no burglar bars and no alarm systems! No real prospect of a robbery or violent home invasion. It would be lovely to live without that stress.

But a declining population brings its own problems:
A reduction in tax revenue with which to maintain roads and infrastructure (already obvious).

Doctors are packing up and leaving, making it harder to find good, accessible health care. And fewer people means fewer economic opportunities.

But it is nice to toy with the idea of such a life.
So many of our peers in **The Republic** are thinking this way.
And as Tom Petty said: *"You don't have to live like a refugee."*

What are you dreaming of Gareth?
Love C

The vacuum created by the arrival of freedom,
And the possibilities it seems to offer, if one can grasp it,
After such a series of shocks and aftershocks.

You can train by shadow boxing
But a real-life adventure is worth more than gold.
Blue sky above and sunlight on your arms.

Chapter 66

The Replies

I wrote an email from Canada to some of my friends back home in Cape Town.

The usual newsy correspondence ended with the following lines:

Today I rode early in the cool.
So happy because of yesterday's news about my friend Gareth's release date from prison in Kuwait.
And so sad because of South Africa today:
Malema's latest Mussolini-style fascist utterances:
"There is no freedom without the shedding of blood ..."
And Zuma appointing a new rotten lawyer Lungisani Mantsha to replace Hulley.

How does one imagine a civilised future for oneself in such a place?
It breaks my heart to think that I might have to move away.
I am so part of it, and it so part of me.
I miss the ocean deeply.
I feel out of place here.
It is not my home.
I ask myself, will South Africa be too intolerably Third World for me to live in, in 15 to 25 years?
This is an honest question.
For decades I have hoped.
Is all this stuff the end for the paleface?

Best Greetings
Carlos

Some of them replied, I will share four:

Reply 1

Greetings Carlos

I too am reflecting.
Sadly, I think our days are limited as the paleface.
History tells us so.
Many Empires have come and gone; Phoenicians. Persians. Greeks. Moghuls.
And so too their people. Some survivors stayed behind to integrate.
Others went home after 100 or 200 years.
And we are indeed the dregs of the Anglo-Dutch empire.
Our turn is over.

We are the blamed ones – the failed state needs a reason. We are the minority.
Like Hitler's Jews.
They died because they were too successful.
They showed the Germans up.
They were the ones blamed for Germany's poverty.
All the ex-colonies above imploded.
The African culture seems to learn nothing from the north.
They will make the same mistakes.
It is a patriarchy culture, a feudal one with very little openness.

Ultimately, we must leave, our forebears did it.
The cycle continues.
And return when we want.
When the transition settles.
But it will take a generation or two.
I don't feel like being part of it.
Having racism against me.
Lived through racism once before.
So I too am in a quandary.

Travel safe.
C

Reply 2

Hi Carlos

I think immigration does leave a kind of amputee longing.
And it is a matter of weighing up pros and cons.
The beauty versus the horror, the excitement versus the madness.
And, of course, the roots of a lifetime of living and *verlangenis*.

What can I say? Often, I feel overwhelmed by the *kak* here.
But there is no shortage of *kak* in the world at the moment and the key, I think, is to do as much living as we can now.

Love to Zaan.

Groete, ou maat.
H

Reply 3

Hi Carlos,

How splendid to hear from you and for some thoughtful musings amongst the noise and chaos of this world.

It is probably part of the complex web known as "the human condition" that what you find dull and mundane there is precisely what we yearn for when we are here.

We find it increasingly difficult when returning from our travels to adapt to the lawlessness of this country. From government and corporate corruption, via taxi and other road-related carnage, to common or garden rapes, robberies and murders.

I like being able to walk down a European or North American street without keeping wallets, keys and phones in white-knuckled grips.

Maybe we are born to "*verlang*"?

I prefer not to express any views on the dire politics of the place.

I am very happy to hear that Gareth is getting out. He was at SACS a few years ahead of me, so I have been following his story. I am sure your letters will have helped him a lot.

B

Reply 4

Hi CDL

15 to 25 years?
Lucky if we see TEN without it becoming a Trumpolian "shithole country".
I do not hold out hope here.
Kak gaan ons kak, *soos die korporaal jare terug so mooi verduidelik het.*

Enjoy your stay in Canada mate – it looks wonderful, peaceful and all about what life is about, focusing on good things, planting ideas in fertile soil, competing on a fair footing and reaping the rewards of an honest day's work without it being stolen, destroyed or you being murdered for your efforts.

A

My sincerest hope is that President Ramaphosa manages to clean up
Zuma's corrupt mess.
But I fear that Zuma is an insane and dangerous wounded lion at large.
Wounded lions should always be finished off properly.
Wounded lions sneak into kraals at night and kill.

26 August 2018   Letter #67

Dear Gareth

Thank you for your email. I cannot believe that you will be a free man walking in London on the 19th of September!

We are all, as you must be, absolutely thrilled! … At last! … A FREE MAN … and this, dear friend, will be the last of my monthly letters to you in prison.

Being a non-religious man, I reflect on a snippet of your Holy Bible …
2 Timothy 4:7. Gareth, **we have kept the faith.**

I hope that you will come back to South Africa soon and have a few days with your old dad, Bonzo – the king of sandwich-making. And your clever son Mikey. And your real friends. "Champagne for my real friends, real pain for my sham friends." As toasted by Francis Bacon. A great triumph.

I arrived back in Cape Town on Wednesday evening and have worked like a maniac for two days to clear the way for a free weekend of writing. So much admin and so many requirements from others. Work stuff. Cashflow, requirements for survival in the modern day.

On Thursday morning, a little later than usual, I went for a run on the loop trail around Lion's Head. The ground I know so well. The familiar smells of pelargoniums. My bird pals. The views of Camps Bay, Clifton, Robben Island and Table Bay. Light rain incoming. Puddles to jump over. A quick chat with trail familiars: Alfred, Anne, Dominic.

Overjoyed! Yes … overjoyed to be back.

Mr Lukas came over. "Mr Karros," he beamed, "how is it going overseas?" We laughed and talked and feasted on fried eggs and butter and toast and I showed him my photos: Gothic cathedrals, neoclassical detail, young people surfing on the Eisbach River in München's Englischer Garten. Summer crowds. Reflections of pre-war buildings, distorted in the glass facades of modern ones, built in the spaces left by bombs.

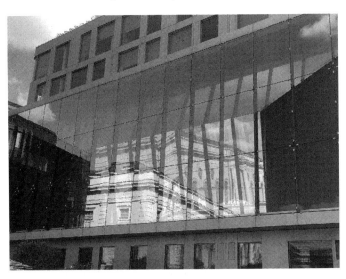

I contemplate the young RAF and USAAF bomber crews, high overhead, by now kings of the sky, and the young Germans running for cover down below. The same age as the carefree kids in my snapshots riding on shiny bicycles through the park.

After some weeks in Europe and now back in the Cape, I realise how Africa and the culture of what was formerly known as Christendom are alloyed in me. It is not possible to separate them. But I need a little more time for my thoughts and feelings to digest before I can spit out a distillation. So for now, I offer only impressions:

One thing I do know for sure is that I do not want to fly on Emirates in the east-west direction again. This is my fifth and final year of that. The north-south "South Africa" route is civilised and clean, but the flights ferrying our contemporary Arab-culture brethren and sistren to and from the North American continent and Europe are disgusting. Noisy, undisciplined children and adolescents run riot. Appallingly chauvinistic men speak rudely to passive cabin crew. And persons unknown foul the lavatories. I know that I have commented on this before, forgive me.

⁓᙮᙮᙮᙮⁓

Here is a brief synopsis of our journey: From Toronto, Zaan and I flew to Iceland. We rented a car at the airport and drove in to Reykjavik. It was a windy day, piercingly polar. "The warmest day so far this summer," the Polish guide at the lava-cave told us. "Make the most of it, stay outdoors for as long as you can." It is a cold and bleak country with snow-covered volcanoes rising in the distance. The vibe is ScandiNord, so I automatically start speaking Norwegian. It is not southern Italy.

After two days in Iceland we flew on to München and railed across to Salzburg where we hired a lovely compact Ford Eco-sport. Zaan then drove us down (via Hitler's Berchtesgaden) to the Austrian Südtirol to join my old friend and mentor Gordon, at his 80th birthday celebration.

We spent a long weekend in a gorgeous traditional hotel, with horses in the paddocks below and tremendous peaks soaring up out of green pastures and steep forests. We enjoyed long peaceful walks and saunas and functions with beer, buffets, a traditional orchestra and bands, bagpipes, lederhosen-clad dancers and fireworks.

Then off to Salzburg via the lake district, and finally Wien/Vienna.

Vienna in August is hot and thick with tourists.
I look darkly at the pedestrian masses on the Graben.
I do not like crowds, they threaten my space.
But, admittedly, they are all extremely well-behaved.
And I must take cognisance of the fact that I am one of their number, and Zaan another.
And I must ask myself, why are they there?
Not for tanning at the beach,
nor to look out over Niagara Falls and then head off to the casino,
Or for the obligatory visit to a crammed viewpoint at the Grand Canyon's rim, stuffing pizza slices into their faces,
Or to hire V8 Cobras and roar around the suburb at night,
Nor for any other thrills.

No, they are there for the culture and the history.
They are there to see Schönbrunn Palace,
And marvel at the paintings of Gustav Klimt,
And to be stunned by the raw power of Egon Schiele,
And the Leopold and the Albertina,
And the Naturhistorische and Kunsthistorische museums:
The staggering collections of the emperors and empresses,
now open for all to see.
And for the concerts and operas and to marvel at the Stephansdom,
And all the other glorious buildings in this,
the capital of the Austro-Hungarian Empire.

My mom and dad met in Vienna in 1955, just ten years after the war.
Just as the Russian occupiers were leaving, my dad told me.

After Wien we railed back to München, going 230km/h at times …
Through the heady late summer countryside.
I am reading the histories again:
As complex as Venetian lace and beset by war.
Europe, playing out in a grand theatre, is the human condition:
Our incredible capacity for creativity and art and adaptation,
Offset against our congenital and unremitting requirement for conflict.

I observe as Vladimir Putin comes over to visit the Austrians. He is the man to watch. An atheist leader conning his people into blind faith. I listened carefully while in Russia and Crimea last year. The rise of the Orthodox Church, the resurgence of Stalin as a national hero. An idol. Monarchist propaganda.

Putin was a KGB man. Sly. Trained. Ruthless. He knows all the tricks. How to manipulate the masses. Not at all like the EU greenhorn idealist civilians turned to leadership. Putin aims to be tsar, maybe he is tsar already. His oligarchs are the new nobility. A new Russian empire, including Ukraine, warmer lands and warmer waters to the south and west. Kiev. A new empire, once again waiting to fall.

See you on the outside.

Love
C

Chapter 67

TL

I spoke to our friends Jennifer and Skip the other day.

We are middle-aged people, I guess.

"TL," they said, "TL is what we are focusing on and how best to use it!"

"What is TL?" I asked, (thinking possibly *true love?*)

"Time Left!" they answered in unison.

"Time Left!"

This is the future ... how best to use it?

Acknowledgements

Thanks to our dear friend Anthony Allen, who recently fell from the sky, for all the photos taken from above.

The balance of the pics were taken by me or other persons untraceable, collected over time in my paper diaries or PC journals or albums. I trust that their use will be accepted in good spirit. I thank the unknown photographers.

Thanks also to the storytellers who have talked to me.

And thanks to the great writers like Sebald, Alexievich, Harari, Fermor, Steinbeck, Chatwin, Thesiger, Melville, Hochschild and Kapuściński who have stimulated my thinking.

And the advocate for all the books.